CONTENTS

LIST OF FIGURES

LIST OF TABLES

FOREWORD

When we began to study Congressional elections around 1970, mastering the literature was a trivial matter. There was a book by Milton Cummings (1966), some relevant chapters in Julius Turner (1951), Lewis Froman (1963), and Wayne Shannon (1968), and a handful of articles, including, of course, several classics based on the representation study carried out by Warren Miller and Donald Stokes (Stokes and Miller, 1962; Miller and Stokes, 1963; Miller, 1970). In the view of most scholars there was a perfectly good reason that the literature was so sparse: Congressional elections simply were not of much interest. The prevailing view was that such elections were "low information, party-line affairs." Election outcomes reflected voters' long-term party allegiances and most seats were safe for one party or the other. On occasion the electoral arena was buffeted by national forces, chiefly the coattails of an attractive presidential candidate or a popular mid-term reaction to the mistakes (usually economic) of an administration (Tufte, 1973). But members of Congress had little or no personal control over their electoral fates. The Miller and Stokes studies had shown that voters generally were ignorant of the characteristics of the congressional candidates and the positions they held, not to mention the voting records of incumbents. Moreover, Bauer, Poole, and Dexter (1968) had shown that interest groups too, were vastly overrated actors in American politics. Thus, the behavior of members of Congress was considered to be primarily determined by the expectations and norms that prevailed within the Congress rather than by pressures emanating from the electoral arena.

By the end of the decade, however, the efforts of a younger generation of scholars raised serious questions about the prevailing portrait and rekindled scholarly interest in the study of congressional elections. A number of factors came together to generate this resurgence of interest. Erikson (1972) and Mayhew (1974) identified a growing electoral advantage of incumbency and succeeding studies described the constituency activities of incumbents, activities that reflected more time and effort than might be expected if incumbents believed they had no influence over their electoral fates. Indeed, rather than resting securely in their seats, Mann (1978) showed that incumbents were nervous, feeling "unsafe at any margin." Moreover, reliable campaign finance data became available in the 1970s, and the National Election Studies expanded to include congressional elections in 1978, enabling researchers to study congressional elections in much greater detail than previously. Scholars like Herbert Asher, Charles Bullock, Lawrence Dodd, Robert Erikson, John Ferejohn, John Jackson, Samuel Kernell, Warren Kostroski, Thomas Mann, Bruce Oppenheimer, Norman Ornstein, Glenn Parker, David Rohde, James Stimson, Herbert Weisberg, Gerald

Wright, and others contributed significantly to a new picture. But no one contributed more than Gary Jacobson, who today stands unchallenged as the leading student of modern congressional elections.

Jacobson (1980) pioneered analysis of the newly available campaign finance data and a generation of undergraduates dutifully learned his surprising conclusion that "the more incumbents spend, the worse they do." Jacobson (1989) emphasized the importance of congressional challengers and documented the decline in their quality as a factor in the growth of the incumbency advantage. Jacobson and Samuel Kernell (1981) analyzed the self-fulfilling interaction between national forces and candidate calculations and showed how such an interaction could amplify or dampen the effect of national forces on election outcomes. Jacobson (1990) explicated the electoral basis of the persistent state of divided government that seemed to take hold during the last half of the twentieth century. And when the portrait of congressional elections that he and his generation had painted grew outdated in the 1990s, Jacobson was among the first to point out how contemporary congressional elections differ from the incumbency dominated elections of the 1970s and 1980s (Jacobson, 2000).

Enough by way of background. For present purposes the important point is not the plethora of original contributions Jacobson has made to the congressional research literature. Rather, in addition to carrying out his own research program, for two decades Jacobson has conscientiously collected and synthesized the work of numerous others as well as his own. That ongoing process of collection and synthesis has appeared regularly as a new edition of his definitive text, *The Politics of Congressional Elections*, the seventh edition of which follows this *Foreword*. The student, layman, journalist or professional looking for the latest word on congressional elections will find it herein. The presentation is clear and concise, the writing graceful, and the coverage comprehensive and up to date. Like some wine, this text gets better with age.

David W. Brady
Morris P. Fiorina
Stanford University

Gary C. Jacobson, "Reveral of Fortune: The Transformation of U.S. House Elections in the 1990s," in *Continuity and Change in Congressional Elections,* David W. Brady, John F. Cogan, and Morris P. Fiorina, eds. (Stanford, CA: Stanford University Press, 2000): 10–38.

PREFACE

This book, like the previous six editions, is about congressional election politics, broadly understood. In writing it, I have tried to keep in mind that elections are means, not ends in themselves. What happens during campaigns or on election days is, of course, fascinating and important, and I do not neglect congressional candidates, campaigns, and voters. But campaigns and elections are more than curious rituals only because they reflect deeper structural patterns and currents in American political life and help determine how-and how well-we are governed. Part of the book is therefore devoted to tracing the connections between the electoral politics of Congress and other important political phenomena. Examining congressional election politics in this way inevitably raises fundamental questions about representation and responsibility, and these are the central normative concerns of the book. My intent here, then, is to offer a systematic account of what goes on in congressional elections and to show how electoral politics reflect and shape other basic components of the political system, with profound consequences for representative government.

Research on congressional elections continues to thrive, and it will quickly become clear to the reader how much I have learned from the work and ideas of other scholars. Information on congressional voters, candidates, and campaign finances becomes richer with each passing election as well; we now have the 1988–1992 Senate Election Studies to go along with the indispensable National Election Studies. When the National Science Foundation decided it would no longer be willing to fund NES midterm elections studies after 2002, other academic research teams picked up the slack, producing two new large-scale survey studies for 2006. These developments, along with the remarkable upheavals produced by the congressional elections of the early 1990s and the Democratic takeover of Congress in 2006, continue to make thinking and writing about congressional elections an intellectual pleasure.

I remain deeply indebted to the many friends and colleagues who have guided and stimulated my thinking about congressional election politics. The genesis of this book was my work as a member of the Committee on Congressional Election Research of the Board of Overseers of National Election Studies, which has designed the congressional component included in National Election Studies since 1978. Everyone I worked with on the committee has contributed to it in some way: Alan Abramowitz, David Brady, Heinz Eulau, Richard Fenno, John Ferejohn, Morris Fiorina, Barbara Hinckley, Malcolm Jewell, Jack Katosh, James Kuklinski, Thomas Mann, David Mayhew, Warren Miller, Glenn Parker, Barbara Sinclair, Michael Traugott, Raymond Wolfinger, and Gerald Wright.

Subsequently, continuing association with the National Election Study Board helped keep me in touch with other scholars who have contributed in various ways to my understanding of congressional elections and politics: Larry Barrels, Richard Brody, Stanley Feldman, William Flanigan, Charles Franklin, Edie Goldenberg, Mary Jackman, Stanley Kelley, Rod Kiewiet, Donald Kinder, David Leege, Douglas Rivers, Steven Rosenstone, Gina Sapiro, Merrill Shanks, Walter Stone, Mark Westlye, and John Zaller. I also wish to thank the many political scientists who used the earlier editions in their teaching and have let me know what they liked and disliked about the book.

I am grateful to all my colleagues at U.C. San Diego for providing an environment wonderfully conducive to scholarly work. Samuel Kemell read and commented on several chapters and has shared some of the research reported in the book. I have also enjoyed instructive and stimulating conversations with Nathaniel Beck, Amy Bridges, Peter Cowhey, Gary Cox, Elizabeth Gerber, Richard Kronick, David Laitin, Skip Lupia, John Mendeloff, Mathew McCubbins, and Samuel Popkin. Mo Fiorina, Herbert Jacob, Burdett Loomis, Tom Mann, and Steve Rosenstone read the entire manuscript of the first edition, and their service continues to register in this one. Jon Bond, Priscilla Southwell, Darrell West, Lynda Powell, Garrett Glasgow, Jamie L. Carson, Timothy Nokken, Michael Tofias, Franco Mattei, and many other anonymous scholars reviewed current and previous editions with an eye to improving this one; the book is clearly better for their suggestions and probably the worse for my not having heeded more of them. I am obliged to Denise Gimlin, Edward Lazarus, Del Powell, and David Wilsford for helping to gather some of the data analyzed in Chapter 6. Greg Bovitz, Mike Dimock, Tommy Kim, and Jeff Lazarus helped with this revision in various important ways (whether they know it or not). I am grateful, too, to colleagues who have generously shared data with me: James E. Campbell, George W. Edwards III, Michael Malbin, and Norman J. Ornstein.

Finally, I want to express my thanks to David Brady and Morris Fiorina for the kind words they have written in the Foreword. I am honored to have two such stellar congressional scholars leading off this edition.

Part of the research reported here was supported by a grant from the National Science Foundation (SES-80-7577), for which I am most grateful. Some of the data used in this book were made available by the Inter-University Consortium for Political and Social Research. The data for the 1978–2004 National Election Studies and the 1988–1992 Senate Election Study were originally collected by the Center for Political Studies of the Institute for Social Research, the University of Michigan, under grants from the National Science Foundation. Neither the original collectors of the data nor the consortium bear any responsibility for the analyses and interpretations presented here, and the same, of course, holds for anyone else I have mentioned.

Gary C. Jacobson
La Jolla, California

Chapter 1

INTRODUCTION

Elections stand at the core of American political life. They provide ritual expression of the myth that makes political authority legitimate: We are governed, albeit indirectly, by our own consent. Elections are also the focus of thoroughly practical politics. They determine who will hold positions of real power in the political system and, by establishing a framework in which power is pursued, profoundly affect the behavior of people holding or seeking power. The mythical and practical components of elections meet at the point where electoral constraints are supposed to make leaders responsive and responsible to the public. How comfortably they fit together has deep consequences for the entire political system. Almost any important development in American political life will be intertwined with the electoral process.

Congressional elections in particular are intimately linked to many basic phenomena of American politics. In countless ways, obvious and subtle, they affect the performance of Congress and, through it, the entire government. At the same time, they reflect the changing political landscape, revealing and shaping its fundamental contours.

The basic questions to be asked about congressional elections are straightforward: Who gets elected to Congress and how? Why do people vote the way they do in congressional elections? How do electoral politics affect the way Congress works and the kinds of policies it produces? What kind of representation do congressional elections really provide? Every answer has further implications for the workings of American politics and many of them must be traced out in order to grasp the deeper role of congressional elections in the political process.

This book aims to explain what goes on in congressional elections and to understand how they are connected in myriad ways to other aspects of American political life. It also has a more pointed intention: to use a careful examination of the complex, multifaceted business of electing Congress to help understand why politicians in Washington find it so difficult to fashion measured solutions to pressing national problems.

A central theme in earlier editions of this book was that political incapacity and stalemate were fostered by an electoral process that gave senators and representatives every reason to be individually responsive but little reason to be collectively responsible. Since the third edition was published, the chickens of collective irresponsibility have come home to roost. First, the 1992 elections brought the highest turnover of House seats in fifty years. Then, the 1994 elections put Republicans in control of both houses of Congress for the first time in forty years. Since then, party loyalty and ideological polarization in Congress have grown apace and imposing collective responsibility on its members has become far more feasible. Republicans maintained control by narrow margins—though losing the Senate for a time in the 107th Congress because of a party switcher—until 2006, when the electorate punished them collectively for supporting the George W. Bush administration and the Iraq War. These developments have raised many new questions and opened many new possibilities for analysis, and I spend a good deal of time in this edition examining their electoral roots.

Congressional elections are complex events and the sources of this complexity are numerous. An important factor is the number of different perspectives from which congressional elections can be examined. Consider the alternative ways the question "How's the congressional election going?" might be answered. A candidate or campaign manager would immediately begin talking about what was going on in the district, who was ahead, what groups were supporting which candidate, how much money was coming in, and what issues were emerging. A national party leader—the president, for example—would respond in terms of how many seats the party might gain or lose in the House and Senate and what that might mean for the administration's programs. A private citizen might grumble about the hot air, mudslinging, and general perfidy of politicians—or might scarcely be aware that an election was taking place.

Similarly, political scientists and other people who study congressional elections do so from a variety of research orientations. Some study voters: Why do people vote the way they do? Why do they vote at all? Others study candidates and campaigns: Who runs for Congress, and why? What goes on in campaigns? How is money raised and spent—and what difference does it make? Or they explore the aggregate results of congressional elections: What accounts for the changes in the distribution of House and Senate seats between the two parties? Still others are interested in representation: How are the activities of members of Congress and the performance of Congress as an institution connected with what goes on in elections? These and other questions are deserving of individual attention. But it is no less essential to understand how they are all interrelated.

People involved in congressional elections are at least implicitly aware of the connections between the different levels of analysis. Voters are interested primarily in the candidates and campaigns in their state or district, but at least some are conscious of the broader political context and may, for example, adapt their congressional voting decision to their feelings about presidential candidates. Presidents worried about the overall makeup of Congress are by no means indifferent to individual races and sometimes involve themselves in local campaigns. Candidates and other congressional activists are mindful of both the national and local political conditions they believe influence election outcomes and, of course, they spend a great deal of time trying to figure out how to appeal effectively to individual voters.

Scholars, too, are fully aware that, although research strategies dictate that the congressional election terrain be subdivided into workable plots, no aspect of congressional elections can be understood in isolation. It is essential to integrate various streams of investigation to obtain a clear account of what is going on. This is no simple task. One difficulty is quite familiar to students of the social sciences: how to connect the accounts of individual behavior to large-scale social phenomena. The problem is one of coordinating the micro- and macro-level accounts of political behavior (there are middle levels, too, of course). But it turns out to be a most fruitful problem. Its solution is a rich source of insight into congressional election processes and their consequences.

The approach taken in this book is to examine congressional elections from several perspectives while attending throughout to the interconnections among them. Chapter 2 sets out the legal and institutional context in which congressional elections take place. This formal context is easily taken for granted and overlooked but it is, on reflection, fundamental. The very existence of congressional elections depends on this structure, which shapes them in a great many important ways. Chapter 2 also briefly surveys the rich variety of social, economic, and ethnic mixes that are found among states and congressional districts, for this diversity underlies many distinctive aspects of congressional election politics.

Chapters 3 and 4 examine, respectively, congressional candidates and campaigns. The pervasive, if variable, effects of incumbency inject a theme common to both of these chapters. The resources, strategies, and tactics of candidates differ sharply, depending on whether a candidate is an incumbent, is a challenger to an incumbent, or is running for an open seat for which neither candidate is an incumbent. They also differ between House and Senate candidates in each of these categories. The strategies of candidates in different electoral situations and the consequences of varying strategies are explored. So are the roles of campaign money, organization, campaign activities and tactics, political parties, outside advocacy groups, and the local political context. Campaigns both reflect and work to reinforce candidates' assumptions about the electorate and they are also closely linked to the behavior in office of those elected.

Chapter 5 deals with voting in congressional elections. Knowing who votes and what influences the voting decision are valuable pieces of information in their own right, but such knowledge is even more important as a means for understanding what congressional elections mean and what they can and cannot accomplish. The way voters react is tied closely to the behavior of candidates and the design and operation of campaigns—and to what members of Congress do in office.

Chapter 6 examines congressional elections as aggregate phenomena. When all of the individual contests are summed up over an election year, the collective outcome determines which party controls the Congress and with how large a majority. It also strongly influences the kinds of national policies that emerge; it is at this level that the government is or is not held responsible. Congressional elections clearly respond to aggregate political conditions. But aggregate outcomes are no more than the summation of individual voting decisions in the districts to election results across all districts. The path that leads from aggregate political conditions to individual voting decisions to aggregate congressional election outcomes is surprisingly complicated; candidates' strategies turn out to provide a critical connecting link. The points in this chapter are illustrated by more detailed accounts of election from 1992 through 2006.

Finally, of course, congressional elections are important for how they influence the behavior of elected leaders and therefore the success or failure of politics. In fact, the knowledge that they are elected officials is the key to understanding why members of Congress do what they do in office—not only *that* they are elected but *how* they are elected matters. How candidates mount their campaigns and how voters choose among them has a crucial effect on what members of Congress do with their time and other resources and with the quality, quantity, and direction of their legislative work. Electoral necessities enhance or restrict in predictable ways the influence of individuals, groups, parties, congressional leaders, and presidents. And all these things affect the performance of Congress as a policy-making institution. These points are argued in Chapter 7, which also examines the electoral basis of increasing partisan polarization in both chambers, illustrated by the attempt to impeach and expel President Bill Clinton in 1998–1999 and by divisions over the Iraq War in 2007; considers congressional reform; and speculates about the elections of 2008 and beyond.

Chapter 2

THE CONTEXT

The ascendant importance of individual candidates and campaigns that characterized the electoral politics of Congress from the 1960s through the 1980s has been challenged since the early 1990s by the growing influence of national and partisan forces. Nonetheless, congressional campaigns continued to be largely candidate-centered affairs. Even when national issues have an unusually powerful influence on the results, as in 1994 and 2006, their effects vary widely according to how they are exploited locally. Although national party organizations have greatly expanded their efforts to recruit and finance candidates in recent elections, their ability to produce victories still depends largely on the decisions of politicians operating as individual political entrepreneurs. Despite the strong national party support, which the most promising congressional aspirants can now expect, individual candidates still absorb the balance of risks, pains, and rewards of mounting a campaign. Most instigate their own candidacies, raise most of their own resources (especially the early money that signals a viable candidacy), and put together their own campaign organizations. Their skills, resources, and strategies have a decisive effect on election outcomes. Even though voters show signs of growing partisan loyalty, ideological consistency, and attentiveness to the national issues, they continue to be influenced strongly by their assessments of the particular candidates running in the state or district.

The focus on individual candidacies has important implications for every aspect of the political process to which congressional elections are relevant. Many are spelled out in subsequent chapters. This chapter traces some of the roots of candidate-centered electoral politics. It examines the constitutional, legal, and political contexts in which congressional elections take place, for they are fundamental sources of the present system and it cannot be understood apart from them.

The Constitutional Framework

Whether to have an elected legislature was never a question during the Constitutional Convention that met in Philadelphia in 1787. The influence of British parliamentary tradition and colonial experience—all thirteen colonies had legislatures with at least one popularly elected house—was decisive. Beyond question, the new government would have one. But not much else about it was certain. Delegates disagreed about how the legislative branch would be organized, what its powers would be, and how its members would be selected.

The matter of selection involved several important issues. The most crucial was the basis of representation: How were seats in the legislature to be apportioned? Delegates from large states naturally preferred representation according to population; otherwise, their constituents would be underrepresented. Those from smaller states were convinced that their interests would be in jeopardy if only size counted, so they proposed equal representation for each state. The controversy coincided with another unsettled and unsettling issue: Was it to be a national government representing a national citizenry, or was it to be a federal government representing sovereign states?[1]

The conflict was resolved by a quintessential political deal. General sentiment was strongly in favor of a bicameral legislature,[2] and this made a solution easier. Each side got what it wanted. Seats in one chamber, the House of Representatives, would be apportioned by population; each state's representation would be determined by its share of the population as measured in a decennial census (Article I, Section 2 of the U.S. Constitution). In the other chamber, the Senate, states would enjoy equal representation, each choosing two senators (Article I, Section 3).

This "great compromise," as it has been called, opened the way to resolving another dispute. At issue was the extent of popular participation in electing officials in the new government. Most delegates were skeptical of democracy as they conceived it, but to varying degrees. A bicameral legislature allowed different levels of popular involvement in choosing members of Congress. Representatives were to be "popularly"[3] chosen in frequent elections. Biennial elections were the compromise choice between the annual elections proposed by many delegates and the three-year term advocated by James Madison.[4] Broad suffrage and short terms were meant to ensure that one branch of government, the House, remained as close as possible to the people.

The Senate, in contrast, was designed to be much more insulated from momentary shifts in the public mood. The term of office was set at six years (another compromise, as terms of three, four, five, six, seven, and nine years had been proposed).[5] Continuity was enhanced by having one-third of the Senate's membership elected every two years. Senators, furthermore, were to be chosen by state legislatures rather than by voters. The Senate could thus act as a stable and dispassionate counterweight to the more popular and radical House, protecting the new government from the volatility thought to be characteristic of democracies. Its structure could also embody the elements of state sovereignty that remained.[6]

The opposition to popular democracy embodied in the indirect election of senators (and the president) diminished during the nineteenth century. Restrictions on suffrage were gradually lifted and more and more offices came to be filled by popular election. The Civil War effectively settled the issue of national sovereignty. By the beginning of the twentieth century, the constitutional method of choosing senators had come to be viewed by most Americans as undemocratic and corrupting; it was replaced, via the Seventeenth Amendment (ratified in 1913), by popular election. Members of both houses of Congress are now chosen in elections in which nearly every citizen past his or her eighteenth birthday is eligible to vote.[7]

Congressional Districts

The Constitution itself apportioned seats among states for the first Congress (Article I, Section 3). Following the initial census in 1790, membership of the House was set at 105, with each state given one seat for each 33,000 inhabitants. From that point on, until 1911, the House grew as population increased and new states joined the nation. Congress sought to limit the politically painful reductions in representation faced by states suffering unfavorable population shifts by adding seats after each decennial census. Eventually a point was reached where further growth could seriously impair the House's efficiency. Membership was set at 435 after the 1910 census and strong opposition developed to any further increase.

A crisis thus arrived with the 1920 census results. Large population shifts between 1910 and 1920 and a fixed House membership would mean that many states—and members of Congress—would lose seats. Adding to the turmoil was the discovery by the census that, for the first time, a majority of Americans lived in urban rather than rural areas. Reapportionment was certain to increase the political weight of city dwellers and reduce that of farmers. The result was an acrimonious stalemate that was not resolved until 1929, when a law was passed establishing a permanent system for reapportioning the 435 House seats after each census; it would be carried out, if necessary, without additional legislation.[8]

The new system took effect after the 1930 census. Because twenty years had passed since the last apportionment, unusually large shifts occurred. California's delegation went from eleven to twenty; other big gainers were Michigan (four), Texas (three), and New York, Ohio, and New Jersey (two each). Twenty-one states lost seats; Missouri lost three; and four other states lost two each.[9] Subsequent shifts have not been so dramatic, but the beginning of each decade still ushers in a period of heightened uncertainty and anxiety among congressional incumbents.

Anxiety is not misplaced. In 2002, redistricting gave thirty-six incumbents the choice of retiring or facing another incumbent in the primary or general election. Some retired; eight ended up losing contests to other incumbents. As in past decades, the new distribution of House seats reflected population shifts since the previous census, redistributing power among states and regions. States in the East and Midwest lost a total of twelve seats to states in the South and West. Arizona, Florida, Georgia, and Texas gained two seats each; California, Colorado, Nevada, and North Carolina each gained one seat. Pennsylvania and New York lost two seats each and Connecticut, Illinois, Indiana, Michigan, Mississippi, Ohio, Oklahoma, and Wisconsin each lost one seat. In the 1950s, states in the South and West controlled 41 percent of House seats; after the latest reapportionment, their share had grown to 55 percent.

At first, federal law fixed only the number of representatives each state could elect; other important aspects of districting were left to the states. Until 1842, single-member districts were not required by law, and a number of states used multimember or at-large districts. Thereafter, apportionment legislation usually required that states establish contiguous single-member districts and, in some years, it required that they be of roughly equal populations and even "compact" in shape. Such requirements were never, when ignored by mapmakers, successfully enforced. Single-member districts became the overwhelming norm, but districts composed of "contiguous and compact territory . . . containing as nearly as practicable an equal number of inhabitants," in the words of the 1901 reapportionment act, did not.[10]

Many states continued to draw districts with widely differing populations. In 1930, for example, New York's largest district (766,425) contained nearly nine times as many people as its smallest (90,671). As recently as 1962, the most populous district in Michigan (802,994) had 4.5 times the inhabitants of its least populous (177,431).[11] Rural populations were usually overrepresented at the expense of people living in cities and suburbs. The Supreme Court's 1964 ruling in *Wesberry v. Sanders*, however, applied the principle of one person–one vote to congressional districts and, since then, malapportioned districts have, under the watchful eye of the courts, become extinct.

The Court's rulings have indeed given more equal weight to each citizen's House vote, but they have also reinforced some less-desirable aspects of the congressional election system. Drawing district lines with an eye to size rather than to natural political communities increases the number of districts composed of people with nothing in common save residence in the district. District boundaries are even less likely than before to coincide with the local political divisions—cities, counties, state legislative districts—around which parties are organized. So a greater number of congressional aspirants become political orphans, left to their own organization devices. More will be said later about the irrelevance of local parties to most congressional candidates; the structure of House districts is clearly one of its sources.

Partisan Gerrymandering

The requirement of equal district populations has encouraged another old political custom: gerrymandering. District boundaries are not politically neutral. Parties controlling state governments are naturally tempted to draw district lines designed to maximize the number of seats the party can win, given the number and distribution of its usual voters. The idea is to concentrate the opposing party's voters in a small number of districts that the party can win by large margins, thus "wasting" many of its votes, and to create as many districts as possible where their own party has a secure, though not overwhelming, majority.[12] Forced by the Court's strict standard of equality to ignore community boundaries in drawing districts, legislators are freer to pursue naked partisan advantage. The use of computers allows precise integration of partisan with egalitarian objectives.[13]

Partisan gerrymanders are easier to calculate than to carry out, however. Arrangements that might add to a party's share of seats often conflict with other political necessities, particularly the protection of incumbents unwilling to increase their own electoral risks to improve their party's collective welfare.[14] Voters more attuned to candidates than to parties sometimes frustrate partisan schemes.[15] But state legislatures still try, when the opportunity arises, to draw lines favoring their party's House candidates—and sometimes they succeed. The redistricting activity that followed the 2000 census offers an example of how consequential partisan gerrymandering can be.

Republicans enjoyed two advantages in redistricting after the 2000 census. First, the states that gained seats after 2000 were more Republican in their voting habits than were states that lost seats. Al Gore won six of the ten states losing seats, while Bush won seven of the eight states gaining seats. Second, Republicans controlled the redistricting process in several of the large states that were set to lose or gain seats, and they used that control effectively to boost their House representation.

A convenient way to assess the redistricting-induced changes in district party balances for 2002 is to compare the distribution of the major-party presidential vote in 2000 in the old and new districts. Short-term partisan forces were evenly balanced in 2000 and party-line voting was the highest in decades, so both the national and district-level presidential vote reflected the underlying national partisan balance with unusual accuracy.[16] The first row of Table 2–1 shows that, according to the Bush–Gore vote division, the net effect of redistricting helped Republicans, raising the number of House districts where Bush won more votes than Gore by ten, from 228 to 238. The data also show that the reduction in

TABLE 2–1 Effects of Redistricting on the 2002 House Elections

I.	**GORE-MAJORITY DISTRICTS**			**BUSH-MAJORITY DISTRICTS**		
	2000	**2002**	**Change**	**2000**	**2002**	**Change**
All seats	207	197	−10	228	238	10
I. Seat Reallocations						
State lost seats	80	65	−15	63	66	3
No change	65	66	1	85	84	−1
State gained seats	62	66	4	80	88	8
II. Partisan Control of Redistricting						
Republicans	41	30	−11	59	68	9
Democrats	64	68	4	69	67	−2
Shared or neither party	100	97	−3	95	98	3
At-large states	2	2	0	5	5	0

II.	**WON BY DEMOCRATS[a]**			**WON BY REPUBLICANS**		
	2000	**2002**	**Change**	**2000**	**2002**	**Change**
All seats	211	205	−6	223	229	6
I. Seat Reallocations						
State lost seats	72	59	−13	71	72	1
No change	70	73	3	79	76	−3
State gained seats	69	73	4	73	81	8
II. Partisan Control of Redistricting						
Republicans	40	31	−9	60	67	7
Democrats	74	79	5	59	56	−3
Shared or neither party	96	94	−2	99	101	2
At-large states	1	1	0	5	5	0

[a]Independent Bernard Sanders, who votes on organizational matters with Democrats, was also reelected.

Gore-majority districts was concentrated in the states that lost seats. The number of Bush-majority districts actually grew in those states, despite their total loss of twelve House seats. This lopsided outcome reflects successful Republican gerrymanders in Michigan, Ohio, and Pennsylvania, as reflected in the data in the second part of this section.[17] Plainly, both parties used control of redistricting to improve their candidates' prospects, but Republicans more so than Democrats, and Republicans also came out ahead in states where neither party had full control of the process.

Part II of Table 2–1 shows that the House election results in 2002 reflected redistricting patterns with remarkable fidelity. Democrats suffered a net decline in states that lost seats (and where redistricting was controlled by Republicans), which was only partially offset by additional victories in states that gained seats. Republicans actually managed to add a seat among the states losing representation and won eight additional seats in the states gaining districts. The similarity between the two sections is not coincidental. Eight of the ten seats switching party control in 2002, including all four seats lost by incumbents, went to the party with the district presidential majority.[18]

Aside from its notable partisan effects, redistricting for 2002 also gave both parties' vulnerable incumbents safer districts. Redistricting gave eight Democrat incumbents who had been representing Bush-majority districts new Gore-majority districts; only one suffered the contrary switch, leaving a net increase of six. All thirteen of the switches involving Republican incumbents were from Gore-majority to Bush-majority districts. Of the twenty-five districts Republicans had won in 2000 with less than 55 percent of the major-party vote, eighteen were strengthened by increasing the proportion of Bush voters; of the nineteen similarly marginal Democratic districts, fifteen were given a larger share of

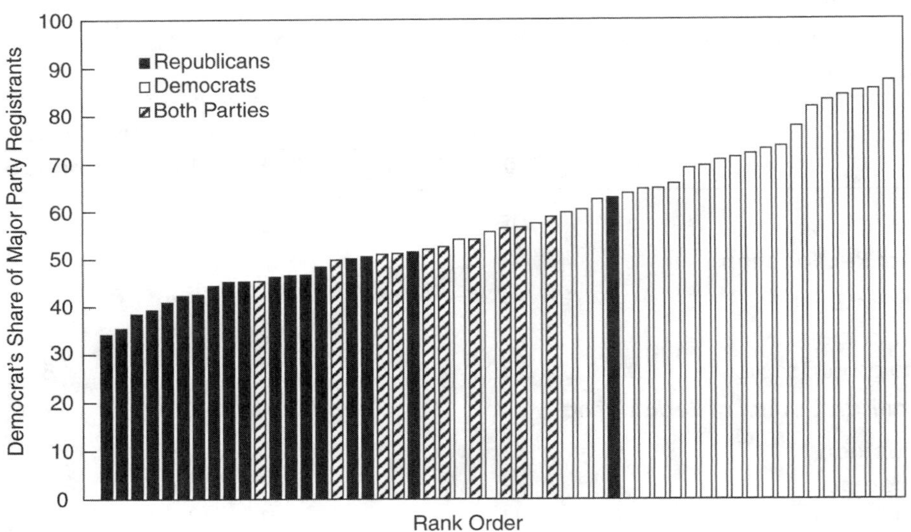

FIGURE 2–1a Registration and Party Control of California House Seats, 1992–2000

Source: Gary C. Jacobson, "All Quiet on the Western Front: Redistricting and Party Competition in California House Elections," in *Redistricting in the New Millennium*, ed. Peter Galderisi (Lanham, Maryland: Lexington Books, 2005); 230.

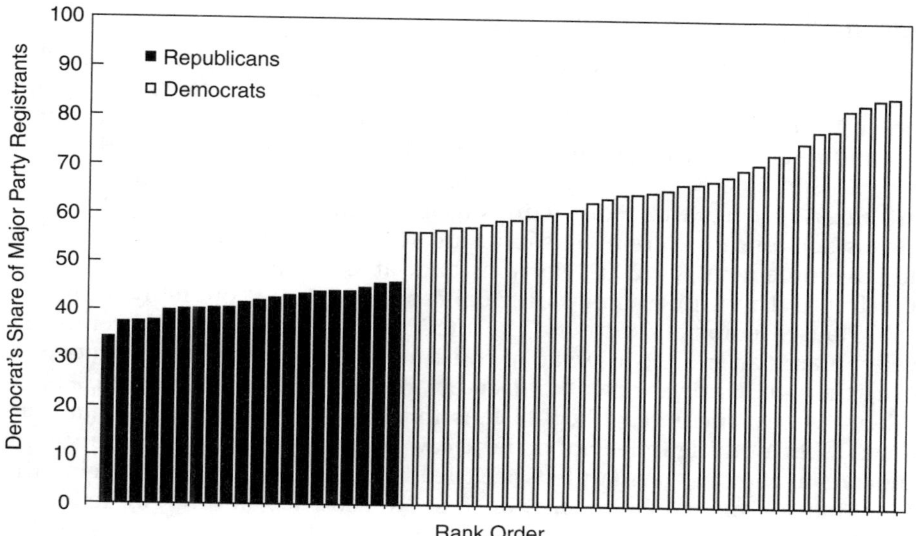

FIGURE 2–1b Registration and Party Control of California House Seats, 2002

Source: Gary C. Jacobson, "All Quiet on the Western Front: Redistricting and Party Competition in California House Elections," in *Redistricting in the New Millennium*, ed. Peter Galderisi (Lanham, Maryland: Lexington Books, 2005); 230.

Gore voters. Thus, three-quarters of the marginal districts were made safer by redistricting.

In addition to giving Republicans more favorable terrain, then, the redistricting for 2002 also dampened competition for House seats. California, where a redistricting scheme endorsed by both parties left not a single one of the state's fifty-three House districts truly competitive, led the way. Figures 2–1a and 2–1b illustrate what happened. Figure 2–1a shows the California House districts as they existed in 2000, ranked in order of the Democratic percentage of major party registrants and indicates the pattern of party control for the 1992–2000 reapportionment cycle. Notice that the competitive range—where both parties have been able to win—generally falls within 45–58 percent Democratic registration. After redistricting, not a single district with registration between 46 and 56 percent Democratic remained.[19] In the 159 House contests held in California from 2002 through 2006, only one of these seats changed party hands: Republican Richard Pombo, beset by personal scandal and a modest increase in Democratic registration in his 11th District, was defeated in 2006.

The Supreme Court declared in 1986 (*Davis v. Bandemer*) that a partisan gerrymander could be unconstitutional if it were sufficiently egregious but has yet to identify any that violated this ambiguous standard. A challenge to the 2002 Republican gerrymander in Pennsylvania was rejected in a 5–4 decision in 2004 (*Vieth v. Jubelirer*). Four justices concluded that political gerrymandering could never be subject to court challenge on the grounds that no coherent standard could be drawn to establish its constitutional limits. A fifth, Justice Kennedy, left open the possibility of finding a standard while rejecting the challenge in the Pennsylvania case. Each of the four dissenters proposed a different set of criteria, underlining the problem that led the first four to throw up their hands.

Redistricting Between Censuses

The issue of partisan gerrymandering arose in another guise when Colorado's Republican government, newly elected in 2002, redrew the state's new court-imposed House districts to make two formerly competitive seats safely Republican, aiming to solidifying the party's 5–2 majority in the delegation. However, the state's supreme court voided the move on the grounds that the Colorado constitution specified that redistricting take place only once every decade.

Texas Republicans were more successful. They won full control of the Texas state government in the 2002 elections and, at the behest of House majority leader Tom DeLay, proposed new district lines that would thoroughly dismantle several House Democrats' districts. The effect would be to give these Democrats largely unfamiliar, more conservative constituencies; to force them to move by placing them in districts with other Democratic incumbents; or, in two cases, to pit them against incumbent Republicans in new, overwhelmingly Republican districts. With nothing in federal or Texas law standing in the Republicans' way, Democrats in the state legislature twice tried to thwart the remap by fleeing the state en masse (once to Oklahoma, once to New Mexico) to prevent action by denying legislative quorums while avoiding arrest under a Texas statute aimed at preventing just this tactic.[20] It took five months and two special legislative sessions before the Democrats capitulated.

The Texas lawmakers did not overestimate the stakes. Prior to the 2003 redistricting, Republicans held fifteen of Texas' thirty-two House seats. After the new map was enacted, one House Democrat (Ralph T. Hall) defected to the Republican Party, another retired, another was defeated in a primary, and four were defeated in the general election. Only one targeted Democrat (Chet Edwards) managed to survive. After the 2004 election, Republicans held twenty-one of Texas's seats, a gain of six. The Texas gerrymander survived U.S. Supreme Court review in 2006 (*League of United Latin American Citizens v. Perry*); the Court ruled that states were free to redistrict as often as they liked but did require the state to adjust several district boundaries because one district was found to discriminate against Latinos in violation of the Voting Rights Act. Substantively, the new Texas map could hardly be tagged unfair, for it actually reversed a court-drawn plan that had amounted to a pro-Democratic gerrymander; in 2002, Democrats had won 53 percent of the Texas seats with 45 percent of the vote in a state where Al Gore had won 41 percent in 2000.

In redrawing new gerrymandered districts between censuses, Texas was actually reviving a practice once common in many states. For example, Ohio's district map was redrawn seven times between 1878 and 1892 as control of its government switched back and forth between the parties.[21] This practice coincided with a period of intense partisan competition for control of Congress, not unlike the present. But obstacles, such as the state constitutional barrier that thwarted the new Colorado gerrymander, make it unlikely that Texas's example will be widely imitated.

Figure 2–2 summarizes the electoral payoffs of partisan redistricting, with the major-party vote for Gore in 2000 serving as the baseline measure of district partisanship. The benefits of partisan gerrymandering are clear in years with (2006) or without (2004) strong partisan national tides. Even after 2006, the best election for Democrats since 1992, Republicans held a larger share of seats in states

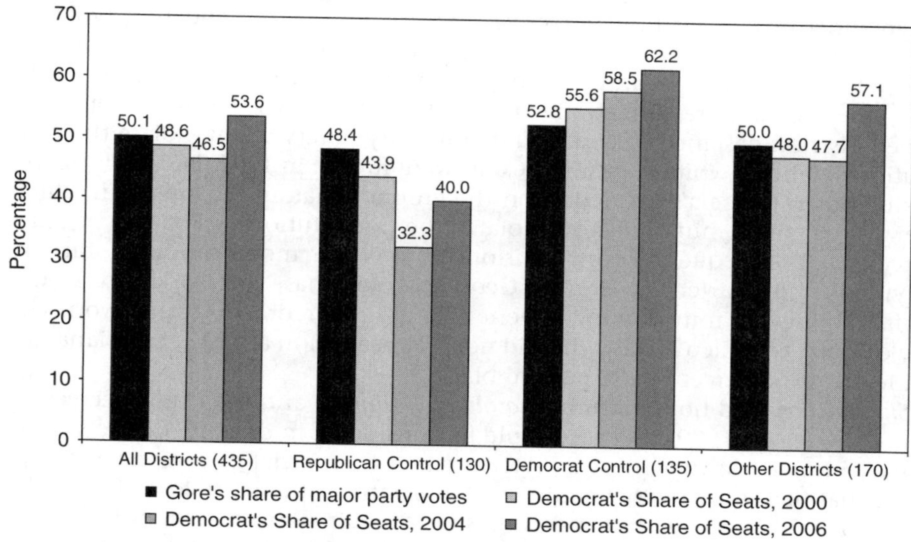

FIGURE 2–2 Control of Redistricting and Change in the Distribution of House Seats, 2000–2006

where they got to draw the lines than they had held in 2000. The Democrats' advantage in seats above their partisan base after 2006 was also highest in states where they controlled redistricting. But also notice that the effects of the strong pro-Democratic national tide registered regardless of who designed the districts.

Racial Gerrymandering

In a 1986 decision (*Thornburg v. Gingles*), the Supreme Court had construed the Voting Rights Act to require that legislative district lines not discriminate, even unintentionally, against racial minorities. The decision was widely interpreted as requiring mapmakers to design districts in which racial or ethnic minorities comprised a majority of voters wherever residence patterns made this feasible. Assiduous pursuit of this goal, backed by modern computer technology, produced some of the strangest looking districts on record.

Gerrymandering often produces bizarrely shaped districts; the term itself comes from a cartoon depicting an odd, salamander-like creature suggested by a district drawn under the administration of Elbridge Gerry, an early governor of Massachusetts. Perhaps the most audacious modern example of partisan gerrymandering was the 6th District of California as drawn in 1982 by Philip Burton for his brother, John (who surprised everyone by retiring from Congress before he could enjoy it). The district was composed of three sections connected only by the waters of San Francisco Bay; two parts of one section were linked only by a narrow strip of land underlying some railroad yards.

Racial gerrymandering after 1990 inspired some equally creative artwork; the 12th District of North Carolina, for example, stitched together African American communities in several of the state's larger cities, using Interstate 85 (northbound lanes in one county, southbound lanes in another) as the thread. Racial gerrymandering was far more effective than partisan gerrymandering typically is—the 1992 elections raised African American representation in the House from twenty-five to thirty-eight and Hispanic representation from ten to seventeen. In 1993, however, a more conservative Court ruled (in *Shaw v. Reno*) that bizarrely shaped districts designed to concentrate minority voters might violate the constitutional rights of white voters. The Court went further in 1995 (*Miller v. Johnson*), striking down Georgia's districting on the grounds that any mapping in which race was the "predominant factor" violated the Constitution's guarantee of equal protection.[22] Subsequent court decisions forced the modification of racially gerrymandered districts in Florida, Georgia, Louisiana, New York, Texas, and Virginia, but every minority incumbent running in a redrawn district won. The only casualty was Cleo Fields, who did not seek reelection after his Louisiana district fell from 55 percent to 28 percent black.[23]

Shaw v. Reno did not overturn *Thornburg v. Gingles*, and the Court decreed in *Hunt v. Cromartie* (1999) that race could be considered in drawing districts if the primary motive was to achieve a partisan rather than racial gerrymander (recognizing that blacks are overwhelmingly Democratic in the party loyalties).[24] The extent to which racial gerrymandering is now required, permitted, or forbidden remains unsettled, guaranteeing further litigation. The Court's restrictions on racial gerrymandering work to the disadvantage of Republicans. Minority voters are primarily Democrats; packing them into minority–majority districts helped Republican candidates elsewhere; racial gerrymandering was responsible for as many as ten of the seats Republicans gained in the South in 1992 and 1994.[25] For the 2002 redistricting, Republican officials again sought to maximize the number of minority–majority districts, but Democrats, including some minority activists who recognized that helping Republicans win more House seats did not serve their interests, resisted, and the Court's decisions precluded the kind of artful line-drawing of a decade earlier.[26] In the end, Republicans did benefit from redistricting, but racial gerrymandering was not a factor.

The Republican Advantage in House Districts

Some demographic features of American political geography give the Republican Party a structural advantage in contests for House seats. The advantage has been in place for decades but only in recent elections have Republicans have been able to exploit it. The Republicans' advantage lies in the fact that their regular voters are distributed more efficiently across House districts than are Democratic voters. To grasp this point, consider the distribution of the major-party vote for president in 2000. Short-term political forces were evenly balanced that year and party-line voting was the highest it had been in decades, so both the national and district-level presidential vote reflected the electorate's underlying partisan balance with unusual accuracy.[27] The Democrat, Al Gore, won the national popular vote by about 540,000 of the 105 million votes cast. Yet the distribution of these votes across current (2008) House districts yields 240, in which Bush won more votes than Gore, compared to 195 districts in which Gore outpolled Bush. The principal reason is that Democrats win a disproportionate share of minority and other urban voters, who tend to be concentrated in districts with lopsided Democratic majorities.[28] But the successful Republican gerrymanders in Florida, Michigan,

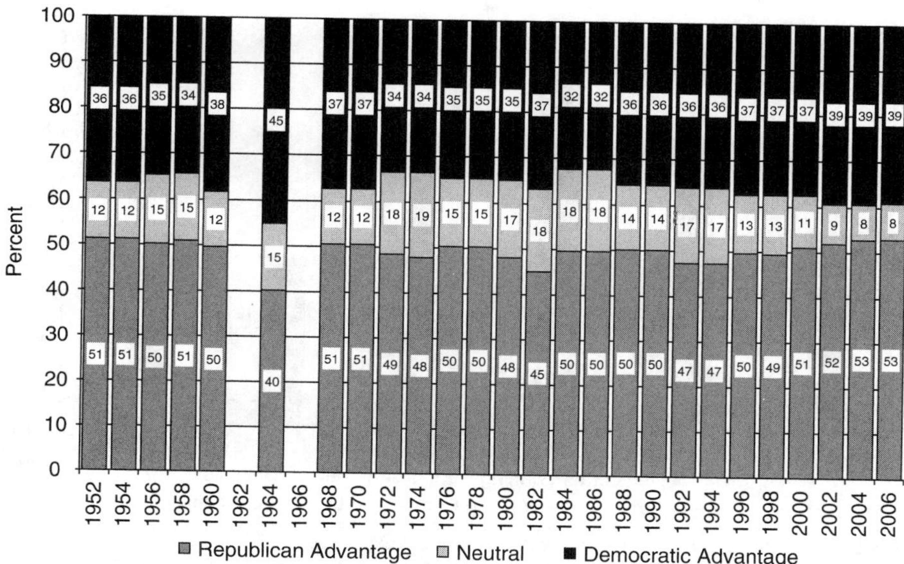

FIGURE 2–3 District Partisan Advantage, 1952–2006

Ohio, Pennsylvania, and, after 2002, Texas did enhanced the party's advantage, increasing the number of Bush-majority districts by 12, from 228 to 240.[29]

The Republicans' structural advantage, though enlarged in the post-2000 redistricting, is nothing new. As Figure 2–3 shows, except after the 1964 election, a larger proportion of House seats have leaned Republican than have leaned Democratic (estimated here as having the district vote for their party's presidential candidate at least 2 percentage points above the national average).[30] In past decades, Democrats were able to win a substantial proportion of these Republican-leaning seats, as high as 43 percent in the 1970s (Figure 2–4). Their ability to win such seats has dropped dramatically since the 1980s, for reasons examined in Chapters 5 and 6. Republicans have never done particularly well in Democratic territory and remain less successful than Democrats remain in this regard—but this is not a problem for them at present because their structural advantage is able to deliver Republican House majorities even if they win only Republican-leaning seats.[31] Figure 2–3 also shows that the proportion of seats falling into the competitive range (by the presidential vote measure) has declined; although critics blame gerrymandering, the main sources of this trend are changes in the behavior of voters, discussed in Chapters 5, 6, and 7.[32]

States as Electoral Units

For the Senate, "districts" are fixed by state boundaries, and the question of reapportionment never arises. It is easy to find examples of state boundaries that, like House district lines, cut across natural economic units—greater New York City, with suburbs in Connecticut and New Jersey, forms such a unit—and states that are sharply divided into distinct and conflicting political regions (Tennessee, for example). But this matters less than for House districts because states are, after

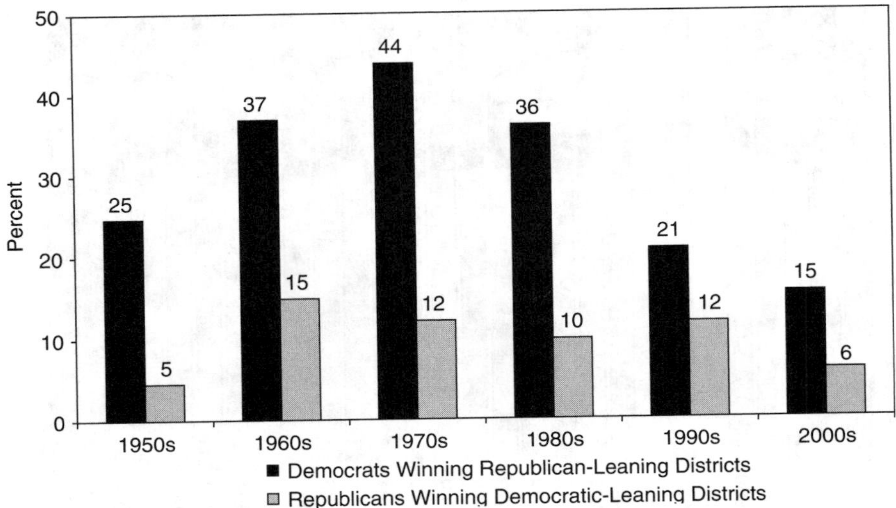

FIGURE 2–4 Winning Against the Partisan Grain, by Decade
Note: Leaning districts are defined as those in which the district-level presidential vote was at least 2 percentage points higher than the national average for that election; decades are defined by the reapportionment cycle (e.g. 1990s is 1992–2000).

all, important political units for purposes other than Senate elections. Indeed, this is an important basis for some of the differences between House and Senate elections that are spelled out in later chapters.

States form an odd set of electoral units for another, quite obvious, reason: their great diversity in population. A senator from California represents more than 71 times as many people as a senator from Wyoming. The nine largest states are home to 51 percent of the population but elect only 18 percent of the Senate; the smallest twenty-six states control 52 percent of the Senate but hold only 18 percent of the population.

The potential electoral bias introduced by unequal state populations has only recently begun to receive careful scholarly scrutiny. During the post–Civil War era, it favored Republicans.[33] Since the advent of popular election of senators, the bias has generally favored whichever party is in the minority nationally: the Democrats between 1914 and 1930, and the Republicans during the New Deal realignment and from 1956 through 1992. At present, it also produces a bias against ideological liberals and racial minorities.[34]

By allowing the minority party to win a share of seats significantly larger than its share of votes, Senate malapportionment makes it harder for popular majorities to rule, just as the framers of the Constitution intended.[35] Indeed, without it, Republicans would not have held the Senate in the early 1980s; they won majority control by taking a disproportionate share of the smaller states, winning twenty-two of thirty-four Senate contests in 1980 while winning less than a majority of Senate votes cast nationwide.[36] Today, with the two parties nearly even in popular support nationally, the Republicans enjoy the same sort of structural advantage in Senate as in House elections. Although Al Gore won more votes than George W. Bush overall in 2000, Bush won more votes in thirty of the fifty states.

Election Laws

The diversity that once characterized state election laws has gradually given way to substantially greater uniformity, but important differences remain. Congress was given the constitutional power to regulate all federal elections (Article I, Section 4) but was in no hurry to do so. Initially, states were allowed to go entirely their own way. For example, at one time many states elected members of Congress in odd years; the practice did not entirely end until 1880. The date of federal elections was not fixed as the first Tuesday after the first Monday in November until 1845, and states could still hold elections on different dates if their constitutions so required. For a time, some states required the winner of a congressional election to receive a majority of all votes cast; now all states except Louisiana permit election by plurality, at least in general elections (Louisiana requires a runoff if no candidate receives an absolute majority). Restrictions on suffrage once varied from state to state; constitutional amendments, court decisions, and federal laws have now eliminated almost every restriction on suffrage for citizens who have passed their eighteenth birthday and who have not been convicted of felonies.[37]

The trend toward more uniform election laws is not merely of historical interest. A single date for all federal elections encourages national campaigns, party tickets, and coattail effects. Each election is more than an isolated, idiosyncratic event, or at least it can be treated as such by voters. The removal of formal and informal barriers to voting has substantially altered the political complexion of some areas, notably in the Deep South, where formerly excluded black voters are now an important political force. Lowering the voting age to eighteen has made the student vote a key factor in districts encompassing large university towns, such as Ann Arbor, Michigan, and Madison, Wisconsin.

The process of voting itself has undergone important changes. Prior to the 1890s, each local party produced its own ballots listing only its own candidates, which were handed to voters outside the polling place. The party ballots were readily distinguishable; voting was thus a public act. Because local parties printed the ballots, internal party rivalries were sometimes fought with multiple or competing party ballots, frustrating state party leaders' pursuit of electoral unity and control.[38] The system invited intimidation of voters and other forms of corruption, and it was expensive for the parties to administer. It was replaced in a remarkable burst of reform between 1888 and 1896, when about 90 percent of the states adopted what was called the Australian ballot (after the country of its origin). An Australian ballot is produced by the government, lists candidates from all parties, and is marked in the privacy of a voting booth.

Although the Australian ballot has been blamed for weakening party loyalty by making it easier for voters to vote for different parties' candidates for different offices,[39] in some forms it increased partisan loyalty, at least initially. In states that adopted the *party column* ballot, which lists candidates by party, ticket-splitting diminished. Beyond using the party column format, the ballot could foster straight-ticket voting by allowing voters to mark a single spot (or pull a single lever on a voting machine) to vote for all the party's candidates. On the other hand, where states adopted the *office bloc* ballot, which lists candidates by office, ticket-splitting was facilitated. The search for partisan advantage led some states to switch back and forth between the two forms, depending on which party or faction was in power.[40] Differences among ballot types, and their consequences, persist to this day.[41] The technology of voting continues to evolve to varying degrees across states and sometimes with considerable controversy—absentee balloting has grown increasingly common; Oregon now conducts all elections exclusively by mail; and the debate over the security and accuracy of computerized touch-screen voting—as well as of older rival balloting systems—has yet to be resolved.

Again, variations in formal procedures can be politically consequential. The effects of ballot formats that make ticket-splitting easier run counter to those of uniform election dates. Easier ticket-splitting weakens coattails and other partisan links between candidates, by making it easier to focus the election on candidates rather than on parties. Early absentee balloting stretches the crucial part of the campaign period when voters are making their final decision, favoring candidates with enough resources to spread their campaign advertising over a longer period.

Political Parties

Without question, the most important additions to the institutional framework established by the Constitution have been political parties. The parties, along with the system of presidential elections that inspired their development, are the formal institutions that contribute most to making congressional elections something other than purely local festivals—and politicians something other than purely independent political entrepreneurs. The long-term atrophy of party organizations and the weakening of partisan ties from the 1950s through the 1970s thus contributed to the detachment of congressional elections from national political forces and to the rise of candidate-centered campaigns. For the same reason, the emergence of more vigorous national party organizations in recent decades has contributed to a significant reversal of these trends. See Chapter 4 for more on this topic.

The decline of parties stemmed from a variety of causes; several of the most important ones are discussed later. A fundamental factor, however, is clearly institutional: the rise and spread of primary elections as the method for choosing party nominees for the general election. Nineteenth-century parties nominated candidates in caucuses and, later, conventions. These were often dominated by self-elected party elites; they came under increasing criticism when the United States entered into a period of sectional one-party dominance following the election of 1896. Parties faced with serious competition found it prudent to nominate attractive candidates; without this constraint—with the assurance of victory because of an overwhelming local majority—they could freely nominate incompetent hacks or worse. With the nomination tantamount to election in so many places, the general election, and therefore the voter, seemed increasingly irrelevant.

The direct primary election was introduced as a way to weaken party bosses by transferring the right to choose the party's nominees to the party's voters and to allow people to cast meaningful votes despite meaningless general elections. It was also an effective method for settling disputes over who was the party's official candidate, which became necessary when states adopted the Australian ballot. In the South, where one-party dominance was most pronounced, most states eventually established a second, runoff primary between the two candidates receiving the most votes when none won a majority on the first ballot. Today, election laws in every state provide for primary elections for House and Senate nominations—although the rules governing them vary from state to state—and party leaders are able to control the nomination in very few places. They can, however, help direct the flow of campaign money to favored candidates, providing an edge if not always a victory.

A few states still hold nominating conventions and require that a candidate receive a minimum vote at the convention (20 percent is the usual threshold) to be eligible for the primary ballot. But even this may not give the party much control. In one convention state, Colorado, the eventual Republican nominee for the Senate in 1980, Mary Buchanan, did not win support of 20 percent of the delegates, but she got on the primary ballot anyway, by petition. She defeated three other Republicans, all of whom were preferred by party leaders, and then lost the general election.[42]

Scattered modern instances of party control over congressional nominations can still be found. When the congressman who represented the 5th District of Illinois (in Chicago) died in 1975, state representative John Fary "was called into Mayor Richard J. Daley's office. At 65, Fary had been a faithful servant of the machine; and he thought the Mayor was going to tell him it was time to retire. Instead, he was told he was going to Congress."[43] He did, declaring on the night of his special-election victory, "I will go to Washington to help represent Mayor Daley. For twenty-one years I represented the Mayor in the legislature, and he was always right."[44] When, in 1982, Fary ignored the party's request that he retire, he was crushed in the primary. More recently, veteran Illinois congressman William Lipinski announced he would not seek reelection only days before the August 26, 2004, deadline for a party to replace any candidate who had withdrawn. Among the local political leaders who gathered to pick his replacement were Lipinski himself, John Daley, son of the late Mayor Daley and brother of the current Mayor Daley, and a number of long-standing stalwarts of Chicago's legendary Democratic organization. To no one's surprise, their unanimous choice was Lapinski's son, Daniel, a political scientist on the faculty of the University of Tennessee who had not lived in Illinois for fifteen years.[45]

Fary's tale and Lipinski's sudden ascent from classroom to Capitol Hill are noteworthy because they are so atypical. The local party organization's influence on congressional nominations varies but is typically feeble. Few congressional candidates find opposition from the local party leaders to be a significant handicap; neither is their support very helpful. National party leaders control more resources and hence potential influence, but they use them sparingly in primaries and are regularly thwarted when they do. Usually, the nomination is not something to be awarded by the party but rather a prize to be fought over (when it seems worth taking) by freebooting political entrepreneurs.

Primary elections have largely deprived parties of their most important source of influence over elected officials. Parties no longer control access to the ballot and, therefore, to political office. They cannot determine who runs under the party's label and so cannot control what the label represents. National parties have never had much of a say in nominations. Although attempts by national party organizations to influence nominations in competitive states and districts are now sometimes successful, party leaders do not threaten primary challenges to keep their current legislators in line, for fear of losing seats to the opposition following divisive intra-party battles. For example, even Lincoln Chaffee of Rhode Island, the least-loyal Republican in the Senate, got full national-party backing when challenged in the 2006 primary (Chaffee won the primary, 54–46, but lost his seat to a Democrat in the general election—just the result the party had sought to avoid). Thus, the primary system has long been an important barrier to strong party discipline in Congress. American parties lack a crucial sanction available to some of their European counterparts; namely, the ability to deny renomination to uncooperative members. State and local parties now typically have even fewer sanctions to discourage maverick behavior.

The primary election system also complicates the pursuit of a congressional career. Candidates must be prepared to face two distinct, if overlapping, electorates. Primary electorates are much more partisan and prone to ideological extremity, and the need to please them is one force behind party polarization in Congress (see Chapter 7).

Differences in primary-election laws underlie much of the diversity among congressional election processes across states. The date of the general election may be fixed, but primaries are held at any time from March through September. The runoff primary used in ten states (nine of them in the South) has already been mentioned; where two-party competition has finally developed, candidates must sometimes win three serious contests to gain office. Washington state holds a *blanket* primary, allowing any voter to vote in any party's primary; registered Democrats, for example, may vote in Republican primaries, and registered Republicans may vote in Democratic primaries. Louisiana has a unique system in which candidates of both parties compete in the same primary; if no candidate receives an absolute majority of votes, the top two vote-getters compete in the general election—even if they are from the same party.

Rules governing access to the ballot also differ. Some states require only a small fee and virtually anyone can run; others require a larger fee or some minimum number of signatures on a petition. Challenges to incumbents, as well as third-party or independent candidacies, are thus encouraged or discouraged to differing degrees.

This discussion of the legal and institutional framework of congressional elections has necessarily been brief; filling in all the details would demand volumes. But it is sufficient to point out some of the important ways in which reference to the formal context is required to account for the activities of candidates, voters, and other participants in congressional elections.

It is important to remember that the formal context does not arrive mysteriously from somewhere outside the political system. Rules and institutions are consciously created and shaped by politically active people to help them achieve their goals. Rules that allow members of Congress to pursue their aims independently of their party evolve when politicians thrive on independence; when loyal partisanship becomes more conducive to political success, rules are altered to encourage party cohesion. Although in the short view it seems that the formal framework establishes a set of independent parameters to which political actors are forced to adapt, it does not. Rather, the framework itself reflects the values and preferences prevalent among politically active citizens, and it changes as those values and preferences change.

Social and Political Contexts

The rules and customs that control districting and primary elections may contribute to the large idiosyncratic component of congressional elections, but the contribution is hardly decisive. Idiosyncrasy is deeply rooted in the cultural, economic, and geographical heterogeneity of the United States. A few short examples will suggest the astonishing variety of electoral conditions that would-be candidates must be prepared to face. States and districts vary in geographical size, population, economic base, income, communications, ethnicity, age, and political habits.[46]

Geography. Simple geography is an abundant source of variation. House districts are as small as 12 square miles (New York's 11th District) or as large as Alaska's 586,000 square miles, where campaigning by airplane is essential and occasionally fatal.[47] Even Michigan has a district that is more than 490 miles from end to end (the 1st). The range in geographical size among states is smaller but still enormous. The purely physical problems of campaigning in or representing constituencies differ greatly and can be quite severe.

Population. Obviously, states vary widely in population, and both districts and states also vary in population density. Imagine the problems faced by California's senators, who are expected to represent 38 million people living more than 2,500 miles from Washington, D.C. It is probably no coincidence that in the past sixty years only four of California's senators have won more than two terms. Alaska's senators serve only 627,000 people, but they are even further from the U.S. capital and are scattered over a far larger area. Rhode Island, in contrast, is a "tiny little city state,"[48] compact, with a relatively small population.

Economic base. The high-tech companies of Silicon Valley dominate the economic life of California's 14th District; 22,000 workers in the 5th District of Michigan get their paychecks from General Motors; Wyoming's prosperity rises and falls with that of the energy and mining sectors; West Virginia's largest employer is Wal-Mart; and 29 percent of the workforce in Maryland's 4th District work for the federal government.[49] Delaware is the home of DuPont, which has far greater revenues than the state government. At the other extreme are states and districts with thoroughly heterogeneous local economies.

Income. According to the 2000 census, the second poorest district in the nation is Kentucky's 5th; its median family income at that time was $26,627. The wealthiest is California's 14th, with a median income of $91,249. The Kentucky district gave George Bush 57 percent of its votes in 2002 and is represented in the House by a Republican; the California district gave Al Gore 65 percent and is represented by a Democrat.

Communications. Districts such as Tennessee's 5th (Nashville) and Oklahoma's 5th (Oklahoma City) coincide with media markets and are covered efficiently by newspapers and television and radio stations. Compare them with any of the thirty-five or so districts that fall in the New York City media market or to a state such as Wyoming, with multiple media markets. Or consider New Jersey, a state of more than 8.4 million people, all of whom live in media markets centered outside the state in neighboring metropolitan areas (specifically, New York and Philadelphia). Campaigning and representing are largely based on communication. It is easy to see how the media-market structure determines which tactical options are available to candidates and how easily they can attract public attention.[50] But more subtle influences operate in the mix as well. In some districts, for example, a member of Congress is a newsworthy politician; in others, he or she is lost in the crowd.

Ethnicity. Some districts are overwhelmingly of one racial or ethnic group, for example: 63 percent of the residents of New York's 10th District are African American; 78 percent in the 15th District of Texas are Hispanic. As of 2002, twenty-four U.S. districts had African American majorities and twenty-seven districts had Hispanic majorities. Other districts are ethnic patchworks. California's 9th was, in 2002, 26 percent African American, 19 percent Hispanic, 16 percent Asian, and 35 percent non-Hispanic white. States, too, have very different ethnic mixes: The political importance of Jews in New York, Irish in Massachusetts, and Hispanics in New Mexico are familiar examples.

Age. The median age in Florida's 13th district (Sarasota) was forty-seven in 2002; 37 percent of the eligible voters were older than sixty-five. Compare this with a district such as Utah's 3rd, where the median age is twenty-four, or with Wisconsin's 2nd, which includes 41,500 university students. Imagine how the dominant political concerns differ among the three.

Political habits. Some districts have historic traditions of strong loyalty to the candidates of one party or the other; others are characterized by intense two-party competition. Still others undergo rapid political flux through demographic shifts created by a restless, mobile population. Voter turnout in recent House elections in which both major parties fielded candidates has ranged from below 20 percent to above 80 percent; for Senate elections, the range is narrower—from 30 percent to 68 percent—but still striking.

Conclusion

These categories and examples do not begin to exhaust the possibilities, but they are sufficient to make the point that politically relevant conditions vary enormously across states and districts and are a potent source of localism and idiosyncrasy in the electoral politics of Congress. The problem for each congressional aspirant is to devise a strategy to win and maintain the support of voters in a particular state or district, and it is not surprising that no common formula has been discovered. Nor is it surprising that candidates try to nurture an image of independence. But recognition of the heterogeneity among states and districts cannot explain why political fragmentation and independence increased during the 1960s and 1970s, nor why it has diminished so much since then.

NOTES

1. See James Madison, Alexander Hamilton, and John Jay, *The Federalist*, ed. Edward Meade Earle (New York: Modern Library, 1937), Nos. 37 and 39.
2. Ten of the thirteen colonies and, of course, Britain, had bicameral legislatures.

3. The Constitution specifies that "Electors in each State shall have the Qualifications requisite for the Electors of the most numerous Branch of the State Legislature" (Article 1, Section 2). Property and other qualifications were, in fact, common in the early years of the nation; universal suffrage was a long time in arriving.
4. *Electing Congress* (Washington, DC: Congressional Quarterly Press, 1978), p. 135.
5. *Electing Congress*, p. 135.
6. Madison, Hamilton, and Jay, *The Federalist*, No. 62.
7. The exceptions are people in penal and other institutions and, in many states, former felons. Senate seats vacated because of retirement, death, or resignation before the end of the term may be filled by special gubernatorial appointment until the next regular general election; vacated House seats are filled by special elections.
8. *Congressional Quarterly's Guide to U.S. Elections* (Washington, DC: Congressional Quarterly Press, 1976), pp. 530–534.
9. *Guide to U.S. Elections*, pp. 530–534.
10. *Guide to U.S. Elections*, p. 528.
11. *Guide to U.S. Elections*, p. 528.
12. Bruce E. Cain, *The Reapportionment Puzzle* (Berkeley: University of California Press, 1984), pp. 148–150.
13. Rob Gurwitt, "Judgment on Gerrymanders Expected from Indiana Case," *Congressional Quarterly Weekly Report* 39 (September 28, 1985): 1939.
14. Cain, *Reapportionment*, pp. 151–157.
15. Richard Born, "Partisan Intentions and Election Day Realities in the Congressional Redistricting Process," *American Political Science Review* 79 (1985): 317.
16. Gary C. Jacobson, "A House and Senate Divided: The Clinton Legacy and the Congressional Elections of 2000," *Political Science Quarterly* 116 (Spring 2001): 5–13.
17. The classification is from Republican National Committee, "Redistricting Party Control," at *http://www.rnc.org/images/congonly.jpg*, September 9, 2002.
18. The victories that defied this trend were those of conservative Democrats Lincoln Davis (Tennessee's 4th District), who won a district where Bush's share of the 2000 vote was 50.5 percent, and Rodney Alexander, who won the December 7 runoff in Louisiana's 5th District, where Bush had won 58.0 percent.
19. Gary C. Jacobson, "All Quiet on the Western Front: Redistricting and Party Competition in California House Elections," in *Redistricting in the New Millennium*, ed. Peter F. Galderisi (Lanham, MD: Lexington Books, 2005), 217–244.
20. DeLay sought help from federal agencies to track the missing Democrats, a move that earned him a formal admonishment from the House Ethics Committee.
21. Erik J. Engstrom and Samuel Kernell, "Manufactured Responsiveness: The Impact of State Electoral Laws on Unified Party Control of the Presidency

and House of Representatives, 1840–1940," *American Journal of Political Science* 49 (July 2005): 535–537.

22. Holly Idelson, "Court Takes a Harder Line on Minority Voting Blocs," *Congressional Quarterly Weekly Report* 53 (July 1, 1995): 1944–1946.
23. Michael Barone and Grant Ujifusa, *The Almanac of American Politics 2000* (Washington, DC: National Journal, 1999), p. 697.
24. Caroline E. Brown, "High Court Upholds Minority Districts," *Congressional Quarterly Weekly Report* 57 (May 22, 1999): 1202.
25. Kevin A. Hill, "Does the Creation of Majority Black Districts Aid Republicans? An Analysis of the 1992 Congressional Elections in Eight Southern States," *Journal of Politics* 57 (1995): 384–401. Professor Hill kindly provided the 1994 update (personal communication). John W. Petrocik and Scott W. Desposato argue that the damage to Democrats from racial gerrymandering was largely indirect (forcing incumbent Democrats to run in new districts with many new constituents) and contingent on the strong pro-Republican tide among white southerners in 1992 and 1994; see their "The Partisan Consequences of Majority–Minority Redistricting in the South, 1992 and 1994," *Journal of Politics* 60 (1998): 613–633.
26. Gregory L. Giroux, "New Twists in the Old Debate on Race and Representation," *Congressional Quarterly Weekly* 59 (August 2001): 1966–1973.
27. Jacobson, "A House and Senate Divided," pp. 5–27.
28. For example, according to the CBS News/*New York Times* Poll of August 20–25, 2004, Democratic identifiers outed Republicans nearly five to one in New York City. See "New York City and the Republican Convention" at *http://www.cbsnews.com/htdocs/CBSNews-polls/nyc.pdf*, November 6, 2004.
29. Jacobson, "The 2004 Elections," pp. 201–203.
30. The substantive point is unchanged if the standard is 5 rather than 2 percentage points.
31. Democrats have also done worse in the dwindling number of evenly balanced districts; from the 1950s through the 1980s, they won 66 percent of these districts; since 1992, they have won 53 percent.
32. Gary C. Jacobson, "Competition in U.S. House Elections," in *The Marketplace of Democracy: Electoral Competition and American Politics*, ed. Michael P. McDonald and John Samples (Washington, DC: Cato Institute and Brookings Institution Press, 2006), pp. 27–52; Alan I. Abramowitz, Brad Alexander, and Mathew Gunning, "Incumbency, Redistricting, and the Decline of Competition in U.S. House Elections," *Journal of Politics* 68 (2006): 75–88.
33. An exception may be the years 1876–1892, when Republicans were able to win the Senate more consistently than the House or the White House by winning a disproportionate share of newly admitted, less populous states in the West. See Charles H. Stewart III, "Lessons from the Post–Civil War Era," in *The Politics of Divided Government*, eds. Gary Cox and Samuel Kernell (Boulder, CO: Westview Press, 1991), pp. 203–238.
34. John D. Griffin, "Senate Apportionment as a Source of Political Inequality," *Legislative Studies Quarterly* 31 (2006): 405–432.

35. Frances E. Lee and Bruce I. Oppenheimer, "Senate Apportionment: Competitiveness and Partisan Advantage," *Legislative Studies Quarterly* 22 (1997): 3–24.
36. John T. Pothier, "The Partisan Bias in Senate Elections," *American Politics Quarterly* 12 (1984): 89–100.
37. Felons are denied the right to vote temporarily in most states and permanently in some.
38. Lisa A. Reynolds, "Reassessing the Impact of Progressive Era Ballot Reform" (Doctoral dissertation, University of California, San Diego, 1995), pp. 23–27.
39. Jerrold G. Rusk, "The Effects of the Australian Ballot Reform on Split Ticket Voting: 1876–1908," in *Controversies in Voting Behavior*, eds. Richard G. Niemi and Herbert F. Weisberg (San Francisco: W.H. Freeman, 1976), pp. 485–486.
40. Reynolds, "Progressive Era Ballot Reform," pp. 77–106.
41. Rusk, "Australian Ballot Reform," pp. 493–509; Angus Campbell, Philip E. Converse, Warren E. Miller, and Donald E. Stokes, *The American Voter* (New York: John Wiley, 1960), p. 276.
42. "The Outlook: Senate, House, and Governors," *Congressional Quarterly Weekly Report* 38 (October 11, 1980): 2999.
43. Michael Barone, Grant Ujifusa, and Douglas Matthews, *The Almanac of American Politics 1980* (New York: E.P. Dutton, 1979), p. 246.
44. Alan Ehrenhalt, ed., *Politics in America: Members of Congress in Washington and at Home* (Washington, DC: Congressional Quarterly Press, 1981), p. 333.
45. Michael Barone with Richard E. Cohen, *The Almanac of American Politics 2006* (Washington, DC: National Journal, 2005), pp. 567–568.
46. Census data are from *http://factfinder.census.gov/home/en/cd108*.
47. House Majority Leader Hale Boggs and Alaska Congressman Nick Begich were killed in a plane crash while campaigning in that state in 1972.
48. Barone, Ujifusa, and Matthews, *Almanac of American Politics 2000*, p. 1410.
49. Michael Barone, Richard E. Cohen, and Grant Ujifusa, *The Almanac of American Politics 2004* (Washington, DC: National Journal, 2004), pp. 202–203, 829, 1721, 1784.
50. Richard G. Niemi, Lynda W. Powell, and Patricia L. Bicknell, "The Effects of Congruity Between Community and District on the Salience of U.S. House Candidates," *Legislative Studies Quarterly* 11 (1986): 190–198; Dena Levy and Peverill Squire, "Television Markets and the Competitiveness of U.S. House Elections," *Legislative Studies Quarterly* 25 (2000): 313–325.

Chapter 3

CONGRESSIONAL CANDIDATES

Each state or congressional district is a unique electoral arena. Diversity among constituencies underlies the astonishing variety of political forces operating in congressional politics. When attention is shifted to particular states or districts, however, as it is when we examine congressional candidates and campaigns—the subjects of this chapter and the next—the local context becomes a constant rather than a variable factor. Its elements are fixed, at least for the short run. Electoral variation originates elsewhere, in changing political conditions and issues, and in the skills, resources, and strategies of candidates and other participants in electoral politics.

The Incumbency Factor

From the 1950s through the 1980s, the electoral importance of individual candidates and campaigns expanded, while that of party labels and national issues diminished. The emergence of a more candidate-centered electoral process helped one class of congressional candidates to prosper: the incumbent officeholders. Indeed, the electoral advantage enjoyed by incumbents, at least as measured by electoral margins, increased so notably after the mid-1960s that it became the main focus of congressional electoral research for the next quarter century. This research leaves little doubt that incumbency confers major electoral benefits, but it also reveals that those benefits are neither automatic, nor certain, nor constant across electoral contexts. Even during the 1970s and 1980s, when House incumbents were riding their highest, impressive reelection rates and expanded electoral margins seemed ever more dearly bought. The pursuit of reelection absorbed a great deal of time, energy, and money, reflecting members' enduring sense of electoral uncertainty and risk. The electoral upheavals in elections since then, particularly 1994 and 2006, show that their worry was not misplaced; the advantages of incumbency proved to be far more contingent than the surface evidence might have suggested.

Nonetheless, incumbency remains a conspicuous factor in congressional elections from almost any perspective. Most obviously, incumbency is a dominant consideration because incumbents are so consistently successful at winning elections—and everyone involved in politics knows it. At a deeper level, nearly everything pertaining to candidates and campaigns for Congress is profoundly influenced by whether the candidate is already an incumbent, is challenging an incumbent, or is pursuing an open seat.

The basic picture seems clear enough. The data in Table 3–1 show just how thoroughly incumbents have dominated postwar House elections. Typically, more than 90 percent of the races have included incumbents, and more than 90 percent of those incumbents have won. During the period 1946–2006, only 1.6 percent of officeholders have been defeated in primary elections, and only 6.0 percent have lost general elections. Even in years very unfavorable to one of the parties, a large majority of its House incumbents return. In 1994, the Democrats' worst year since 1946, 84 percent of the House Democrats who sought reelection won. In 2006, a bad year for Republicans, 90 percent of the Republican incumbents who ran were returned to office.

TABLE 3–1 Reelection Rates of House and Senate Incumbents, 1946–2006

Year	Seeking Reelection	Defeated in Primaries	Defeated in General Elections	Percentage Reelected
House				
1946	398	18	52	82
1948	400	15	68	79
1950	400	6	32	91
1952	389	9	26	91
1954	407	6	22	93
1956	411	6	16	95
1958	396	3	37	90
1960	405	5	25	93
1962	402	12	22	92
1964	397	8	45	87
1966	411	8	41	88
1968	409	4	9	97
1970	401	10	12	95
1972	390	12	13	94
1974	391	8	40	88
1976	384	3	13	96
1978	382	5	19	94
1980	398	6	31	91
1982	393	10	29	90
1984	409	3	16	95
1986	393	2	6	98
1988	408	1	6	98
1990	406	1	15	96
1992	368	19	24	88

1994	387	4	34	90
1996	384	2	21	94
1998	402	1	6	99
2000	403	3	6	99
2002	398	8	8	96
2004	402	2	7	98
2006	398	3	22	94
Senate				
1946	30	6	7	57
1948	25	2	8	60
1950	32	5	5	69
1952	31	2	9	65
1954	32	2	6	75
1956	29	0	4	86
1958	28	0	10	64
1960	29	0	1	97
1962	35	1	5	83
1964	33	1	4	85
1966	32	3	1	88
1968	28	4	4	71
1970	31	1	6	77
1972	27	2	5	74
1974	27	2	2	85
1976	25	0	9	64
1978	25	3	7	60
1980	29	4	9	55
1982	30	0	2	93
1984	29	0	3	90
1986	28	0	7	75
1988	27	0	4	85
1990	32	0	1	97
1992	28	1	4	82
1994	26	0	2	92
1996	21	1	1	90
1998	29	0	3	90
2000	29	0	6	79
2002	27	1	3	85
2004	26	0	1	96
2006	29	1[a]	6	79

[a]Senator Joseph Lieberman Connecticut lost in the Democratic primary but won reelection as an independent.

Sources: Norman J. Ornstein, Thomas E. Mann, and Michael J. Malbin, *Vital Statistics on Congress 2001–2002* (Washington, D.C.: American Enterprise Institute, 2002), Tables 2–7 and 2–8. Data for 2002–2006 compiled by author.

The story is rather different for Senate incumbents. Although the odds still favor them, senators have not been as consistently successful at winning reelection as representatives have been. During the postwar period, 79.0 percent have won reelection; 4.7 percent have lost primaries; and 16.3 percent have lost general elections. Moreover, their electoral fortunes have fluctuated much more widely from year to year. In 1980, for example, only 55 percent of the incumbent Senate candidates won reelection. In 1986, more incumbent senators than representatives were defeated, even though fourteen times as many of the latter were running. Yet in 1982, 1990, and 1994, Senate incumbents were more difficult to defeat than House incumbents. This is only the first of many instances of greater variability to be observed among Senate elections.

Figure 3–1 displays graphically the fluctuations in the success rates of House and Senate incumbents in elections from 1946 through 2006. The sharp swings in the fortunes of Senate incumbents are clearly visible. House incumbents were much more vulnerable in 1946 and 1948 than in later elections; after 1948, their fortunes have varied, with notably high rates of success sustained in elections from 1984 through 1990 and again from 1998 through 2004.

Measuring the Value of Incumbency

The most straightforward measure—the mean percentage of the two-party vote won by incumbent House candidates in contested elections from 1946 through 2006—is displayed in Figure 3–2. The average incumbent's vote share rose dramatically from the late 1940s to the late 1980s, from about 60 percent to about

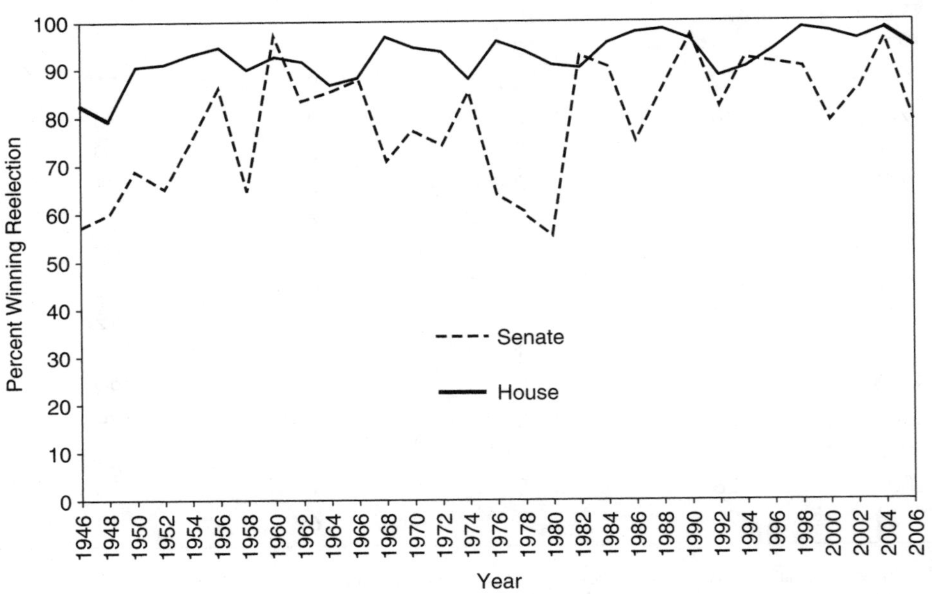

FIGURE 3–1 Success Rates of House and Senate Incumbents Seeking Reelection, 1946–2006

Source: Data in Table 3–1.

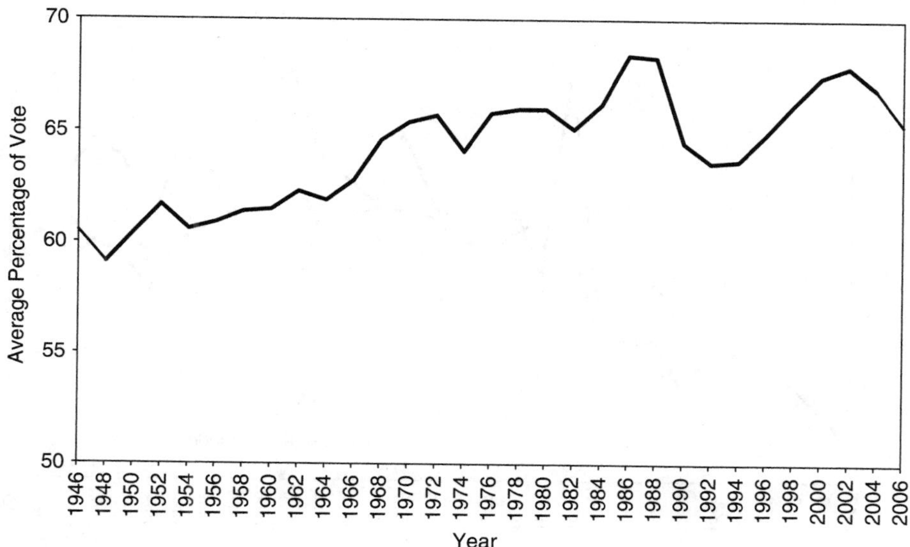

FIGURE 3–2 Average Percent of the Major Party Vote Won by House Incumbents in Contested Elections, 1946–2006
Source: Compiled by Author.

68 percent. After its peak in 1986 and 1988, it dropped back below 65 percent for the next four elections, before rising again between 1998 and 2004; in 2006 it was back down to 65 percent.

The incumbent's vote share is an ambiguous measure of the incumbency advantage, however. Some proportion of it reflects the partisan makeup of the district, votes that would go to any candidate with the same party label; conceivably, all an incumbent's votes could fall into this category.[1] The incumbency advantage must therefore be gauged by how much better candidates do running as incumbents than they would do running as nonincumbents. Scholars have taken several approaches to estimating this difference, but all of them support the same conclusion: The electoral value of incumbency, measured in votes, increased sharply during the 1960s.

The simplest approach is to look at what happens to the district vote in adjacent elections with and without the incumbent. Thus scholars initially estimated the incumbency advantage by calculating the *sophomore surge* (the average gain in vote share won by candidates running as incumbents for the first time compared to their vote share in the initial election) and *retirement slump* (the average drop in the party's vote from the previous election when the incumbent departs and the seat becomes open).[2] Averaged together into a single index, they form the *slurge*.[3] More elaborate approaches have sought to refine estimates by eliminating selection bias and other sources of error in the components of the slurge.[4] Although consensus has yet to emerge on which technique is most appropriate, the choice makes little practical difference. All the indices tell the same basic story.

Figure 3–3 displays the postwar trends in two popular measures, the slurge and Gelman and King's index.[5] Both show the growing value, in votes, of holding a House seat; both show a particularly sharp increase in the mid-1960s; and both show that the incumbency advantage, so measured, persisted at the higher level

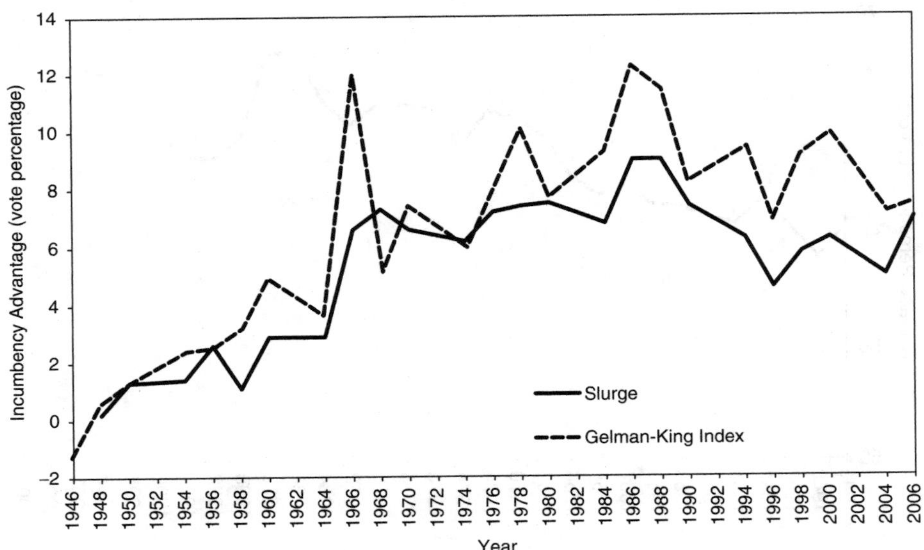

FIGURE 3–3 Incumbency Advantage in House Elections, 1946–2006
Source: Compiled by Author.

into the 1990s. According to the slurge, the value of incumbency, in votes, jumped from an average of 1.6 percent in the 1946–1964 period to 7.2 percent for 1966–1984 and to 8.5 percent for 1986–1990; according to Gelman and King's index, it jumped from 2.2 percent to 8.2 percent and then to 10.6 percent over the same time spans. Both indices show a modest decline in the value of incumbency since 1990, to averages of 5.8 percent for the slurge and 8.3 percent for the Gelman King index.

The value, in votes, of Senate incumbency also increased during the 1960s. Trends in Senate elections are more difficult to detect than trends in House elections because the number of contests is much smaller (33 or 34 in most election years) and only one-third of the Senate's seats are automatically up for election in any election year. Still, careful analysis suggests that Senate incumbency, worth a little more than 2 percent of the vote in elections from 1914 (when Senators first became subject to popular election) to 1960, rose to 7 percent for the 1962–1992 period.[6] Why this change did not make Senate elections involving incumbents any less competitive is an issue I shall address later.

The Vanishing Marginals

David Mayhew identified and named one effect of the augmented House incumbency advantage: the "vanishing marginals."[7] Increased vote shares meant that fewer incumbents held *marginal seats*—those taken with narrow margins of victory and therefore thought to be at heightened risk for future losses. Conventionally, seats won with less than some specified share of the two-party vote are designated marginal; 60 percent is the most common break point. Figure 3–4 shows how the proportion of incumbents whose vote lifted them out of the marginal range (60 percent or less) varied over the postwar period. Until 1966, an average of 61

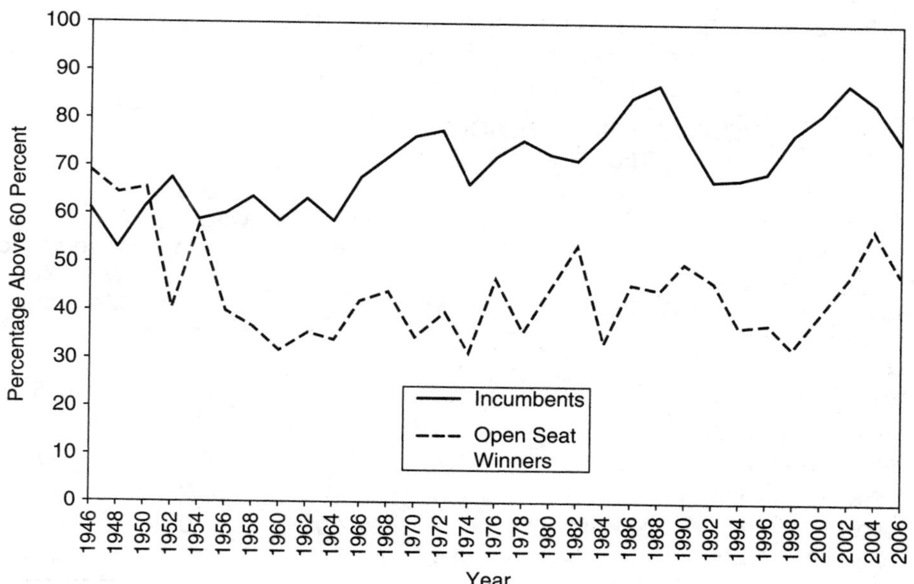

FIGURE 3–4 House Candidates Receiving More Than 60 Percent of the Major-Party Vote, 1946–2006

percent of House incumbents won in excess of 60 percent of the vote; the proportion jumped to 73 percent for the 1968–1982 period (the jump that caught Mayhew's eye) and higher still, to 83 percent, for 1984–1988. For the 1990–1998 period, it dropped back down to 71 percent, rose to an all-time high of nearly 88 percent in 2002, and fell off again slightly in 2004 and 2006. As Mayhew also pointed out (and Figure 3–4 shows), most contests for open seats have remained in the marginal range, so the vanishing marginals were *not* simply the effect of a more general decline in closely contested elections. Incumbency itself had something to do with it.

Scholars who first noticed the rise in the value of incumbency according to these measures understandably took it to signify a decline in electoral competition. With wider margins of safety, fewer incumbents should lose, turnover should decline, and therefore so should the *swing-ratio*—the percentage of seats changing hands for a given percentage swing in the national partisan vote.[8] Remarkably, none of these things occurred until more than a decade after they were anticipated, and not for the reasons initially proffered. House incumbents were not significantly less likely to lose in the 1970s than they were in the 1950s. Neither—if marginality is defined correctly—did the number of marginal House seats decline over this period. And seat swings remained nearly as sensitive to vote swings as before.

Measures of marginality are, in essence, estimates of vulnerability. Members of Congress who win with less than some specified share of votes supposedly have a higher risk of defeat in the next election. Such thresholds are arbitrary, however, and make sense only if they are, in fact, stable indicators of vulnerability. Table 3–2, which lists the percentage of incumbents at various margins who lost in the next election, shows that they are not. As the "marginal" incumbents

TABLE 3–2 Incumbents Defeated in General Elections to the U.S. House of Representatives, by Previous Vote Margin and Decade (in percentages)

	VOTE MARGIN IN PREVIOUS ELECTION:					
Decade	**50.0–59.9%**	**60.0–64.9%**	**>65%**	**Standard Deviation of Vote Swing**	**Loser's Mean Vote in Prior Election**	**Losers Who Were Not Marginal**
1940s	27.7	4.2	1.2	5.1	54.5	7.8
1950s	13.4	1.9	0.8	5.0	54.1	10.5
1960s	13.3	3.3	1.5	6.0	55.6	17.9
1970s	12.6	8.0	2.7	8.5	58.0	35.7
1980s	8.0	2.4	0.6	7.4	56.2	28.9
1990s	10.7	4.2	0.2	6.0	55.0	18.1
2000s	9.0	7.8	0.5	5.5	59.1	54.1

Note: Includes only incumbents who faced major party opponents in stable (non-redistricted) districts. Decades are defined by reapportionment cycles; for example, the 1950s include 1952 through 1960; the exceptions are the 1940s (1946 through 1950) and 2000s (2002 through 2006).

Source: Compiled by author.

(by the customary 60 percent standard) became safer, nonmarginal incumbents became more vulnerable. Indeed, an incumbent elected in the 1970s with between 60 and 65 percent of the vote was more likely to lose in the next election than an incumbent in the 1950s who had been elected with 55 to 60 percent of the vote (8.0 percent compared with 6.9 percent).

Although the mean incumbent's vote increased by about 5 percentage points during the 1960s, incumbents added almost nothing to their electoral security in the 1970s because they were little safer with a 65 percent margin than they had been in the 1950s with a 60 percent margin; their comparative risk at higher margins (above 65 percent) was also greater. Because incumbent defeats did not diminish and marginal seats—correctly defined—did not dwindle, there was no reason to expect the swing ratio to have been significantly lower during this time, and it was not.[9]

How could vote margins increase without adding to House incumbents' security, diminishing competition, or dampening swings? The answer lies in another crucial change, first noticed by Thomas E. Mann: an attendant increase in the heterogeneity of inter-election vote swings among districts.[10] Consider a hypothetical case. Suppose the average incumbent wins with 55 percent of the vote and the inter-election vote swing is normally distributed with a standard deviation of 5 percentage points. This means that, other things being equal, an incumbent with the average margin has about .84 chance of winning in the next election because .16 of the normal curve falls one standard deviation below the mean (that is, in this case, below 50 percent). Now suppose the average incumbent's vote increases to 60 percent. If the standard deviation of the inter-election vote swing does not change, the average incumbent's probability of winning next time jumps to .98 because only .02 of the normal curve falls two standard deviations below the mean. But if the standard deviation increases to 10 percentage points, the incumbent's seat is just as much at risk as it was before.

With this in mind, observe the fifth column in Table 3–2. The table lists the standard deviation of inter-election swings in the Democratic vote across incumbent-held House districts, averaged by decade. As the average incumbent's vote margin grew, so did the heterogeneity of inter-election vote swings. In the 1940s and 1950s, the standard deviation of the swing averaged 5.1; in the 1970s, it averaged 8.5. Vote margins could increase without making incumbents significantly safer because electorates became more volatile and electoral change more idiosyncratic across districts.[11]

Additional evidence that larger vote margins did not necessarily enhance electoral safety appears in the final two columns of Table 3–2. The sixth column lists the mean vote share losing incumbents had won in the election immediately prior to their defeat. In the earlier decades, the typical loser had won about 54 percent of the vote in the previous election; in the 1970s, the loser's previous vote averaged 58 percent. The seventh column lists the percentage of losing incumbents whose previous vote had put them out of the marginal range as it is customarily defined (60 percent or less of the vote); in the 1970s and 1980s, a sharply higher proportion of losers had held seats by what was once thought to be a safe margin.

In the late 1980s, some of the effects anticipated from the vanishing marginals finally came to pass. Incumbents were reelected at record rates in 1986 and 1988. The swing ratio finally underwent a statistically significant decrease (of about 25 percent).[12] Critics proclaimed the end of electoral competition; President Ronald Reagan, among others, made the invidious observation that there was "less turnover in Congress than in the Supreme Soviet."[13] Incumbency, it seems, had finally overwhelmed all other electoral forces. In retrospect, however, the elections of the late 1980s did not establish a new norm; all the relevant figures and tables in this chapter show a sharp revival of electoral competition for incumbent-held seats in the mid-1990s. Why did the predicted collapse of competition take so long to happen? Why did competition revive so vigorously in the mid-1990s? Why has it continued to vary from election to election?

These questions are merely the beginning of the list of what we want to know about the nature of the incumbency advantage in congressional elections. Why do incumbents usually do so well? Why do House incumbents do so much better than Senate incumbents? Why did House incumbents' vote margins increase sharply in the mid-1960s and what explains their ups and downs since then? Why did district electorates become more, and then less, volatile in their voting patterns across the last five decades? The answers are crucial to understanding congressional politics and congressional elections. They involve a complicated, interlocking set of institutional, behavioral, and contextual elements that we begin to examine in this chapter but that will take the rest of the book to explicate fully.

Sources of the Incumbency Advantage

The Institutional Characteristics of Congress

The search for an explanation for the sharp rise in the incumbency advantage during the 1960s proceeded on several fronts. One major focus was the institutional characteristics of Congress. David Mayhew, summarizing the results of his close examination of Congress as of the early 1970s, put it succinctly: "If a group of planners sat down and tried to design a pair of American national assemblies with the goal of serving members' reelection needs year in and year out, they would be hard pressed to improve on what exists."[14]

The congressional system that Mayhew described permitted the widest individual latitude for pursuing reelection strategies. For example, a highly decentralized committee and subcommittee structure allowed members to specialize in legislative areas where they could best serve local interests. It also provided most members with a solid piece of legislative turf. The operative norm for writing legislation was similar: something for everyone. Positive-sum distributive politics, represented by pork barrel legislation and the Christmas tree bill (one with separate little "gifts" for a variety of special interest groups), were much more prevalent than the zero-sum competition for scarce resources. Members deferred to each other's requests for particular benefits for their states or districts in return for deference to their own.

The parties also bowed to the varied electoral needs of members. Party discipline within Congress was lightly applied. In the face of controversial and divisive issues, Mayhew noted, "the best service a party can supply to its congressmen is a negative one: it can leave them alone. And this is in general what the congressional parties do."[15] Party leaders, taking the position that the first duty is to get reelected, encouraged members to vote the district first; members happily complied.

The system allowed members to take the "right" positions, make pleasing statements, and bring home the bacon while avoiding responsibility for the collective performance of Congress. It provided a setting for emphasizing individual achievements while insulating members from blame for the general failures and inadequacies of the institution, which were at least in part a consequence of the patterns of individual behavior encouraged by the system itself. This is important because the public's assessment of the performance of Congress was often strongly negative. Ratings of Congress actually declined while House incumbents were increasing their vote margins in the late 1960s and early 1970s. Disdain for Congress did not extend to its individual members; people generally rated their representatives far higher than they did their Congress.[16]

Members of Congress also voted themselves an astonishing array of official resources that could be used to pursue reelection. These include salary, travel, office, staff, and communication allowances that are now, by a conservative estimate, worth more than $1 million per year for each House member and up to several times that much for senators (whose allowances vary by state population).[17] All these perquisites were augmented dramatically in the 1960s and 1970s, with trends flattening out in the 1980s. The expansion of personal staffs of House and Senate members since 1930 is documented in Figure 3–5. The sharpest increase occurred between the 1950s and the late 1970s. The value to members of personal staff was underlined in 1994 when the new Republican House majority voted to slash committee staff by one-third but rejected a proposal to reduce personal staff from eighteen to sixteen.[18] Travel allowances grew in comparable fashion (see Table 3–3; before travel allowances became so generous, members would, of course, return to their districts on occasion at their own expense).

The growth of other official resources kept pace. The most important congressional perquisite is the franking privilege, which allows members to use the mails free of charge for "official business," which is broadly interpreted to include most kinds of communications to constituents. Figure 3–6 reveals that franked mail grew

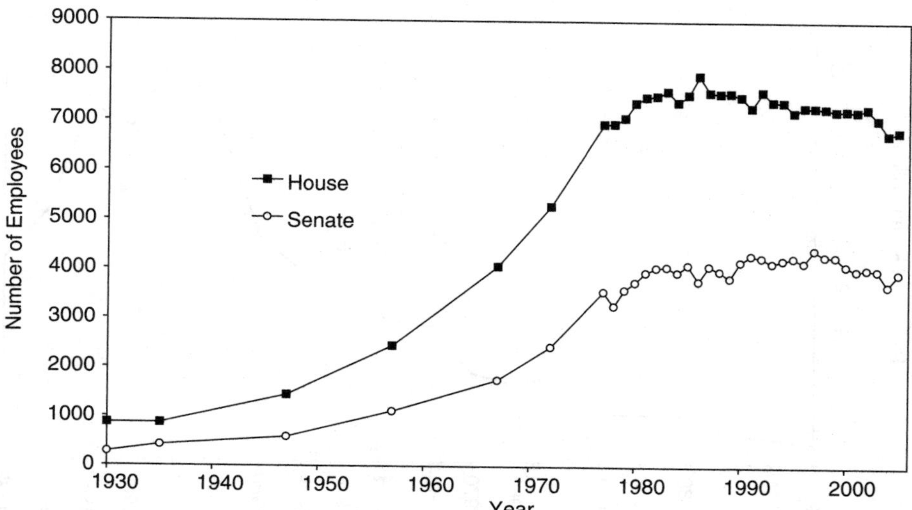

FIGURE 3–5 Personal Staff of House and Senate Members, 1930–2005

Source: Norman J. Ornstein, Thomas E. Mann, and Michael J. Malbin, *Vital Statistics on Congress, 2001–2002* (Washington, D.D.: American Enterprise Institute, 2002), Table 5–2.; 2002–2005 from Norman J. Omstein, personal communication.

by more than an order of magnitude between the 1950s and 1980s. Public criticism led both houses to tighten up the rules governing franked mail in 1990, so the volume fell substantially from its peak in 1984. Even tighter rules were proposed by Republican reformers in 1994, but reforms were successfully opposed by newly elected members representing large Western districts.[19] It is easy to understand members' reluctance to deny themselves such a serviceable tool. Other media have not been overlooked. Facilities for preparing radio and television tapes and films are

TABLE 3–3 House Members' Paid Trips to Their Districts, 1962–2007

YEAR	TRIPS TO DISTRICT
1962	3
1966	5
1968	12
1973	18
1975	26
1977	33
1978 and later	unlimited

Note: Since 1978, travel expenses have been included in an overall lump sum for offices, equipment, supplies, postage, communications, etc., which members may budget as they see fit. The lump sum total for 2007 averaged more than $1 million per member.

Sources: Morris P. Fiorina, *Congress: Keystone of the Washington Establishment*, 2nd edition (New Haven, Connecticut: Yale University Press, 1989), p. 61; Norman J. Ornstein, Thomas E. Mann, and Michael J. Malbin, *Vital Statistics on Congress 2001–2002* (Washington, D.C.: American Enterprise Institute, 2002), Table 5–12.

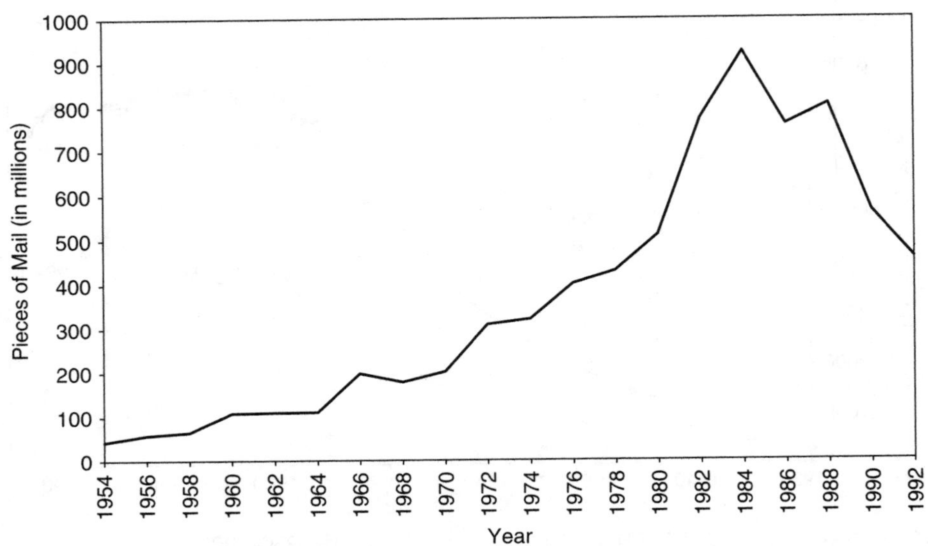

FIGURE 3–6 Election-Year Congressional Mailings, 1954–1992
Source: Norman J. Ornstein, Thomas E. Mann, and Michael J. Malbin, *Vital Statistics on Congress, 1997–1998* (Washington, D.D.: Congressional Quarterly Press, 1988), p. 172. Data are not available after 1992.

available to members free of charge. In 1977, members voted themselves unlimited WATS line service for long-distance telephone calls. Their offices are now linked to the Internet and nearly all of them maintain professionally designed websites.

Changes in Voting Behavior

Obviously, one major advantage of incumbency is control of extensive official resources for reaching and serving constituents. The remarkable expansion of these resources during the 1960s thus offered a ready explanation for larger incumbent vote margins: more vigorous exploitation of ever-expanding communications resources.[20] The accepted ideas about voting behavior in congressional elections lent support to this view. Voters were known to favor candidates with whom they were familiar (that is, whose names they could recall when asked), so more extensive self-advertising by members could be expected to have direct electoral payoffs, assuming that it made them more familiar to voters. Apparently, it did not. John Ferejohn showed that the proportion of voters who could recall incumbents' names did not increase between 1958 and 1970, nor did incumbents' familiarity advantage over their challengers grow. He proposed that a change in voting behavior was behind the enlarged incumbency advantage. Voters had become substantially less loyal to political parties during the 1960s and early 1970s. Perhaps they were merely substituting one simple voting cue, incumbency, for another, party.[21]

This explanation reflected a conception of voters as remarkably uninformed and superficial in their approach to voting decisions. As Chapter 5 will report in greater detail, later research challenged this view of congressional voters. If the congressional electorate is at least modestly more sophisticated and better informed than was once commonly thought, voters' preference for incumbents must arise from something more than the simple fact of incumbency.

Constituency Service

Morris Fiorina argued that members of Congress had enhanced their own electoral fortunes, not simply by advertising themselves more extensively but also by changing the focus of their activities and thus the content of the message they sent to voters. Essentially, they created needs and then reaped the rewards of spending more time and energy catering to them. In the three decades following World War II, Congress enacted legislation that greatly increased the size and scope of the federal government. Government growth generated an increasing volume of demands from citizens for help in coping with bureaucratic mazes or in taking advantage of federal programs. Members responded to the demand by continually adding to their capacity to deliver assistance, including the previously mentioned growth of personal staffs. The placement of new staff was equally significant; a disproportionate share went into augmenting members' capacity to provide services to constituents. In 1972, 13 percent of personal Senate staff and 23 percent of personal House staff worked in district or state offices; by 2001, the proportions had grown to 31 percent and 42 percent, respectively.[22]

The greater demand for services and the greater resources for providing them created more opportunities for building credit with constituents. For electoral purposes, Fiorina noted, "the nice thing about case work is that it is mostly profit; one makes many more friends than enemies."[23] Casework is also nonpartisan. The party affiliation of the member delivering the assistance, or of the constituent receiving it, is irrelevant. What counts is the members' ability to deliver services, which increases with tenure in Washington and consequent seniority and familiarity with the administrative apparatus. It is, therefore, perfectly reasonable for voters to prefer candidates on the basis of their incumbency rather than on their party label or policy positions. And it is equally reasonable for members to concentrate on providing services rather than on making national policy as a strategy for staying in office.

The evidence regarding Fiorina's thesis has been equivocal. The amount of time spent in the district appears to have little effect on the incumbent's vote margin, for example.[24] The value of pork barrel legislation has also been called into doubt, although some research suggests that Democrats, at least, benefited from delivering local projects.[25] Nor is it fully established that personal and district services persuade voters to prefer incumbents, although again, some research, including some clever experimental studies, indicates that they do.[26] Part of the analytical problem is that if members work the district harder the more insecure they are, then harder work may be associated with narrower electoral margins, even if it is what keeps the member in office.[27]

As originally proposed, none of these explanations took note of the fact that, despite wider reelection margins, House incumbents kept losing at about the same rate as before until the late 1980s. Once this is recognized, the evidence marshaled on their behalf takes on a rather different cast. For example, it is striking that the steep increase in staff, travel, and communications allowances during the 1960s and 1970s failed to produce any net improvement in incumbents' reelection prospects at the time they were occurring. Not until the late 1980s—well after the growth in official resources had flattened out—did the average incumbent's probability of reelection actually grow, and that change was reversed in the early 1990s. Considered in this light, it appears that incumbents spent a decade running ever harder just to stay in the same place.

Similarly, the idea that incumbents prospered by exploiting the decline of partisanship among voters needs to be amended. The basic argument is that a less-partisan, more candidate-oriented electorate favors incumbents. Diminished partisanship means fewer automatic votes against an incumbent, so personal cultivation of the district can pay off in a wider vote margin—but it also means fewer automatic votes for an incumbent and, thus, larger potential vote losses, should local electoral circumstances change.[28] A less-partisan electorate is more fickle; the vote is less stable from one election to the next; and a wide margin in one election is a weaker guarantee of success in the next.[29]

Although it, too, was proposed as part of an explanation for greater incumbent security, Fiorina's main point—that incumbents' increased emphasis on nonpartisan district services has altered the meaning of the electoral choice—is not necessarily blunted if incumbents' security has been exaggerated. Attention to constituency service plainly does command an enlarged share of the time of members and their staffs.[30] Members elected since the mid-1970s in particular have "exhibited great ingenuity and phenomenal tenacity in 'cultivating' their districts."[31] Fiorina's thesis thus helps explain why first-term House members, who were once much more vulnerable than more senior incumbents, became considerably more difficult to defeat.

Prior to the changes of the 1960s, new members were often swept into the House on a partisan tide and then swept out again two years later as it receded. Between 1946 and 1966, for example, 20.4 percent of all new House members lost their first reelection bids, a rate of defeat nearly quadruple that of members who had served two or more terms (5.2 percent). Since then, first-termers have held on to newly won seats much more consistently; only 6.6 percent have lost, compared with 3.3 percent of more senior incumbents. Indeed, between 1968 and 1980, the defeat rates of newcomers (5.6 percent) and senior members (4.4 percent) did not differ significantly ($p = 0.24$). Since then, the greater vulnerability of new members has returned; in elections from 1982 through 2006, 7.5 percent of first-termers lost, compared with only 2.8 percent of senior members.

Until the late 1980s, then, declining partisanship and more assiduous cultivation of House districts enhanced the reelection prospects mainly of first-term incumbents. After the first reelection, House members were actually more vulnerable in the 1970s than they had been before the changes of the 1960s. The advent of more candidate-centered politics did not automatically favor incumbents. A less-partisan electorate may have made it easier for a representative to develop the kind of personal hold on a district that insulates him or her from external political forces. But a less-partisan electorate is also more fickle; support from constituents is easier to lose as well as to win; an easy victory in one year does not guarantee reelection the next time.

In addition, greater insulation from outside forces did not reduce uncertainty or risk. The locus of competition merely shifted to the district. The incumbent assumed a larger burden of responsibility for winning reelection. Before the mid-1960s, House members who lost could put much of the blame on forces beyond the district and hence their control. On average, their inter-election vote swing was only 4.6 percentage points worse than their party's mean swing. Since 1968, the average loser's vote swing has been 8.7 percentage points worse than their party's mean.

The Variability of the Incumbency Advantage

As we shall see in Chapter 5, partisan loyalty in the electorate has grown since the early 1990s—which is one reason that electoral volatility (Table 3–2) and, to a degree, the incumbency advantage have diminished (Figure 3–3) from their peaks in the 1980s. Incumbency remains a powerful advantage, to be sure. But its electoral value is clearly not a constant. It depends in part on what the incumbent does with the resources available and on how hard and shrewdly he or she works to build and maintain support in the district. And this varies among members, although the degree of variation declined during the 1970s and 1980s, as members less inclined to endless pursuit of reelection quit or were weeded out. It depends even more on the kind of opposition the incumbent faces; as we shall see, differences in the skills and resources of challengers are a primary source of variation over time in incumbents' electoral fortunes. And it depends on what competing considerations shape voters' judgments, as the 1994 and 2006 elections made clear (see Chapter 6).[32]

It is safe to assume that incumbents who seek reelection want to stay in Congress. Why do some exploit the resources of office more vigorously than others to this end? The principal reason is that they have other important things to do with their time, energy, and staff. Single-minded pursuit of reelection detracts from work in Washington and therefore from a member's power and influence in Congress and impact on public policy. Reelection is an instrumental, not ultimate, goal. Sometimes opportunities to build support back in the district must be foregone if a member is to share in governing the country. And the longer a member is in office, the more opportunities he or she has to influence policy and to gain the respect of others in government. Members very soon find that they have to balance their desire for electoral security against their desire for a successful career in Washington.

One reelection strategy might diminish this tradeoff. For incumbents who stake their electoral futures on their party's performance, cultivating the district could lose some of its urgency. Many of the Republicans taking office for the first time in 1994 initially wedded their fortunes to the party's "Contract with America," dedicating their energies to dismantling welfare and regulatory programs and balancing the budget. Pledged to limiting their stay in Congress, they claimed to want careers that were, in the words of one of them, Steve Largent of Oklahoma, "brilliant but brief."[33] But even members far more interested in revolutionizing government than in lengthy congressional careers did not necessarily pay less attention to their districts. Losing would jeopardize the revolution. Insofar as supporting fundamental change forces members to cast politically dangerous votes, members have all the more reason to please constituents in every other way they can. The Republican incumbents elected in the 1990s thus continued to provide constituents with the services they had come to expect from their representatives and to work energetically to maintain a strong district presence.

Discouraging the Opposition

Casework, trips back to the district, issuing newsletters, and all the other things members do to promote reelection are not aimed merely at winning votes in the next election. They are also meant to influence the perceptions formed by politically active people of the member's hold on the district. The electoral value of incumbency lies not only in what it provides to the incumbent but also in how it affects the thinking of potential opponents and their potential supporters. Many incumbents win easily by wide margins because they face inexperienced, sometimes reluctant, challengers who lack the financial and organizational backing to mount a serious campaign for Congress. If an incumbent can convince potentially formidable opponents and people who control campaign resources that he or she is invincible, he or she is very likely to avoid a serious challenge and so will be invincible—as long as the impression holds.

This is so because politically skilled and ambitious nonincumbents follow rational career strategies; people who control campaign resources make strategically rational decisions about deploying them; and the volume of campaign resources at the disposal of a nonincumbent candidate has a great deal to do with how well he or she does at the polls.

Other things being equal, the strongest congressional candidates are those for whom politics is a career. They have the most powerful motive and the greatest opportunity to master the craft of electoral politics. They are most likely to have experience in running campaigns and in holding elective office. They have the incentive and opportunity to cultivate other politically active and influential people and to put them under some obligation.

Ambitious career politicians also have the greatest incentive to follow a rational strategy for moving up the informal, but quite real, hierarchy of elective offices in the American political system. An experienced politician will have acquired valuable political assets—most typically, a lower elective office—that increase the probability of moving to a higher office. However, these assets are at risk and may be lost if the attempt to advance fails. Thus, the potentially strongest congressional aspirants will also make the most considered and cautious judgments about when to try for a congressional seat.[34]

Incumbency is central to their strategic calculations. Politically knowledgeable people are fully aware of the advantages of incumbency and of the long odds that challengers normally face, and they adjust their behavior accordingly. Hence, for example, typically more than half of the candidates for open House seats have previously held elective offices, whereas such experienced candidates comprise fewer than one-quarter of the candidates challenging incumbents. Within this larger pattern, experienced challengers are more likely to run against incumbents who had closer contests in the last election. Table 3–4 presents the evidence for these points and shows the close association between the prospects for victory and the presence of experienced House candidates.[35]

The career strategies of potential congressional candidates are complemented and reinforced by those of individuals and groups that control campaign resources. The most important of these resources is money, although other forms of assistance can also be valuable. People and groups contribute to congressional campaigns for reasons ranging from selfless idealism to pure venality. Regardless of the purpose, however, most contribute more readily to nonincumbent candidates in campaigns that are expected to be close.[36] So do political parties. (The situation regarding incumbents is somewhat different and will be discussed later.) Resources are limited and most contributors deploy them where they have the greatest chance of affecting the outcome; donors naturally try to avoid wasting money on hopeless candidates. Figure 3–7 displays the consequences of this tendency.

TABLE 3–4 The Probability of Victory and the Quality of Nonincumbent Candidates for the U.S. House of Representatives, 1946–2006

Type of Race	Number of Cases	Winners (%)	Former Officeholders (%)
Open Seats			
No general election opponent	88	100.0	71.6
Held by candidate's party	1,168	73.0	69.1
Held by neither party	268	50.0	49.0
Held by opposite party	1,168	27.0	38.8
Total	2,692	51.6	54.0
Challengers to Incumbents			
Incumbent's vote in last election (%)			
50.0–54.9	1,931	19.0	44.2
55.0–59.9	1,891	7.9	28.8
60.0–64.9	1,887	4.3	18.5
65.0–69.9	1,687	1.9	14.3
70.0 or more	2,536	0.4	8.1
unopposed	1,898	0.9	5.3
Total	11,830	5.6	19.4

Source: Compiled by author.

Candidates for open seats typically have substantially more money to spend than those challenging incumbents, and more money is available to challengers who face incumbents who had smaller margins of victory in the previous election (the simplest measure of electoral vulnerability). Notice also that as funds available to nonincumbent candidates have increased over these three decades, they have also become increasingly concentrated in marginal districts and open seats; challengers to nonmarginal incumbents have become relatively weaker by this standard.

As party loyalty among voters has grown over the past two decades, largely reversing its earlier decline (see Chapter 5), the partisan makeup of the district has become an increasingly important indicator of electoral prospects. In contests involving incumbents, prospects are governed by an additional consideration: the availability of issues—personal, local, and national—that the candidate and campaign might use effectively to undermine the support that the incumbent has enjoyed in past elections.

Expectations about the likelihood of electoral success, then, influence the decisions of potential candidates and campaign contributors. The better the electoral odds, the more likely the race is to attract a strong challenger, and the more money will be contributed to his or her campaign. Furthermore, strong candidates themselves attract campaign money, and the availability of campaign money attracts strong candidates. A system of mutually reinforcing decisions and expectations thus links nonincumbent candidates and contributors with each other and with perceived electoral prospects.

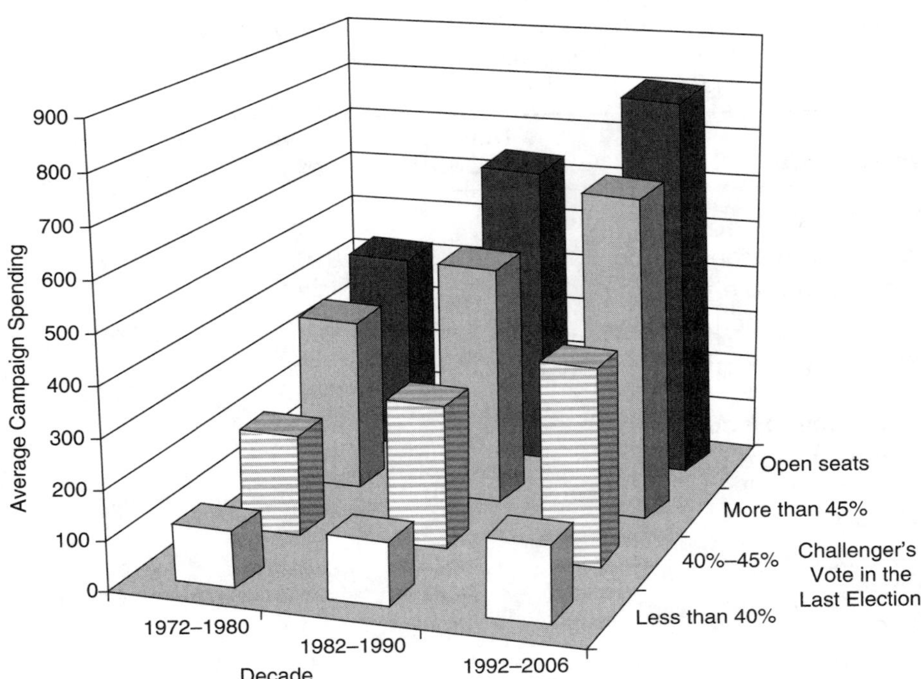

FIGURE 3–7 Electoral Competition and Spending by Nonincumbent House Candidates, 1972–2006 (in thousands of dollars, adjusted for inflation, 2006 = 1.00)

Source: Compiled from data supplied by Common Cause, *1972 Congressional Campaign Finances*, 10 vols. (Washington D.C., 1974) and *1974 Congressional Campaign Finances*, 3 vols. (Washington D.C., 1976), and the Federal Election Commission (1978–2006).

The strategies pursued by prospective congressional candidates and their prospective backers matter a great deal in a candidate-centered election process because the quality and experience of challengers, and the campaign resources made available to them, have a powerful effect on election results. I present a variety of evidence for this conclusion in the following pages. For now, the relevant point is that variations in the quality and resources of challengers offer an alternative explanation of increased vote margins enjoyed by incumbents since the 1960s.

Gary Cox and Jonathan Katz, for example, parsed the House incumbency advantage into *direct*, *scare-off*, and *quality* effects. *Direct effects* are those derived from the expansion of resources and district activities we have already discussed. *Scare-off effects* contribute to the incumbency advantage when strong challenges are successfully discouraged. *Quality effects* measure the difference that candidate experience makes. (All incumbents are, by assumption, high-quality candidates; variation is supplied by nonincumbents, many of whom have never before held elective office.) Cox and Katz concluded that the most important source of growth in the incumbency advantage was an increase in the electoral effect of quality differences. The value of incumbency grew not because of greater resources or more effective deterrence of quality challengers but because the difference in electoral performance between experienced and inexperienced candidates grew. Cox and Katz attributed this change to the weakening of party ties and the consequent growth of candidate-centered electoral politics.[37] One attraction of this explanation is that it is consistent with evidence that the incumbency advantage also increased in elections for state legislature, governor, and other statewide offices during the same period.[38]

David Brady, Brian Gaines, and Douglas Rivers's analysis, using somewhat different methods, reached a similar conclusion. Moreover, they found that the effect of the challenger's quality on the incumbent's vote had grown by about the same amount in Senate and House elections. Senators did not become more secure, however; unlike House districts, states became more competitive—that is, more evenly balanced in a partisan sense—over the same time span, offsetting the growing incumbency advantage.[39] This research suggests that the incumbency advantage depends not so much on what incumbents do as on what potential opponents do, and that it has grown because the impact of the opposition's level of mobilization has grown.[40]

Money in Congressional Elections

Mobilization requires money. Congressional aspirants are wise, indeed, to worry about the availability of money for a campaign. How well nonincumbent candidates do on election day is directly related to how much campaign money they raise and spend. The precise relationship between campaign spending and election results is difficult to pin down, however, because most candidates and contributors act strategically. Potential donors try to avoid wasting their money on hopeless causes. The better a candidate's prospects, the more contributors of all kinds are willing to invest in the campaign. The connection for nonincumbents between spending and votes is therefore at least potentially reciprocal: Money may help win votes, but the expectation that a candidate can win votes also brings in money. To the degree that (expected) votes influence spending, ordinary measures will exaggerate the effects of spending on votes.

Spending by incumbents is also reciprocally related to the vote, but in a rather different way: The higher the incumbent's expected vote, the *less* money flows into the campaign. This is not because secure incumbents have trouble raising money; quite the contrary. Many interest groups contribute to campaigns not so much to influence the outcome as to gain influence with, or at least access to, people who are likely to be in a position to help or hurt them. They waste no money on sure losers but have no qualms about giving money to sure winners, even when it is not really needed. Whether incumbents tap this source of funds depends on whether they think they need the money (or may some time in the foreseeable future).

Most members of Congress do not particularly enjoy asking for money, and most limit their fundraising efforts if they do not see a pressing need for additional campaign cash (given the strength of the opposition they are facing). If they feel threatened, though, incumbents have sources that are not nearly so readily available to challengers. In addition to groups seeking access, party committees and ideological interest groups rally to support threatened incumbents of the preferred party or ideology on the grounds that it is easier to hold on to a seat than to take one from the opposition. Incumbents, then, can generally raise as much campaign money as they think they need. Again, the anticipated vote affects spending—but for incumbents, the relationship is negative: The larger their expected vote, the less they raise and spend. To the degree that (expected) votes influence spending, ordinary measures will underestimate the effects of incumbent spending on votes.

To measure the effect of campaign spending on votes or victories, then, it is necessary to subtract the reciprocal effect of (expected) votes or victories on spending. Although theoretically feasible, this turns out to be extremely difficult in practice and, after thirty years of research, the appropriate solution remains elusive. We simply do not know the extent to which analyses that ignore the problem overestimate the effects of challenger spending or underestimate the effects of incumbent spending—if at all.

The Connection between Money and Success

Nonetheless, certain things are clear. First, congressional challengers rarely win if they do not spend a substantial amount of money, and the more they spend, the more likely they are to win. Figures 3–8 and 3–9 leave no doubt on this point. Figure 3–8 displays the percentage of winning challengers in House elections from 1972 through 2006 at ascending levels of campaign spending (adjusted for inflation, 2006 = 1.00). It also displays the proportion of challengers at each level of spending. The odds against challengers who spent less than $100,000 were long indeed; only 1 of 3,027 was successful. A majority (54 percent) of all House challengers fell into that category. Chances were only slightly better for challengers who spent between $100,000 and $200,000; they and the first group include two-thirds of all challengers. Prospects improved with increased spending. The most extravagant challengers (spending $1 million or more) won almost one-third of their races.

Of course, not all election years are alike. Some elections feature national political tides—driven by recessions, scandals, unpopular wars, presidential politics, and the like—that strongly favor one party's candidates. Conditions in other years seem nearly neutral between parties. Intuitively, a House challenger's chances of winning should vary with the strength and direction of national partisan tides.

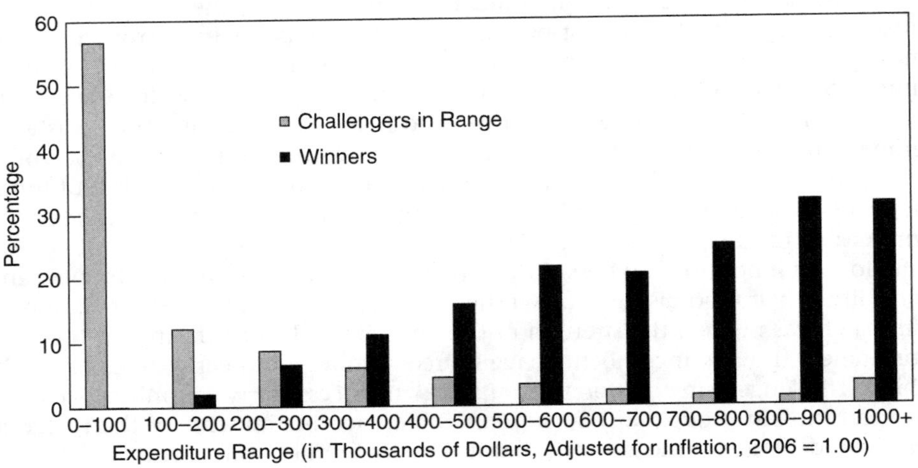

FIGURE 3–8 Challengers' Expenditures and Victories in House Elections, 1972–2006
Source: Compiled by author.

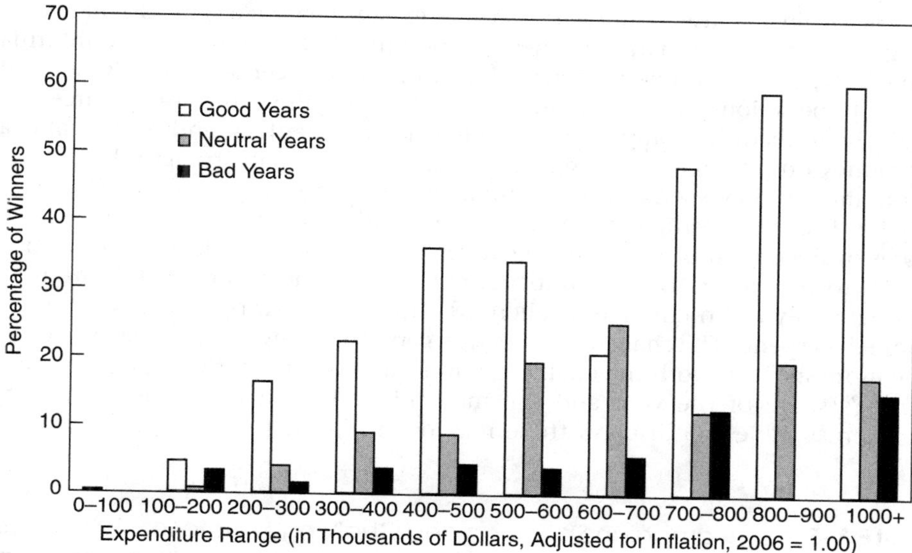

FIGURE 3–9 Winning House Challengers, by Level of Campaign Spending, 1972–2006
Source: Compiled by author.

Figure 3–9 shows that challengers favored by national conditions—Democrats in 1974, 1982, 1996, and 2006; Republicans in 1980, 1984, and 1994—won more frequently at every level of campaign spending. Anything over $300,000 was enough to make a race of it; those spending more than $500,000 won 37 percent of their contests, and those spending more than $1 million won more than half of the time. In addition, challengers were able to spend more money in good election years; for example, 30 percent spent more than $500,000 in the good years, compared with 16 percent in neutral years and 13 percent in bad years. This is further evidence of strategic behavior on the part of contributors.

In the absence of strong partisan tides, challengers have a much harder time winning and need to spend more than $600,000 to enjoy at least a one-in-ten chance of winning. Against contrary partisan tides, challengers raise the least amount of money and find it very difficult to win no matter what they spend.

What do these data tell us about the cost of a minimally competitive challenge? Obviously, it varies from district to district and from state to state, depending on the structure and cost of mass media advertising, the vigor of local parties and other politically active organizations, and local campaign styles. It also varies with national partisan tides and it has certainly grown over time (even taking inflation into account). Still, if we set an arbitrary but reasonable standard for a competitive campaign as one giving the challenger at least a 20 percent chance of winning, $600,000 (in 2006 dollars) is a plausible estimate for the threshold for the entire period. Only 10 percent of all House challengers crossed this threshold; a large majority spent far too little to make a contest of it. If we confine analysis to more recent elections, the minimum price tag for a competitive House campaign under average conditions today is probably closer to $800,000; sixty-two of the sixty-four challengers who defeated incumbents from 1996 through 2006 spent more than that amount.

Defeating a House incumbent is clearly expensive (and a serious Senate campaign can cost more than ten times as much in a large state such as California, New York, or Texas); relatively few challengers have been able to raise enough funds to be serious threats. Challengers who do acquire sufficient resources can make incumbents feel anything but safe. For incumbents, spending a great deal of money on a campaign is a sign of weakness rather than strength. In fact, the more money they spend on the campaign, the worse they do on election day. That is, the relationship between the incumbent's level of spending and share of votes or likelihood of victory is negative. Spending money does not cost them votes, to be sure; rather, incumbents raise and spend more money the more strongly they feel themselves challenged. The more their opponent spends, the more they spend. The challenger evidently gets more bang for the buck; therefore, the more spent by both the challenger and the incumbent, the greater the challenger's share of the vote and the more likely the challenger is to win the election.[41] Table 3–5 displays these relationships, much simplified. It lists the

TABLE 3–5 Campaign Spending and Challenger Victories, 1986–2006

	CHALLENGER'S SPENDING[a]						
	<200	200–400	400–600	600–800	800–1,000	>1,000	Row Average
***Incumbent's Spending*[a]**							
Percent of Victories							
< 200	0.0	0.0	0.0	0.0	0.0	0.0	0.0
200–400	0.0	0.0	0.0	0.0	0.0	0.0	0.0
400–600	0.0	4.7	11.1	14.3	0.0	25.0	1.1
600–800	0.0	2.1	2.2	17.7	42.9	22.2	1.7
800–1,000	0.0	5.5	4.4	25.0	15.4	30.8	3.8
>1,000	0.3	4.5	3.5	11.2	17.4	27.4	9.7
Column Average	0.04	3.9	3.9	13.5	17.7	26.9	4.0
Number of Cases							**Row Total**
<200	147	1	1	2	3	0	154
200–400	462	26	8	1	3	3	503
400–600	572	64	18	7	1	4	666
600–800	480	97	46	17	7	9	656
800–1,000	288	73	45	20	13	13	452
>1,000	392	155	114	116	92	245	1,114
Column Total	2,341	416	232	163	119	274	3,545

[a]In thousands of dollars, adjusted for inflation 2006 = 1.00.

percentage of winning challengers at different combinations of incumbent and challenger spending in elections since 1986. The column average shows that the more challengers spent, the more likely they were to win. Only 1 of the 2,341 who spent less than $200,000 won, while 27 percent of those spending more than $1 million replaced the incumbent. The row average shows that the more incumbents spent, the more likely they were to lose. None in the lowest category of spenders failed to win reelection; 10 percent in the highest category did so. At any given level of incumbent spending, challengers do better the more they spend; at any given level of challenger spending, the incumbent's spending makes little apparent difference in the outcome. The variation across every row (except the first two) is statistically significant at $p < 0.001$; the variation down every column is insignificant ($p > 0.45$).

More elaborate multivariate models that analyze votes or victories as a function of campaign spending and other variables (national tides, district partisanship, and so forth) tell exactly the same story.[42] This pattern appears in Senate elections, as well.[43] Unfortunately, the problem of reciprocal causation renders all such results suspect. Because challengers raise more money the better they are expected to do, this kind of analysis exaggerates the effects of their campaign spending. Because incumbents raise *less* money the better they are expected to do (remember, their spending is reactive), the analysis underestimates the effects of their spending. What we do not know is by how much.

Scholars have estimated a variety of models designed to take reciprocal causation into account, but the findings vary widely. At one extreme, results simply reinforce the original findings; at the other, they suggest that marginal returns on spending are as high for incumbents as for challengers. Most often, however, they suggest that the marginal returns on spending are indeed greater for challengers than for incumbents, but to a lesser degree than the original findings would indicate. Also, at least two studies have found that the returns on spending by first-term incumbents are about as large as the returns on spending by their opponents—and much larger than the returns on spending by more senior members.[44] The results from an alternative approach to the problem—using panel or multiple-wave surveys to measure the effects of spending on changes over time in popular support for candidates—are considerably more consistent in finding that the marginal returns on spending are substantially higher for challengers than for incumbents.[45]

Despite the uncertainties that remain, several things are abundantly clear. Challengers (and candidates for open seats who face well-financed opponents) rarely win without spending a great deal of money. Even rarer is a losing incumbent who might plausibly blame defeat on a shortage of funds.[46] Moreover, there are solid reasons challengers should get a larger return on their spending than do incumbents. However, there are also good reasons for believing that, under some circumstances, the incumbent's spending should affect the outcome as well.

Why Campaign Money Is More Important to Challengers than to Incumbents

Campaign spending is subject to diminishing returns; the more dollars spent, the less gained by each additional dollar. Congressional incumbents usually exploit their official resources for reaching constituents so thoroughly that the additional increment of information about their virtues put forth during the campaign adds comparatively little to what is already known and felt about them. As we shall see in Chapter 5, the extent to which voters know and like incumbents is unrelated to how much is spent on the campaign. The situation is quite different for nonincumbents. Most are largely unknown before the campaign, and the extent to which they penetrate the awareness of voters—which is crucial to winning votes—is directly related to how extensively they campaign. The money spent on nonincumbents' campaigns buys the attention and recognition that incumbents already enjoy at the outset of the campaign.

If this is true, we would expect spending by both candidates to affect the outcomes of contests for open seats, and indeed it does. Table 3–6 displays the relationships in their most elementary form: Democrats do better the more they spend, and Republicans do better the more they spend. Democrats thrive in the combinations appearing in the upper-right section of the matrix (winning

TABLE 3–6 Campaign Spending and Democratic Victories in Open House Seats 1986–2006 (in Percentages)

	DEMOCRAT'S SPENDING ($1,000s)[a]						
	< 200	200–400	400–600	600–800	800–1,000	>1,000	Row Average
PERCENT OF VICTORIES							
Republican's Spending ($1,000s)							
Percent of Victories							
< 200	75.0	100.0	100.0	100.0	100.0	100.0	98.7
200–400	0.0	66.7	83.3	55.7	75.0	83.3	69.0
400–600	7.1	16.7	33.3	75.0	50.0	87.5	44.4
600–800	0.0	22.2	26.3	21.4	44.4	89.5	39.7
800–1,000	0.0	0.0	14.3	30.0	25.0	52.6	27.3
>1,000	3.8	0.0	0.0	9.5	21.4	47.4	29.1
Column Average	7.8	33.3	43.1	50.6	52.9	61.6	46.7
Number of Cases							**Row Total**
< 200	4	7	15	23	12	14	75
200–400	1	3	6	9	4	6	29
400–600	14	6	6	12	8	8	54
600–800	8	9	19	14	9	19	78
800–1,000	11	4	7	10	4	19	55
>1,000	26	7	12	21	14	95	175
Column Total	64	36	65	89	51	164	466

[a]In thousands of dollars, adjusted for inflation 2006 = 1.00; the number of case appears in parentheses.

79 percent of the time); Republicans thrive in the lower-left section (winning 83 percent of the time). Along the diagonal, results are split (Democrats win 44 percent overall). Multivariate analyses recapitulate these results.[47]

In general, then, spending should matter more to nonincumbent candidates than to incumbents because they have yet to get their message out, and getting a message out costs money. Spending may also matter to incumbents if they have to get out a *new* message. That is, when an incumbent is in trouble for some reason—personal, such as involvement in the House Bank scandal in 1992, or political, as with Democrats facing the Republican tide in 1994 or Republicans saddled with an unpopular president and war in 2006—and needs to counter with a new pitch, campaign money is essential. It comes down to this: Regardless of their potential, if challengers cannot raise lots of money, they can forget about winning. If incumbents are strongly challenged, raising and spending lots of money may not help them much, although there is no reason to think it hurts. Even if the marginal return on spending by incumbents is very small, spending a great deal of money is probably a rational strategy because even a small number of votes may make the difference between winning and losing.

Plainly, though, spending huge sums of money does not ensure reelection. What matters much more is the amount spent by the challenger (and, related to it, how qualified and skillful he or she is). This means that *the incumbent's most effective electoral strategy is to discourage serious opposition.* The most effective way to do this is to avoid showing signs of electoral vulnerability. Even the most implacable political enemies will not mobilize their full range of resources against an incumbent if they see no prospect of success. Maintaining an active presence in the district helps to discourage the opposition.[48] So does working to maintain the electoral coalition that put the member into office in the first place. Because elections are the most pertinent source of information on a member's electoral strength, it is particularly important to avoid slippage at the polls. An unexpectedly weak showing in one election inspires even stronger opposition in the next. As one incumbent put it, "It is important for me to keep the young state representatives and city councilmen away. If they have the feeling that I'm invincible, they won't try. That reputation is very intangible. [But] your vote margin is part of it."[49]

It is also shrewd strategy for incumbents to diminish the intensity of opposition in the district. No one can please everyone, and nothing is to be gained by alienating one's supporters, but occasional friendly gestures to potentially hostile political interests may be sufficient to dampen their enthusiasm for organizing an all-out campaign against the member. From an incumbent's perspective, then, elections are not merely discrete hurdles to be cleared at regular two-year intervals. They are, as Richard F. Fenno Jr.'s unique research showed, a series of connected events that form part of a "career in the district," which parallels the career in Washington.[50] Winning is always crucial, of course, but winning in a way that minimizes future opposition is just as desirable in the long run.

The Career in the District

Other important insights into congressional election processes emerge from thinking in terms of congressional careers rather than single elections. Fenno's observations in the 1970s led him to conclude that House members' careers in the district passed through identifiable stages. In the first, the *expansionist phase,* members devoted a great deal of time and energy to building up their base of regular supporters. Beginning with a core of solid backers, they worked to reach additional individuals and groups in the district that they hoped to incorporate into their electoral coalitions. The expansionist phase began before the first election and continued for at least a few more. The capacity of first-term members to increase their electoral margins, even in the face of strongly contrary electoral tides, was a sign of this effort and its efficacy.

Fenno observed that at some point, after a few elections, members typically entered into a *protectionist phase,* during which they work to maintain the support they have built up over the years but no longer attempt to add to it. By this time, they had often discouraged serious opposition through a show of growing electoral strength, and they have been in Washington long enough to have acquired some influence and responsibility. Working the district became a less-attractive alternative to making policy and exercising legislative skills. It is at this stage that members risked "losing touch with the district," to use the politicians' cliche. If they did, they could become vulnerable at the polls. But their vulnerability might not become apparent at all until it was tested.

The stages of congressional career development may no longer be so clear-cut, as most members now show little sign of diminishing attention to district matters as their seniority grows. Still, the pattern influences the strategies pursued by nonincumbents seeking congressional seats. The best opportunity arises when the incumbent dies or retires, and it is not uncommon to find ambitious young politicians biding their time until a seat becomes open, after which a lively scramble ensues among them for the nomination and election.[51] First-term members also attract unusually vigorous opposition; their challengers are twice as likely to have held elective public office and spend, on average, nearly twice as much money as challengers to more senior incumbents. The strategic assumption is that newly elected members do not have as firm a hold on their districts as they will later develop, so it is better to go after them now than later.[52] Politicians who use electoral margins as evidence of electoral vulnerability will focus on these new incumbents because so many of them initially win office in close elections. Although for a time, during the 1970s, first-term incumbents were not really any easier to knock off, their greater vulnerability has since returned.

Incumbents who survive the first bid for reelection should be most vulnerable in the protectionist stage of their careers. Electoral support is not won once and for all. It requires continual renewal and reinforcement, especially at times when party loyalties are weaker and the incumbent's personal performance is more central to voters' decisions. Members who work merely to maintain their base of support may actually let it slip, especially if they enjoy a few elections with feeble opposition that disguises any weakening of their hold on the district. A challenger who, through luck or cleverness, puts together a serious campaign against a member whose hold on the district has imperceptibly atrophied may surprise everyone, including the incumbent and challenger.

One example is Duncan Hunter, who defeated Democratic incumbent Lionel Van Deerlin in the 1980 contest for the 42nd District of California. Van Deerlin had not been seriously challenged in years; he was unaware of his own electoral weakness and of the progress his challenger was making until it was too late to do anything about it. Hunter had decided to run only at the last minute and then on the theory that, although he was likely to lose, he would be in a stronger position to take the seat in 1982, especially if, as many anticipated, Van Deerlin retired. Hunter's hesitation did not prevent a vigorous and well-financed campaign, and he wound up with 53 percent of the vote, compared with the 24 percent won by the token Republican challenger in 1978—a shift of 29 percentage points between the two elections.

Van Deerlin was only the most surprised of a number of senior House Democrats in 1980. Republican challengers defeated fourteen incumbents who had served at least five terms, eight who had served at least nine terms. The 1992, 1994, and 2006 elections also proved disastrous for some entrenched members, in the first instance largely because of the House Bank scandal (of which I have more to say in Chapter 6) and in the second because of the powerful Republican tide. Among the victims (all Democrats) in 1994 were Tom Foley of Washington, Speaker of the House (fifteen terms); Jack Brooks of Texas, chairman of the Judiciary Committee (twenty-one terms); Neal Smith of Iowa, Appropriations Subcommittee chairman (eighteen terms); and Dan Glickman of Kansas, chairman of the Intelligence Committee (nine terms). Twelve of the twenty-two Republican incumbents defeated in 2006 had served six or more terms, and four had served ten or more terms.

The 1992, 1994, and 2006 elections offer a powerful illustration of how fickle district electorates can be. A member's personal relationship with constituents can keep the district safely in his or her hands—but only through a continuing high level of personal attention, and only if potent new issues detrimental to the incumbent do not intrude. Mayhew noted that to say "Congressman Smith is unbeatable" means only that he "is unbeatable as long as he continues to do the things he is doing."[53] After the 1994 and 2006 elections, we should add, "and only as long as what he is doing is what voters care about when deciding how to vote." A wide reelection margin is maintained only through unrelenting entrepreneurial effort; allow for a letup or a slipup that attracts and is exploited by a formidable opponent wielding a potent issue, and it can evaporate quickly. Personal ties to the district pays electoral dividends, but only as long as members are willing to invest the time and energy required to maintain them. Even then, there are no guarantees that personal ties will prevail in the face of troublesome new issues or a contrary partisan tide.

Motivating Challengers

Most senators and representatives are willing to pay the price to remain members of Congress, at least for a time; retirement or defeat awaits those who refuse.[54] Because most incumbents work hard to remain in office and are therefore extremely difficult to defeat, it is not absurd to ask why, under most circumstances, anyone challenges them at all. Part of the answer is that a fair proportion of incumbents are not challenged. In 2002, a record eighty-one House incumbents had no major-party opponent in the general election, and almost all of them were spared primary opposition as well. But most are challenged, even those who appear to be unbeatable. Why?

One reason suggested by studies of congressional challengers is naïveté. As David Leuthold noted in his study of San Francisco–area congressional campaigns, "Inexperienced candidates often did not realize that they had no chance of winning."[55] Most challengers recognize that the odds are against them, of course, but their hopes may be buoyed by the inherent uncertainties of electoral politics and a large dose of self-deception. Writing from personal experience—he is a political scientist who ran for Congress but did not get past the primary—Sandy Maisel pointed out that "politicians tend to have an incredible ability to delude themselves" about their electoral prospects.[56]

Maisel's report of his own and other congressional primaries in 1978 provides several additional insights into the question. Many congressional candidates had planned for years to run for Congress—someday. The only question was "When?"; then, when circumstances seemed only a little bit more favorable than usual, their thinking was, "If not now, when?" or, more desperately, "Now or never."[57]

Candidates can delude themselves all the more easily when they lack the resources to discover just how difficult their task is; impoverished candidates cannot afford top-quality polls to gauge their status with the electorate. They most often rely instead on their own political intuition and, to a lesser degree, on the opinions of local political activists.[58] Both sources are inclined to tell them what they want to hear, so it is not difficult to see why they might overestimate their chances.

Other scholars, though, discern rationality rather than naïveté when inexperienced candidates challenge entrenched incumbents. Jeffrey Banks and D. Roderick Kiewiet argue that inexperienced challengers choose to run when their prospect of defeating the incumbent appears dim because this nonetheless maximizes their probability of getting elected to Congress. Because the long odds deter ambitious career politicians, political neophytes are much more likely to win the nomination than they would be if conditions were more promising (had, for example, the incumbent retired). Their much-greater chance of winning the nomination more than offsets the smaller chance of knocking off the incumbent in the general election. The odds may be very long but they are still the best an inexperienced amateur can envision.[59]

At least a few such candidates are rewarded with unanticipated success, and that no doubt encourages others to take the plunge. In 1988, for instance, Ronald Matchley, a political novice, was nominated unopposed (the expected nominee, a former state party chair, inexplicably failed to meet the filing deadline) to face Democratic Representative Fernand J. St Germain, the powerful chairman of the Committee on Banking, Finance, and Urban Affairs. Matchley was able to exploit St Germain's ethical problems to achieve "the most improbable triumph in recent Rhode Island history."[60] In 1990, first-time candidates managed to defeat Douglas Walgren of Pennsylvania and Robert Kastenmeier of Wisconsin, although there was little prior indication that these veteran House incumbents were vulnerable.

Moreover, elections such as those in 1992, 1994, and 2006 show that boldness is sometimes rewarded across the board. Challengers who had put themselves in a position to exploit the House Bank scandal, popular disgust with Clinton and gridlock, or discontent with Bush and the Iraq War ended up with a great shot at the brass ring. No doubt many of the Republican newcomers elected in 1994 were surprised to find themselves in the House, let alone in the majority, as were some of the Democratic challengers in 2006. Their experience serves as a seductive object lesson for prospective challengers who can imagine that they, too, might find themselves in the right place at the right time to beat the long odds against defeating an incumbent.

Even candidates who are certain they will not win find motives for running. The most common reason given is to provide some opposition, to make sure the party is represented on the ballot, "to demonstrate that the party [has] a spark of life in the district."[61] Local party leaders may run themselves when they are unable to find anyone else willing to face a drubbing.[62] Some run to build for their own or the party's future, as did many southern Republicans in the 1950s and early 1960s. Others run to promote strongly held ideological beliefs. Opponents of abortion and other religious conservatives have swelled the ranks of Republican challengers in recent years; in 1992, several of them used the legal requirement that TV stations run uncensored campaign ads in order to broadcast anti-abortion messages featuring graphic footage of aborted fetuses.[63] Still others evidently run to advertise themselves in their professions; this reason is not often volunteered, and with the profession of politics in such low repute, it may no longer be very common. But for much of the postwar period, a remarkable proportion of young attorneys, insurance agents, and real-estate brokers turned up as challengers in districts where they had little hope of winning. Finally, some apparently find the process of running itself reward enough.[64]

Challengers who are naïve, inexperienced, or self-deceiving or who run without hope of winning do not make particularly formidable opponents. Incumbents blessed with such opposition win reelection easily. Still, every so often one is rudely surprised, for uncertainty is an inevitable component of congressional election politics. In important respects, electoral uncertainty has actually increased in recent years. Congressional incumbents have no monopoly on entrepreneurial electoral politics. They now face institutional players—political action committees, national party campaign committees, professional campaign outfits, independent spenders, polling and direct-mail firms—that are equally adept at exploiting current technologies and electoral habits. The next chapter explores how these have affected campaign politics.

NOTES

1. John R. Alford and David W. Brady, "Personal and Partisan Advantage in U.S. Congressional Elections, 1846–1990," in *Congress Reconsidered*, 5th ed., ed. Lawrence C. Dodd and Bruce I. Oppenheimer (Washington, DC: Congressional Quarterly Press, 1993), pp. 146–147.
2. Albert D. Cover and David R. Mayhew, "Congressional Dynamics and the Decline of Competitive Congressional Elections," in *Congress Reconsidered*, 2nd ed., ed. Lawrence C. Dodd and Bruce I. Oppenheimer (Washington, DC: Congressional Quarterly Press, 1981), p. 70; see also Robert S. Erikson, "Malapportionment, Gerrymandering, and Party Fortunes in Congressional Elections," *American Political Science Review* 66 (1972): 1240.
3. David W. Brady, Brian Gaines, and Douglas Rivers, "The Incumbency Advantage in the House and Senate: A Comparative Institutional Analysis" (manuscript, Stanford University, 1994).
4. Andrew Gelman and Gary King, "Measuring Incumbency without Bias," *American Journal of Political Science* 34 (1990): 1142–1164; Michael Krashinsky and William J. Milne, "The Effects of Incumbency in U.S. Congressional Elections, 1950–1988," *Legislative Studies Quarterly* 18 (1993): 321–344; and Brady, Gaines, and Rivers, "Incumbency Advantage."

5. Gelman and King compute the incumbency advantage by regressing the Democrat's share of the two-party vote on the Democrat's vote in the previous election, the party holding the seat, and incumbency (which takes a value of 1 if the Democratic candidate is an incumbent, –1 if the Republican is an incumbent, and 0 if the seat is open). The coefficient on the incumbency variable estimates the value (in percentage of votes) of incumbency for each election year. The index cannot be calculated for elections in years ending in 2 because of redistricting.
6. Brady, Gaines, and Rivers, "Incumbency Advantage," Table 3.
7. David R. Mayhew, "Congressional Elections: The Case of the Vanishing Marginals," *Polity* 6 (1974): 295–317.
8. To calculate the swing ratio, simply divide the change in the percentage of seats a party wins by the change in the percentage of votes it wins; for example, if one party's share of seats rises from 45 percent to 55 percent when its share of the vote rises from 47 percent to 52 percent, the swing ratio is 2.0 [(55 − 45)/(52 − 47) = 2.0]; see Erikson, "Malapportionment," pp. 1240–1241; Edward R. Tufte, "The Relationship between Seats and Votes in Two-Party Systems," *American Political Science Review* 67 (1973): 540–554; and Mayhew, "Vanishing Marginals," pp. 312–314; Cover and Mayhew, "Congressional Dynamics," p. 78; Morris P. Fiorina, "The Case of the Vanishing Marginals: The Bureaucracy Did It," *American Political Science Review* 71 (1977): 177.
9. John A. Ferejohn and Randall Calvert, "Presidential Coattails in Historical Perspective," *American Journal of Political Science* 28 (1984): 131; and Gary C. Jacobson, "The Marginals Never Vanished: Incumbency and Competition in Elections to the U.S. House of Representatives, 1952–1982," *American Journal of Political Science* 31 (1987): 126–141.
10. Thomas E. Mann, *Unsafe at Any Margin: Interpreting Congressional Elections* (Washington, DC: American Enterprise Institute for Public Policy Research, 1977), p. 90.
11. The increase in volatility remains when effects of changes in the sophomore surge and retirement slump are removed; see Gary C. Jacobson, *The Electoral Origins of Divided Government: Competition in U.S. House Elections, 1946–1988* (Boulder, CO: Westview Press, 1990), pp. 17–18.
12. Jacobson, *The Electoral Origins of Divided Government*, pp. 82–93.
13. Judy Mann, "Eyes Turn to Hill's Fortress of Incumbency," *Washington Post*, May 24, 1989, p. B3.
14. David R. Mayhew, *Congress: The Electoral Connection* (New Haven, CT: Yale University Press, 1974), pp. 81–82.
15. Mayhew, *Congress*, pp. 99–100.
16. Glenn R. Parker and Roger H. Davidson, "Why Do Americans Love Their Congressmen So Much More Than Their Congress?" *Legislative Studies Quarterly* 4 (1979): 53–61.
17. Roger H. Davidson and Walter J. Oleszek, *Congress and Its Members*, 6th ed. (Washington, DC: Congressional Quarterly Press, 1998), p. 145.
18. "GOP's House-Cleaning Sweep Changes Rules, Cuts Groups," *Congressional Quarterly Weekly Report* 52 (December 10, 1994): 3487.

19. "GOP's House-Cleaning Sweep Changes Rules, Cuts Groups."
20. Mayhew, *Congress*, p. 311.
21. John A. Ferejohn, "On the Decline of Competition in Congressional Elections," *American Political Science Review* 71 (1977): 174.
22. Norman J. Ornstein, Thomas E. Mann, and Michael J. Malbin, *Vital Statistics on Congress 2001–2002* (Washington, DC: American Enterprise Institute, 2002), Tables 5–3 and 5–4.
23. Fiorina, "The Bureaucracy Did It", p. 180.
24. Glenn R. Parker and Suzanne L. Parker, "The Correlates and Effects of Attention to District by U.S. House Members," *Legislative Studies Quarterly* 10 (1985): 239; R. Michael Alvarez and Jason L. Saving, "Deficits, Democrats, and Distributive Benefits: Congressional Elections and Pork Barrel Politics in the 1980s," *Political Research Quarterly* 50 (1997): 809–831.
25. Paul Feldman and James Jondrow, "Congressional Elections and Local Federal Spending," *American Journal of Political Science* 28 (1984): 152; Patrick Sellers, "Fiscal Consistency and Federal District Spending in Congressional Elections" (Paper delivered at the Annual Meeting of the Midwest Political Science Association, Chicago, April 14–16, 1994); Alvarez and Saving, "Deficits, Democrats, and Distributive Benefits"; and Kenneth N. Bickers and Robert M. Stein, "The Electoral Dynamics of the Federal Pork Barrel," *American Journal of Political Science* 40 (November 1996): 1300–1326.
26. See John R. Johannes and John C. McAdams, "The Congressional Incumbency Effect: Is It Casework, Policy Compatibility, or Something Else?"; Morris P. Fiorina, "Some Problems in Studying the Effects of Resource Allocation in Congressional Elections"; Diana Evans Yiannakis, "The Grateful Electorate: Casework and Congressional Elections"; and John C. McAdams and John R. Johannes, "Does Casework Matter? A Reply to Professor Fiorina," all in *American Journal of Political Science* 25 (1981): 512–604. See also Lynda W. Powell, "Constituency Service and Electoral Margin in Congress" (Paper delivered at the Annual Meeting of the American Political Science Association, Denver, September 2–5, 1982); John R. Johannes and John McAdams, "The Effect of Congressional Casework on Elections" (Paper delivered at the Annual Meeting of the American Political Science Association, New Orleans, August 29–September 1, 1985); Albert C. Cover and Bruce S. Brumberg, "Baby Books and Ballots: The Impact of Congressional Mail on Constituent Opinion," *American Political Science Review* 76 (1982): 347–359; John R. Johannes, *To Serve the People: Congress and Constituency Service* (Lincoln: University of Nebraska Press, 1984); Morris P. Fiorina and Douglas Rivers, "Constituency Service, Reputation, and the Incumbency Advantage," in *Members of Congress at Home and In Washington*, ed. Morris P. Fiorina and David Rohde (Ann Arbor: University of Michigan Press, 1989); George Serra and Albert D. Cover, "The Electoral Consequences of Perquisite Use: The Casework Case," *Legislative Studies Quarterly* 17 (1992): 233–246; George Serra, "What's in It for Me? The Impact of Congressional Casework on Incumbent Evaluation," *American Politics Quarterly* 22 (1994): 403–420; and David W. Romero, "The Case of the Missing Reciprocal Influence: Incumbent Reputation and the Vote," *Journal of Politics* 58 (November 1996): 1198–1207.

27. Fiorina, *Congress: Keystone of the Washington Establishment* (New Haven: Yale University Press, 1989), 94–97; and Fiorina, "Resource Allocation in Congressional Elections," pp. 545–550; Bickers and Stein, "The Electoral Dynamics of the Federal Pork Barrel."
28. Morris P. Fiorina, "The Incumbency Factor," *Public Opinion* (September/October, 1978): 42–44.
29. Jacobson, *The Electoral Origins of Divided Government*, pp. 15–19, 56–57.
30. Parker and Parker, "Attention to District by U.S. House Members," p. 229; see also Glenn R. Parker, *Homeward Bound: Explaining Changes in Congressional Behavior* (Pittsburgh, PA: University of Pittsburgh Press, 1986).
31. Charles M. Tidmarch, "The Second Time Around: Freshman Democratic House Members' 1976 Reelection Experiences" (Paper delivered at the Annual Meeting of the American Political Science Association, Washington, DC, September 1–4, 1977), p. 27.
32. For an analysis of the varying effects of incumbency based on NES survey data, see John R. Petrocik and Scott W. Desposato, "Incumbency and Short-Term Influences on Voters," *Political Research Quarterly* 57 (2004): 363–373.
33. "Freshmen: New Powerful Voice," *Congressional Quarterly Weekly Report* 53 (October 28, 1995): 3251.
34. Gary C. Jacobson and Samuel Kernell, *Strategy and Choice in Congressional Elections*, 2nd ed. (New Haven, CT: Yale University Press, 1983), Chapter 3; Bruce W. Robeck, "State Legislator Candidates for the U.S. House: Prospects for Success," *Legislative Studies Quarterly* 7 (1982): 511–512; Thomas A. Kazee, "Ambition and Candidacy: Running as a Strategic Calculation," in *Who Runs for Congress? Ambition, Context, and Candidate Emergence*, ed. Thomas A. Kazee (Washington, DC: Congressional Quarterly Press, 1994), pp. 171–177; and L. Sandy Maisel and Walter P. Stone, "Determinants of Candidate Emergence in U.S. House Elections: An Exploratory Study," *Legislative Studies Quarterly* 22 (February 1997): 79–96.
35. For additional evidence of strategic behavior among potential challengers, see Jon R. Bond, Cary Covington, and Richard Fleisher, "Explaining Challenger Quality in Congressional Elections," *Journal of Politics* 47 (1985): 523; William T. Bianco, "Strategic Decisions on Candidacy in U.S. Congressional Districts," *Legislative Studies Quarterly* 9 (1984): 360; Gary C. Jacobson, "Strategic Politicians and the Dynamics of U.S. House Elections, 1946–1986," *American Political Science Review* 83 (1989): 773–793; David Lublin, "Quality, Not Quantity: Strategic Politicians in U.S. Senate Elections," *Journal of Politics* 56 (1994): 228–241; Marc J. Hetherington, Bruce Larson, and Suzanne Globetti, "The Redistricting Cycle and Strategic Candidate Decisions in U.S. House Races, "*Journal of Politics* 65 (2003): 1221–1234; Walter J. Stone and L. Sandy Maisel, "The Not-So-Simple Calculus of Winning: Potential U.S. House Candidates' Nomination and General Election Prospects," *Journal of Politics* 65 (2003): 951–977; Andrew J. Taylor and Lowell W. Barrington, "The Personal and the Political in Repeat Congressional Candidacies," *Political Research Quarterly* 58 (2005): 599–605; Cherie D. Maestas, Sarah Fulton, L. Sandy Maisel, and Walter J. Stone, "When to Risk It? Institutions, Ambitions, and the Decision to Run for the House," *American Political Science Review* 100 (May 2006): 195–208; and

Jamie L. Carson, "Strategy, Selection, and Candidate Competition in U.S. House Elections," *Journal of Politics* 67 (2005): 1–28.

Candidates who have held elective office are not the only high-quality challengers, to be sure; some "ambitious amateurs" are equally effective and equally strategic in their behavior. See David T. Canon, *Actors, Athletes, and Astronauts: Political Amateurs in the United States Congress* (Chicago: University of Chicago Press, 1990). Decisions to contest open House seats are also strategic; see Jon R. Bond, Richard Fleisher, and Jeffrey C. Talbert, "Partisan Differences in Candidate Quality in Open Seat House Races, 1976–1994," *Political Research Quarterly* 50 (1997): 281–299.

36. Gary C. Jacobson, *Money in Congressional Elections* (New Haven, CT: Yale University Press, 1980), pp. 72–101.
37. Gary W. Cox and Jonathan Katz, "Why Did the Incumbency Advantage in U.S. House Elections Grow?" *Journal of Politics* 40 (1996): 478–497.
38. Stephen Ansolabehere and Jams M. Snyder Jr., "The Incumbency Advantage in U.S. Elections: An Analysis of State and Federal Offices, 1942–2000," *Election Law Journal* 1 (2002): 315–338.
39. Brady, Gaines, and Rivers, "Incumbency Advantage," p. 14.
40. Marcus Prior has offered an alternative explanation for the rise of the incumbency advantage—the spread of television—but other research has not supported his hypothesis. See Marcus Prior, "The Incumbent in the Living Room: The Rise of Television and the Incumbency Advantage in U.S. House Elections," *Journal of Politics* 68 (2006): 657–673, and Stephen Ansolabehere, Erik C. Snowberg, and James M. Snyder Jr. "Television and the Incumbency Advantage in U.S. Elections, *Legislative Studies Quarterly* 31 (2006): 469–490.
41. Jacobson, *Money in Congressional Elections*, pp. 136–145; Gary C. Jacobson, "Money and Votes Reconsidered: Congressional Elections, 1972–1982," *Public Choice* 47 (1985): 16–40; Gary C. Jacobson, "Enough Is Too Much: Money and Competition in House Elections, 1972–1984," in *Elections in America*, ed. Kay L. Schlozman (Boston: Allen and Unwin, 1987), pp. 173–195; and Gary C. Jacobson, "The Effects of Campaigning in House Elections: New Evidence for Old Arguments," *American Journal of Political Science* 34 (1990): 334–362.

    For the contrary argument that incumbent spending has powerful effects, see Donald P. Green and Jonathan S. Krasno, "Salvation for the Spendthrift Incumbent: Reestimating the Effects of Campaign Spending in House Elections," *American Journal of Political Science* 32 (1988): 884–907; and Donald P. Green and Jonathan S. Krasno, "Rebuttal to Jacobson's 'New Evidence for Old Arguments,'" *American Journal of Political Science* 34 (1990): 363–372.
42. Jacobson, *Money in Congressional Elections*, pp. 136–146; Alan I. Abramowitz, "Incumbency, Campaign Spending, and the Decline of Competition in U.S. House Elections," *Journal of Politics* 53 (1991): 34–56; and Stephen Ansolabehere and Alan Gerber, "The Mismeasure of Campaign Spending: Evidence from the 1990 U.S. House Elections," *Journal of Politics* 56 (1994): 1106–1118. Ansolabehere and Gerber show that the result holds if only the money spent directly on campaign communications is measured as

spending, although the coefficient on communications spending is naturally larger than the coefficient on total spending in their model.

43. Alan I. Abramowitz, "Explaining Senate Election Outcomes," *American Political Science Review* 82 (1988): 385–403; and Jacobson, *Money in Congressional Elections*, pp. 152–155.
44. Robert S. Erikson and Thomas Palfrey, "Campaign Spending and Incumbency: An Alternative Simultaneous Equation Approach," *Journal of Politics* 60 (1998): 355–373; Robert K. Goidel and Donald A. Gross, "A Systems Approach to Campaign Finance in U.S. House Elections," *American Politics Quarterly* 22 (1994): 125–153; Christopher Kenny and Michael McBurnett, "An Individual Level Multi-equation Model of Expenditure Effects in Contested House Elections," *American Political Science Review* 88 (1994): 669–707; and Larry Bartels, "Instrumental and 'Quasi-instrumental' Variables," *American Journal of Political Science* 35 (1991): 777–800.
45. Gary C. Jacobson, "Campaign Spending Effects in U.S. Senate Elections: Evidence from the National Annenberg Election Study," *Electoral Studies* 25 (2006): 195–226; Gary C. Jacobson, "Measuring Campaign Spending Effects in U.S. House Elections," in *Capturing Campaign Effects*, ed. Henry E. Brady and Richard Johnston (Ann Arbor: University of Michigan Press, 2006), pp. 199–220; Jacobson, "New Evidence," pp. 334–362.
46. Losing House incumbents 1986–2006 spent an average of more than $1.7 million in inflation-adjusted dollars (2006 = 1.00); 76 percent spent more than $1 million; 78 percent outspent their victorious challengers.
47. Jacobson, "Money and Votes Reconsidered," pp. 28–30.
48. Or so politicians think. One empirical study found that district attention, variously measured, had no discernible effect on the quality of the challenger or the money spent against the incumbent; see Bond, Covington, and Fleisher, "Challenger Quality in Congressional Elections," p. 523. However, this study is subject to the same doubts raised about negative findings in other studies on the effects of district attention, discussed earlier.
49. Quoted in Richard F. Fenno Jr., *Home Style: House Members in Their Districts* (Boston: Little Brown and Company, 1977), p. 13.
50. Fenno, *Home Style*, Chapter 6.
51. See Robeck, "State Legislator Candidates," p. 511; Harvey L. Schantz, "Contested and Uncontested Primaries for the U.S. House," *Legislative Studies Quarterly* 5 (1980): 550; and David T. Canon, "Contesting Primaries in Congressional Elections: 1972–1988" (Paper delivered at the Annual Meeting of the American Political Science Association, Atlanta, August 31–September 3, 1989), p. 14.
52. For example, here is Martin Franks, then executive director of the Democratic Congressional Campaign Committee, on why first-termers head the Democrats' target list: "The best chance of getting them is now. Every day they are here they become harder to unseat." Quoted in David Kaplan, "Freshmen Find It Easier to Run as Incumbents," *Congressional Quarterly Weekly Report* 43 (November 2, 1985), p. 2225.
53. Mayhew, *Congress*, p. 37.

54. See, for example, the story of how Fred Eckert, a first-term incumbent Republican, managed to lose a Republican district in upstate New York, in Linda L. Fowler and Robert D. McClure, *Political Ambition: Who Decides to Run for Congress?* (New Haven, CT: Yale University Press, 1989).
55. David A. Leuthold, *Electioneering in a Democracy: Campaigns for Congress* (New York: John Wiley, 1968), p. 22.
56. L. Sandy Maisel, *From Obscurity to Oblivion: Running in the Congressional Primary* (Knoxville: University of Tennessee Press, 1982), p. 23.
57. Maisel, *From Obscurity to Oblivion*, p. 17.
58. Maisel, *From Obscurity to Oblivion*, Table 2.2; see also Fowler and McClure, *Political Ambition*, p. 68.
59. Jeffrey S. Banks and D. Roderick Kiewiet, "Explaining Patterns of Candidate Competition in Congressional Elections," *American Journal of Political Science* 33 (1989): 997–1015. For a contrary view, see David C. Canon, "Sacrificial Lambs or Strategic Politicians? Political Amateurs in U.S. House Elections," *American Journal of Political Science* 37 (1993): 1119–1141.
60. "Rhode Island—1st District," *Congressional Quarterly Weekly Report* 46 (December 31, 1988), p. 3618.
61. Robert J. Huckshorn and Robert C. Spencer, *The Politics of Defeat* (Amherst: University of Massachusetts Press, 1971), p. 75.
62. For an example, see John F. Bibby, "The Case of the Young Old Pro: The Sixth District of Wisconsin," in *The Making of Congressmen: Seven Campaigns of 1974*, ed. Alan L. Clem (North Scituate, MA: Duxbury Press, 1976), p. 216.
63. "Campaign Crusaders Air Graphic Anti-Abortion Ads," *Congressional Quarterly Weekly Report* 50 (September 26, 1992): 2970–2971.
64. Canon, *Actors, Athletes, and Astronauts*, pp. 38–39.

Chapter 4

CONGRESSIONAL CAMPAIGNS

It should be apparent by now that much of the action in congressional election politics takes place outside of the formal campaigns and election periods. This in no way implies that campaigns are inconsequential. The bottom line is that votes must be sought and the most concentrated work to win them takes place through the campaign. The formal campaign is, of course, crucial to those candidates, including most nonincumbents, who have not been able to match the more-or-less incessant campaigning now typical of congressional incumbents.

Despite the dramatically expanded involvement of national organizations in recent years, congressional election campaigns have not lost their predominantly candidate-centered focus. To be sure, party committees, political action committees (PACs), and other types of organizations have become major players, but mainly by learning to operate effectively in an electoral system where candidates rather than parties are normally the centers of attention. Credit belongs to parties and PACs, along with independent professional campaign consultants, for the continuing stream of innovations in campaign technology and strategy that have transformed congressional campaigning in recent years. They also, consequently, share responsibility for higher costs, harsher rhetoric, greater partisan polarization, and the effects that all of these things have had on how members of Congress do their job.

Election campaigns have a simple dominant goal: to win at least a plurality of the votes cast and thus the election. Little else is simple about them, however. Campaigns present candidates difficult problems of analysis and execution, which, even in the best of circumstances, are mastered only imperfectly.

The analytical work required for an effective congressional campaign is suggested by the variety of campaign contexts set forth in Chapter 2. States and districts are not homogeneous lumps; voters do not form an undifferentiated mass. They are divided by boundaries of community, interest, class, race, ideology, moral values, and geography. Candidates (and those who help them put campaigns together) need to recognize these myriad boundaries and to understand their implications for building winning electoral coalitions. Often, those without political experience do not understand these intricacies—and this in itself guarantees failure.[1]

The basic questions are straightforward: Which constituents are likely to become solid supporters? Who might be persuaded? Which groups are best written off as hopeless, and how can they be discouraged from voting? How can potential supporters be reached? How can they be induced to show up at the polls on election day? What kinds of appeals are likely to attract their support? All these questions must be answered twice, and in different ways, if there is a primary contest. They cannot be addressed at all without some cognitive handle on the constituency: Campaigners are necessarily theorists.

Successful campaigners recognize this, at least implicitly. Members of the House develop highly differentiated images of their constituencies. Their behavior is guided by a coherent diagnosis of district components and forces. Knowledge is grounded in experience; they learn at least as much about their constituents from campaigning and from visiting the district between elections as their constituents learn about them. This kind of learning takes time, and its necessity is another reason for viewing House elections from a time perspective longer than a campaign period or a two-year term.[2] It is also one source of the incumbency advantage and helps to explain why politically experienced nonincumbents make superior House candidates.

The analytic tasks facing Senate candidates are, in most states, substantially more formidable than those facing House candidates. Senate candidates normally deal with larger and more diverse constituencies, scattered over much wider areas. Incumbents as well as challengers usually suffer far more uncertainty about how to combine constituent groups into winning coalitions. Few have the opportunity to know their states as intimately as House candidates may know their districts.

In earlier times, candidates could sometimes get a feel for unfamiliar neighborhoods and communities from local party activists who were a part of them. Now they are more likely to rely on professional research—if, of course, they can afford it. Commercial vendors offer detailed voter lists, complete with information on family income, demographics, consumption patterns, group memberships, voting history, addresses, and phone numbers. Professionally conducted polls probe the opinions and attitudes of district residents. Focus groups—small groups of ordinary citizens brought together to mull over candidates and issues under the guidance and observation of experienced researchers—provide a sense of what lies behind the polling results. Intelligence gathering, like every other aspect of campaigning, can now be farmed out to specialists if a campaign has enough money to hire them.[3]

The deepest understanding of the political texture of a state or district will not, by itself, win elections. Effective campaigns require a strategy for gathering at least a plurality of votes and the means to carry out that strategy. The central problem is communication. As Chapter 5 will show, what voters know about candidates has a strong effect on how they decide to vote. Voters who have no information about a candidate are much less likely to vote for him or her than those who do. The content of the information is equally consequential, to be sure, but no matter how impressive the candidate or persuasive the message, it will not help if potential voters remain unaware of them.

Two resources are necessary to communicate with voters: money and organization. They may be combined in different ways, but overcoming serious opposition requires adequate supplies of both. Money is crucial because it buys access to the media of communication: radio, television, newspapers, direct mail, pamphlets, videos, billboards, bumper stickers, bullhorns, websites, and so on. Organization is necessary to design and execute campaign strategy, to raise money, to schedule the candidate's use of personal time devoted to cultivating voters and contributors, and to help get out the vote on election day.

Campaign Money

Raising money is, by consensus, the most unpleasant part of a campaign. Many candidates find it demeaning to ask people for money and are uncomfortable with the implications of accepting.[4] Most do it, however, because they cannot get elected without it. The trick, neophyte campaigners are advised, is to "learn how to beg, and do it in a way that leaves you with some dignity."[5]

Congressional campaign finances are supposed to be regulated by the Federal Election Campaign Act (FECA) and its amendments, enforced by the Federal Election Commission. The law requires full disclosure of the sources of campaign contributions and also restricts the amount of money that parties, groups, and individuals may give to congressional candidates.[6] The FECA was originally intended to limit campaign costs and to reduce the influence of wealthy contributors in electoral politics. The opposite occurred, partly because the Supreme Court declared limits on campaign spending to be an unconstitutional violation of the First Amendment,[7] partly because the act itself, by establishing a clear legal framework for campaign finance activities, invited parties and PACs to flourish.[8]

In response to concerns that party contribution limits were choking off traditional local party activity in federal elections, Congress liberalized the FECA in 1979 to allow unrestricted spending for state and local party-building and get-out-the-vote activities. In 1996, a Supreme Court decision freed parties to engage in unfettered independent spending for their candidates.[9] Funds for these activities were commonly called "soft money," as distinguished from the "hard money" raised and spent under the FECA's limitations. Other groups may also finance independent campaigns either explicitly (in which case their spending has to be reported to the Federal Election Commission) or under the guise of "issue advocacy" or "voter education" (which need not be reported, as long as the campaign does not explicitly urge a vote for or against a particular candidate). Organizations taking the latter route are called "527"or "501(c)" groups, after the sections in the tax code regulating them. The details of a group's organization determine the section under which they fall; 527s are purely political organizations, whereas 501(c) groups include social welfare organizations, labor unions, and business associations.

Unrestricted raising and spending of soft money, along with unregulated issue advocacy and voter-education campaigns, effectively destroyed the limits on campaign money in federal elections. The Bipartisan Campaign Reform Act (BCRA), enacted in 2002, attempted to put the lid back on by banning soft money and regulating independent spending on issue advocacy and voter education. But the explosive growth of campaigning by 527 groups in 2004 and of independent party spending in 2006, discussed below, shows that, while BCRA may have affected the sources of money spent outside the candidates' official campaigns, it could not prevent the injection of massive, essentially unregulated sums into election politics.[10]

Contributions to Candidates

Aggregate figures on the amounts and sources of money contributed to House and Senate campaigns from 1972 through 2006 are presented in Table 4–1. Average campaign receipts have grown steadily, although the growth rate is considerably less impressive than these nominal dollar figures would suggest if

TABLE 4–1 Sources of Campaign Contributions to House and Senate Candidates, 1972–2006

		PERCENTAGE OF CONTRIBUTIONS FROM:				
	Average Contributions	**Individuals**	**Parties**	**PACs**	**Candidates[a]**	**Unknown**
House						
1972	$ 51,752[b]	60[c]	27	14	—	9
1974	$ 61,084	73	4	17	6	—
1976	$ 79,421	59	8	23	9	—
1978	$ 111,232	61	5	25	9	—
1980	$ 148,268	67[c]	4	29	—	—
1982	$ 222,260	63[c]	6	31	—	—
1984	$ 240,722	51	3	39	6	—
1986	$ 280,260	52	2	39	7	—
1988	$ 282,949	49	2	43	6	—
1990	$ 291,246	48	1	44	7	—
1992	$ 358,925	50	1	39	10	—
1994	$ 414,812	54	1	37	8	—
1996	$ 510,997	55	1	34	7	3
1998	$ 544,349	53	1	36	6	4
2000	$ 661,472	53	1	35	7	4
2002	$ 699,736	50	1	37	9	3
2004	$ 766,752	57	0.6	36	4	3
2006	$ 953,044	54	1	35	5	5
Senate						
1972	$ 353,933[b]	67	14	12	0.4	8
1974	$ 455,515	76	6	11	1	6
1976	$ 624,094	69	4	15	12	—
1978	$ 951,390	70	6	13	8	—
1980	$ 1,079,346	78[c]	2	21	—	—
1982	$ 1,771,167	81[c]	1	18	—	—
1984	$ 2,273,635	68	1	20	11	—
1986	$ 2,721,793	69	1	25	6	—
1988	$ 2,649,492	68	1	26	6	—
1990	$ 2,166,031	70	1	24	5	—
1992	$ 2,638,964	68	1	25	6	—
1994	$ 3,659,650	61	1	17	22	—
1996	$ 3,274,940	63	1	19	13	4
1998	$ 3,530,099	62	1	19	12	6
2000	$ 5,305,051	55	0.2	14	25	6

TABLE 4–1 Continued

	Average Contributions	PERCENTAGE OF CONTRIBUTIONS FROM: Individuals	Parties	PACs	Candidates[a]	Unknown
2002	$ 4,013,845	68	0.9	20	8	3
2004	$ 5,418,860	76	0.6	17	4	2
2006	$ 7,943,400	68	0.3	13	13	5

[a]Includes candidates' loans unrepaid at time of filing.
[b]Some contributions before April 7, 1972, may have gone unrecorded.
[c]Includes candidates' contributions to their own campaigns.

Sources: Compiled by author from data supplied by Common Cause (1972 and 1974) and the Federal Election Commission (1976–2006).

inflation is taken into account. In real dollars, contributions to House candidates have grown an average of 9 percent and those to Senate candidates rose an average 12 percent, from election year to election year over this period.

Private individuals contribute the greatest share of campaign money; Senate candidates are especially dependent on individual donations. PACs are the second most important source of campaign funds. Their share grew rather steadily until the early 1990s, peaking at 44 percent for House candidates (1990) and 26 percent for Senate candidates (1988) before falling back in the four most recent elections to averages, respectively, of 36 percent and 18 percent. This category includes the various committees organized by unions, corporations, trade and professional associations, ideological and issue-oriented groups of many kinds, and political leaders.

PACs

There is a simple explanation for the growth and then modest decline in the financial importance of PACs. As campaign costs increased and the real value of the dollar declined (losing more than three-quarters of its value between 1974 and 2006), candidates, constrained by the FECA's fixed contribution limits, naturally put more effort into soliciting funds from sources that may legally contribute up to $10,000—the PACs—and less into soliciting private individuals, who may contribute only one-fifth as much. As Figures 4–1 and 4–2 indicate, the number of PACs available for solicitation also grew dramatically during the first decade under the FECA, as did the amount of money at their disposal. This growth flattened out in the mid-1980s while campaigns continued to raise larger sums, eventually reducing the PACs' share of the total. After BCRA raised the ceiling on individual contributions but not on PAC donations in 2002 (from $1,000 to $2,000 per campaign, effectively $2,000 and $4,000 when the primary is included) and allowed them to rise with inflation (hence a limit of $2,300 for 2008), the relative efficiency of soliciting PACs rather than individuals declined.

Business-oriented PACs have grown the most in both numbers and total contributions to congressional candidates under the FECA. The number of corporate PACs rose from 89 to 1,816 between 1974 and 1988 before falling off somewhat, ending up at 1,622 in 2006; corporate PAC contributions have multiplied more

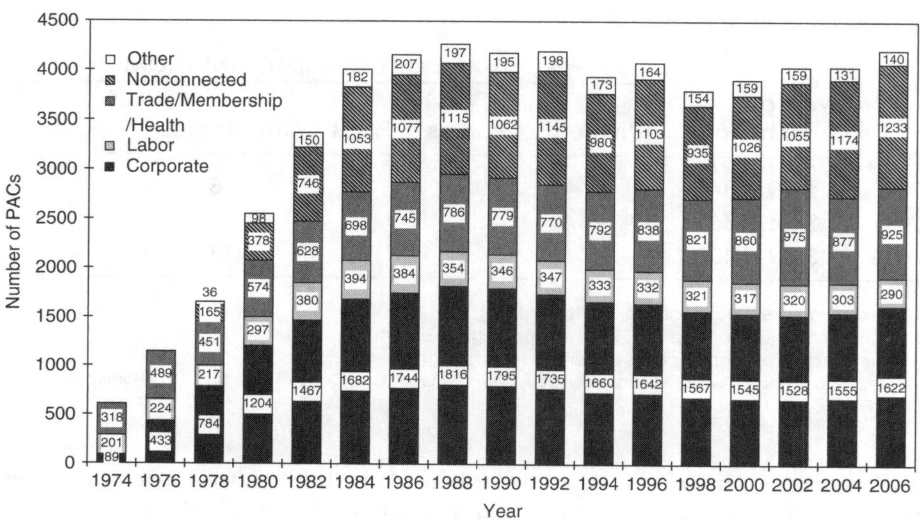

FIGURE 4–1 Political Action Committees, 1974–2006
Source: Federal Election Commission.

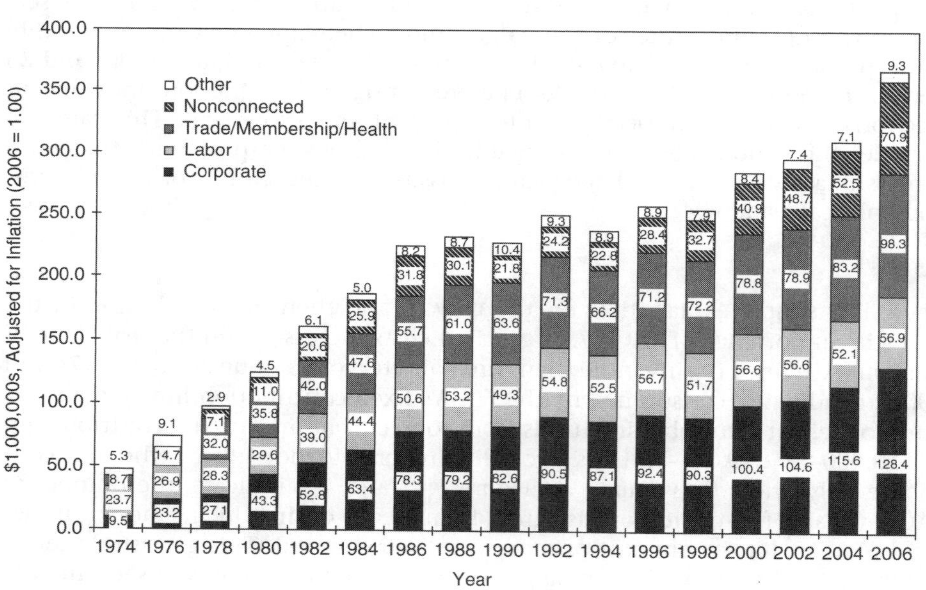

FIGURE 4–2 Contributions by Political Action Committees, 1974–2006
Source: Federal Election Commission.

than twelvefold in real (inflation-adjusted) dollars since 1974. Corporate PAC contributions surpassed those of labor PACs in 1980, and because business associations dominate in the trade/membership/health category, labor's importance relative to business as a source of campaign funds has declined.

This development created a potential problem for Democrats. Organized labor has traditionally been the Democrats' principal source of PAC funds, and only labor PACs have shown much inclination to supply the venture capital so important to the party's nonincumbent candidates. Figures 4–3a and 4–3b document the overwhelming preference of labor PACs for Democratic candidates. The growing financial strength of corporate and trade association PACs during the first decade after passage of the FECA was expected to benefit Republicans, and according to the data in Figures 4–4a-b and 4–5a-b, this expectation was borne out in 1978 and 1980. Republican challengers in both House and Senate contests

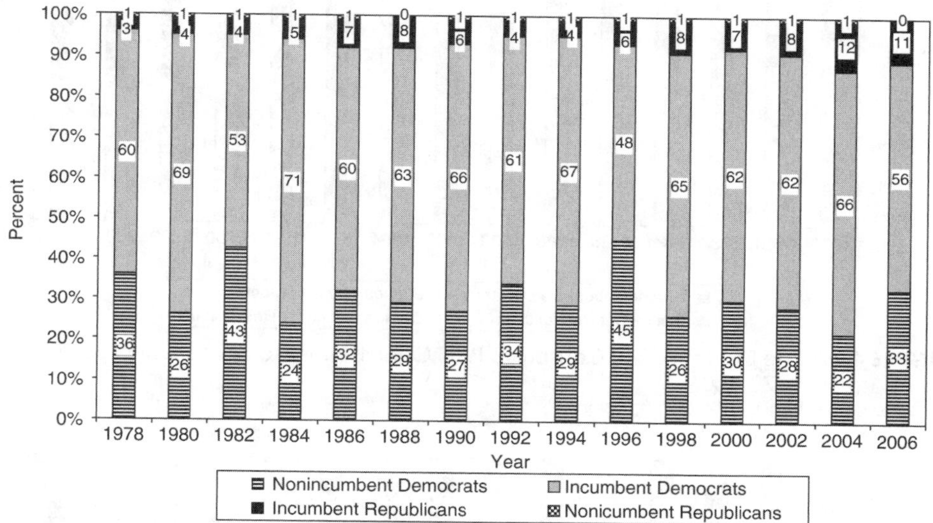

FIGURE 4–3a The Distribution of Labor PAC Contributions to House Candidates, 1978–2006

Source: Federal Election Commission.

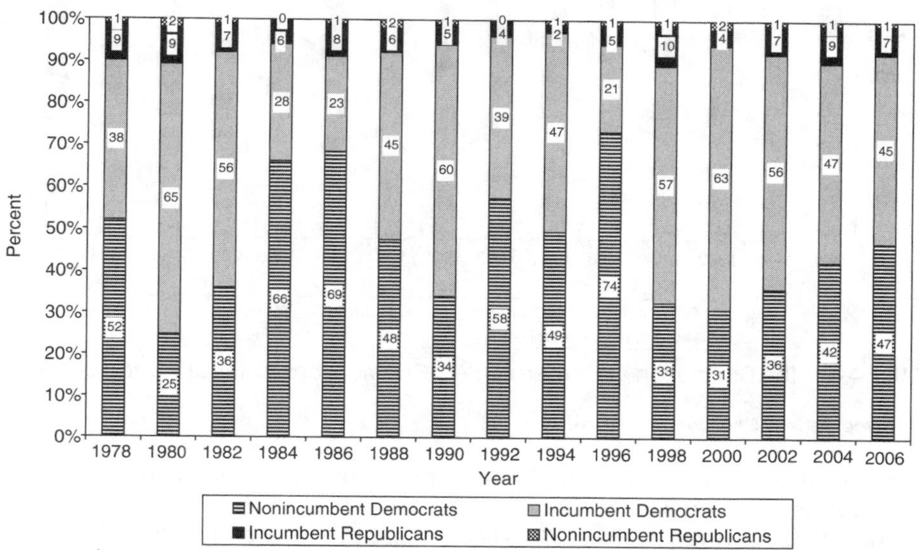

FIGURE 4–3b The Distribution of Labor PAC Contributions to Senate Candidates, 1978–2006

Source: Federal Election Commission.

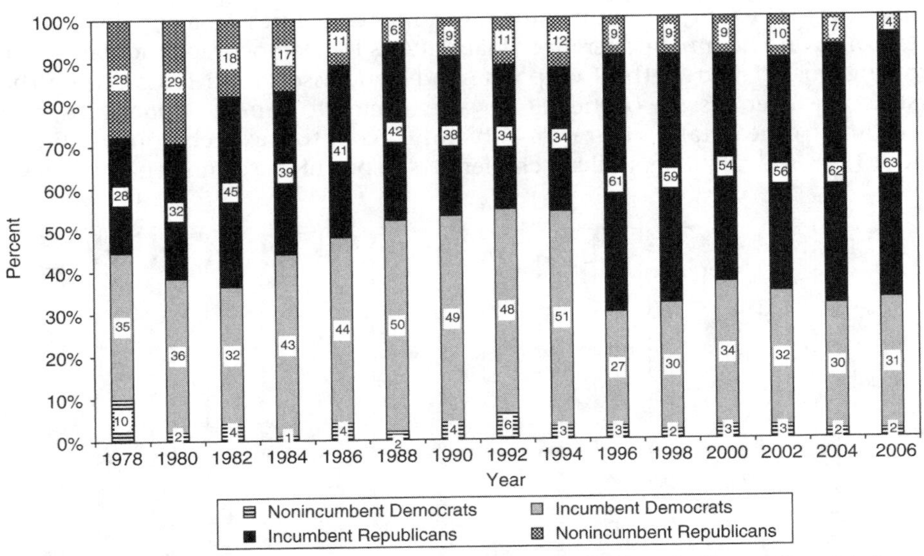

FIGURE 4–4a The Distribution of Corporate PAC Contributions to House Candidates, 1978–2006
Source: Federal Election Commission.

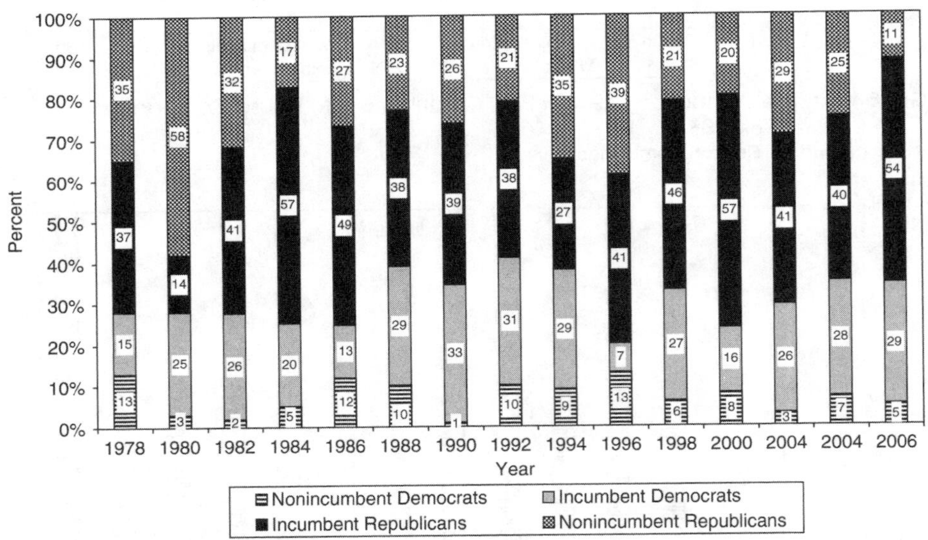

FIGURE 4–4b The Distribution of Corporate PAC Contributions to Senate Candidates, 1978–2006
Source: Federal Election Commission.

were treated generously (compared to other election years) by business-oriented PACs in those elections.

After 1980, however, business PACs became grew more even-handed; 49 percent of corporate and 54 percent of trade association PAC dollars went to Democrats in 1994, for example—but only because so many of them pursued a dual strategy.

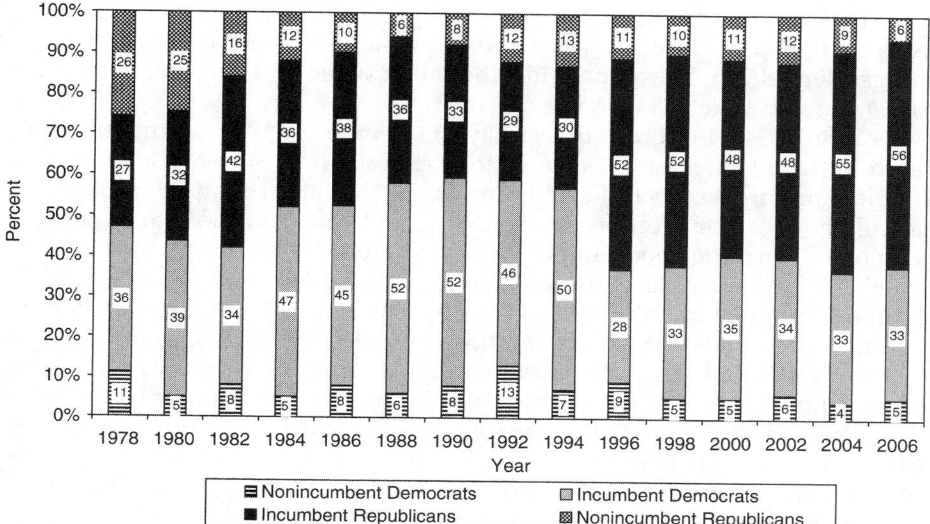

FIGURE 4–5a The Distribution of Trade/Membership/Health PAC Contributions to House Candidates, 1978–2006

Source: Federal Election Commission.

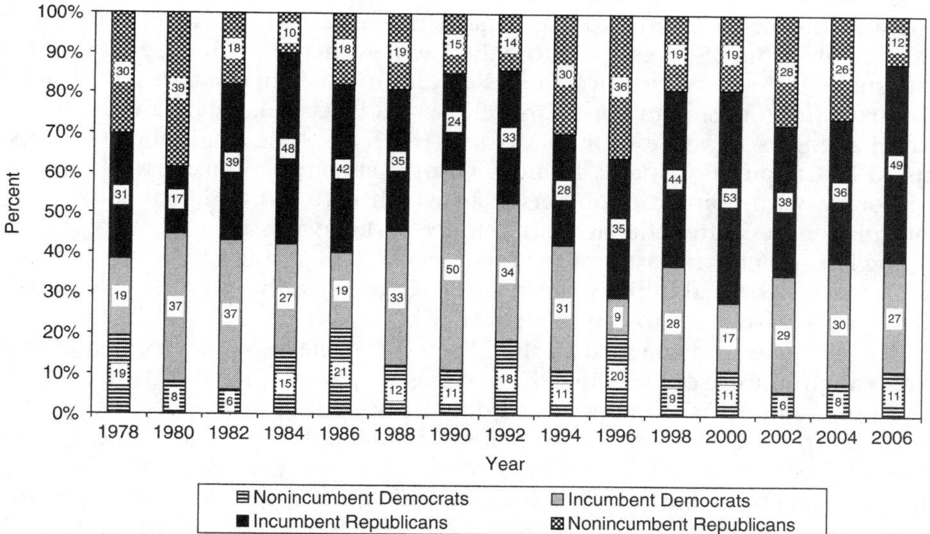

FIGURE 4–5b The Distribution of Trade/Membership/Health PAC Contributions to Senate Candidates, 1978–2006

Source: Federal Election Commission.

They were generous to incumbents of either party who were in positions to help or hurt their interests and were likely to remain there. As long as Democrats controlled Congress, business-oriented PACs sought to keep doors open and to avoid antagonizing Democratic members who look unbeatable—hence, their generosity to incumbent Democrats and stinginess with Republican challengers. They were, however, also willing to support promising nonincumbent Republicans—insofar as they could find any—as part of a long-term strategy aimed at electing a stronger Republican, hence more ideologically congenial, Congress. Nonincumbent Democrats were given very short shrift.

Because PACs contribute strategically, the pattern of PAC contributions displayed in these figures varies with electoral expectations. Business-oriented PACs give more to nonincumbent Republicans when Republican prospects look bright, particularly in Senate elections (note 1980 and 1994), and more to Republican incumbents when the opportunities for taking seats from Democrats look dim and Republican incumbents face strong Democratic challenges, as in 1982, or 2006.[11]

Labor does the same thing from the opposite side, investing relatively more in Democratic challenges when conditions favor Democrats (for example, 1982, 1996 and 2006) and relatively less when they do not. Because it matters a great deal how much challengers raise and spend, strategic contributions by PACs and other donors reinforce national partisan trends, with important consequences (discussed at length in Chapter 6). Both business and labor PACs tend to give lavishly to candidates for open seats of their preferred party; the absence of an incumbent makes for a more competitive election and the best opportunity to take a seat from the other party.

Several notable trends appear in these data. Note the sharp decline in the proportion of corporate and trade association PAC money given to nonincumbent Republican House candidates (from more than 25 percent in 1978 and 1980 to a paltry 6 percent in 1988) and the parallel rise in money given to Democratic incumbents (from 35 percent to more than 50 percent) through the 1980s. These patterns reflect several realities. First, Republican challengers, as a group, were unusually unpromising in the 1986–1990 period.[12] Second, and related, Republican challengers lacked exploitable issues. (Both of these phenomena are discussed in Chapter 6.) Finally, Democratic officials pursued business PAC funds vigorously, with pointed reminders as to which party, in all likelihood, would control Congress after the election.[13] Indeed, Democrats were so successful at raising PAC money, at least for their incumbents, that by the late 1980s, Republican leaders—who had initially celebrated PACs as a healthy expression of pluralist democracy—wanted to ban them outright.[14]

The 1994 election changed all that. Even before election day, the Republican surge caught the eye of PAC officials, who began opening their coffers to competitive nonincumbents. Some were no doubt responding to prospective Speaker Newt Gingrich's October threat that those who did not join the Republican cause could expect "the two coldest years in Washington" after the election.[15] After the election, pragmatic business PACs scrambled to atone for years of supporting incumbent Democrats by helping newly elected Republicans to retire their campaign debts and prepare for 1996. Willing to make a marriage of convenience with Democrats as long as Democrats were running the show, the PACs were now free to pursue a love match with the ideologically more compatible Republicans; who no longer talked of banning PACs.[16] Without their majority status and committee power to attract PAC contributions from business interests, the balance of PAC campaign resources shifted against the Democrats.

The shift is clearly evident in Figures 4–4a-b and 4–5a-b, most strikingly in the data for House elections. In the period 1988–1994, corporate PACs gave an average of 53 percent of their money to Democrats, 49 percent of their money to

Democratic incumbents. For elections following the Republicans' takeover of Congress in 1994, the comparable figures have been 34 percent and 31 percent, respectively. A nearly identical shift occurs in the pattern of trade association PAC donations. Of course, some of this change reflects the increase in the relative number of Republican incumbents; but a more detailed analysis, taking this and other relevant factors into account, found that loss of majority status cost Democratic incumbents an average of roughly $36,000 in corporate and trade association PAC contributions, a reduction of about 19 percent in money from these sources.[17] If history is any guide, the balance will shift back toward the Democratic incumbents for 2008.

PAC contributions to Senate candidates are also influenced by majority status, although contribution patterns are a good deal more variable across election years, reflecting variations in the incidence of competitive campaigns and in the set of states holding Senate elections. Over the years covered by Figures 4–4b and 4–5b, Democrats running for reelection to the Senate got an average of 47 percent of corporate and 42 percent of trade association PAC contributions when Democrats controlled the Senate, compared with 21 percent and 22 percent, respectively, when they did not. Again, a more detailed analysis indicates that, all else being equal, Senate majority status is worth an average of about $51,000 in corporate and trade association PAC contributions.[18]

The "nonconnected" category is made up largely of PACs with clear ideological or issue agendas, many of which therefore care more about influencing the makeup of Congress than about having access to officeholders. They thus comprise the only set with any inclination to be more generous to nonincumbents than to incumbents. The notable shift over time among nonconnected PACs, displayed in Figures 4–6a-b—from a strongly pro-Republican to a pro-Democratic

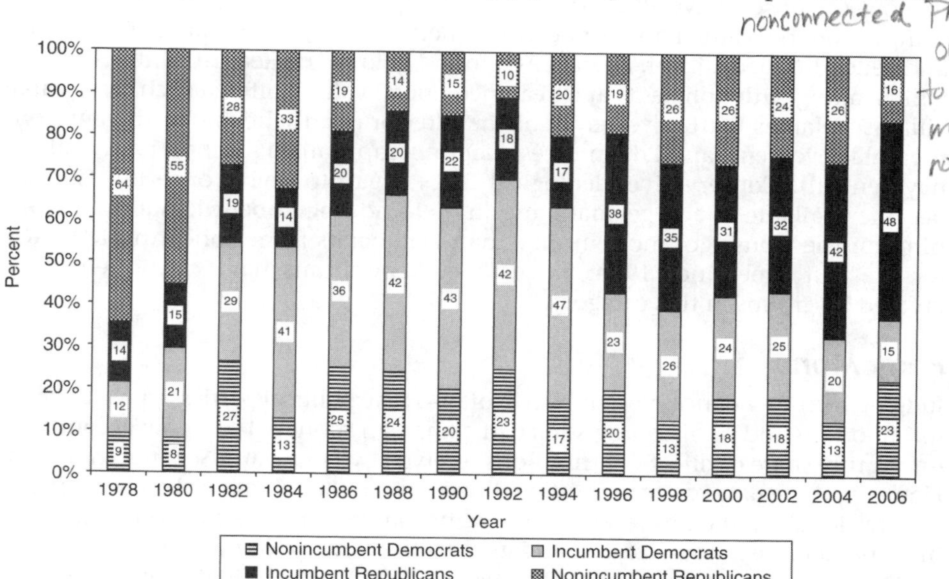

FIGURE 4–6a The Distribution of Nonconnected PAC Contributions to House Candidates, 1978–2006

Source: Federal Election Commission.

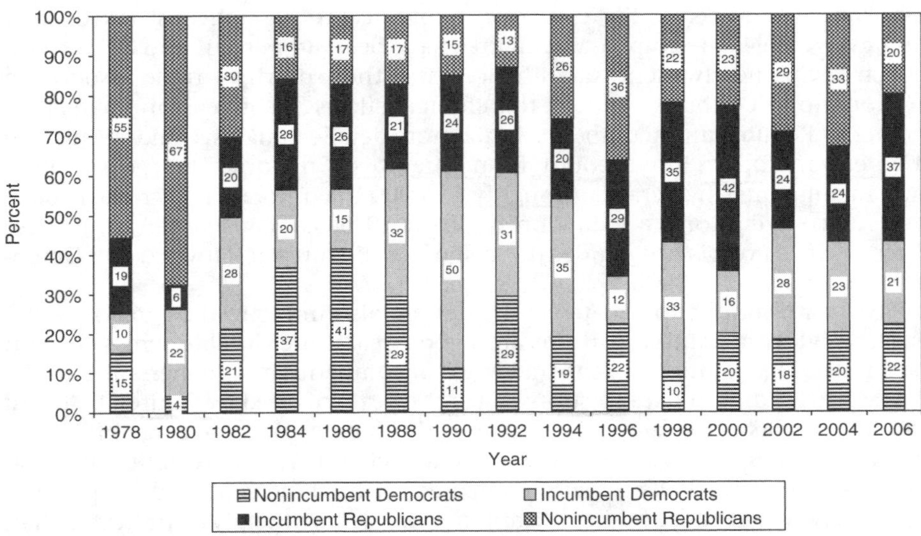

FIGURE 4–6b The Distribution of Nonconnected PAC Contributions to Senate Candidates, 1978–2006
Source: Federal Election Commission.

bias and then back to favoring Republicans—reflects changes in the composition of this category. Many of these groups raise their money through direct-mail appeals, which are most effective when they invoke threats that make people fearful or angry enough to send a check, which is easier to do in opposition than in power. Conservative PACs thus flourished in the late 1970s, when all bad things could be blamed on Democratic leaders such as Jimmy Carter, Tip O'Neill, and Teddy Kennedy. Later, liberal PACs found gold in the Reagan administration, which, along with policies that threatened liberal values, offered such serviceable villains as James Watt (a secretary of the interior openly hostile to the environmental movement) and Edwin Meese (an uncompromisingly conservative attorney general). Conservative ideological PACs began to revive once Bill Clinton became available as a bogeyman, and in 1994 nonincumbent Republicans running for the House got more money than Democrats from nonconnected PACs for the first time since 1984. Since then, Republicans have continued to be favored by groups in this category.

Party Money

Judging by the evidence presented in Table 4–1, the political parties appear to be an unimportant and diminishing source of campaign money. They now account for only a tiny share of direct contributions received by House and Senate candidates. However, these data vastly understate the amount of help, financial and otherwise, congressional candidates receive from party sources. In close elections, the party may spend more in total for a candidate than the candidate's own campaign.

Direct party contributions are limited to $5,000 per candidate per election for House candidates. This means that any party committee can give, at most, $10,000 to a candidate in an election year ($15,000 if there is a primary runoff). Both the national committees and the congressional campaign committees of each party can contribute this amount, so direct national party contributions can amount to $20,000 in House campaigns, a small fraction of what it costs to run a minimally serious campaign. The maximum allowable contribution to Senate candidates from all national party sources is only $44,500. Parties cannot be a major source of *direct* campaign contributions because the FECA will not allow it.

The FECA contains a special provision allowing party committees to spend money *on behalf of* congressional candidates, however. This *coordinated spending* is also limited, but the limits are higher and, unlike contribution limits, rise with inflation. The original limit of $10,000 set in 1974 for House campaigns had grown to $39,600 by 2006. The ceiling on coordinated party spending for Senate candidates varies with the state's population; in 2006, it ranged from $79,200 in the seven least populous states to $2,093,800 in California. The Senate limit applies to House candidates in any state with a single House seat.[19] State party committees are permitted to spend the same amount as national party committees on coordinated campaign spending but rarely have the money to do so. The parties have solved this problem by making the national party committee the state party's agent for raising and spending the money. In practice, this loophole doubles the amount the national party may spend on its candidates.

National party committees may thus play an important part in financing congressional campaigns. In 2006, for example, national party sources could give as much as $188,000 worth of assistance to a House candidate (direct donations of $5,000 in both the primary and general elections from the party's national committee, the congressional campaign committee, and the state party committee, plus twice $79,200 in coordinated expenditures). For Senate candidates, the total varied from about $200,000 to $4.2 million, depending on the state's voting-age population. Although these are significant sums, they still amount to no more than 20 percent of what it costs to mount a competitive campaign.

Of course, national party committees can spend money for candidates only after they have raised it. Following the FECA's enactment, Republican committees quickly outstripped their Democratic counterparts in raising funds. Between 1976 and 1984, total receipts for the National Republican Congressional Committee (NRCC) and National Republican Senatorial Committee (NRSC) grew from $14 million to $140 million. Over the same period, total receipts of the Democratic Congressional Campaign Committee (DCCC) and Democratic Senatorial Campaign Committee (DSCC) increased only from $195,000 to $19 million. Subsequently, Democratic fundraising picked up, but Republican committees enjoyed a large fundraising advantage in every election cycle until 2005–2006, when the parties' Hill committee fundraising was nearly even ($260 million for the DCCC and DSCC, and $268 million for the NRCC and NRSC).

Republican superiority in fundraising initially gave the party's congressional candidates a considerable advantage in party contributions and coordinated spending, but the Democrats closed some of the gap in the 1990s. Both parties now raise enough money to support all of their competitive candidates to the legal limit in direct contributions and coordinated spending. Between them, the Hill committees spent $22.3 million on assistance of this kind in 2006.

Coordinated party expenditures can be made for almost any campaign activity. The only condition is that the party as well as the candidate have some control over how the money is spent. The party committees typically foot the bill for conducting polls, producing campaign ads, and buying broadcast media time—major expenses in areas where technical expertise is essential. In 1992, for example, the NRCC conducted polls for 117 Republican House candidates and produced 188 TV ads for 45, including 22 nonincumbents. The DCCC itself produced no ads for Democratic candidates, but 240 used the party's media center to create their own. Party committees compile lists of voters to target, develop and hone campaign issues, and conduct "opposition research"—combing the public (and sometimes private) records of the other party's candidates to find weak points to attack. Both parties' committees also scrutinize the records of their own incumbents to detect points of vulnerability that might require special defenses.[20]

Coordinated spending does not begin to exhaust the services now performed by the Hill committees; indeed, it comprises a decreasing portion of their assistance to candidates. They run programs to train candidates and campaign managers in all aspects of campaigning: fundraising, personnel management, legal compliance, advertising, press relations, and so on. For example, prior to the 1996 elections, the Republican National Committee (RNC) held training seminars in forty-one states involving 6,000 Republican candidates and activists, the NRCC conducted three four-day candidate schools, and the NRSC offered seminars on fundraising and campaign techniques attended by representatives of twenty-two Senate campaigns. The Democratic National Committee (DNC) organized training sessions for 3,000 campaign operatives, and the DCCC and DSCC conducted training seminars for nonincumbent candidates and their campaign staffs.[21] Especially on the House side, the Hill committees have become trade schools of modern electoral politics.

The Hill committees have also assumed a central role in helping candidates raise money from PACs and other contributors. In addition to advising on fundraising techniques and targets, they serve as matchmakers between potential contributors and promising but needy candidates. PACs use party cues in making strategic investment choices, so getting onto their party's "watch list" of competitive races has become crucial to the prospects of nonincumbent candidates. The Hill committees also arrange to have safe incumbents use their fundraising prowess to help their party's other candidates (see the next section, Contributions from Other Members of Congress). Hill committee staffs also help candidates find suitable managers, consultants, pollsters, media specialists, direct-mail outfits, and other campaign professionals.

Beginning in 1996, the national party committees began exploiting the soft money option more intensely and, by 2002, transfers of both soft and hard money to state parties to be used to promote the election of House and Senate candidates had come to dwarf all other party assistance. Figures 4–7 and 4–8 display the trends in soft and hard money expenditures from 1988 through 2006. After BCRA banned the transfer of soft money to state parties for federal campaign activities following the 2002 elections, the parties adapted by ratcheting up their hard money fundraising. They also redirected their efforts into independent campaigns, which in 2004 and 2006 absorbed by far the largest share of national party resources (Figures 4–9 and 4–10). This avenue had been neglected while the soft money spigot was still open (note the low sums for 1998–2002) but was exploited with a vengeance once it was closed off.

With independent spending added to the mix, national party committees have become responsible for a substantial share of the funds spent on serious

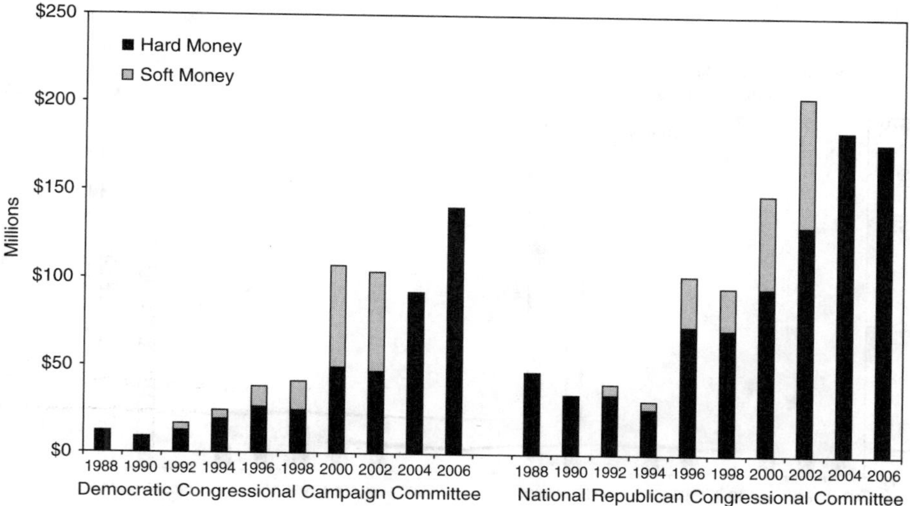

FIGURE 4–7 Hard and Soft Money Spent by House Campaign Committees, 1988–2006
Source: Compiled by Author from Federal Election Commission Data.

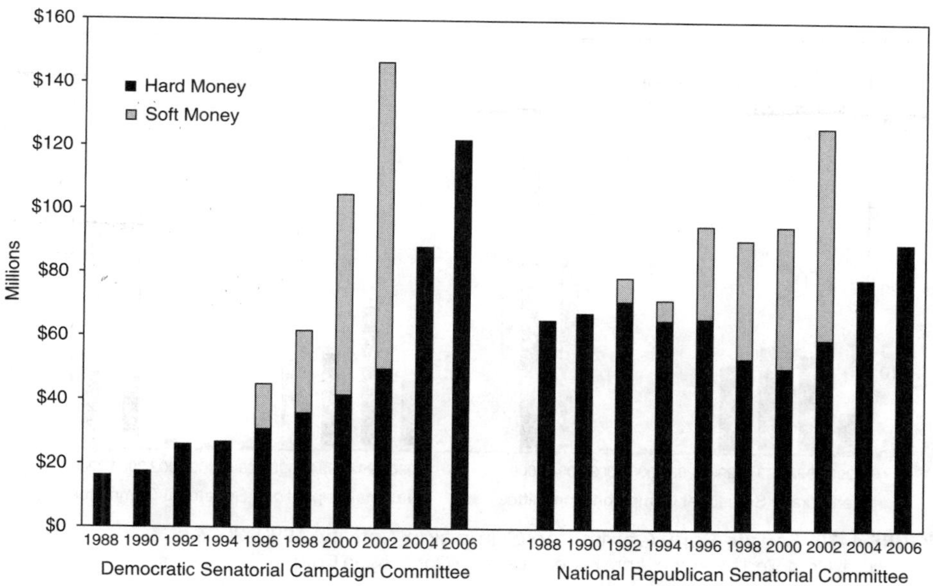

FIGURE 4–8 Spending by Senatorial Campaign Committees, 1988–2006
Source: Federal Election Commission.

congressional campaigns. Table 4–2 lists the average spending by the candidate's campaigns and by the party committees in the most hotly contested House and Senate races in 2006.[22] Clearly, the national parties provide a large supplement to these already generously financed campaigns. Most of the money they spend independently is used to attack their candidates' opponents rather than support their own candidates. The party committees have contributed to the

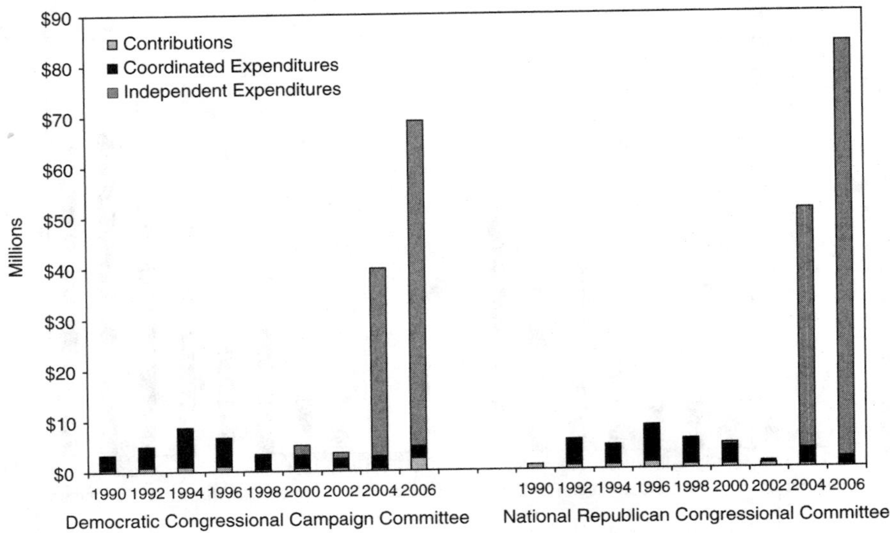

FIGURE 4–9 House Party Committee Campaign Activity, 1990–2006

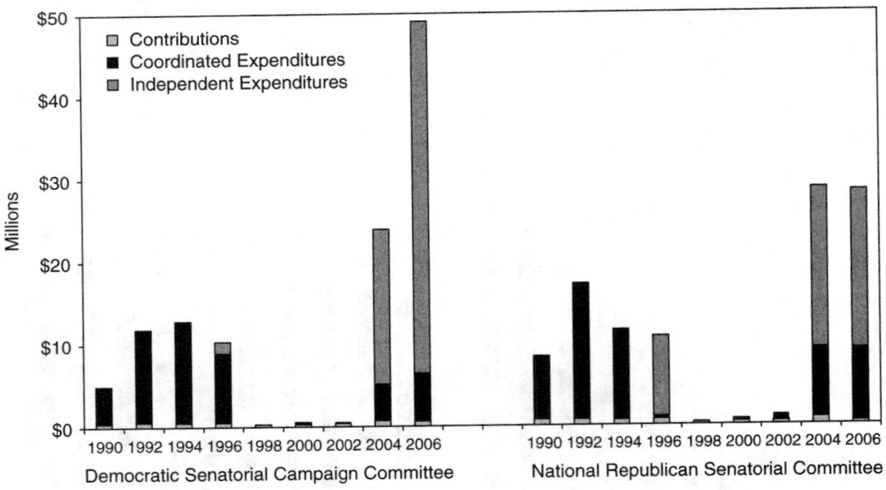

FIGURE 4–10 Senate Party Committee Campaign Activity, 1990–2006
Source: Compiled by Author from Federal Election Commission Data.

ever-growing concentration of funds in the most competitive races, since, like other strategic participants in congressional campaign finance, they invest almost exclusively in what they anticipate to be close campaigns, where the funds might therefore actually affect the outcome. In the 2006, between 88 and 99 percent of party spending was concentrated in these contests.

Party money does not come without strings. For example, in the extremely tight race for Colorado's 7th District in 2002, NRCC officials funneled about $2.4 million into the campaign of Republican Bob Beauprez, eventual victor by

TABLE 4–2 Party Money in Competitive House and Senate Races (2006)

	Republicans	Democrats
House of Representatives (63 races)		
Average candidate spending	$2.680 million	$1.919 million
Average party spending	$1.178 million	$ .910 million
Percent added by party spending	44%	47%
Percent of party independent spending for the party's candidate	6%	11%
Percent of party independent spending against the opponent	94%	89%
Percent of total party spending invested in competitive contests	88%	85%
Senate (10 races)		
Average Candidate Spending	$13.443 million	$11.259 million
Average party committee spending	$3.238 million	$4.622 million
Percent added by party spending	24%	41%
Percent of party independent spending for party's candidate	25%	25%
Percent of party money spent against opponent	75%	75%
Percent of total party spending invested in competitive contests	97%	99%

Source: Compiled by author from Federal Election Commission data.

a mere 121 votes. Along with the money came continuing NRCC oversight of Beauprez's campaign; as his annoyed campaign manager put it, "they crawl up our ass on a daily basis."[23] The state party's executive director reported that the NRCC instructed how the money was to be spent "down to the dollar."[24] The national party used its clout to shape the content of the campaign—the results were not always pretty. One direct-mail piece featured "side-by-side photographs of a cigar-chomping lobbyist and a rabid dog. The oversized postcard inveighed, 'what do you get when you cross this [cigar-chomping lobbyist] with this [rabid dog]? You get Mike Feeley [Beauprez's opponent]. And he wants to be your congressman.'"[25]

The Beauprez–Feeley race was not unique in this regard. National parties invest millions in congressional campaigns with the sole purpose of winning, and their inclination is to do whatever it takes to come out ahead. In doing so, they may even ignore their own candidate's preferences or reelection strategies. When Republican representative Jim Leach of Iowa was running for reelection in 2002, he publicly asked the party to stop running TV ads against his opponent because he thought them distorted and unfair. Leach also sought to position himself as a moderate (his district had given Al Gore 56 percent of its votes in

2000) but some national party–driven Republican ads extolled his support of "Iowa's Conservative Values." Despite Leach's protest, the party committees kept on broadcasting ads, spending $1.5 million in the process. The national party may have made Leach the winner in spite of himself; one close observer of this contest concluded that "it is doubtful that he would have won without" its unwanted help.[26] In 2006, Republican committees spent only $21,000 for Leach, none against his opponent, and he lost the seat.

Contributions from Other Members of Congress

In an era of very narrow legislative majorities, when control of both the House and Senate is up for grabs every two years, members have powerful interest in helping fellow partisans win elections. Many of them also aspire to leadership positions in their party. Because in any given election most members face little electoral risk themselves, they can use their fundraising prowess as incumbents to help their party and themselves by funneling money into the campaigns of colleagues in competitive races. They may form their own "leadership" PACs to pass out funds, contribute directly from their own campaign committees, or help attract contributors to other candidates' fundraising events.[27] When successful, the strategy increases their party's representation and puts some of the winners in their debt. For example, Susan Davis, Adam Schiff, and Jane Harman, three California Democrats who defeated Republican incumbents in 2000, received $130,000, $170,000, and $130,000, respectively, from members' PACs and campaign committees. It is far from coincidence that Nancy Pelosi was elected minority leader for the 108th Congress (2003–2004) on her way to becoming Speaker of the House for the 110th (2007–2008) after having contributed more than any other Democrat to other House candidates over the previous two election cycles, about $1.9 million.[28]

As Figure 4–11 shows, members' donations to other candidates have grown steeply in the past decade; in 2006, safe incumbents contributed $56 million to colleagues' campaigns. Both parties have participated in the trend, although Democrats were playing catch-up during the years when Republicans controlled Congress (Figure 4–12). At the same time, in response to heavy pressure from congressional leaders, members have also been transferring increasing sums to their party's campaign committees (Figure 4–13); in 2006, such contributions accounted for 17 percent of NRCC and 24 percent of DCCC receipts, for example.[29]

Plainly, the growing awareness of the stakes involved in the party's collective electoral performance has led to a steep increase in national party involvement in congressional campaigns. However, this activity has not necessarily shifted the focus of electoral politics away from individual candidates and back to parties. Rather, most of the parties' activities are explicitly designed to produce candidates who are more competitive in the candidate-centered system as it currently operates. Republicans in particular set a high priority on recruiting and training candidates because their "farm team"—candidates holding the lower elective offices that serve as stepping stones to Congress—was, at least prior to the 1990s, much thinner than that of the Democrats. During the 1980s, national-level Republican committees even invested in state legislative races, not only to elect more Republicans to the bodies that draw congressional district lines, but also to expand their pool of seasoned candidates. (State legislatures are the single most important source of future members of Congress; half the present members of the House have served in them.) Gingrich, while serving as minority

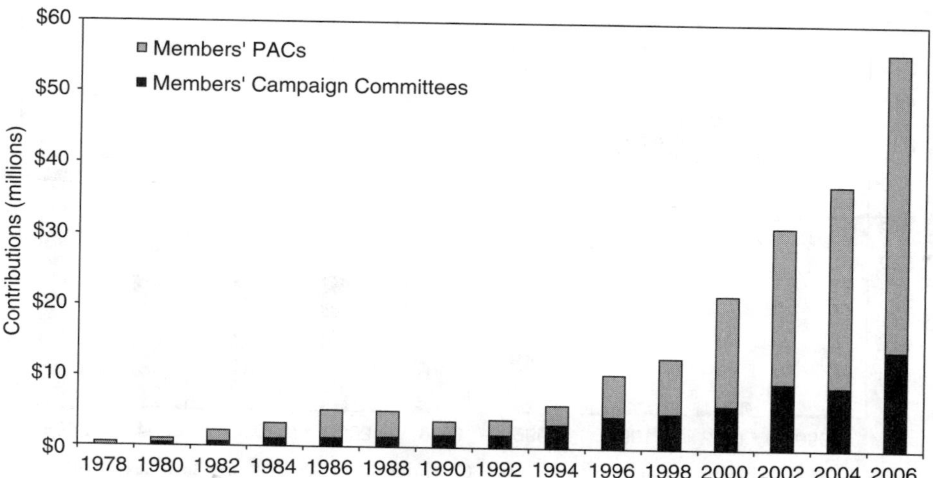

FIGURE 4–11 Contributions of Members' Campaign Committees and PACs to House and Senate Candidates, 1978–2006

Sources: 1978–2002, Anne Bedlington and Michael J. Malbin, "The Party as Extended Network: Members Giving to Each Other and to their Parties." in Michael J. Malbin, ed., *Life After Reform: When The Bipartisan Campaign Reform Act Meets Politics* (Roman and Littlefield, forthcoming), Figure 7–1; 2004–2006, Center for Responsive Politics, "Spreading the Wealth," at *http://www.opensecrets.org/bigpicture/wealth.asp?type=lead2cand,* accessed October 26, 2007.

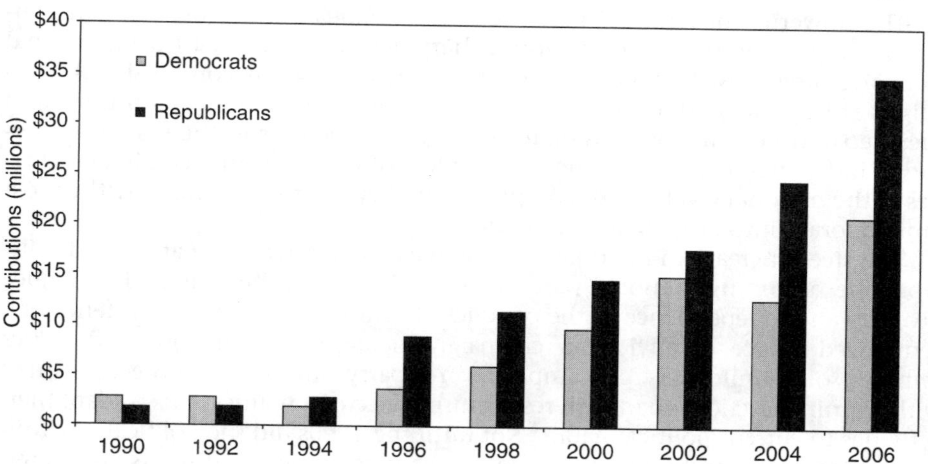

FIGURE 4–12 House and Senate Members' Contributions to Other Candidates' Campaigns, 1990–2006

Source: Center for Responsive Politics, "Spreading the Wealth," at *http://www.opensecrets.org/bigpicture/wealth.asp?cycle=2006,* accessed October 26, 2007.

leader, formed a PAC (referred to as the GOPAC) to recruit, train, and finance candidates for state legislatures; Republicans whose initial forays into state politics were sponsored by Newt Gingrich's GOPAC swelled the ranks of the majority that elected him Speaker in 1995.[30] Today, both parties are heavily involved in candidate recruitment, again with a focus on potentially competitive seats; one important source of the Democrats' success in 2006 lay in finding and nurturing

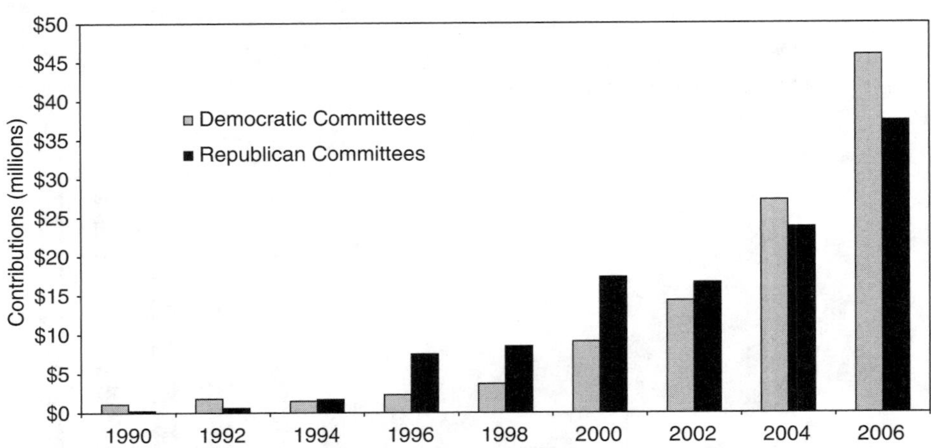

FIGURE 4–13 House and Senate Members' Contributions to Congressional Campaign Committees, 1990–2006

Sources: 1990–1996: Center for Responsive Politics, "Spreading the Wealth," at *http://www.opensecrets.org/bigpicture/wealth.asp?cycle=2006*, accessed October 26, 2007; 1998–2006, Anthony Corrado and Katie Varney, "Party Money in the 2006 Election," Campaign Finance Institute Report, 2007, p. 13.

House candidates who were sufficiently conservative to win some Republican-leaning districts.

The flowering of national party activity—financial and otherwise—in congressional election politics represents a sharp departure from past congressional campaign practices. Formerly, parties were most active in congressional campaigns at the state and local levels. The declining vigor of these party units and their separation from congressional campaigns helped foster the system of personal, independent campaigning now typical of congressional candidates. Parties at the national level focused on presidential elections, making only the most limited forays into other federal elections.

The steep increase in national party activity has altered this pattern radically. From the beginning, national party activities have had the potential to reduce diversity and independence in the conduct of campaigns; the mere existence of a centralized source of advice on campaign management, strategy, and tactics imposes some uniformity on campaigns. Yet party officials are more concerned with winning elections than with restructuring electoral politics and so adapt their activities to current political habits. Not until the 1990s did the political environment offer campaign themes that resonated across numerous districts and states, and not until 1994 did these themes have a strong partisan thrust. However, once conditions were right, the Republicans' national party infrastructure helped individual candidates take full advantage of their extraordinary opportunity and the party enjoyed a historic victory. In 2006, it was the Democrats' turn and they, too, proved organizationally capable of exploiting national issues locally to great effect.

Self-Financing by Candidates

Aside from individuals, PACs, and parties, candidates can also obtain campaign money from their own pockets. The Supreme Court's 1976 decision in *Buckley v.*

Valeo overturned limits on how much of their own money candidates may spend to get elected, which gives no small advantage to wealthy candidates. They can finance as lavish a campaign as the family fortune allows without the aggravation fundraising entails, while their opponents must spend time hustling limited donations from a large number of individuals and groups. The most notorious example is Jon Corzine, who made a fortune in investment banking and spent a fair chunk of it—$60.2 million—to win a New Jersey Senate seat in 2000. Another example is Peter Fitzgerald, who spent $13.8 million of his own money in defeating incumbent Carol Moseley-Braun in a 1998 race for an Illinois Senate seat.

Tapping the family fortune does not guarantee victory, to be sure; in 1994, Michael Huffington spent $28.4 million from his own pocket in a failed attempt to take a California Senate seat from Dianne Feinstein. Pursuing West Virginia's 2nd District, Democrat James Humphreys spent $6.1 million in 2000 and another $7.8 million in 2002, but he lost both contests to Shelly Moore Caputo, whose total campaign spending was less than one-third as much. In fact, wealthy self-financed candidates lose far more often than they win. Jennifer Steen found that in elections from 1990 through 1998, only five each of the top twenty self-financers in both House and Senate contests were successful (and two of the Senate winners were incumbents).[31] Of the twenty-eight House candidates spending more than $1 million of their own on general election campaigns between 2000 and 2006, only four won, all taking open seats. Only six of the eighteen similarly self-financed Senate candidates were successful over this period, and two were already incumbents. Steen found that, on average, candidates contributing substantial sums to their own campaigns did only slightly better than candidates financed by others.[32]

Despite this unimpressive record, BCRA's designers thought it necessary to accommodate the incumbent's nightmare of facing a multimillionaire opponent by including a provision that raised contribution and party spending limits for candidates facing self-financed opponents. The limits are raised on a sliding scale depending on the level of self-financing; at maximum, the limits for individual contributions to Senate candidates may be increased sixfold and the limits on party support are entirely eliminated. The provision has yet to have a discernable effect beyond some minor adjustments in the funding of a few campaigns.[33] The BCRA also tried to discourage high levels of self-financing by limiting the amount candidates may loan their campaigns to $250,000; anything more must be a personal donation to the campaign that cannot be recouped from contributors later (something winners would have been able to do before BCRA).

Obviously, great personal wealth is not a prerequisite to winning a seat in Congress. But candidates not enjoying the fundraising advantages that come with incumbency normally must be prepared to invest some of their own money—perhaps $50,000—to pay startup costs and to demonstrate commitment, with little hope of recouping any of it if they lose.

Fundraising Tactics

The most important aspect of fundraising is convincing potential donors that their money will not be wasted. Donors must be persuaded that the candidate has a plausible chance of winning and would be more attentive to their values and interests than would the opponent. Incumbents are, of course, in the best position to be persuasive. For nonincumbents, techniques of persuasion range from polls and old election returns to a smooth tongue backed by a lively imagination, and from recitation of a political record to solemn promises. PACs and other contributors, understandably wary of such salesmanship, often take cues from each other and, more importantly, from party campaign committees in deciding who is worth an investment.

With or without party matchmaking, large contributions must usually be solicited face-to-face by the candidate or a prominent, high-status fundraiser. Smaller contributions are sought at meetings, rallies, dinners, through direct-mail appeals sent to individuals at home, and on campaign websites. Direct mail can be expensive; in 1992, Congressman Robert Dornan of California spent $1,151,338 to raise $1,407,922; $967,650 of the total went to direct-mail solicitation.[34] This form of fundraising has raised some concern because direct-mail pleas are the most successful when they play on strong emotions, such as anger, fear, or frustration, to convince people to support the candidate. Extremist candidates—Dornan, a flamboyant conservative firebrand, again serves as an example—are thus best able to exploit this method.[35] Internet fundraising, by comparison, is very cheap but requires even more intense commitment on the part of donors; as one veteran direct-mail fundraiser put it, "You think of the mail as fundraisers as chasing donors. The Internet, when it works, is donors chasing fundraisers, which is a truly unnatural act."[36]

No matter how candidates raise the money, timing is crucial. It is as important to have money available when it is needed as it is to have it in the first place. In general, money available early in the campaign is put to much better use than money received later. Early money is seed money for the entire campaign effort; it is needed to organize, plan, and raise more money. This circumstance adds to the advantage of personal wealth; it also enhances the importance of national party and other organizations that are willing to make contributions and provide help early in the campaign. Emily's List, a PAC devoted to electing pro-choice women to Congress, takes its name from an acronym extolling this approach: "Early money is like yeast (it makes the dough rise)." Emily's List is also the premiere proponent of "bundling"; rather than contribute money directly to candidates, the PAC directs the individual contributions of its members to designated candidates. That way, it can provide help in excess of the $5,000 PAC contribution limit. In 2006, for example, Emily's List channeled $11 million to the campaigns of pro-choice women via bundling.[37]

Independent, "Voter Education," and "Issue Advocacy" Campaigns

Candidates and parties have never enjoyed exclusive control over congressional campaigns; independent campaigns conducted by PACs and other organizations have been part of the process since the adoption of the FECA. But until the 1990s, their part was minor, with independent spending never accounting for more than 3 percent of total campaign spending, and in most elections it was closer to 1 percent. In the 1990s, however, interest groups developed a new avenue for large-scale involvement in electoral politics beyond the control of the candidates. The Court's *Buckley* decision construed the FECA "to apply only to expenditures for communications that in express terms advocate the election or defeat of a clearly identified candidate for federal office." Subsequent decisions have confirmed that the First Amendment protects the right to conduct unrestricted so-called voter-education or issue-advocacy campaigns, even if clearly intended to influence voters (by, for example, tendentious comparisons of candidates' issue positions), as long as such terms as "vote for," "elect," "vote against," "defeat," and "reject," are not used.[38] The Supreme Court's decision in *Federal Election Commission v. Wisconsin Right to Life*, announced in June 2007, overturned BCRA's attempt to limit the effect of these campaigns through a ban on mentioning candidates' names in them during a fixed pre-election period (30 days for primaries, 60 days for general elections). Although such ads must still refrain from specifically advocating a vote for or against a candidate, foreswearing the Court's forbidden "magic words" does not prevent the production of ads that are indistinguishable from ordinary campaign ads.[39]

Independent spending by PACs must be reported to the FEC. The totals these groups spent for and against congressional candidates from 1978 through 2006 are shown in Figures 4–14 and 4–15. The sums have become significant only recently, and there is considerable variation from year to year as groups adopt independent spending practices to changing legal and political circumstances. Democratic House candidates got a particularly large boost from this source in 2006. Precise figures on spending by 527 and 501(c) groups are often unavailable because they do not come under the FEC's jurisdiction, but there is no question that sums have become substantial. One informed estimate has the total spending on congressional races by 527s at $143 million and by 501(c) groups at $90 million in 2006.[40] Table 4–3 puts these numbers into context. Overall, about 71 percent of total spending in 2006 came from candidates' campaigns; independent groups (15 percent) were as prominent as the parties (14 percent) in accounting for the rest.

Such prominent organizations as the Christian Coalition, AFL-CIO, Sierra Club, the United States Chamber of Commerce, and Americans for Limited Terms, as well as more shadowy groups such as Americans for Job Security, have

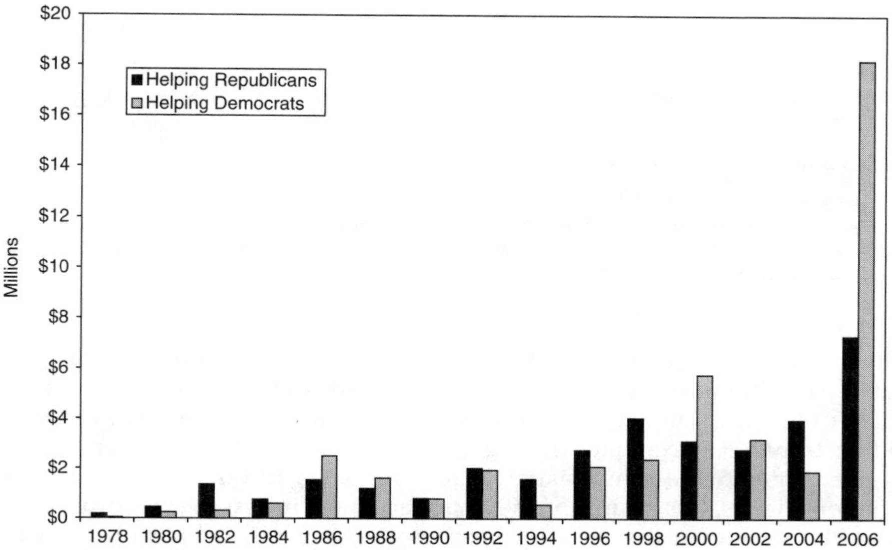

FIGURE 4–14 Non-Party Independent Spending in House Elections, 1978–2006
Source: Federal Election Commission.

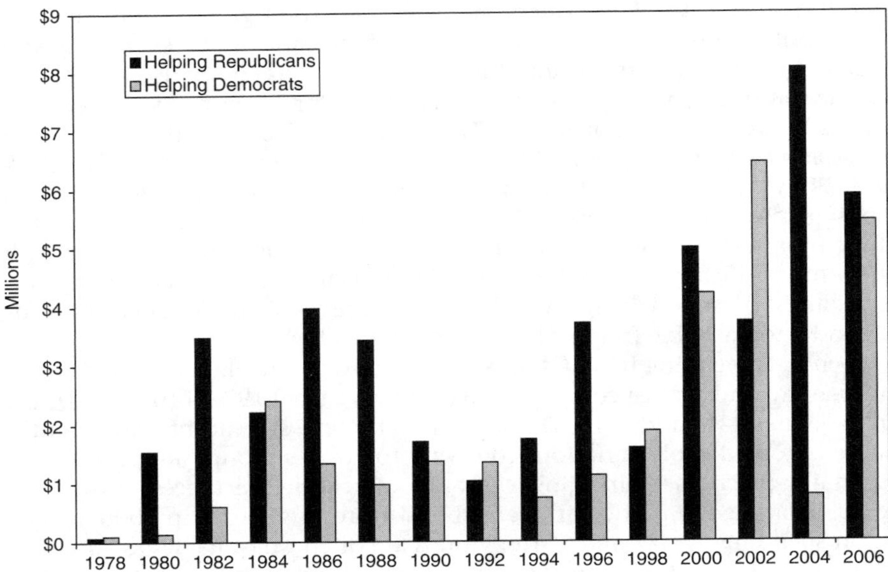

FIGURE 4–15 Non-Party Independent Spending in Senate Elections, 1978–2006
Source: Federal Election Commission.

TABLE 4–3 Sources of Total Campaigns Spending in the 2006 Congressional Races

	Spending in $ Millions	Percent
Candidates' Campaigns[a]	1,273	71.7
Parties[a]	225	12.7
Independent Committees[a]	44	2.5
527 Groups[b]	143	8.1
501(c) Organizations[b]	90	5.1
Total	1,775	100.0

[a]Compiled by author from Federal Election Commission data.
[b]Stephen R. Weissman and Kara D. Ryan, *Soft Money in the 2006 Election and the outlook for 2008: the Changing Nonprofits Landscape* (Report, Campaign Finance Institute, 2007), p. 7. The authors note that the 501(c) figure is an underestimate because of lax disclosure rules for such organizations.

invested heavily in "voter education" and "issue advocacy" in recent campaigns. By taking this route, groups can spend unlimited and unregulated sums on behalf of candidates. They can also conduct stealth campaigns behind innocuous-sounding fronts. For example, three groups active in 2002 on the Republican side—the United Seniors Association, the Seniors Coalition, and the 60 Plus Association—were all creatures of the pharmaceutical industry, promoting candidates who supported the industry's prescription drug plan.[41] Stealth was carried to an extreme in some House races in 2002. Jill Long Thompson, Democratic candidate for Indiana's 2nd District, was hammered during the last three weeks of the campaign in a series of twelve automated phone calls, each of which reached at least 40,000 households. The calls, including one featuring the voice of Barbara Bush, the president's mother, reiterated Long Thompson's Republican opponent's campaign theme.[42] Chris Kouri, Democrat competing for North Carolina's 8th District, faced a similar automated onslaught.[43] In neither case did anyone admit responsibility for the phone calls and their origin remains a mystery. Both Long Thompson and Kouri lost. More systematic evidence that "voter education" campaigns can be effective comes from a study of the AFL-CIO's $25–$35 million campaign against sixty-four Republican incumbents in 1996; the campaign deprived targeted freshmen of their sophomore surges and, arguably, cost as many as seven of them their seats.[44]

Independent groups usually coordinate their campaigns with those of the parties and candidates, albeit tacitly, in order to stay within the law. But some have their own agendas and are willing to sacrifice a party's interest to further their own. The Club for Growth, for example, a group dedicated to electing anti-tax purists, has mounted primary campaigns against Republican incumbents it considers insufficiently conservative. Contrary to the wishes of national Republican leaders, the group sponsored a primary challenge to moderate Republican Senator Lincoln Chaffee of Rhode Island in 2006. The challenge fell short, 46–54, but it probably helped weaken the incumbent, who lost the general election to Democrat Sheldon Whitehouse by a similar margin. Had the conservative Republican backed by the Club for Growth won the nomination, he would certainly have done even worse than Chaffee. Thus the Club was willing to sacrifice Republican control of the Senate (which the Democrats won by a single seat in 2006) in order to move the Republican Party rightward.

Campaign Organizations

Campaigns require organization. Raising funds, handling the legal formalities, gathering intelligence, designing and executing advertising strategies, holding events, and identifying supporters and getting them to the polls on election day are complex and demanding tasks that have to be carried out in a brief and inflexible time frame. It takes experience and savvy to do any one of them well. It is neither easy nor cheap to build a good campaign organization.

Many incumbents keep at least an embryonic campaign organization permanently in place, often as personal staff. Other candidates must normally build organizations from scratch—one reason seed money is so important. There was a time when, in many places, vigorous party organizations operated on a permanent basis and worked for entire party tickets. This is rarely the case now. Even when parties were robust, congressional candidates were not centers of attention, since local parties were interested primarily in patronage and members of Congress controlled little of that. Now that local party organizations have lost much of their value as campaign allies (at least until the national party decides to finance their federal campaign activities), congressional candidates are even more on their own when it comes to mounting a campaign.

For candidates who can afford it, the easiest way of acquiring a campaign organization is to buy one. Professional campaign specialists have taken over many of the functions formerly performed by local parties and have pioneered a variety of new electoral techniques adapted to an age of television and computers. It is possible for a candidate to hire a single outfit that will handle the entire campaign. More commonly, candidates engage a team of specialists—campaign managers, accountants, media consultants, pollsters, fundraisers, researchers, and the like. Professional services do not come cheap. Incumbents can afford them; often challengers cannot and must soldier on without much professional assistance. A 1992 study, for example, found that virtually every incumbent had a paid campaign manager, while 35 percent of challengers' House campaigns were managed by volunteers.[45] No doubt most poorly financed challengers—and 110 reported spending less than $25,000 in 2006—continue to run campaigns without professional help. Senate challengers, with larger campaigns and bigger budgets, are much more likely to make use of professional campaign services. Hiring experienced professionals is now one sign of a serious campaign, and candidates who cannot afford to do so are unlikely to attract much attention from PACs or party committees.[46]

Short of buying a complete team package, the only way most nonincumbent congressional candidates can have an adequate campaign organization is to assemble one themselves (although the most promising candidates can expect extensive help from national party officials). Close political friends, the "personal constituency" that Fenno noticed all of his congressmen had acquired, form the core. Other components are added as they are available. Some Democrats, for example, receive extensive organizational help from labor unions. Fragments of local parties can sometimes be used. Inner-city African American candidates may work through neighborhood churches. Republican candidates espousing "family values" are helped by Christian fundamentalist congregations and other conservative organizations. Single-issue groups, such as environmentalists, opponents of gun control, or those on opposite sides of the abortion issue, provide organizational help to supporters of their causes. Almost any existing group with political interests can be absorbed into a campaign organization. In some Florida districts, condominium activists form a cadre of "articulate people with organizational literacy, an interest in issues, a knack for politics, and plenty of time on their hands" that can be recruited into congressional campaigns.[47] The kind of organization a candidate assembles depends on what kinds of groups are available, which ones he or she can appeal to, and the candidate's range of contacts, resources, and level of political skill.

The campaign organizations of poorly funded House challengers tend to be personal, ephemeral, and dependent on volunteers. Because they are ephemeral and rely on people giving their time and energy without pay, a great deal of effort goes into internal organizational maintenance. Xandra Kayden observed that "most of the campaign staff devotes most of its time to creating and maintaining the campaign organization."[48] Such campaign organizations cannot be hierarchical because sanctions are so few. They cannot learn from their mistakes because they exist for such a short time and go out of business at the very time the real effectiveness of their work is measured—on election day. It is not surprising that so few are successful.

Campaign Strategies

In a broad sense, everyone knows what campaigns are supposed to do: find and expand the pool of eligible voters favoring the candidate and make sure that they vote. Figuring out just *how* to do it is another matter. As one political veteran told

John Kingdon, "I don't know very much about elections. I've been in a lot of them."[49] In fact, the central motif of almost every discussion of campaign strategy is uncertainty.

What is the most efficient way to reach voters? No one knows for sure. The conventional view is that "half the money spent on campaigns is wasted. The trouble is, we don't know which half."[50] The effects of uncertainty about what works and what does not pervade campaign decision making. Successful candidates are inclined to do what they did in the past—they must have done something right, even if they cannot be sure what; a degree of superstition is understandable. Other candidates follow tradition. Kayden concludes that, "basically, campaigns produce literature because campaigns have always produced literature."[51] The same may be said of yard signs, bumper stickers, and campaign buttons. They appear in every election year, not so much because they have ever been shown to be effective but because everyone expects them and their absence would be noticed, if only by the campaign's activists (hence, they may be part of organizational maintenance).

On the other hand, uncertainty also invites innovation. Challengers, underdogs, and former losers have an incentive to try new tactics, if only to get desperately needed attention from the news media. For example, Lawton Chiles won a surprise victory in the 1970 Florida Senate election by walking the length of the state, talking and listening to people along the way. Other candidates quickly imitated him. While it was still fresh, the tactic generated abundant free publicity and far more attention than Chiles and the other candidates could afford to buy. Similarly, Tom Harkin, challenging the Republican incumbent for Iowa's 5th District in 1972, made news by working for one day at a time in a variety of blue-collar jobs, ostensibly to get close to the common experience. Others soon picked up the idea. Senator Bob Graham of Florida made such workdays his political trademark, logging more than 385 between his first successful campaign in 1978 (for governor) through the end of his third and final Senate term in 2004.[52]

Whatever seems to work for one is imitated by others,[53] so the novelty and therefore effectiveness of such tactics fade. But there is always something new. In 1980, Kenneth Snider, Democratic challenger in Indiana's 8th District, dropped in on voters with the helicopter he had purchased especially for the campaign; the news media loved it.[54] Snider lost the election but won a respectable 45 percent of the vote. Two years later, Republican Dan Burton, campaigning in his 1948 fire engine, was more successful; he has represented Indiana's 5th District ever since.[55]

Other modes of transportation have not been overlooked. Challenger Gene Freund undertook what might be called the "Tour d'Iowa," pedaling his bicycle 800 miles through twenty-seven counties of Iowa's 5th district in 1988.[56] In 1986, another challenger had been desperate enough for publicity to bicycle 340 miles across the Nevada desert along the shoulder of Interstate 80 in August.[57] Neither of these cyclists crossed the finish line first, but David Minge's 500-mile bike tour through forty-seven towns in nine days helped him win Minnesota's 2nd District in 1992. Minge repeated the tactic in 1994, narrowly holding off a challenger who, among other things, campaigned from a train.[58]

Sometimes a vehicle can even embody the campaign's central theme. In 1994, Greg Ganske campaigned for Iowa's 4th District in the "Nealmobile," a DeSoto made in 1958, the year the incumbent, Neal Smith, was first elected to the House. A sign on the roof asked: "WHY is it still running?"[59] In a year when *career politician* was a nasty epithet, Ganske drove the Nealmobile right in to the House. Candidates also travel in battered pickup trucks, old station wagons, and other humble vehicles to show that they are just plain folks, not out-of-touch Washington insiders. In 2006, as voters watched gas prices rise above $3.00 per gallon nationally, the fuel rather than the vehicle provided the gimmick. Mike Weaver, Democratic challenger to Ron Lewis in Kentucky's 2nd, "filled motorists' gas tanks for $1.20 per gallon, the price gasoline cost when Lewis was first elected to Congress in 1994," paying the difference out of pocket; Lewis thereupon accused Weaver of the federal crime of trying to buy votes.[60]

Campaign Media

Two groups of activities are common to all full-scale campaigns. One is mass media advertising, which absorbs about 45 percent of a typical campaign budget.[61] The candidate's name and perhaps a short message are presented to voters via some combination of television, radio, newspaper advertisements, billboards, mass mailings, automated telephone calls, emails, and instant messaging. The choice of media is partly strategic and partly dictated by cost and available resources. About one-third of House campaigns, for example, do not use paid television.[62] In large metropolitan areas, it is inefficient and too expensive for candidates without extraordinarily ample funds. Candidates must pay for the audience they reach; at the extreme (the greater New York City media market), constituents may comprise less than 5 percent of the audience. The more efficiently television markets fit a district, the more likely House candidates are to use television advertising.[63]

Still, House candidates with enough money buy television time even if it is very inefficient, for it may be the only way to reach many potential voters. So do parties and organizations spending independently of candidates' campaigns. The notion that television advertising is essential regardless of price is one important force driving up the cost of campaigning. In the hotly contested campaigns that attract the national parties' attention, multimillion-dollar broadcast campaigns that saturate the airwaves in the weeks leading up to the election are not uncommon. Radio advertising is also "wasteful" in large media markets, but the costs are much lower than those for TV, and radio audiences sort themselves out demographically for targeting, so campaigns often use radio ads where TV is beyond their means.

Senate campaigns are usually able to use television much more efficiently than House campaigns because constituencies are entire states, though cost and efficiency still vary considerably across states.[64] The use of television helps candidates who are not already well known (i.e., challengers) and can be added to the list of factors that make Senate campaigns so much more competitive, on the average, than House campaigns.

With enough money on both sides, a television campaign can take on the character of an ongoing debate, where "one day's set of TV ads for one candidate [is] followed soon after by his opponent's set of counterads, and the process [is] repeated several times in an intricate series of tactical moves."[65] There is no apparent limit to how much television advertising voters will tolerate. Back in 1984, Senator Jesse Helms's reelection campaign in North Carolina was on the air almost continuously for the eighteen months preceding the election; 150 different ads were produced for the campaign. His opponent, James Hunt, also saturated the airwaves, though for a shorter period.[66] Helms won, spending $16.5 million to Hunt's $9.5 million in what was up to then the most expensive Senate contest ever held. Twenty years later, John Tune won a narrow victory in South Dakota over Tom Daschle, then Democratic majority leader of the Senate, in a contest in which the candidates managed to spend more than $34 million between them in a state with fewer than 502,000 registered voters. The total amounted to a record $68 per voter. More than $9 million was spent on broadcast ads in a state where airtime is relatively cheap.[67]

Well-funded House campaigns in districts with inefficient television coverage often rely heavily on direct mail, which can pinpoint the district's voters. House and Senate campaigns also use direct mail to send messages targeted to specific subgroups in the electorate. In a sample of hotly contested races in 2002, the candidates and parties combined to send an average of forty-four unique mail pieces during the campaign; voters reported receiving three or four pieces a day during the last week of the campaign. Some campaigns greatly exceeded these averages; in the contest for South Dakota's Senate seat, won by incumbent Democrat Tim Johnson by a margin of only 524 votes, some voters reported receiving as many as ten pieces of mail per day. A total of 174 unique direct-mail pieces were distributed during this race:

> The blizzard of messages became intrusive and it was hard to break through the clutter and process all of the brief messages. The direct mail pieces were primarily visual, usually filled with distorted images of opponents, babies, or the candidate and his family. The messages lacked substance and most were brief enough to be read on the way to the trash can.[68]

The growing sophistication of both data processing and lists segmenting the voting population into distinct subgroups has greatly increased the efficiency with which direct-mail appeals can be targeted to specific audiences.[69] Improved databases and much cheaper technology have also led to increased use of the telephone to get out campaign messages and mobilize voters. "A telephone call, as unwelcome as it may be, cuts through . . . apathy and cynicism by forcing voters to listen to a political message," or so its practitioners claim.[70]

Congressional candidates have also discovered the Internet. A study of the 2002 campaigns found that 70 percent maintained websites, and 55 percent sought to raise funds online (via credit card transactions). Most sites featured newsletters and action alerts, as well as information about the candidates.[71] By 2006, campaign websites and Internet fundraising efforts were virtually universal. They are a boon to researchers looking for a quick way to check out the candidates, but it is hard to gauge how effectively they serve the campaigns. Websites no doubt help to coordinate the candidate's active supporters, making it easy for them to keep in touch and send money. That said, whether they attract the uncommitted in sufficient numbers to matter is questionable. In any case, as anyone who sifts through them soon learns, at least the truly flaky websites do expose some of the truly flaky candidates.

Email is also now part of the campaign arsenal, although some care has to be taken to avoid irritating voters with unwanted spam. So is text-messaging. For example, Rick Santorum, running (unsuccessfully) for reelection to his Pennsylvania Senate seat in 2006, encouraged attendees at a woman's outreach breakfast "to text 'LEADING' to a PA phone number to receive a return text message that read: 'From Keeping Women's Docs in PA to Allowing Parents the Freedom to Work from Home, Rick Santorum is Leading 4 Women. Look 4 Msgs with More Information.'"[72] Because cell-phone users have to sign up to receive the messages, the medium is better suited to rallying the faithful than to attracting the undecided.

Regardless of which combination of media is chosen, a fundamental goal is to get the candidate's name before the public. Although little else is certain about the effects of mass communications, it is well established that mass media coverage is positively related to public awareness of people, products, messages, and events. As we shall see in Chapter 5, the more nonincumbent candidates spend on a campaign, the more voters are likely to know who they are. Getting voters' attention is only one hurdle, of course, but clearing it is essential.

Personal Campaigning

The second basic type of campaign activity centers around the candidate's personal contact with potential voters. Most politicians have faith in the personal touch; if they can just talk to people and get them to listen, they can win their support. There is some evidence behind this notion. Larry Pressler, who represented South Dakota in Congress from 1974 to 1996, won his first House election with a campaign that consisted largely of meeting people one-on-one. "I tried to shake 500 hard hands a day," Pressler has said. "That is where you really take their hand and look at them and talk to them a bit. I succeeded in doing that seven days a week. I put in a lot of twelve-hour days, starting at a quarter to six in the morning at some plant in Sioux Falls or Madison."[73] Pressler estimates that he shook 300 to 500 hands per day on about eighty days. "You would not believe the physical and mental effort this requires."[74] Shaking one hand per minute, a candidate would have to work for more than eight hours without stop to reach 500 people.

The difficulty with this approach is that even the average House district now contains nearly 700,000 people, and states can be much more populous than this. It is simply impossible to meet more than a small fraction of the electorate during a single campaign. But candidates often agree with Pressler that it is worth trying—especially challengers whose only advantage may be the time they can devote to one-on-one campaigning. Some go door-to-door, "shoe-leathering" the neighborhoods; in his first House campaign in 1990, candidate Rick Santorum rang 25,000 doorbells in his upset victory over the incumbent in Pennsylvania's 18th District[75]; four years later, he won election to the Senate.

Many candidates greet the early shift at the factory gate, shaking hands, passing out leaflets, showing workers they care enough to get up as early as the workers must. Most will accept any opportunity to speak to a group, and it is not uncommon for candidates to show up wherever people congregate in sufficient numbers: shopping malls, community picnics, parades, sporting events, and the like. As Santorum proved, energetic grassroots campaigns of this sort are occasionally successful even in this high-tech era[76] and, because they offer about the only hope to unknown candidates not blessed with great personal wealth, they remain common.

Even lavishly funded campaigns use the personal touch when it is feasible, and with adequate research resources, the touch can be personal indeed. Tim Johnson's successful campaign for reelection to the Senate in 2002

> made an effort to personally visit as many households as [it] could. When either the candidate or campaign worker was going door to door, they carried nine different scripts that contained different issues. Before knocking on the door they already knew something about the occupant and selected the script designed for that demographic.[77]

Many of a candidate's activities are designed to reach voters beyond those in the immediate audience by attracting the attention of the news media. Indeed, campaigns work so hard to get "free" media exposure that campaign professionals commonly refer to it as "earned" media.[78] The main reason for walking the length of the state or pedaling across the district is that it makes news. Campaign events are designed not so much for the immediate audience as for the larger audience watching television or reading the newspaper at home. The temptation to resort to gimmickry is not always resisted. Ronald Machtley began his successful campaign to replace Fernand St Germain accompanied by a "250-pound hog named Lester H. Pork ('Les Pork') to symbolize his opposition to St Germain's big spending policies."[79] Mark Sanford donned camouflage hunting clothes to declare "a war on career politicians" in his successful bid for South Carolina's 1st District in 1994.[80]

Paid campaign ads may also be used to gain media exposure; one consultant recommends using "shock mailers" to provoke opponents into outraged responses, which then give the charges much wider publicity when the news media report the squabble.[81] A gentler tactic was used in Russ Feingold's successful challenge to Wisconsin Senator Bob Kasten in 1992: humorous ads, including one featuring a mock personal endorsement by Elvis, that delighted the media. Kasten eventually countered with his own Elvis spot attacking Feingold on the issues.[82]

A candidate's time is a scarce resource, so an important function of a campaign organization is to arrange for it to be used effectively. An exhausting day of travel and meetings that results in few contacts with voters or little money raised is a campaign manager's nightmare. Time wasted cannot be retrieved. The reality of campaigns is that candidates and their aides cannot tailor the social and political world to suit their needs; they have to be ready to exploit opportunities for meeting people and making news as they arise.

Campaign Messages

Along with letting voters know who the candidate is, a campaign is designed to persuade them to vote for him or her. Uncertainty dominates here, as well. There is no magic formula for appealing to voters; what works in one district or election year may not work in another. Nonetheless, according to campaign professionals, to be effective, every campaign needs to develop and project *some* consistent campaign theme. The theme explains why the candidate should be elected and why the opponent should not. It attempts to frame the choice—to establish what the election is *about*—in a way that underlines the candidate's strengths and plays down the candidate's weaknesses. The goal is not to change people's political attitudes, but rather to define the choice so that a vote for the candidate is consistent with existing attitudes.[83] The available themes and approaches are often rather different for incumbents, challengers, and candidates for open seats, so it is best to consider these categories separately.

Challengers' Campaigns

Challengers certainly hope to convince people of their own virtues—at minimum, that they are qualified for the office—but they are not likely to get far without directly undermining support for the incumbent. The trick is to find some vulnerable point to attack, and challengers are happy to exploit whatever is available. There are inevitably at least a few members beset with scandal—moral or ethical lapses, felony convictions, signs of senility or alcoholism—that offer obvious targets, although a surprising number of incumbents with such liabilities manage to win reelection.[84] Democratic challengers to several Republicans defeated in 2006—including Richard Pombo (California 11th), J. D. Hayworth (Arizona 5th) and Senator Conrad Burns (Montana)—successfully exploited the incumbent's close association with convicted influence-peddler Jack Abramoff. But William Jefferson, a Democrat representing Louisiana's 2nd District, won reelection despite the discovery in his home freezer of $90,000 in marked bills from a FBI sting operation; Jefferson was indicted eight months after the election on multiple corruption charges.[85] In 1992, the House Bank scandal provided ammunition to challengers of the more than 200 incumbents seeking reelection who had written unfunded checks on their House Bank accounts. Individual political failings—excessive junketing, lack of attention to the district or to legislative duties—also invite attack. The defeat of incumbent Walter Huddleston in Kentucky's 1984 Senate race is widely attributed to a television ad that featured a pack of bloodhounds searching for him in places far from Washington, DC, and underlined the charge that Huddleston had neglected his duties. Congressional travel became a common target in the 1990s, as challengers used it to symbolize insulation of "career politicians" from lives of ordinary people.

Challengers also routinely try to show that incumbents are out of touch with district sentiments by attacking specific roll-call votes, the ideological or partisan pattern of votes, or a combination of the two. They also try to hang unpopular policies or politicians around their necks. Although cases are known in which a single "wrong" vote led to defeat, it is by no means easy to nail members with their voting records. Members are aware that they may be called to answer for any vote and on controversial issues take pains to cast an "explainable" vote.[86] That is, any vote likely to offend important groups in the member's electoral coalition or in the district at large will be cast only if it can be supported by a plausible explanation, one that does not make the member look bad if it is questioned.

Normally, a few wrong votes do not seriously weaken an incumbent, although a string of them lends plausibility to the charge that a member is mismatched with the constituency and ought to be replaced. On occasion, challengers have been able to turn one or two key votes into potent symbols of the incumbent's divided loyalties. House Democrats running for reelection in 1994 did significantly worse than others if they had supported President Clinton's 1993 budget (containing "the biggest tax increase in history"), the North American Free Trade Agreement Implementation Bill, or the Omnibus Anti-Crime Bill (opposed by the gun lobby for its ban on assault weapons and depicted by Republicans as "larded with pork"). The more loyal they were to president and party on these votes, the more electoral damage they suffered; the more Republican the district's voting patterns in presidential elections, the more severe the damage.[87] Democratic challengers also effectively used the strategy of tying the incumbent to a locally unpopular president in 2006; a number of their campaigns featured ads depicting the president in close proximity to the incumbent, sometimes digitally "morphing" one into the other, to suggest that the two were indistinguishable. Incumbents are also attacked for opposing locally popular presidents; several Republicans who voted to impeach Bill Clinton in 1998 despite representing districts he had won handily in 1996 paid the price in 2000.

General ideological or partisan attacks have been a mainstay of challengers' campaigns for decades. Incumbents are criticized for being too liberal or too conservative for the constituency or for their guilt by association with unpopular parties, causes, or leaders. This approach lost some of its punch in the 1960s and 1970s, as members strove to avoid ideological categorization or personal responsibility for party decisions when it would hurt them politically back home. By soliciting support as individuals rather than as representatives of a party or cause, they sought to undermine the force of such charges. As electoral politics took on a more ideological and partisan cast in the 1980s, incumbents—particularly Democrats—found it more difficult to sidestep attacks of this sort. Since then, the number of members representing districts where their party label suggests a poor ideological fit has dwindled (see Figure 2–3 in Chapter 2), but as the congressional parties have become increasingly polarized along ideological lines (see Chapter 7), charges of extremism continue to be plausible.

Going Negative

Until the 1980s, harsh personal attacks on an opponent were considered a sign of desperation, ineffective, and likely to backfire. Challengers on the ropes sometimes resorted to them; incumbents ignored the attacks on the theory that reacting would only bring them unwarranted attention. They were most common in campaigns of "sure losers."[88] No longer. Campaign professionals have become convinced that negative advertising works—although academic studies have yet to confirm this belief.[89] One Democratic consultant put it this way: "People say they hate negative campaigning. But it works. They hate it and remember it at the same time. The problem with positive is that you have to run it again and again to make it stick. With negative, the poll numbers will move in three or four days."[90] *Campaigns & Elections*, which bills itself as "The Magazine for Political Professionals," devoted several articles in its July 1995 issue to helpful hints on "going negative" (for example, "Attack Mail: The Silent Killer").[91] Campaign professionals distinguish between accurate *comparative* ads that highlight differences between the candidates (fair) and strictly personal attacks of questionable accuracy or relevance (unfair), although voters may not always appreciate the distinction.

In close races where party organizations are heavily involved, a division of labor usually emerges: The candidate's campaign takes the high road, while the party does the dirty work. Commenting on the 2002 campaign in New Mexico's 2nd District, the Democrats' political director asserted that "the party's job was to act 'as the bad guy,' so Democratic candidates could focus on a more positive message." His Republican counterpart agreed: "negative advertising is the job of the party, leaving candidates to stay above the fray longer."[92] Independent groups are even freer to sling mud; as the late Terry Dolan, whose National Conservative PAC pioneered independent campaigning in the early 1980s, observed in a moment of candor, "a group like ours could lie through its teeth and the candidate it helps stays clean."[93] The BCRA has reinforced this division of labor by requiring candidates to say on camera—in every ad their campaigns broadcast—that they authorized and approved it. Still, candidates are not above going negative themselves; Saxbe Chambliss's successful Senate challenge of Georgia Democrat Max Cleland, who lost both legs and an arm in Vietnam, featured a television ad that followed footage of Osama bin Laden and Saddam Hussein with an unflattering shot of Cleland and a voiceover claiming that he had "voted against the president's vital homeland security efforts."[94]

The logic, if not the civility, of attacking opponents is compelling in a system of candidate-centered electoral politics. If members of Congress win and hold office by eliciting trust and regard as individuals, then the way to undermine their support is to destroy their constituents' trust and regard. Even national issues unfavorable to the incumbent's party—bad economic news, scandals, failed policies, an unpopular president—need to be personalized to be used effectively to weaken an incumbent. When national issues are scarce or favor the other party, character assaults are about the only tactic readily available.[95]

National issues helpful to challengers did become available in the early 1990s, and they were quick to exploit them. Intense public dissatisfaction with Congress's performance offered a potent theme to those challengers who could demonize the incumbent as a career politician guilty by association with the government's failings. Demonizing *individual* incumbents, as opposed to the class of officeholders, is not easy, however. For years, members of Congress managed to avoid the fallout from the public's routine dissatisfaction with Congress's institutional performance. Rather than defend the place, they would join in the criticism: "Members of Congress run *for* Congress by running *against* Congress."[96] They defended their own personal performances vigorously but not at all the collective actions of Congress.

The effectiveness of this strategy began to break down in 1990, when voters reacted to an unpopular October budget deal that cut programs and raised taxes by reducing their support for incumbents of both parties.[97] It was further undermined in 1992, when the House Bank scandal allowed challengers to connect members personally, through their record of bad checks, with congressional malfeasance.[98] It also failed conspicuously for Democrats in 1994, when Republicans succeeded in turning hostility to government into hostility to Democrats by depicting them as adherents of an intolerable status quo, exemplified by their unpopular president's "big government" solution to the health care system's shortcomings.[99] Nor did it work in 2006, when Democrats succeeded in framing the choice in national terms—as a referendum on the performance of the president and the Republican Congress—rendering the Republican incumbents' emphasis on local service and political independence ineffective (see Chapter 6).[100]

In the search for campaign issues, then, challengers are necessarily opportunists. It is a matter of finding and exploiting the incumbent's mistakes—neglect of the district, personal lapses, "bad" votes—or discovering a way to saddle the incumbent with personal responsibility for Congress's or the administration's shortcomings. A challenger cannot hope to win without reordering the campaign agenda. Incumbents thrive on campaigns that center around personal performance, experience, and services. Few members are vulnerable if they can persuade voters that this is what the contest is about; even losing incumbents get high marks on these dimensions. Challengers succeed only when they can frame issues in a way that makes these dimensions less relevant and other considerations more salient.

From this perspective, the burgeoning role of party committees and other institutional participants in congressional election politics takes on added importance. National campaign committees have helped their challengers by polling between elections to probe for soft spots in incumbents' support, tracking their votes to store up ammunition for the next election, attacking them between elections with negative advertising, and quickly spreading the word about successful innovations in strategy and tactics. Dozens of groups now rate roll-call votes, target incumbents opposing their views, advise favored challengers on tactics, and mobilize campaign volunteers—in addition, of course, to providing campaign money. All of these things add to the uncertainty and worry of incumbents; aware of the resources available to be mobilized against them, most act as if they were anything but safe.

Incumbents' Campaigns

Incumbents pursue reelection throughout their terms in office, so their campaign strategies are visible in all their dealings with constituents. Naturally, they try to avoid mistakes that would give opponents campaign issues, but in an uncertain and complicated political world, in which the pressure for party loyalty is now higher than it has been in decades, that is not always possible. They therefore work to maintain the kind of relationship with constituents that will allow them to survive a damaging vote or contrary political tide. Fenno's insightful account of how House members do this, in fact, describes effective campaigning by any congressional candidate, incumbent or challenger.[101]

Fenno traveled extensively with eighteen House members as they made the rounds of their districts. He found that each member projected a personal *home style* that defined his relationship to the groups he relied on for political support. Home styles varied according to the character of the district and the personality of the individual member, but in one way or another, all members basically sought to inspire *trust* among their constituents. They did this by emphasizing their personal qualifications, including moral character, by identifying with their constituents ("I am one of you," they implied, "so you can trust me to make the right decisions—those you would make under the same circumstances"), and by working to develop bonds of empathy with the groups and individuals they met.

For most of the members Fenno watched, issues, policy, and partisanship were not prominent objects of discussion with constituents and were not used to elicit support. Even members who did display issue-oriented home styles used issues primarily to cement ties of trust; *how* they addressed the issues rather than the issues themselves was what mattered. Members used issues to show themselves to be the kind of people constituents would want in Washington.

Along with trust, members emphasized their *accessibility*. Constituents were reminded continually that lines of communication were open, that they had access to the member whenever they needed it. The payoffs are clear. A member who is trusted, accessible, and thought to be "one of us" will have much less trouble defending him- or herself against personal attacks. His or her explanations for controversial votes will be heard more sympathetically; institutional or partisan failures and even notorious ethical lapses may go unpunished.

This kind of relationship cannot be developed overnight, nor can it be maintained without continual reinforcement. Its importance is the reason that, as one congressman put it, "it's a personal franchise you hold, not a political franchise."[102] Nonincumbents may aspire to it, but they have little chance to achieve it in the brief period of a single election campaign. Those who have held other elective offices in the district or who are already familiar to district voters for other reasons—a previous campaign, family name, or celebrity status as an athlete, entertainer, or newscaster—have a head start.

The personal connection so important to Fenno's subjects is no doubt harder to cultivate now that districts contain 50 percent more constituents than when he did his research, but members continue to try.[103] In addition to keeping district connections in good repair, incumbents have now begun to deal with the growing threat of harsh personal and political attacks and well-financed challenges by campaigning preemptively. Incumbents have always raised and spent money reactively, in proportion to what their challengers raise and spend against them. They now spend increasing amounts of money preemptively in order to inoculate voters against anticipated attacks.

Both patterns are evident when incumbents' expenditures are regressed on challengers' expenditures in House elections from 1972 through 2006; the results are reported in Table 4–4. For comparison, the dollar figures have been adjusted for inflation (2006 = 1.00). First, look at the intercept, which indicates how much, on average, an incumbent would spend if the challenger spent nothing at all. It has increased dramatically, from $158,000 to $940,800 (in 2006 dollars) between 1972 and 2006; the average increase from one election to the next is about 12 percent. House incumbents have been raising and spending increasing sums of money, regardless of the kinds of challenges they face. Second, the regression coefficients (slopes) vary but average around 0.69, indicating that, on top of their initial level of spending, an incumbent matches an average of a little more than two-thirds of the challenger's spending.

The same campaign professionals who promote negative campaigns recommend a preemptive strategy to cope with them. "Inoculation and preemption are what win campaigns," according to one Republican consultant. Said another, "If you know what your negatives are and you know where you are vulnerable, you can preempt it."[104] Hence, for example, Republican Senator James Abdnor of South Dakota, expecting to be challenged by the state's governor for renomination on grounds of ineffectiveness, began broadcasting ads in November 1985 that had prominent Republican senators bearing witness to his effectiveness. Another Republican thought to be in trouble for the 1986 election, Senator Paula Hawkins of Florida, also began airing commercials in 1985. A year before the election she had already spent $750,000 on media advertising alone.[105] Both these attempts at preemption failed, however; evidently, the candidates' real weaknesses could not be masked by rhetoric. More successful was Democratic Senator Patrick Leahy, who ran an ad warning his Vermont constituents, "Oh boy, it's going to get knee deep around here. Dick Snelling has hired some famous dirty tricksters to foul the airwaves with a big-bucks, political smear campaign. . . . Do we really have to go through this in quiet, sensible, beautiful Vermont?"[106]

Although incumbents, at least in the House, engage more or less continuously in activities aimed at assuring reelection—including, now, preemptive

TABLE 4–4 Incumbents' Expenditures as a Function of Challengers' Expenditures in House Elections, 1972–2006

Year	Number of Cases	Intercept		Regression Coefficient: Challenger's Expenditures		R^2
1972	319	158.0	(14.8)	.56	(.04)	.34
1974	323	156.4	(10.4)	.63	(.04)	.41
1976	332	201.2	(11.5)	.55	(.04)	.36
1978	312	262.0	(14.5)	.50	(.04)	.38
1980	338	253.8	(20.7)	.74	(.05)	.41
1982	315	382.2	(19.8)	.58	(.05)	.34
1984	341	428.7	(19.4)	.63	(.04)	.39
1986	319	501.6	(29.3)	.73	(.07)	.27
1988	328	528.9	(25.0)	.79	(.06)	.32
1990	320	560.4	(22.8)	.70	(.07)	.24
1992	312	655.8	(31.8)	.82	(.08)	.23
1994	336	599.0	(30.0)	.64	(.06)	.23
1996	358	595.9	(32.3)	.86	(.06)	.40
1998	306	740.3	(43.4)	.46	(.06)	.14
2000	336	721.4	(35.8)	.88	(.05)	.51
2002	302	895.9	(34.4)	.43	(.04)	.26
2004	332	867.2	(37.1)	.91	(.06)	.40
2006	347	940.8	(34.9)	.92	(.04)	.57

Note: Expenditures are in thousands of dollars, adjusted for inflation (2006=1.00); standard errors are in parentheses; all coefficient are significant beyond $p < .001$.

campaigning—their real campaigns start when it becomes clear who the challenger will be in the primary or general election or both. Different challengers present different problems and inspire different campaign strategies. Inept, obscure, or underfinanced opponents can be dealt with via routine maintenance of ties with groups in the electoral coalition, and they can otherwise be ignored. Senator Daniel Inouye, for example, had little reason to mention his 1998 opponent, Crystal Young, who spent no money on the campaign but got some publicity when she "alleged that actress Shirley McLaine implanted electromagnetic needles in her."[107]

Ignoring the opposition is a standard tactic of incumbents who feel relatively secure: Why give an unknown opponent free publicity? More serious opponents compel more vigorous campaigns, with the strategy adapted to the relative strengths and weaknesses of both candidates. Incumbents also adjust to opponents' campaign tactics once their effectiveness has been demonstrated. For example, counterattack or, better yet, preemptive assaults on the challenger's character and credibility has replaced the older practice of ignoring personal attacks. Expecting to be on the defensive because of adverse national conditions in 2006, many Republican incumbents followed this stratgegy. Those who did so had plenty of help and encouragement from their party. As early as the summer of 2005, the RNCC began investigating prospective Democratic challengers, looking for anything that could be used to discredit them: Unpaid student loans, bankruptcies, op-ed pieces written in college advocating legalized pot, defending criminals in court, tax delinquencies; anything from a challenger's past that could be portrayed as unsavory was collected and catalogued. Indeed, in an era of Google, Facebook, and YouTube, prospective candidates are on notice that no youthful indescretion is safe from wide public exposure. Representative Thomas Reynolds (New York–26), the NRCC's chair, boasted that "these candidates have been out there doing other things—they have never seen anything like this before. We haven't even begun to unload this freight train."[108] An example that went awry:

> In New York, the NRCC ran an ad accusing Democratic House candidate Michael A. Arcuri, a district attorney, of using taxpayer dollars for phone sex. "Hi, sexy," a dancing woman purrs. "You've reached the live, one-on-one fantasy line." It turns out that one of Arcuri's aides had tried to call the state Division of Criminal Justice, which had a number that was almost identical to that of a porn line. The misdial cost taxpayers $1.25.[109]

Incumbents also adapt their strategies to the president's current standing with the public. Many Democrats who had been happy to link themselves with their party and Bill Clinton in 1992 sought to declare their independence in 1994. Similarly, many Republicans who had celebrated their connection with George Bush in 2002, when his approval ratings were in the mid-60s, emphasized their differences with the president and avoided appearing with him at campaign events in 2006, when his ratings were about 25 points lower.

Common to most incumbents' campaigns are an emphasis on the value of experience and seniority (for the capacity it gives members to serve the district more effectively) and reminders of the things that the member has done over the years for constituents. When the *insider* image these accomplishments evoked became a potential liability in the early 1990s, some switched to emphasizing their status as *outsiders* opposed to the status quo by advocating term limits, balanced budgets amendments, and the end to congressional perks. This was a favorite (and uniformly successful) tack taken by Republican incumbents in 1994. In special circumstances, special ploys may be necessary. Senator Milton Young, running for reelection to the Senate from North Dakota in 1974 at the age of seventy-six, countered suggestions that he was getting too old by running a TV spot showing him splitting a block of wood with a karate chop.[110]

Despite the knowledge members acquire of their constituencies, uncertainty plagues incumbents as well as nonincumbents. Each election may present a new challenge and a new set of electoral variables. Because incumbents are not sure which of their actions got them elected previously, they cannot be sure what combination of campaign activities will serve them in altered circumstances. Although in a normal election year most members are reelected easily (at least in the House), most of them have had close calls at one time or another, and all have vivid memories of seemingly entrenched colleagues who suffered sudden massive vote losses and unexpected defeats.

Because of uncertainty, members tend to exaggerate electoral threats and overreact to them. They are inspired by worst-case scenarios—what would they have to do to win if everything went wrong?—rather than objective probabilities. Hence, some members conduct full-scale campaigns even though the opposition is nowhere to be seen. The desire to win decisively enough to discourage future opposition also leads many incumbents to campaign a good deal harder than would seem objectively necessary. The sense of uncertainty and risk felt by incumbents has grown in recent years, along with the money, professional talent, and technology potentially available to their opponents. The specter of fickle electorates, combined with active organizations ready to mobilize extensive campaign resources against them should they show signs of vulnerability, undermines whatever confidence comfortable reelection margins might otherwise inspire. The electoral shake-ups of the early 1990s and of 2006 are a reminder that they are wise to take nothing for granted.

Candidates for Open Seats

Candidates for open seats face somewhat different electoral situations because none of the contestants is an incumbent or a challenger with the accompanying advantages or disadvantages. They are much more likely to face difficult primary contests because the opportunity offered to ambitious politicians by an open seat attracts more and better-qualified candidates. Indeed, the primary is often a more difficult hurdle than the general election.[111]

Both candidates are likely to have some experience in elective office and, therefore, some familiarity with at least a part of the constituency and some useful relationships with electorally important segments of it (recall Table 3–4). Both are likely to have adequate campaign resources because contests for open seats are expected to be competitive; the best chance by far to take a seat from the opposing party occurs when no incumbent is involved. As a consequence, candidates for open seats are typically better known and better liked than challengers—but not as well as incumbents.[112] No particular pattern of campaign strategy is typical of candidates for open seats other than a highly variable mixture of the approaches used by incumbents and challengers that coincides with the electoral position between the two.

Because candidates competing for open seats are normally much more closely balanced in skills and resources than are challengers and incumbents, the outcome is more strongly influenced by partisan trends, both local and national. Without the pull of incumbency, votes are cast more consistently along party lines, so election results reflect state or district partisanship more consistently. Presidential coattails (discussed more fully in Chapter 6) are stronger; that is, voters are more likely to cast congressional votes consistent with their presidential votes, so the fates of candidates for open seats are tied more closely to the top of the ticket in presidential election years.[113] Open seats also register partisan tides more strongly; in years with big swings, such as 1974 and 2006 (pro-Democratic) or 1980 and 1994 (pro-Republican), a disproportionate share of the winning party's gains come from open seats.[114]

Senate Campaigns

As we observed in Chapter 3, Senate elections are, on average, considerably more competitive than House elections. Senate incumbents win less consistently and by narrower margins than do House incumbents. Nearly every state is potentially winnable by either party. Thirty-nine states have chosen senators from both parties in elections since 1984, and all the remaining states have elected governors of the party opposite their senators' during this time. Greater partisan balance by itself makes Senate elections more competitive than House elections, but it also creates a strategic electoral environment that enhances competition in several ways.

First, Senate incumbents are usually faced with formidable opponents.[115] About two-thirds of Senate challengers in recent elections had previously held elective office. Among the successful first-time candidates have been two former astronauts (John Glenn and Harrison Schmitt), a former basketball star (Bill Bradley), a lawyer-turned-actor (Fred Thompson), and several prominent multi-millionaire businessmen.

Formidable challengers attract campaign resources. Senate campaigns in general attract proportionately greater contributions because the donations are, in a sense, more cost-effective, especially in smaller states.[116] Senate contests are usually closer, so campaign resources are more likely to affect the outcome. Parties and groups with particular policy agendas are aware that, when it comes to passing legislation, one senator is worth 4.35 representatives. A party has to defeat far fewer incumbents to take over the Senate than to take over the House. It makes strategic sense for campaign contributors to focus on the Senate, and that is what they have done. The campaign finance laws also make it easier for national party organizations to participate extensively in Senate contests. Thus, Senate challengers are much more likely than House challengers to enjoy adequately funded campaigns.

Senate challengers can also use their campaign resources more effectively than House challengers. Most Senate constituencies have the size and structure to make television advertising cost-efficient. Resources are usually sufficient to justify using campaign professionals and the technical paraphernalia of modern campaigns: computers, polls, direct-mail advertising and solicitation, and so forth. The news media are much more interested in Senate campaigns, so much more free attention and publicity is bestowed on Senate candidates than on their House counterparts.[117] It is little wonder that Senate challengers and other nonincumbents are much better known by voters than are House challengers.[118]

Furthermore, Senate incumbents find it much more difficult to develop and maintain the kind of personal relationships with constituents that Fenno observed among House incumbents. The reason is obvious. Senate districts—states—are, with seven exceptions (the states with a single representative) , more populous than congressional districts, often very much so. The opportunities for personal contacts with constituents and attention to individual problems are proportionately fewer. It also follows that the larger the state, the more difficult it is for a senator to cultivate firm ties to constituents. The larger Senate staffs cannot make up the difference.[119]

Senators' activities in Washington are also more conspicuous than those of representatives. Action in the Senate is more visible than action in the House; the Senate has fewer members and they are given more attention by the news media.[120] Senators are thus more likely than representatives to be associated with controversial and divisive issues.[121] Senators do not have the pressure of a two-year election cycle to keep them attuned to the folks back home. Electoral coalitions may fall into disrepair, and a careless senator may discover that he or she must begin almost from scratch when reelection time rolls around.

Lavishly funded and professionally run Senate campaigns have been the proving ground for the latest innovations in campaign tactics and techniques. One development is interactive campaigning, in which the campaign themes and messages of each candidate are rapidly altered in response to what the opposition is saying and, more importantly, to what their tracking polls tell them about the effectiveness of both campaigns. Polling technology is the key. In the words of a Democratic consultant, "It's relatively simple and not very expensive now to sample public opinion. In the last month of a campaign, both sides will poll nightly, test how that day's media and campaigning has played, and trace the results."[122] Instead of planning and executing a single strategy over the course of an entire campaign, *strategic flexibility* is now the catchphrase. Observed another consultant, "When candidates come in here now, their first questions to me are: Can you respond quickly? Can you attack quickly? Can you do a fast turnaround?"[123] With enough money, turnaround can be fast indeed. In California's 1994 Senate campaign, Dianne Feinstein saw her campaign ads answered within twenty-four hours by new commercials produced and distributed statewide by Michael Huffington's lavishly funded campaign team.[124]

Manipulating Turnout

The advent of multimillion-dollar media campaigns has not made organized, grassroots-level efforts to get out the vote any less crucial. In fact, campaigns that deluge voters with broadcast ads, mailings, and phone calls may just turn them off. Reviewing the 2002 South Dakota Senate campaign, in which candidates, parties, and interest groups spent some $24 million in a state with fewer than 476,000 registered voters, Meader and Bart concluded that "in the end, most voters probably tuned out the commercials, turned off the phone, and placed all the mail in the trash," citing as an example "one woman [who] wrote and explained that she started to watch public television and stopped answering the phone in the evening."[125] Thus, the effort to mobilize potential supporters to vote either through absentee ballots (increasingly common) or at the polls on election day may be essential to offset voters' inclination to withdraw from the barrage of conflicting, often mean-spirited messages showered on them in competitive races.

For years, labor unions led the effort to get out the Democratic vote in many areas and were responsible for the Democrat's traditional superiority in this area. But Republicans have now caught up. In elections since 2002, the RNC has financed extensive pre-election drives to mobilize voters in key contests, using thousands of volunteers and paid workers. In 2006, it spent $30 million on the effort, which included, according to it's organizer, "35 million live calls and door knocks with one-third of that (13 million) in the last 96 hours."[126] Such campaigns can be effective; Gerber and Green's experimental study indicates that face-to-face mobilization can raise turnout by as much as 9 percentage points, although telephone and direct mail have little apparent effect.[127] Both parties and their interest group allies now mount extensive mobilization drives wherever tight competition makes them necessary.

For purposes of winning an election, however, reducing the other side's vote by a given number is as valuable as raising one's own by the same number. Thus, campaigns have an incentive to discourage the turnout of voters who would, if they participated, vote for the opposition. Because voting, as a duty and a right, is such a potent symbol of democracy, no campaign ever admits openly to trying to keep people from the polls. Nonetheless, Republican activists are regularly accused of trying to dampen turnout in minority neighborhoods, which tend to be overwhelmingly Democratic. For example, an unsigned flyer appeared in minority neighborhoods in Baltimore in 2002 reading, "URGENT NOTICE. Come out to vote on November 6th. Before you come to vote make sure you pay your parking tickets, motor vehicle tickets, overdue rent and most important any warrants"[128] The election was actually on November 5. No one took credit but it is not hard to guess which party's allies put out the flyer.

Negative ads are also used to depress opposition turnout; voters who could never be attracted to a candidate may nonetheless be induced stay home if the alternative is discredited. The dirty work in most often done by supposedly independent groups conducting "voter education" campaigns and thus immune from Federal Election Commission (FEC) reporting requirements. In 2002, one such organization, calling itself the Council for Better Government, ran ads on urban radio stations accusing Democrats of taking African American voters for granted and making such accusations as "Each year the abortion mills diminish the human capital of our community by another 400,000 souls. The Democratic Party supports these liberal abortion laws that are decimating our people."[129]

It is not clear, however, that negative campaigning actually does depress turnout; they may even enhance it.[130] The intensely polarized and competitive electoral environments that encourage campaigns to go negative also excite voters and spur efforts to mobilize them. The 2006 campaigns, conducted in what has been characterized as "the most toxic midterm campaign environment in memory,"[131] featured an abundance of scurrilous and often dishonest attack ads from both sides. Yet turnout was the highest for any midterm since 1982 and the second highest since eighteen-year-olds got the vote.

Concluding Observations

Congressional election practices have undergone a period of rapid development, as organizational, technical, and financial innovations have turned the closest contests into remarkably extravagant affairs. The emergence of evenly matched, strongly polarized national parties has put control of Congress up for grabs in every election since 1994, raising the stakes in competitive races. Campaigns in such contests are no longer controlled or even dominated by the candidates and their organizations; the national parties and outside interest groups, with their own resources and agendas, strongly influence the tone and content of campaigns. Meanwhile, the number of competitive districts, if not states, has fallen, leaving more and more resources concentrated in fewer and fewer contests. From an incumbent's perspective, the value of scaring off serious opposition has never been higher, since abundant, centrally disposed resources are available to be mobilized against them quickly on any sign of vulnerability. New techniques and tactics may hold unpleasant surprises, and strategies for coping with them are still unsure. Sharpened sensitivity to the electoral implications of their activities in office is a natural result; so too is intensified partisan animosity on the Hill. Both of these developments have, as we shall see in Chapter 7, important effects on how the House and Senate work as legislative institutions.

That said, it is also important to emphasize that the large majority of incumbents in the House, and many Senate incumbents, escape serious competition altogether and so win by quite comfortable margins. Indeed, the post-2000 redistricting actually raised the number of secure representatives. The impressive new technology for probing electorates, along with the growing cost of competitive campaigns and the growing number of seats securely in one party's hands, has led to a sharp bifurcation of effort. Electoral resources (including high-quality candidates) are increasingly concentrated in a small subset of House districts and in selected Senate races, making life more difficult for those incumbents who appear sufficiently vulnerable to invite an all-out challenge. But those who avoid becoming targets face increasingly feeble opposition because promising challengers have little incentive to incur the growing cost in money, time, privacy, and family life of conducting a serious challenge unless the prospects for victory are very good.

NOTES

1. See Linda L. Fowler, "Candidate Perceptions of Electoral Coalitions: Limits and Possibilities" (Paper presented at the Conference on Congressional Elections, Rice University and the University of Houston, January 10–12, 1980).
2. Richard F. Fenno Jr., *Home Style: House Members in Their Districts* (Boston: Little, Brown, 1978), pp. 171–172.
3. See any edition of *Campaigns & Elections* for the ads of vendors of these and all other campaign services.
4. Gary C. Jacobson, *Money in Congressional Elections* (New Haven, CT: Yale University Press, 1980), pp. 170–171; Martin Schram, *Speaking Freely: Former Members of Congress Talk about Money in Politics* (Washington, DC: Center for Responsive Politics, 1995), pp. 71–76.
5. Diane Granat, "Parties' Schools for Politicians Grooming Troops for Election," *Congressional Quarterly Weekly Report* 42 (May 5, 1984): 1036.
6. Before the passage of the Bipartisan Campaign Reform Act of 2002, individuals could give no more than $1,000 per candidate per campaign (the primary and general election campaigns are considered separate campaigns), up to a total of $20,000 in an election year; nonparty PACs could give no more than $5,000 per candidate per campaign (other party contribution limits are discussed later in this chapter). Under the BCRA, individual contributions limits were raised to $2,000, to be adjusted for inflation after 2002; for the 2008 elections the limit is $2,300 (see *http://www.fec.gov/pages/brochures/contriblimits.shtml*). The inflation-adjusted maximum that may be donated to all candidates by an individual in 2008 is $42,700. The PAC limits were not changed and not indexed.
7. *Buckley v. Valeo* (96 S. Ct. 612, 1976).
8. Gary C. Jacobson, "Parties and PACs in Congressional Elections," in *Congress Reconsidered*, 4th ed., ed. Lawrence C. Dodd and Bruce I. Oppenheimer (Washington, DC: Congressional Quarterly Press, 1988), pp. 117–121. For a balanced and thorough account of all aspects of campaign finance in the 1980s, see Frank J. Sorauf, *Money in American Elections* (Glenview, IL: Scott, Foresman, 1988).

9. *Colorado Republican Federal Campaign Committee v. Federal Election Commission*, 518 U.S. 604 (1996).
10. Robert G. Boatright, Michael J. Malbin, Mark J. Rozell, and Clyed Wilcox, "Interest Group and Advocacy Organizations After BCRA," in *The Election After Reform: Money, Politics and the Bipartisan Campaign Reform Act*, ed. Michael J. Malbin (New York: Rowman & Littlefield, 2006), pp. 137–138.
11. Theodore J. Eismeier and Philip H. Pollack III, *Business, Money, and the Rise of Corporate PACs in American Elections* (New York: Quantum Books, 1988), pp. 79–94.
12. Gary C. Jacobson, *The Electoral Origins of Divided Government: Competition in U.S. House Elections, 1946–1988* (Boulder, CO: Westview Press, 1990), pp. 62–64.
13. For a fascinating account of how Tony Coelho, chairman of the Democratic Congressional Campaign Committee, persuaded business PACs to support Democratic candidates, see Brooks Jackson, *Honest Graft: Big Money and the American Political Process*, updated ed. (Washington, DC: Farragut Publishing Company, 1990).
14. Chuck Alston and Glen Craney, "Bush Campaign-Reform Takes Aim at Incumbents," *Congressional Quarterly Weekly Report* 47 (July 1, 1989): 1648–1659.
15. "Momentum Helps GOP Collect Record Amount from PACs," *Congressional Quarterly Weekly Report* 52 (December 3, 1994): 3457.
16. "To the '94 Victors Go the Fundraising Spoils," *Congressional Quarterly Weekly Report* 53 (April 15, 1995): 1055–1059.
17. Gary W. Cox and Eric Magar, "How Much Is Majority Status in the U.S. Congress Worth?" *American Political Science Review* 93 (June 1999): 302–303.
18. Cox and Magar, "How Much Is Majority Status in the U.S. Congress Worth?" pp. 304–306.
19. Federal Election Commission, *Federal Election Commission Record*, June 2007, pp. 16–17.
20. Paul Herrnson, *Congressional Elections: Campaigning at Home and in Washington* (Washington, DC: Congressional Quarterly Press, 1995), pp. 88–92.
21. Herrnson, *Congressional Elections*, p. 86.
22. Competitive races are defined here as those won with less than 55 percent of the major-party vote or in which the incumbent was defeated.
23. Daniel A. Smith, "Strings Attached: Outside Money in Colorado's Seventh District," in *The Last Hurrah? Soft Money and Issue Advocacy in the 2002 Congressional Election*, ed. David B. Magleby and J. Quin Monson (Provo, UT: Center for the Study of Elections and Democracy, Brigham Young University, 2003), p. 194.
24. Smith, "Strings Attached," p. 196.
25. Smith, "Strings Attached," p. 198.
26. David Redlawsk, "The 2002 Iowa Senate and Congressional Elections," in *The Last Hurrah?*, ed. Magleby and Monson, pp. 74, 84, 85.
27. For a general analysis of these practices, see Eric S. Heberlig and Bruce A. Larson, "Redistributing Campaign Funds by U.S. House Members:

The Spiraling Costs of the Permanent Campaign," *Legislative Studies Quarterly* 30 (2005): 597–624.

28. Anne Bedlington and Michael J. Malbin, "The Party as Extended Network: Members Giving to Each Other and to Their Parties," in *Life After Reform: When the Bipartisan Campaign Reform Act Meets Politics*, ed. Michael J. Malbin (Lanham, MD: Rowman & Littlefield, 2003), p. 179.
29. For an analysis of the sources of members' generosity to the Hill committees, see Bruce A. Larson, "Incumbent Contributions to the Congressional Campaign Committees, 1990–2000," *Political Research Quarterly* 57 (2004): 155–161.
30. John F. Persinos, "The GOP Farm Team," *Campaigns & Elections*, March 1995, p. 20.
31. Jennifer Steen, "Self-Financing Candidates in American Elections" (Dissertation website, http://socrates.berkeley.edu/jsteen/facts.htm, November 4, 1999).
32. Steen, "Self-Financing Candidates"; see also Jennifer Steen, *Self-Financed Candidates in Congressional Elections* (Ann Arbor: University of Michigan Press, 2006).
33. Jennifer Steen, "Self-Financed Candidates and the 'Millionaires' Amendment,'" in *The Election After Reform: Money, Politics, and the Bipartisan Campaign Reform Act*, ed. Michael J. Malbin (New York: Rowman & Littlefield, 2006), pp. 204–218.
34. Dwight Morris and Mureille E. Gamache, *Handbook of Campaign Spending: Money in the 1992 Congressional Elections* (Washington, DC: Congressional Quarterly Press, 1994), p. 29.
35. Xandra Kayden, "The Nationalizing of the Party System," in *Parties, Interest Groups, and Campaign Finance Laws*, ed. Michael J. Malbin (Washington, DC: American Enterprise Institute for Public Policy Research, 1980), p. 266.
36. David B. Magleby, Kelly D. Patterson, *War Games: Issues and Resources in the Battle for Control of Congress* (Provo, UT: Brigham Young University, Center for the Study of Elections and Democracy, 2007), p. 20.
37. Some of this money went to gubernatorial candidates; see "EMILY's List Remains Top PAC in the Country," News Release, February 7, 2007, *http://www.emilyslist.org/newsroom/releases/20070201.html* (October 15, 2007). See also Ilka M. Knepper, "Emily's List: Verdraengen Political Action Committees Amerikanische Parteien?" (Master's thesis, Zentrum fuer Europa und Nordamerikastudien, Fachbereich Politikwissenschaft, Georg-August-Universitaet Goettigen, 1994).
38. Jonathan D. Salant, "GOP Bumps Up Against Court Precedent in Trying to Block AFL-CIO," *Congressional Quarterly Weekly Report* 54 (April 13, 1996): 996–997.
39. One study found that fewer than 10 percent of *candidates'* broadcast ads used any of the words deemed by the Court to be out of bounds for issue advocacy campaigns; see "Straight Talk on Campaign Finance: Separating Fact from Fiction.," Paper No. 5, The Brennen Center for Justice (undated), at *http://www.brennancenter.org/dynamic/subpages/paper5.pdf* (July 2, 2007).

40. The 527 groups spent much more in 2004, but mostly in the presidential race.
41. "Pulling Strings from Afar," *AARP Bulletin Online*, February 3, 2003, at *http://www.aarp.org/bulletin/consumer/a2003-06-30-pullingstrings.html* (October 15, 2007).
42. John Roos and Christopher Roderiguez, "Indiana Second District—Hoosier Values and Outside Money," *The Last Hurrah?* p. 22.
43. Eric S. Heberlig, "North Carolina's Eighth and Ninth Districts," *The Last Hurrah?* p. 260.
44. Gary C. Jacobson, "The Effect of the AFL-CIO's 'Voter Education' Campaign on the 1996 House Elections," *Journal of Politics* 61 (1999): 185–194.
45. Herrnson, *Congressional Elections*, p. 64.
46. Paul S. Herrnson, "Do Parties Make a Difference? The Role of Party Organizations in Congressional Elections," *Journal of Politics* 48 (1986): 612–613.
47. Michael Barone and Grant Ujifusa, *The Almanac of American Politics 1990* (Washington, DC: National Journal, 1989), p. 279.
48. Xandra Kayden, *Campaign Organization* (Lexington, MA: D.C. Heath, 1978), p. 61.
49. John W. Kingdon, *Candidates for Office: Beliefs and Strategies* (New York: Random House, 1968), p. 87.
50. One of Fenno's congressmen raised it to 75 percent; see Fenno, *Home Style*, p. 17.
51. Kayden, *Campaign Organization*, p. 120.
52. Michael Barone and Richard Cohen with Charles E. Cook Jr., *The Almanac of American Politics 2004* (Washington, DC: National Journal, 2003), pp. 384–385.
53. Marjorie Randon Hershey, *Running for Office: The Political Education Campaigners* (Chatham, NJ: Chatham House, 1984), pp. 69–79.
54. "The Outlook: Senate, House, and Governors," *Congressional Quarterly Weekly Report* 38 (October 11, 1980): 3014, 3017.
55. Alan Ehrenhalt, "House Freshmen: Campaign Traditionalists," *Congressional Quarterly Weekly Report* 41 (January 8, 1983): 30.
56. Jonathan Roos, "Freund Hopes to Grab Coattails," *Des Moines Register* (August 23, 1988), p. A2.
57. "Outlook: Nevada," *Congressional Quarterly Weekly Report* 44 (October 11, 1986): 2453.
58. Michael Barone and Grant Ujifusa, *The Almanac of American Politics 1994* (Washington, DC: National Journal, 1993), p. 691; "Minnesota," *Congressional Quarterly Weekly Report* 52 (October 22, 1994): 3032.
59. "Challenger Hits Iowa's Smith with Incumbency, Earmarks," *Congressional Quarterly Weekly Report* 52 (September 10, 1994): 2533.
60. Nicole Duran "GOP: Gas Gimmick Is Illegal," *Roll Call*, September 5. 2006.
61. Morris and Gamache, *Handbook of Campaign Spending*, Tables 1–5 and 1–6.
62. Herrnson, *Congressional Elections*, p. 183.

63. Edie N. Goldenberg and Michael W. Traugott, *Campaigning for Congress* (Washington, DC: Congressional Quarterly Press, 1984), p. 120; and Stephen Ansolabehere, Alan Gerber, and James M. Snyder Jr., "Television Costs and Greater Congressional Campaign Spending: Cause and Effect or Coincidence?" (Manuscript, August 1999).
64. Charles Stewart III and Mark Reynolds, "Television Markets and Senate Elections," *Legislative Studies Quarterly* 15 (1990): 495–523.
65. Alan Ehrenhalt, "Technology, Strategy Bring New Campaign Era," *Congressional Quarterly Weekly Report* 43 (December 7, 1985): 2559.
66. Ehrenhalt, "Technology, Strategy," p. 2563.
67. Elizabeth Theiss Smith and Richard Braunstein, "The Nationalization of Local Politics in South Dakota," in *Dancing Without Partners: How Candidates, Parties, and Interest Groups Interact in the New Campaign Environment*, ed. David B. Magleby, J. Quin Monson, and Kelly D. Patterson (Provo, UT: Brigham Young University, Center for the Study of Elections and Democracy, 2005), p. 246.
68. James Meader and John Bart, "South Dakota: At-Large and Senate Race 2002," in *The Last Hurrah?* ed. Magleby and Monson p. 164.
69. "We've Got Mail," *Campaigns & Elections* (June 1999), p. 22.
70. John Jameson, Chris Glaze, and Gary Teal, "Effective Phone Contact Programs and the Importance of Good Data," *Campaigns & Elections* (July 1999), pp. 64–71.
71. Phil Noble, "Internet and Campaign 2002 Analysis," at *http://www.politicsonline.com/pol2000/specialreports/campaign_analysis_2002* (May 15, 2003).
72. "Consultants Corner: Sending Out An SMS," Hotline On Call, July 14, 2006, at *http://hotlineblog.nationaljournal.com/archives/2006/07/consultants_cor_2.html* (July 2, 2007).
73. Alan L. Clem, "The Case of the Upstart Republican," in *The Making of Congressmen: Seven Campaigns of 1974*, ed. Alan L. Clem (North Scituate, MA: Duxbury Press, 1976), p. 140.
74. Clem, "The Case of the Upstart Republican."
75. Barone and Ujifusa, *Almanac of American Politics 1994*, p. 1119.
76. Ehrenhalt, "House Freshmen," pp. 37, 41.
77. Meader and Bart, "South Dakota," p. 165.
78. Craig Varoga, "Lone Star Upset," *Campaigns & Elections* (March 1995): 35.
79. Barone and Ujifusa, *Almanac of American Politics 1990*, p. 1087.
80. Maureen Groppe, "South Carolina," *Congressional Quarterly Weekly Report* 52 (October 22, 1994): 3050.
81. Eva Pusateri, "Shock Mailers That Jolt Your Audience," *Campaigns & Elections* (May 1995): 41.
82. Barone and Ujifusa, *Almanac of American Politics 2000*, p. 1446.
83. Joel Bradshaw, "Who Will Vote for You and Why: Designing Campaign Strategy and Theme" (Paper presented at the Conference on Campaign Management, The American University, Washington, DC, December 10–11, 1992).

84. For example, Robert Leggett won reelection to the 4th District of California in 1976, even after having been a principal subject of the "Koreagate" investigation and having it known publicly that he had fathered two children by an aide, had been supporting two households for years, and had even forged his wife's name to the deed for the second house. For a more general analysis of the electoral effects of corruption charges, see John G. Peters and Susan Welch, "The Effects of Charges of Corruption on Voting Behavior in Congressional Elections," *American Political Science Review* 74 (1980): 697–708; Susan Welch and John R. Hibbing, "The Effects of Charges of Corruption on Voting Behavior in Congressional Elections, 1982–1990," *Journal of Politics* 59 (1997): 26–39; and Stephen C. Roberds, "Incumbent Scandals in U.S. House Elections" (Paper presented at the Annual Meeting of the Midwest Political Science Association, Chicago, April 15–17, 1999).
85. "Louisiana Congressman Indicted in Bribery Probe." CNN.com, June 5, 2007 at *http://www.cnn.com/2007/POLITICS/06/04/jefferson.probe.ap/index.html* (July 3, 2007).
86. John Kingdon, *Congressmen's Voting Decisions* (New York: Harper and Row, 1973), pp. 46–53.
87. Gary C. Jacobson, "The 1994 Elections in Perspective," *Political Science Quarterly* 111 (1996): 203–223.
88. Goldenberg and Traugott, *Campaigning for Congress*, p. 123.
89. Richard R. Lau and Gerald M. Pomper, *Negative Campaigning: An Analysis of Senate Elections* (Lanham, MD: Rowman & Littlefield, 2004), p. 91.
90. Ehrenhalt, "New Campaign Era," p. 2561.
91. Richard Schlackman and Jamie "Buster" Douglas, "Attack Mail: The Silent Killer," *Campaigns & Elections* (July 1995): 25.
92. Lonna Rae Atkeson, Nancy Carrillo, and Margaret C. Toulouse, "The 2002 New Mexico Federal Races," in *The Last Hurrah?* ed. Magleby and Monson, p. 276.
93. Myra MacPherson, "The New Right Brigade," *Washington Post*, August 10, 1980, p. F1.
94. "Big Brother Lends a Hand," *http://www.cbsnews.com/stories/2002/10/28/politics/main527101.shtml* (May 15, 2003).
95. Paul Taylor, "Accentuating the Negative," *Washington Post* national weekly edition, October 20, 1986, p. 6.
96. Fenno, *Home Style*, p. 168; emphasis is Fenno's.
97. Gary C. Jacobson, "Deficit Cutting Politics and Congressional Elections," *Political Science Quarterly* 108 (1993): 390–396.
98. Gary C. Jacobson and Michael A. Dimock, "Checking Out: The Effects of Bank Overdrafts on the 1992 House Elections," *American Journal of Political Science* 38 (1994): 601–624; see also Chapter 6.
99. Gary C. Jacobson, "The 1994 Congressional Elections in Perspective," *Political Science Quarterly* 111 (1996): 203–223.
100. Gary C. Jacobson, "Referendum: The 2006 Midterm Congressional Elections," *Political Science Quarterly* 122 (2007): 1–24.

101. Fenno, *Home Style*, p. 55.
102. Fenno, *Home Style*, p. 114.
103. Richard F. Fenno Jr., *Congress at the Grassroots: Representational Change in the South, 1970–1998* (Chapel Hill: University of North Carolina Press, 2000), pp. 129–140.
104. Ehrenhalt, "New Campaign Era," p. 2563.
105. Ehrenhalt, "New Campaign Era," pp. 2563–2564.
106. Taylor, "Accentuating the Negative," p. 6.
107. Barone and Ujifusa, *Almanac of American Politics 2000*, p. 497.
108. Adam Nagourney, "The Theme of the Ads: Don't Be Nice," *New York Times*, September 27, 2006, at *http://www.nytimes.com/2006/09/27/us/politics/27ads.html?ex=1317009600&en=5b29b3a6fe35f5cc&ei=5088&partner=rssnyt&emc=rss* (July 3, 2007).
109. Michael Grunwald, "The Year of Playing Dirtier: Negative Ads Get Positively Surreal," *Washington Post*, October 27, 2006, A1.
110. Michael Barone, Grant Ujifusa, and Douglas Matthews, *The Almanac of American Politics 1980* (New York: E.P. Dutton, 1979), p. 669.
111. Harvey Schantz, "Contested and Uncontested Primaries for the U.S. House," *Legislative Studies Quarterly* 5 (1980): 550; and Jeffrey S. Banks and D. Roderick Kiewiet, "Explaining Patterns of Candidate Competition in Congressional Elections," *American Journal of Political Science* 33 (1989): 997–1015.
112. The evidence is in Chapter 5.
113. Jeffrey Mondak, "Presidential Coattails in Open Seats: The District-Level Impact of Heuristic Processing," *American Politics Quarterly* 21 (1993): 307–319; and Gregory H. Flemming, "Presidential Coattails in Open Seat Elections," *Legislative Studies Quarterly* 20 (1995): 197–211.
114. See Ronald Keith Gaddie, "Congressional Seat Swings: Revisiting Exposure in House Elections," *Political Research Quarterly* 50 (1997): 699–710.
115. Peverill Squire, "Challenger Quality and Voting Behavior in U.S. Senate Elections," *Legislative Studies Quarterly* 17 (1992): 247–264; and David Lublin, "Quality, Not Quantity: Strategic Politicians in U.S. Senate Elections," *Journal of Politics* 56 (1994): 228–241.
116. David Magleby, "More Bang for the Buck: Campaign Spending in Small-State U.S. Senate Elections" (Paper presented at the Annual Meeting of the Western Political Science Association, Salt Lake City, March 30–April 1, 1989).
117. Kim Fridken Kahn, "Senate Elections and the News: Examining Campaign Coverage," *Legislative Studies Quarterly* 16 (1991): 349–374.
118. John R. Alford and John R. Hibbing, "The Disparate Electoral Security of House and Senate Incumbents" (Paper presented at the Annual Meeting of the American Political Science Association, Atlanta, August 31–September 3, 1989), pp. 17–19; see also Table 5–3.
119. Gary C. Jacobson and Raymond E. Wolfinger, "Information and Voting in California Senate Elections," *Legislative Studies Quarterly* 14 (1989): 518–519; John R. Hibbing and John R. Alford, "Constituency Population

and Representation in the United States Senate," *Legislative Studies Quarterly* 15 (1990): 581–598; and Bruce I. Oppenheimer and Frances Sandstrum, "The Effect of State Population on Senate Elections" (Paper presented at the Annual Meeting of the Midwest Political Science Association, Chicago, April 6–8, 1995). However, one careful study found little difference in the level of regard voters have for senators compared to representatives and little disadvantage for senators from large states compared to senators from small states. See Jonathan Krasno, *Challengers, Competition, and Reelection: Comparing Senate and House Elections* (New Haven, CT: Yale University Press, 1994), Chapter 3.

120. Timothy Cook, "House Members as Newsmakers: The Effects of Televising Congress," *Legislative Studies Quarterly* 9 (1986): 211.
121. Barbara Sinclair, "Washington Behavior and Home-State Reputation: The Impact of National Prominence on Senators' Visibility and Likability," *Legislative Studies Quarterly* 15 (1990): 486–490.
122. Ehrenhalt, "New Campaign Era," p. 2560.
123. Ehrenhalt, "New Campaign Era," p. 2560.
124. David Lesher, "TV Blitz Fueled by a Fortune," *Los Angeles Times*, September 12, 1994, p. 1.
125. Meader and Bart, "South Dakota," p. 170.
126. Magleby and Patterson, *War Games*, p. 34.
127. Alan S. Gerber and Donald P. Green, "The Effects of Personal Canvassing, Telephone Calls, and Direct Mail on Voter Turnout: A Field Experiment," *American Political Science Review* 94 (September 2000): 653–663.
128. Howard Tibit and Tim Craig, "Allegations Fly as Election Day Nears," *http://www.baltimoresun.com/news/elections/bal-te.md.turnout04nov04, 0,732693.story?coll=bal-election-governor* (May 16, 2003).
129. Jay Barth and Janine Parry, "Provincialism, Populism, and Politics: Campaign Spending and the 2002 U.S. Senate Race in Arkansas," in *The Last Hurrah?* ed. Magleby and Monson, p. 61.
130. Lau and Pomper, *Negative Campaigning*, pp. 76–85.
131. Nigourney, "Theme of Campaign Ads.," *New York Times*, September 27, 2006.

Chapter 5

CONGRESSIONAL VOTERS

Virtually every issue raised in the previous two chapters was examined from the perspective of some implicit notions about how congressional voters operate. Discussions of the sources of the incumbency advantage, the importance of campaign money, and House–Senate electoral differences, to mention a few examples, were grounded in particular assumptions about voting behavior in congressional elections. So, too, are the campaign and career strategies of congressional candidates. Their activities are guided by beliefs about what sways voters and, at the same time, help to define what voters' decisions are supposed to be about. An adequate understanding of voting behavior in congressional elections is important to congressional scholars and politicians alike.

Neither political scientists nor candidates have reason to be fully satisfied; voters continue to surprise them both on election day. Studies over the past three decades have produced a great deal of fresh information about congressional voters, however, and we know much more about them than we once did. This chapter examines voting behavior in congressional elections and how it relates to the other phenomena of congressional election politics. It begins with a discussion of voter turnout and then turns to the fundamental question of how voters come to prefer one candidate over another.

Turnout in Congressional Elections

Voting requires not only a choice among candidates but also a decision to vote in the first place. A majority of adult Americans do not, in fact, vote in congressional elections (see Figure 5–1). Obviously, participation in congressional elections is strongly influenced by whether there is a presidential contest to attract voters to the polls; turnout drops by an average of 13 percentage points when there is not. Even in presidential election years, House voting is about 4 percentage points lower than presidential voting. To be sure, these percentages underestimate turnout by 3 or 4 percentage points because the denominator includes voting-age adults ineligible to register or vote (noncitizens and former felons).[1] Nonetheless, turnout has fallen off since the 1960s, and rarely does more than half of the eligible electorate cast a House vote.

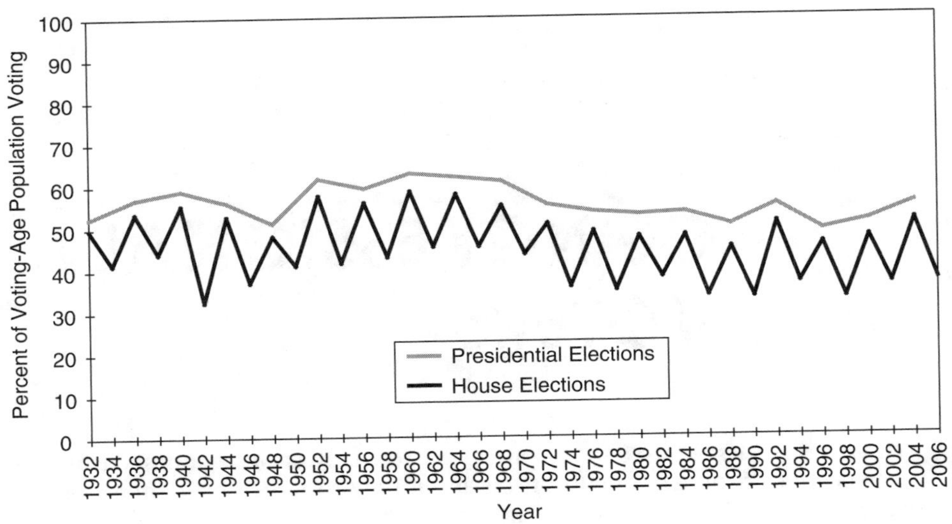

FIGURE 5–1 Voter Turnout in Presidential and Midterm Election Years, 1932–2006

Sources: Norman J. Ornstein, Thomas E. Mann, and Michael J. Malbin, *Vital Statistics on American Congress 2001–2002* (Washington, D.C.: Congressional Quarterly Press, 2002), Table 2–1. Data for 2002–2006 are from Michael P. McDonald, reported at http://elections.gmu.edu/VAP_VEP.htm.

The question of why turnout declined between the 1950s and the 1970s has been the subject of intensive investigation but political scientists have yet to agree on a definitive answer.[2] The mystery grows all the deeper because the single demographic factor most strongly linked to participation—level of education—has been increasing in the population at the same time that voting participation has been stagnant or dropping. The most thorough examination of the question to date, undertaken by Steven Rosenstone and John Mark Hansen, places most of the blame on a decline in grassroots efforts by parties and other organizations (e.g., unions, social movements, and others) to get voters to the polls.[3] A full review of the question would take us too far afield; it is enough for our purposes to recognize that members of Congress are elected by an unimpressive proportion of eligible voters. In midterm elections, little more than 35 percent of the adult population shows up at the polls.

Who Votes?

The low level of voting in congressional elections raises a second question: Who votes and who does not? This question is important because politicians wanting to get into Congress or to remain there will be most responsive to the concerns of people they expect to vote. If voters and nonvoters have noticeably different needs or preferences, the former are likely to be served and the latter slighted.

Raymond Wolfinger and Stephen Rosenstone have most thoroughly studied the question of who votes and who does not. They report that turnout is affected most strongly by education; the more years of formal education one has, the more likely one is to vote. Voting also increases with income and occupational status, but these are themselves strongly related to education and have only a modest influence on turnout once education is taken into account.[4] Voting also increases with age and some occupational groups—notably farmers and government workers—show distinctly higher levels of participation than their other demographic characteristics would lead us to expect. Other things being equal, turnout is about 6 percentage points lower among people living in the South, a residue of the era when one-party rule was fortified by formal and informal practices that kept African Americans and poor whites from the polls.[5]

Wolfinger and Rosenstone's demonstration that turnout varies most strongly with education comes as no surprise because every other study of American voting behavior has found this to be the case. The accepted explanation is that education imparts knowledge about politics and increases one's capacity to deal with complex and abstract matters such as those found in the political world.[6] People with the requisite cognitive skills and political knowledge find the cost of processing and acting on political information lower and the satisfaction greater. Politics is less threatening and more interesting. Similarly, learning outside of formal education can facilitate participation. People whose occupations put them in close touch with politics or whose livelihoods depend on governmental policy—government workers and farmers, for example—vote more consistently, as do people who are older and simply have longer experience as adults.

Curiously, the connection between education and voting participation does not hold in most other Western-style democracies. Western Europeans of lower education and occupational status vote at least as consistently as the rest of the population. The reason, according to Walter Dean Burnham, is that the strong European parties of the left provide the necessary political information and stimuli to their chosen clientele. The sharply lower turnout at the lower end of the American socioeconomic scale can thus be interpreted as another consequence of comparatively weak parties interested mainly in electoral politics and patronage.[7]

Better educated, wealthier, higher-status, and older people are clearly overrepresented in the electorate. When their preferences and concerns substantially differ from those of nonvoters, governmental policy will be biased in their favor. Wolfinger and Rosenstone, citing survey data from the 1970s, argued that the views of voters were not very different from those of the population as a whole, so differential participation did not impart any special bias.[8] In the 1980s and 1990s, policy issues that divided people according to economic status became more prominent and the underrepresented groups suffered. Cuts in government spending to reduce federal budget deficits hit welfare recipients far harder than they hit senior citizens or business corporations. Some evidence suggests that legislators are more attuned ideologically to voters than to nonvoters.[9] Yet research continues to show that the policy preferences of voters and nonvoters are not very different and that few, if any, election results would change if every eligible person voted.[10]

Another question posed by the turnout data is whether congressional electorates differ between presidential and midterm election years. Do the millions of citizens who only vote for congressional candidates because they happen to be on the same ballot with presidential candidates change the electoral environment in politically consequential ways? One prominent study, based on surveys of voters taken in the 1950s, concluded that they did. The electorate in presidential years was found to be composed of a larger proportion of voters weakly attached to either political party and subject to greater influence by political phenomena peculiar to the specific election, notably their feelings about the presidential candidates. At the midterm, with such voters making up a much smaller proportion of the electorate, partisanship prevailed. This resulted in a pattern of "surge and decline," in which the winning presidential candidate's party picked up congressional seats (the surge), many of which were subsequently lost at the next midterm election when the pull of the presidential candidate was no longer operating (the decline). The theory of surge and decline explained why, in every midterm election between 1934 and 1998, the president's party lost seats in the House.[11]

Aggregate shifts in congressional seats and votes from one election to the next will be examined at length in Chapter 6. At this point, suffice it to say that the view of electorates underlying this theory has not been supported by subsequent evidence. More recent research suggests that midterm voters are no more or less partisan than those voting in presidential years and that the two electorates are demographically alike.[12] The addition or subtraction of voters drawn out by a presidential contest does not seem to produce significantly different electorates.[13]

These observations about turnout refer to the electorate as a whole, but congressional candidates are, of course, much more concerned about the particular electorates in their states and districts. As noted in Chapter 2, turnout is by no means the same across constituencies; it varies enormously. One obvious source of variation is the demographic makeup of the district: average level of education, income, occupational status, age distribution, and so on. These factors are, at least in the short run, fairly constant in any individual state or district but turnout also varies in the same constituency from election to election (quite apart from the presidential year–midterm difference)—and these variations are, for our purposes, the most interesting.

The generally low level of voting in congressional elections means that a large measure of the fundamental electoral currency—votes—lies untapped. This affects campaign strategy in several ways. Even incumbents who have been winning by healthy margins recognize that many citizens did not vote for them (even if they did not vote against them) and that they could be in for trouble if an opponent who can mobilize the abstainers comes along. This is not an idle worry. Generally, the higher the turnout, the closer the election; the lower the turnout, the more easily the incumbent is reelected.[14] Successful challengers evidently draw to the polls people who normally do not bother to vote. The wisdom of defusing the opposition and discouraging strong challenges is again apparent. Experienced campaigners know that getting one's supporters to the polls is as important as winning their support in the first place; as we saw in Chapter 4, well-organized campaigns typically devote a major share of their work to getting out the vote.

The effort to get out the vote presupposes that there is a vote to be gotten out, that people brought to the polls will indeed support the candidate. After all, what finally matters is what voters do in the voting booth. And this raises a question of fundamental interest to politicians and political scientists alike: What determines how people vote for congressional candidates? What moves voters to support one candidate rather than the other? The entire structure of congressional election politics hinges on the way voters reach this decision.

Partisanship in Congressional Elections

The first modern survey studies of congressional elections identified partisanship as the single most important influence on individuals' voting decisions, and it has remained so even through the period of weakened party influence in the 1960s and 1970s. The pioneering survey studies of voting behavior in both presidential and congressional elections conducted in the 1950s found that a large majority of voters thought of themselves as Democrats or Republicans and voted accordingly. Particular candidates or issues might, on occasion, persuade a person to vote for someone of the other party but the defection was likely to be temporary and did not dissolve the partisan attachment.[15]

Alternative Interpretations of Party Identification

The leading interpretation of these findings was that voters who were willing to label themselves Democrats or Republicans identified with the party in the same way they might identify with a region or an ethnic or religious group: "I'm a Texan, a Baptist, and a Democrat." The psychological attachment to a party was rooted in powerful personal experiences (best exemplified by the millions who became Democrats during the Depression) or was learned, along with similar attachments, from the family. In either case, identification with a party was thought to establish an enduring orientation toward the political world. The result, in aggregate, was a stable pattern of partisanship across the entire electorate. Thus, from the New Deal onward, the Democrats enjoyed consistent national majorities. Individual states or congressional districts were, in many cases, "safe" for candidates of one party or the other.

This did not mean that the same party won every election, of course. Some voters did not think of themselves as belonging to a party, and even those who did would defect if their reactions to particular candidates, issues, or recent events ran contrary to their party identification strongly enough. But once these short-term forces were no longer present, the long-term influence of party identification would reassert itself and they would return to their partisan moorings. For most citizens, only quite powerful and unusual experiences could inspire permanent shifts of party allegiance.

This interpretation of party identification has been undermined from at least two directions since it was developed. First, the electoral influence of partisanship diminished steadily throughout the 1960s and 1970s. Fewer voters were willing to consider themselves partisans; the party attachments of those who did were likely to be weaker. The percentage of people declaring themselves to be strong partisans fell from 36 in 1952 to 23 in 1978; the percentage declaring themselves to be weak or strong partisans fell from 75 to 60 over the same period. Even those who still admitted to partisan attachments were a good deal more likely to defect to candidates of the other party than they had been earlier.[16]

Although no definitive explanation for the period of decline in electoral partisanship has been developed, it is no doubt related to political events of the 1960s and 1970s. Each party brought disaster upon itself by nominating a presidential candidate preferred only by its more extreme ideologues—the Republicans with Goldwater in 1964, the Democrats with McGovern in 1972. In 1968, the Vietnam War and the civil rights issue split the Democrats badly and fostered the strongest third-party showing since 1924. Republicans suffered in turn, as the Watergate revelations forced their disgraced president from office. Jimmy Carter's inept handling of the economy and troubles with Iran laid the Democrats low in 1980. More generally, the political alliances formed in the battle over the New Deal were fractured along multiple lines as new problems and issues—most notably social issues concerning abortion, crime, and sexuality—forced their way onto the political stage.

Voters responded to these political phenomena as they were expected to respond to short-term forces, defecting when their party preferences were contradicted strongly enough. As defections become more widespread and partisanship, in general, continued to decline, an interpretation of party identification that, among other things, more easily accommodated change gained plausibility. The alternative interpretation emphasizes the practical rather than psychological aspects of party identification. It has been presented most fully by Morris P. Fiorina, who argues that people attach themselves to a party because they have found, through past experience, that its candidates are more likely than those of the other party to produce the kinds of results they prefer.

Because it costs time and energy to determine the full range of information on all candidates who run for office, voters quite reasonably use the shorthand cue of party to simplify the voting decision. Past experience is a more useful criterion than future promises or expectations because it is more certain. Party cues are recognized as imperfect, to be sure, and people who are persuaded that a candidate of the other party would deal more effectively with their concerns vote for him or her. More important, if cumulative experience suggests that candidates of the preferred party are no longer predictably superior in this respect, the party preference naturally decays.[17] Party ties are subject to modification, depending on the answer to the proverbial voters' question "What have you done for me lately?"[18]

The virtue of this alternative interpretation is that it can account for both the observed short-run stability and the long-run lability of party identification evident in individuals and the electorate. For example, it offers a plausible explanation for the evidence of a significant shift in party identification away from the Democrats and toward the Republicans during the 1980s. According to National Election Studies (NES) data, the 52–33 advantage in percentage share of party identifiers held by Democrats in 1980 had, by 1994, shrunk to 47–42.[19] The biggest change took place in the South, where the proportion of white voters identifying themselves as Republicans grew from less than 30 percent in 1980 to 43 percent in 1994 (on the way up to 59 percent in 2004).[20] Moreover, self-described Republicans turned out to vote in higher proportions than did Democrats in 1994, so that for the first time in the forty-two-year history of the National Election Studies, Republicans enjoyed a lead in party identification among voters, 48–46.

The Republicans' gains in party identification were not fully sustained, however. The Democrats' advantage expanded to 52–38 in 1996 and to 53–37 in 1998, as House Republicans' missteps on the budget in 1995 and the unpopular attempt to impeach and convict Bill Clinton in 1998 cost their party public support (see

Chapter 6). Republicans closed the gap slightly in 2000 (50–38 Democratic advantage) and even more so in 2004 (50–41). The Democrats still hold a lead, but it is narrower than it was before the Reagan administration; because Republican identifiers tend to turn out at higher levels and to vote more loyally for their party, the national partisan division remains closely balanced.[21] These swings show that party identification can change in response to political experiences far less earthshaking than the Great Depression, and partisanship appears to be rather more sensitive to short-term influences than the psychological model would predict.[22]

Partisanship and Voting

The issue of which interpretation makes more empirical sense (or which combination of the two views—they are by no means irreconcilable) will not be settled here. What matters most for our purposes is that however party identification is interpreted, it remains an important influence on congressional voters, although that influence has varied in strength over time. Figures 5–2 and 5–3 display the trends in partisan voting in House and Senate elections since 1956. Notice that despite the common perception that voters have become increasingly detached from parties, the share of the electorate composed of voters who label themselves as pure independents, leaning toward neither party, has not grown. What did grow for a time was the proportion of voters who vote contrary to their expressed party affiliation. By the end of the 1970s, defections in House elections were typically twice as common as they were in the 1950s. Since the 1970s, party loyalty has recovered all of the lost ground. In recent elections, about 80 percent of House

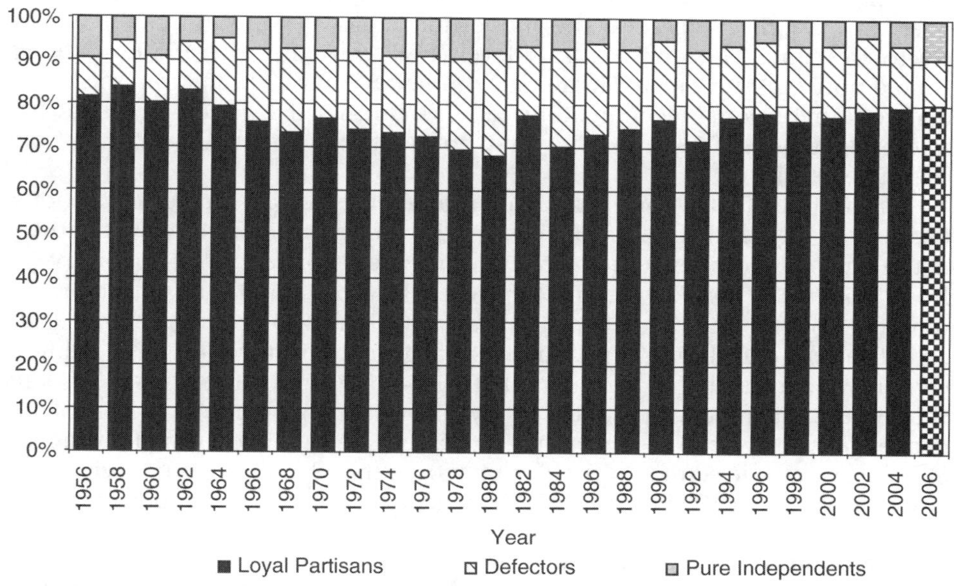

FIGURE 5–2 Party Line Voters, Defectors, and Independents in House Elections, 1956–2006

Source: 1956–2004: National Election Studies; 2006: Cooperative Congressional Election Study.

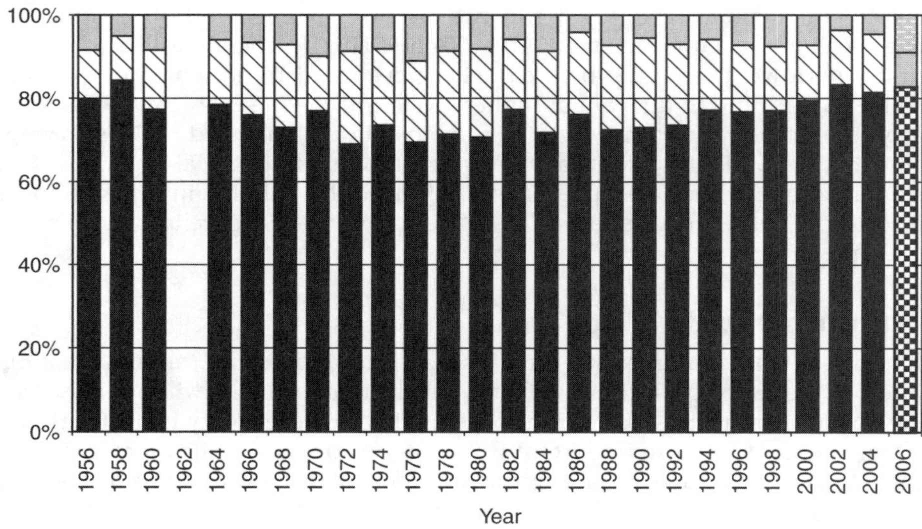

FIGURE 5–3 Party-Line Voters, Defectors, and Independents in Senate Elections, 1956–2006

Source: 1956–2004: National Election Studies; 2006: Cooperative Congressional Election Study.

voters have been loyal partisans, about 15 percent, partisan defectors. The trends for Senate electorates have been similar, with a visible increase in party loyalty over the past three decades; the proportion of loyal partisans in the Senate electorates since 2002 has reached levels not seen since the 1950s. (Readers should note that the data in Figures 5–2 through 5–5 for 2006 are from the Cooperative Congressional Election Study rather than the NES, which did conduct a midterm study in 2006; thus, they may not be strictly comparable to data from earlier years.[23])

The decline of party loyalty had important consequences for House elections, because, as Figures 5–4 and 5–5 show us, the growth in defections was entirely at the expense of challengers. The crucial evidence is from the 1956–1976 surveys; from 1978 to 1998, the vote question was asked in a way that exaggerates the reported vote for the incumbent (typically by about 8 percentage points). The actual rate of defections to incumbents has thus been lower—and has almost certainly fallen further since the mid-1970s—than the figure suggests.[24] Voters sharing the incumbent's party are as loyal now as they ever were. Voters of the challenger's party have become much less faithful (even discounting for exaggeration), generally defecting at very high rates from the 1972 through 1992 elections. Only beginning in 1994 do we see a sustained reduction in defections to incumbents. Defections also clearly favor Senate incumbents but by a considerably narrower and, since 1990, decreasing margin.

Figures 5–4 and 5–5 display, at the level of individual voters, the change in the vote advantage of House incumbents that was evident in the aggregate

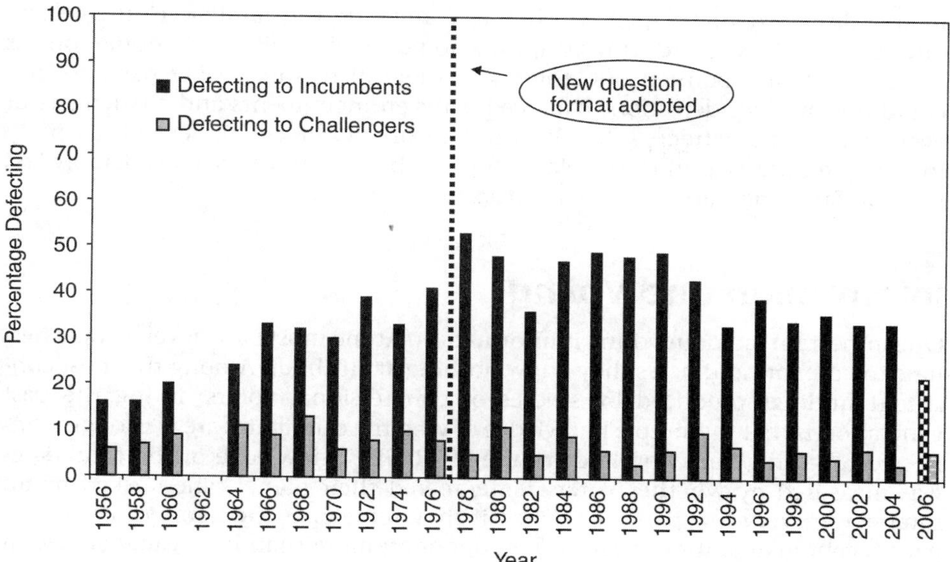

FIGURE 5–4 Partisan Voters Defecting to Incumbents and Challengers in House Elections, 1958–2006

Source: 1956–2004, National Election Studies; 2006: Cooperative Congressional Election Study.

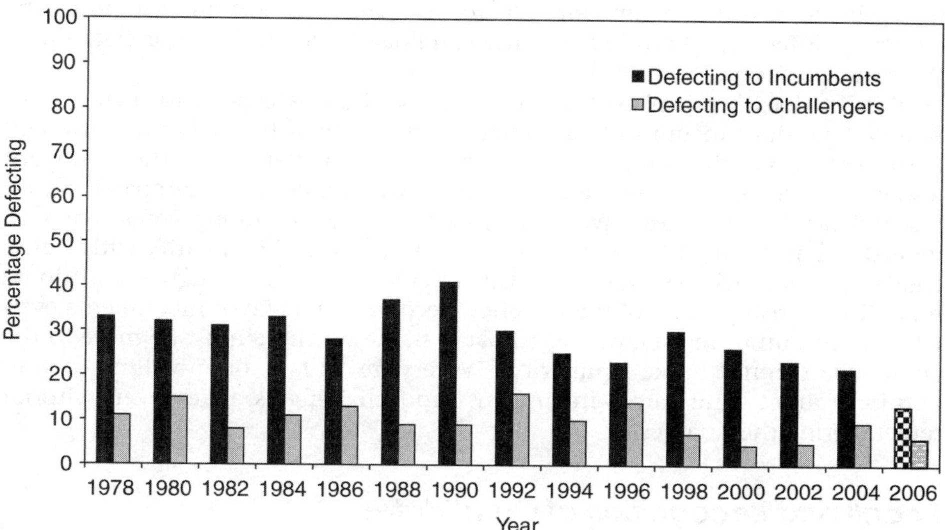

FIGURE 5–5 Partisan Voters Defecting to Incumbents and Challengers in Senate Elections, 1978–2006

Source: 1956–2004, National Election Studies; 2006: Cooperative Congressional Election Study.

figures discussed in Chapter 3. They also reiterate the familiar House–Senate differences in this regard. However, they do not explain either phenomenon. As Albert Cover has pointed out, there is no logical reason weaker party loyalty could not produce defections balanced between incumbents and challengers or even favoring the latter.[25] After all, voters are about as likely to desert their party in Senate elections as in House elections, but the defections are considerably less likely to favor incumbents. Other factors must be involved.

Information and Voting

One important factor in voting is information. At the most basic level, people hesitate to vote for candidates they know nothing at all about. Among the most consistent findings produced by studies of congressional voters during the past generation is that the simple knowledge of who the candidates are is strongly connected to voting behavior. Prior to the 1978 NES, knowledge of the candidates was measured by whether voters remembered their names when asked by an interviewer. Very few partisans defect if they remember the name of their own party's candidate but not that of the opponent; more than half usually defect if they remember only the name of the other party's candidate; defection rates of voters who know both or neither names fall in between. The pattern holds for both Senate and House candidates.[26]

This suggested one important reason that incumbents do so well in House elections: Voters are much more likely to remember their names. In surveys taken during the 1980–2000 period, for example, from 41 to 54 percent (average, 46 percent) could recall the incumbent's name, but only 10 to 26 percent (average, 16 percent) that of the challenger. If only one of the two candidates is remembered, it is the incumbent 95 percent of the time. But understanding the effects of differential knowledge of the candidate's names does not clear up all the basic questions.

First, it does not explain the growth in partisan defections to incumbents. Beyond question, incumbents are comparatively much better known, through both past successful campaigns and vigorous exploitation of the abundant resources for advertising themselves that come with office. But as campaign spending and official resources have grown, their familiarity among voters has not; indeed, it has declined, as Figure 5–6 illustrates.[27] Voters' familiarity with House challengers declined even more, but the difference was not enough to contribute much to the rising value of incumbency. Second, voters favor incumbents even when they cannot recall either candidate's name, so there must be more to the choice than simple name familiarity.[28] Voters are, in fact, often willing to offer opinions about candidates—incumbents and challengers alike—even without remembering their names.[29]

Recall and Recognition of Candidates

Such discoveries forced scholars to reconsider what is meant by "knowing" the candidates. Thomas Mann was the first to show that many voters who could not recall a candidate's name could recognize the name from a list—information always available in the voting booth.[30] Beginning in 1978, the National Election

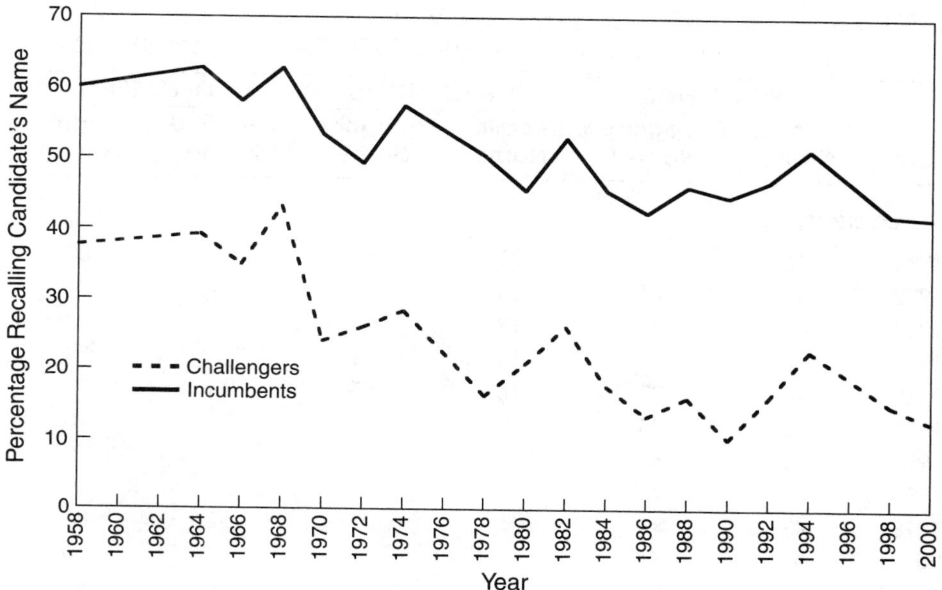

FIGURE 5–6 Name Recall of House Challengers and Incumbents, 1958–2000 (Voters Only)

Source: American National Elections Studies; comparable data are not available for 1960, 1962, 1976, 1996, and 2002–2006.

Studies have thus included questions testing the voters' abilities both to recall and to recognize each candidate's name. The studies have also included a battery of questions designed to find out what else voters know about the candidates, what sort of contact they have had with them, and what they think of them on a variety of dimensions. The data collected since 1978 allow a much more thorough examination of voting behavior in congressional elections than was previously possible and such data are the focus of the rest of this chapter. Unfortunately, however, these newer data cannot cast much light on what changes have occurred in patterns of congressional voting because comparable data from earlier elections do not exist, and they do not cover the 2006 midterm election.[31]

Modern studies of congressional voters leave no doubt that voters recognize candidates' names much more readily than they recall them. Table 5–1 shows that voters are twice as likely to recognize as to recall House candidates in any incumbency category. The same is true for Senate candidates, except in the case of incumbents and candidates for open seats, whose names are already recalled by more than half the voters. These figures also leave no doubt that the House incumbent's advantage in recall is matched by an advantage in recognition. More than 90 percent of voters recognize the incumbent's name. The shift in focus from name recall to name recognition nicely resolves the apparent anomaly of voters favoring incumbents without even knowing who they are. Many more voters also recognize the challenger than recall his or her name, but these voters still amount to little more than half the electorate. Candidates for open seats are better known

TABLE 5–1 Incumbency Status and Voters' Familiarity with Congressional Candidates, 1980–2004 (in percentages)

	INCUMBENTS		CHALLENGERS		OPEN SEATS	
Year	**Recalled Name**	**Recognized Name[a]**	**Recalled Name**	**Recognized Name[a]**	**Recalled Name**	**Recognized Name[a]**
House Elections						
1980	46	92	21	54	32	82
1982	54	94	26	62	29	77
1984	45	91	18	54	32	80
1986	42	91	13	46	43	84
1988	46	93	16	53	33	71
1990	45	93	10	37	26	78
1992	43	87	15	56	23	79
1994	51	93	22	57	36	82
1998[b]	42	91	15	45	52	83
2000	42	91	13	57	29	80
2002[d]	—	95	—	58	—	90
2004[d]	—	92	—	64	—	84
Mean:	*46*	*92*	*17*	*54*	*34*	*81*
Senate Elections						
1980	61	99	40	81	47	89
1982	61	97	37	78	73	95
1986[c]	61	97	41	77	61	94
1988	51	96	30	74	73	97
1990	57	98	31	69	31	86
1992	55	96	33	82	59	93
1994[d]	—	98	—	84	—	92
1998[b,d]	—	96	—	71	—	77
2000[d]	—	93	—	73	—	90
2002[d]	—	99	—	84	—	97
2004[d]	—	92	—	69	—	92
Mean:	*58*	*96*	*35*	*77*	*57*	*91*

[a]Includes only respondents who reported voting and who could recognize and rate the candidates on the feeling thermometer or, if they could not rate the candidates, could recall the candidates' names.
[b]Comparable data are not available for 1996.
[c]Data are not available for 1984 Senate candidates.
[d]Recall question not asked.

Source: American National Election Studies.

than challengers but not so well known as incumbents; indeed, the data show that they fall between incumbents and challengers on almost every measure. This is exactly what we would expect, knowing the kinds of candidates and campaigns typical of open-seat contests.

Senate candidates are better known than their House counterparts in each category, and Senate incumbents are clearly better known than their challengers (though the more populous the state, the lower the proportion of voters who can recall the senator's name[32]). But the gap is smaller than it is for House candidates. Again, this is the kind of pattern we would anticipate, owing to the distinctive circumstances of Senate electoral politics outlined in Chapter 4.

Familiarity is supposed to matter, of course, because of its connection to the vote; Table 5–2 displays the connection for some recent elections.[33] In both House and Senate elections, the more familiar voters are with a candidate, the more likely they are to vote for him or her, with the effect also depending, symmetrically, on the degree of familiarity with the other candidate. Defections are concentrated in the upper-right corner of each table; party loyalty predominates in the lower-left corner. Only about 3 percent of House voters and 13 percent of Senate voters defected to candidates who were less familiar than their own; more than half of both Senate and House voters defected to candidates who are more familiar. Independent voters, omitted from this table, voted for the better-known candidate 84 percent of the time in House races and 82 percent of the time in Senate contests.

TABLE 5–2 Familiarity with Candidates and Voting Behavior in Congressional Elections (Percentage of Voters Defecting)

	FAMILIARITY WITH OWN PARTY'S CANDIDATE		
	Recalled Name	**Recognized Name**	**Neither**
House Elections (2000)			
Familiarity with other party's candidate:			
Recalled name	13	34	84
Recognized name[a]	5	22	43
Neither	0	7	10
Senate Elections (1988–1992)			
Familiarity with other party's candidate:			
Recalled name	20	49	75
Recognized name[a]	9	30	63
Neither	8	7	25

[a]Recognized name and could rate candidate on the thermometer scale but could not recall candidate's name.

Sources: National Election Study, 1998, and Senate Election Studies, 1988, 1990, and 1992.

Why is familiarity of so much benefit to congressional candidates? The answer proposed by Donald Stokes and Warren Miller, that "in the main, to be perceived at all is to be perceived favorably," has not found much support in later work.[34] It does not work so simply. From 1978 through 2000, the NES surveys asked respondents what they liked and disliked about House candidates; the same questions were asked about Senate candidates in the 1988–1992 Senate Election Studies. As the numbers in Table 5–3 indicate, the more familiar voters are with candidates, the more likely they are to discover things they both like and dislike. Familiarity by no means breeds only favorable responses. More important, the benefits of incumbency obviously extend well beyond greater familiarity. Incumbents are better liked—by a wide margin—as well as better known than challengers. At any level of familiarity, voters are more inclined to mention something they like about the incumbent than about the challenger; negative responses are rather evenly divided, so the net benefit is clearly to the incumbent. Voters tend to favor Senate as well as House incumbents on this dimension, though the difference is smaller; Senate candidates tend to attract a higher proportion of negative responses, reflecting the greater average intensity of these contests.

Another survey question allows further comparison of voters' feelings about House and Senate candidates. Respondents were asked to rate candidates they recognized on a "thermometer" scale of 0 to 100 degrees, with 0 as the most unfavorable, 100 as the most favorable, and 50 as neutral. The mean temperatures for House and Senate candidates in different incumbency categories are shown in Figures 5–7 and 5–8.

House and Senate challengers are, on average, rated about the same (the important difference lying in the proportion of voters who could rate them at all), as are candidates for open seats. However, House incumbents are more warmly regarded than Senate incumbents and so the average gap between House incumbents and their challengers (13.8 degrees) is larger than that between Senate incumbents and their challengers (7.9 degrees). Notice that the House incumbents' advantage has shrunk in recent elections, averaging 12 degrees in 1992–2004 compared to 16 degrees in the earlier years covered.

The Senate figures tend to mirror aggregate election results. Recall from Table 3–1 that more than one-quarter of Senate incumbents lost general elections in 1980 and 1986, two years in which the Senate incumbents' advantage in thermometer ratings was much narrower than usual. Indeed, Democratic challengers in 1986 were, on average, rated higher (60.6 degrees) than their incumbent Republican opponents (57.7 degrees), an indication of unusual weakness among the Republican Senate class of 1980 (the Democrats retook control of the Senate in 1986). Overall, the average difference between thermometer ratings of incumbent Senators and their challengers across election years is correlated with the number of incumbents defeated at $-.73$ ($N = 12$, $p < .01$).

Contacting Voters

Why are House incumbents so much better known and liked than their opponents? Why are Senate challengers more familiar to voters than House challengers? One obvious explanation focuses on the frequency with which messages

TABLE 5–3 Incumbency Status and Voters' Likes and Dislikes of House and Senate Candidates (in Percentages)

Year	RECALLED NAME		RECOGNIZED NAME[a]		NEITHER		MARGINAL TOTALS	
	Like Something	Dislike Something	Like Something	Dislike Something	Like Something	Dislike Something	Like Something	Dislike Something
House 1978–2000								
Incumbents	71	32	49	15	11	7	56	22
Challengers	43	35	28	15	2	2	16	13
Open seats	59	37	33	21	6	3	37	23
Senate 1988–1992								
Incumbents	67	43	50	22	17	3	59	34
Challengers	52	49	26	26	4	3	31	29
Open seats	56	48	36	27	4	3	43	35

[a]Includes only respondents who reported voting and who could recognize and rate the candidate on the feeling thermometer or, if they could not rate the candidate, could recall the candidate's name.

Sources: National Election Studies, 1978–2000, and Senate Election Studies, 1988, 1990, and 1992.

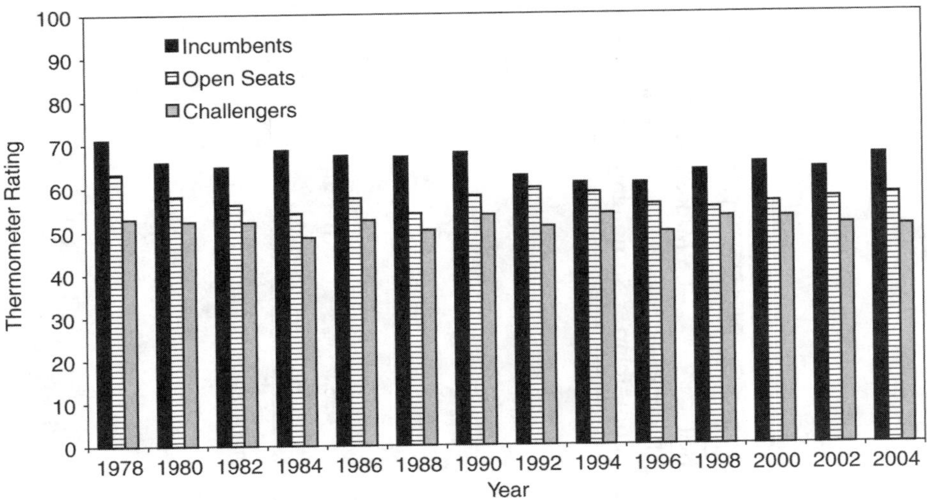

FIGURE 5–7 Voters' Ratings of House Candidates on the 100-Point Thermometer Scale, 1978–2004

Source: American National Election Studies.

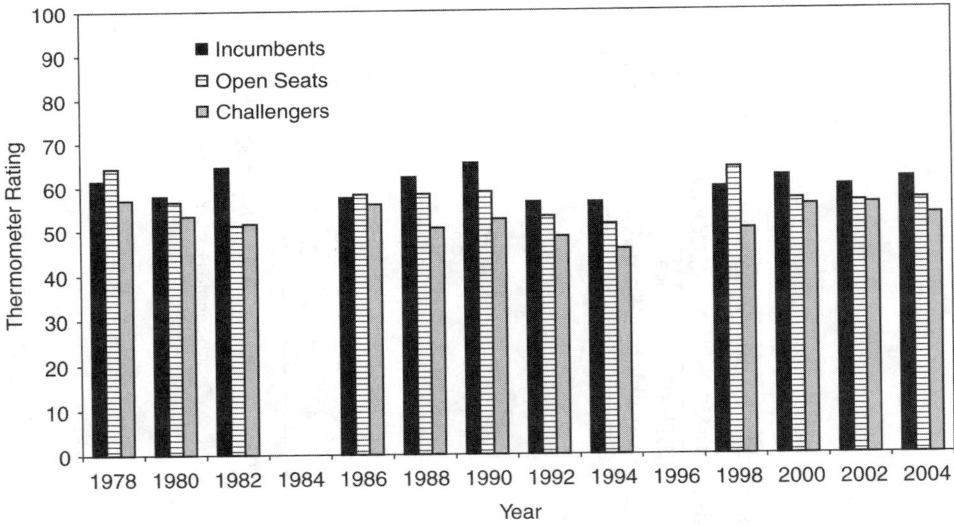

FIGURE 5–8 Voters' Ratings of Senate Candidates on the 100-Point Thermometer Scale, 1980–2004

Source: American National Election Studies.

about members of the various categories reach voters. The percentages of voters reporting contact with House and Senate candidates are listed in Table 5–4. The table lists entries for two separate House election years so that we may compare the frequencies of contacts reported in a year with unusually obscure and underfinanced challengers (1990) with those reported in a year with a relatively high

TABLE 5–4 Voters' Contacts with House and Senate Candidates (in percentages)

Type of Contact	INCUMBENT 1990	INCUMBENT 1994	CHALLENGER 1990	CHALLENGER 1994	OPEN SEAT 1990	OPEN SEAT 1994
House Candidates						
Any	92	90	29	52	81	80
Met personally	20	15	2	4	10	7
Saw at meeting	19	14	3	3	10	7
Talked to staff	13	14	2	5	4	7
Received mail	70	63	12	25	48	49
Read about in newspaper	67	65	20	34	59	55
Heard on radio	30	33	7	18	20	27
Saw on TV	51	61	16	34	58	57
Family or friend had contact	38	32	7	9	21	16
Senate Candidates (1988–1992)						
Any	99		85		96	
Met personally	25		9		10	
Saw at meeting	26		9		11	
Talked to staff	21		7		12	
Received mail	83		51		66	
Read about in newspaper	93		75		85	
Heard on radio	60		45		55	
Saw on TV	94		75		85	

Sources: National Election Studies, 1990 and 1994, and Senate Election Studies, 1988–1992.

proportion of well-financed and successful challengers (1994, the last time these questions were asked). Voters were twice as likely to report contact of every kind with incumbents as with challengers in House races. Almost every voter was reached in some way by the incumbent, while even in a year with unusually vigorous challenges, barely half the voters reported contact of any kind the challenger. Still, the two election years look quite different for challengers, with much higher levels of contact reported in 1994.

Senate incumbents had a substantially smaller advantage over their challengers in frequency of reported contacts. The differences between House and Senate challengers were sharpest in the area of mass media publicity. Notice especially the difference in the proportion of voters reached through television. Richard Fenno's observations of senators and Senate candidates led him to conclude that a major difference between House and Senate elections is the much greater importance of the mass media in the latter. The news media are much more interested in Senate candidates than in House candidates because they are much more interested in senators.[35] As noted in Chapter 4, Senate campaigns are also wealthier and can use paid television more extensively and more efficiently than can House campaigns. The consequences are evident in the survey data; both factors enhance the Senate challenger's ability to catch the attention of voters, an essential ingredient of electoral success.

Although it is no surprise that senators and Senate candidates reach a larger proportion of voters through the mass media, it is certainly a surprise that more voters report meeting them personally and talking to their staffs than report equivalent contacts with their counterparts in the House. We would expect that the much larger constituencies represented by senators would make personal contacts less common. Part of the reason these data show the opposite pattern is that the Senate Election Study has equal-sized samples from every state, so voters from smaller states are overrepresented. Even adjusting for state size, however, House members and candidates evidently have no advantage in personal contacts. Only in the very largest states—those with voting-age populations in excess of five million—do voters report significantly fewer personal contacts with Senate candidates than with House candidates.[36]

The main House–Senate difference, then, is in mass media contacts. For Senate incumbents, the news media's greater interest is a mixed blessing. Senators are accorded more attention but are also subject to higher expectations. A House member running for the Senate explained it to Fenno this way:

> People don't treat me differently. They don't see any difference between the two jobs. Maybe they think it's a higher office, but that doesn't make any difference. But the media hold me to a much higher standard than they did as a House member. They expect me to know more details. Am I treated differently running for the Senate? By the people, no; by the media, yes.[37]

House incumbents who avoid scandal normally do not attract much attention from the news media. This means that, except during campaigns, they produce and disseminate much of the information about themselves that reaches the public. To a large extent, they control their own press; no wonder it is a good press and no wonder voters tend to think highly of them.[38] In most cases, only a vigorous campaign by the challenger spreads information critical of the incumbent's performance, with effects that are analyzed later in this chapter.

Table 5–4 also reinforces the vital point that not all nonincumbent candidates are alike. Voters report more contact of all sorts with candidates for open seats than with challengers. The figures for open-seat candidates are sometimes closer to those for incumbents than to those for challengers. House incumbents hold a wide advantage over challengers in these categories, but not simply because they are incumbents and their opponents are not. Their opponents are, rather, much weaker candidates than they might be—or than appear when no incumbent is running. This is a natural consequence of the strategies followed by potential House candidates and their potential supporters, as discussed in Chapter 3.

Incumbents benefit from their superior ability to reach voters—the more ways voters come into contact with a candidate, the more likely they are to remember the candidate and to like (but also dislike) something about him or her. To see this, we will examine the results of some probit equations estimating the effects of contacts on voter awareness and evaluations of House candidates. Probit analysis is a standard procedure for estimating the effects of independent variables on a categorical dependent variable—that is, one that takes only a small number of discrete values. Here, all the dependent variables happen to be dichotomous; that is, each takes only two values. For example, a voter either recalls the candidate's name or does not; the voter either likes something about the candidate or does not.

Probit allows us to estimate how changes in the independent variables affect the probability of one outcome as opposed to the other. The procedure is analogous to regression analysis, with the important differences being that the estimated probability is constrained to take a value between 0.0 and 1.0 (and so always makes sense as a "probability") and that the relationships are nonlinear: The effect of any independent variable depends interactively on the current levels of the other independent variables.[39] This makes it difficult to interpret the coefficients directly, so the results are also displayed in tables that show the estimated probabilities at various settings of the independent variables. All of this will be clearer with specific examples. The variables used in this and subsequent analyses here and in the next chapter can be seen in Table 5–5.

TABLE 5–5 Definitions of Probit Equation Variables

VARIABLE	DEFINITION
Respondent's House vote	1 if Democratic, 0 if Republican
Recall candidate/recognize candidate	1 if respondent recalled (recognized) candidate, 0 otherwise
Type of contact:	
Personal	1 if respondent has met candidate, attended a meeting where candidate spoke, or had contact with staff, 0 otherwise
Mail	1 if respondent received anything in the mail about the candidate, 0 if not
Mass media	1 if respondent learned about candidate by reading newspapers, listening to the radio, or watching television, 0 otherwise
Indirect	1 if respondent's family or friends had any contact with the candidate, 0 if not
Party identification	1 if strong, weak, or independent Democrat, 0 if independent-independent, −1 if strong, weak, or independent Republican
Democrat is incumbent	1 if Democrat is incumbent, 0 otherwise
Republican is incumbent	1 if Republican is incumbent, 0 otherwise
Familiarity with Democrat Familiarity with Republican	1 if respondent recalls candidate's name, .5 if name is recognized but not recalled, 0 if name is not recognized or recalled
Likes something about candidate/dislikes something about candidate	For each variable, 1 if respondent mentions anything liked (or disliked) about the candidate, 0 otherwise
Presidential vote	1 if for Al Gore, 0 if for George W. Bush

The connection between various kinds of contact (combined into four basic modes[40]) and voters' knowledge and evaluations of the candidates is shown in Tables 5–6 and 5–7.[41] Table 5–6 lists the probit coefficients (with their standard errors) estimating the effects of each mode of contact on the likelihood that a voter would recall, recognize, and like or dislike something about a House challenger or incumbent in 1988. Although weakly intercorrelated, each of these modes of contact is independently related to the probability that voters know and like or dislike something about both types of candidates. All but a handful of the coefficients are larger than twice their standard errors and so achieve at least a 0.05 level of statistical significance.

A comparison of the coefficients suggests that, in general, mass media contact has the strongest effect on these probabilities for challengers. This is confirmed by Table 5–7, which interprets the probit equations for various combinations of the independent variables. The table lists the probability of each response, depending on the modes of contact individually and in combination. Note that respondents are twice as likely to recognize, recall, and evaluate challengers if they report contact with them through the mass media. For incumbents, each type of contact has about the same size effect. Notice the significant effect for both incumbents and challengers of indirect contact (word-of-mouth contact through experiences of family or friends), confirming politicians' faith in the ripple effects of their work to reach voters.

TABLE 5–6 Probit Equations Estimating the Effects of Contacts on Voters' Knowledge and Evaluations of House Candidates, 1994

Independent Variable	DEPENDENT VARIABLE: Recall	Recognize	Like Something	Dislike Something
Challengers				
Intercept	−1.53 (.10)	−.51 (.07)	−1.90 (.13)	−1.83 (.12)
Personal	42 (.21)	.90 (.40)	.76 (.21)	−.09 (.23)
Mail	.25 (.14)	30 (.16)	.39 (.15)	.27 (.15)
Mass media	1.03 (.13)	1.30 (.12)	1.04 (.16)	.92 (.16)
Indirect	.47 (.20)	1.34 (.41)	.81 (.21)	.38 (.22)
Incumbents				
Intercept	−.82 (.13)	.58 (.14)	−.70 (.13)	−1.17 (.14)
Personal	.24 (.13)	.60 (.40)	.70 (.13)	.11 (.13)
Mail	.55 (.11)	.72 (.19)	.44 (.11)	.28 (.11)
Mass media	.44 (.14)	.66 (.18)	.27 (.13)	.47 (.15)
Indirect	.26 (.12)	.68 (.35)	.40 (.12)	.00 (.12)

Note: Standard errors are in parentheses; any coefficient larger than twice its standard error is statistically significant at $p < .05$.

TABLE 5–7 The Effects of Contacts on Voters' Knowledge and Evaluation of House Candidates, 1994

	PROBABILITY OF VOTER'S RESPONSE TO CANDIDATE			
Type of Contact	**Recall**	**Recognize**	**Like Something**	**Dislike Something**
Challengers				
None	.17	.37	.13	.14
Personal	.25	.60	.24	.13
Mail	.22	.45	.18	.17
Mass media	.38	.69	.30	.29
Indirect	.26	.70	.25	.13
Any two[a]	.30–.49	.66–.89	.32–.49	.16–.36
Any three[a]	.40–.59	.88–.95	.52–.67	.22–.43
All four	.60	.96	.75	.41
Incumbents				
None	.30	.64	.33	.24
Personal	.36	.63	.50	.26
Mail	.43	.79	.44	.29
Mass media	.40	.78	.39	.33
Indirect	.36	.78	.42	.24
Any two[a]	.42–.54	.86–.88	.49–.61	.26–.40
Any three[a]	.53–.60	.93–.93	.60–.70	.31–.42
All four	.65	.96	.75	.42

[a]Range of values listed because the probability depends on pair or trio chosen.
Source: Probit equations in Table 5–6.

The effects of different modes of contact are cumulative. The more contacts voters have had with a House candidate, the more likely they are to know and like or dislike something about the candidate. Voters who were reached through all four modes are far more likely to be aware of candidates and to offer evaluative comments about them than voters not reached at all—and among such voters, the incumbent's advantage in recognition and affect disappears. Note also that the probability of both liking and disliking something about a candidate increases with contact but that the increase is greater for positive comments. The net effect of successful attempts to reach voters is clearly helpful to candidates.

The Effects of Campaign Spending

The impact of contacts on familiarity and evaluations—and the importance of these to the vote choice—help to explain why campaign money is so important to challengers. The connection between a House challenger's level of campaign spending and the probability that a voter will report having had contact with the candidate (through each of the basic modes, or any of them) is shown in Table 5–8. The likelihood of every kind of contact increases with expenditures, though at a decreasing rate. For example, as spending goes from $30,000 to $500,000, the probability of any contact at all increases from 0.42 to 0.70, the likelihood of contact through mass media goes from 0.39 to 0.66, and the probabilities of personal contact, contact via mail, and indirect contact through family and friends all increase as well.

TABLE 5–8 Campaign Expenditures and Voters' Contacts and Familiarity with Challengers, 1994

	TYPE OF CONTACT						
Campaign Expenditures	**Any**	**Personal**	**Mail**	**Mass Media**	**Indirect**	**Recall Name**	**Recognize Name**
$ 10,000	.32	.13	.20	.29	.12	.18	.36
$ 30,000	.42	.16	.26	.39	.16	.24	.47
$ 50,000	.48	.18	.29	.44	.18	.27	.52
$ 80,000	.52	.19	.32	.48	.19	.30	.57
$100,000	.55	.20	.34	.50	.20	.32	.59
$150,000	.59	.21	.37	.54	.22	.35	.63
$ 200,000	.62	.22	.39	.57	.24	.37	.65
$ 250,000	.64	.23	.40	.59	.25	.39	.67
$ 300,000	.66	.24	.42	.61	.26	.40	.69
$ 400,000	.68	.25	.44	.64	.27	.42	.71
$ 500,000	.70	.26	.46	.66	.28	.44	.73
Incumbents[a]	*.90*	*.27*	*.63*	*.81*	*.32*	*.51*	*.94*

Note: Table entries are probabilities derived from probit estimates. The intercepts, the probit coefficients on campaign expenditures (natural log of expenditures), and standard errors from the probit equations are:

Type of Contact	Intercept	Coefficient	Standard Error
Any	−4.58	.41	.03
Personal	−3.78	.21	.05
Mail	−4.25	.31	.04
Mass Media	−4.47	.39	.03
Indirect	−4.47	.27	.05
Recall	−4.48	.32	.04
Recognize	−4.21	.40	.03

[a]Mean for all incumbents; voters' contacts with incumbents vary little or not at all with the incumbent's campaign expenditures.

Notice, however, that the incumbent retains a lead in every measure of contact except personal, even if the challenger spends $500,000. This is not merely a consequence of the incumbent's usual financial advantage; the incumbent's level of spending has only a modest and often statistically insignificant effect on these variables. Rather, it is a consequence of past campaigns and the district-oriented activities engaged in by House members whether or not an election is imminent.

For challengers, greater spending produces greater familiarity among voters as well; a high-spending campaign can cut the incumbent's lead in voter recall and recognition by more than half.[42] The data in Table 5–8 help to explain why campaign money is crucial to challengers and other nonincumbent House candidates. Without it, they cannot reach voters, they remain obscure, and so they are swamped by the opposition. Similar data for incumbents show that they receive comparatively little benefit from campaign expenditures; the campaign adds little to the prominence and affection they have gained prior to the campaign by cultivating the district and using the many perquisites of office.

The same situation holds among Senate candidates, although the analysis is more complicated because state populations vary so widely.[43] Controlling for the voting age population of the state, the probability of a respondent's recalling a 1988–1992 Senate challenger rises from 0.18 to 0.75 as the challenger's per-voter spending rises from its lowest to its highest observed level; the probability of a respondent's recognizing the challenger rises from 0.34 to 0.94. For incumbent Senate candidates, the equivalent increases are much smaller: from 0.53 to 0.61 and from 0.91 to 0.94, respectively. Again, campaign spending has a bigger payoff to challengers than to incumbents; if they spend enough, Senate challengers become as well known as incumbents.

Models of Voting Behavior

How well voters know and like the candidates matters, finally, because familiarity and evaluations are directly related to the vote. The series of probit equations reported in Table 5–9, based on analysis of data from several House and Senate elections, suggest how these relationships work. More importantly, they make a fundamental point about the electoral effects of incumbency.

The first equation treats the vote choice as a function of party identification and incumbency status. Not surprisingly, these variables have a strong impact on the vote. Estimates of the size of the impact appear in Table 5–10, which interprets the equations in Table 5–9 by showing how much the probability of voting for the Democrat varies between the most pro-Democratic and pro-Republican setting on the independent variable of interest, with the values of the other variables set at their means. For example, the first equation indicates that in 2000, the probability of voting for the Democrat in a House race was 0.47 higher when the respondent identified with the Democratic rather than the Republican Party. Incumbency has a large effect as well in these elections, the probability of voting for the Democrat being, for example, 0.31 higher if the Democrat rather than the Republican was the incumbent in 2000. In the other election years, party identification has a somewhat larger effect on the vote, although incumbency remains a potent factor as well.

TABLE 5–9 Probit Models of the Voting Decision in Recent House and Senate Elections

	HOUSE			SENATE
	1996	1998	2000	1988–1992
Equation 1				
Party identification	1.05 (.06)	.86 (.07)	1.01 (.06)	.69 (.02)
Intercept	.31 (.18)	−.11 (.18)	−.16 (.16)	.00 (.05)
Democrat is incumbent	.27 (.20)	.78 (.21)	.79 (.18)	.56 (.06)
Republican is incumbent	−1.17 (.19)	−.61 (.20)	−.48 (.18)	−.51 (.07)
Equation 2				
Intercept	.41 (.21)	−.55 (.24)	−.04 (.20)	−.10 (.08)
Party identification	1.04 (.06)	.86 (.07)	1.00 (.07)	.69 (.03)
Democrat is incumbent	.07 (.20)	.63 (.23)	.23 (.20)	.41 (.07)
Republican is incumbent	−1.02 (.20)	−.15 (.21)	−.30 (.19)	−.37 (.08)
Familiarity with Democrat	.83 (.18)	1.54 (.21)	1.50 (.21)	.95 (.08)
Familiarity with Republican	−.95 (.19)	−.93 (.25)	−1.46 (.21)	−.79 (.09)
Equation 3				
Intercept	.51 (.26)	−.60 (.26)	.01 (.23)	−.12 (.10)
Party identification	.95 (.08)	.73 (.08)	.85 (.07)	.59 (.03)
Democrat is incumbent	.03 (.26)	.64 (.27)	.05 (.23)	.31 (.08)
Republican is incumbent	−1.04 (.25)	−.07 (.24)	−.27 (.21)	−39 (.08)
Familiarity with Democrat	.38 (.23)	1.30 (.24)	1.15 (.25)	.79 (.11)
Familiarity with Republican	−.64 (.24)	−.82 (.30)	−1.09 (.24)	−.57 (.11)
Likes something about Democrat	1.53 (.17)	1.14 (.19)	1.07 (.17)	1.09 (.06)
Dislikes something about Democrat	−1.25 (.19)	−1.00 (.23)	−.78 (.20)	−.82 (.07)
Likes something about Republican	−1.20 (.16)	−.59 (.18)	−1.07 (.17)	−1.15 (.06)
Dislikes something about Republican	1.09 (.19)	.51 (.19)	.72 (.20)	.86 (.07)

Note: The dependent variable is vote for Democrat. Standard errors are in parentheses. A coefficient that is at least twice its standard error is statistically significant at $p < .05$.

Source: National Election Studies, 1994, 1996, and 1998, and Senate Election Studies, 1988, 1990, and 1992.

The second equation in Table 5–9 adds a composite familiarity variable for each candidate to the set of explanatory variables. The effect of partisanship is unchanged, but the impact of incumbency shrinks; the probit coefficients are smaller, and four of the six are statistically insignificant. The entries in Table 5–10 indicate that the difference made by incumbency status (when familiarity and party identification are set at their mean values) now ranges between 0.13 and

TABLE 5–10 Probit Estimates of the Effects of Party Identification, Incumbency and Candidate Familiarity, and Affect in Congressional Elections

	HOUSE ELECTIONS			SENATE ELECTIONS
	1996	1998	2000	1988–1992
Equation 1				
Party identification	.47	.40	.47	.33
Incumbency	.35	.33	.31	.26
Equation 2				
Party identification	.47	.40	.46	.33
Incumbency	.27	.19	.13	.19
Familiarity	.42	.55	.63	.41
Equation 3				
Party identification	.44	.34	.40	.29
Incumbency	.26	.17	.08	.17
Familiarity	.25	.48	.61	.33
Likes/dislikes	.85	.65	.72	.75

Note: Entries are the difference in the probability of voting for the Democrat between the most pro-Democratic and the most pro-Republican settings on the indicated variables, with the other variables in the equation set at their mean values. For example, in Equation 2 for the Senate elections, a respondent who recalled the Democrat but did not even recognize the Republican would, other things being equal, have a probability of voting for the Democrat .41 higher than would one who recalled the Republican but did not recognize the Democrat.

Source: Estimated from the equations in Table 5–9.

0.27, depending on the year and office. Familiarity has a large effect, far larger than that of incumbency; it would seem that a substantial portion of the incumbency advantage derives from the greater familiarity incumbents enjoy—the conventional hypothesis. But the third equation suggests further that the incumbency variables are, in part, surrogates for voters' evaluations of the candidates.

Each of the four evaluative variables derived from the likes/dislikes questions has a strong impact on the vote. Cumulatively, these evaluations make an enormous difference; a respondent who likes something about the Democrat and dislikes something about the Republican (without also liking something about the Republican and disliking something about the Democrat) has a probability ranging from 0.65 to 0.85 higher of voting for the Democrat than a respondent who takes the opposite position on all four variables. That is, voters who have only good things to say about one candidate and bad things to say about the other are almost certain to vote for the favored candidate, regardless of party identification or incumbency status. Clearly, some of this effect may be rationalization; respondents, when prodded, will come up with reasons for their vote preference. Even discounting for rationalization, however, the impact of candidate evaluations measured in this way is still very impressive.

Two points are clear from this analysis. The first is that voters are not strongly attracted by incumbency per se, nor does the incumbency advantage arise merely from greater renown. Of greater proximate importance are the very favorable public images most House members acquire and the relatively negative images—if any—projected by their opponents.[44] The second is that there is little difference in the patterns for House and Senate elections. In particular, the effect of incumbency is no smaller in Senate than in House elections, confirming the point that the greater vulnerability of Senate incumbents derives not from the behavior of voters but from the context of the elections (for example, a more even partisan balance, or more talented and better-funded challengers).

Evaluating Incumbents

Voters respond positively to House and Senate incumbents for a variety of reasons. NES survey respondents between 1978 and 2000 were asked a number of general and specific questions about the incumbent's performance in serving the state or district and as a legislator in Washington. Table 5–11 presents data on responses from some of the more recent House and Senate election surveys. The left-hand columns in the table list the percentage of voters who were able to offer a response to each question. For example, 20 percent had asked the House incumbent for assistance or information, received some reply, and therefore were able to indicate their level of satisfaction with it (Item 3). The distribution of responses on this question shows that 56 percent of those who could respond on this question were very satisfied, and the right-hand column in the table indicates that 90 percent of those who were very satisfied with the incumbent's response voted for the incumbent. Dissatisfied voters were much less likely to vote for the incumbent. Notice the *absence* of a House–Senate difference on this and all the other questions. Again, voters respond to senators and representatives in the same way.

It is apparent from the left-hand columns that a large majority of voters could evaluate incumbents' general job performance and diligence at keeping in touch and could offer an opinion on whether they would be likely to help with a problem if asked to do so. Forty-six percent were able to determine whether they generally agreed with the way the House incumbent voted, 56 percent, with the way the Senate incumbent voted. Fewer—from 18 to 32 percent—were able to respond in terms of more specific personal and district services and voting and policy items. But most voters could respond in terms of at least one of them. That is, a majority of voters were able to evaluate incumbents in other than broad, general terms.

Reactions to incumbents, both general and specific, were largely favorable. Four-fifths of the voters offering a response approved of the incumbents' performance in both offices. Despite a decline in the level of approval enjoyed by House incumbents in recent years (it averaged 88 percent from 1980 through 1990, and 83 percent from 1992 through 2004), they still attract far more approval than does the body in which they serve. More than 80 percent of respondents thought that the incumbent would be helpful or very helpful if they brought a problem to him or her. Satisfaction with the incumbents' response to voter requests ran very high indeed; most were "very satisfied," as were friends who made similar requests. Far more voters generally agreed with the incumbent's votes than disagreed with

TABLE 5–11 Evaluations of the Incumbent's Performance and the Vote in House and Senate Elections (in Percentages)

Criterion	RESPONDING			RESPONSE		VOTE FOR INCUMBENT	
	House	Senate		House	Senate	House	Senate
General job performance	91	90	Approve	85	80	88	86
			Disapprove	15	20	12	8
District Services							
1. How good a job of keeping in touch with people	95	94	Very good	33	29	88	87
			Fairly good	46	53	80	72
			Fairly poor	12	11	41	40
			Very poor	9	7	24	21
3. Expectations about incumbent's helpfulness in solving voters' problems	91	93	Very helpful	29	35	95	90
			Somewhat helpful	53	47	67	70
			Not very helpful	14	5	29	24
			It depends	4	3	58	54
3. Level of satisfaction with response to voter-initiated contact	20	19	Very satisfied	56	55	90	90
			Somewhat satisfied	35	30	63	70
			Not very satisfied	8	9	18	40
			Not at all satisfied	11	7	13	26
4. Level of friend's satisfaction with response to voter-initiated contact	19	23	Very satisfied	57	53	88	88
			Somewhat satisfied	32	34	62	75
			Not very satisfied	5	8	57	37
			Not at all satisfied	6	5	13	14
5. Could voter recall anything special incumbent did for the district?	27	32	Yes	27	32	77	78
			No	73	68	63	64
6. General agreement or disagreement with incumbent's votes	46	56	Agreed	55	50	96	92
			Agreed, disagreed about equally	36	34	79	64
			Disagreed	9	16	16	11
7. Agreed or disagreed with vote on a particular bill	18	—	Agreed	71	—	93	—
			Disagreed	29	—	43	—
8. Which candidate would a better job on the most important problem?	26	—	Incumbent	72	—	97	—
			Challenger	28	—	11	—

Sources: The Senate data are from the pooled 1988–1992 Senate Election Studies. The House data are from the 1998 National Election Study for general job performance for Question 1; from the 1994 National Election Study for Questions 3, 4, and 5; from the 1990 National Election Study for Questions 2, 7, and 8; and from the 1988 National Election Study for Question 6. In every case, I include the most recent responses available for the particular question.

them, although most agreed with some and disagreed with others. In 1990, 72 percent of respondents thought the incumbent would do a better job dealing with what they considered to be the most important problem facing the nation, though this figure was well below the 93 percent who thought so in 1988, just two years earlier.

The significance of these positive responses is apparent from their association with the vote. On every question, the more positive the reaction to the incumbent, the more likely the respondent was to vote for him or her. The pattern is very similar for both House and Senate candidates. Naturally, respondents' assessments of incumbents on these dimensions were overlapping and interrelated, but they had a cumulative effect as well. If the positive and negative responses are summed up, the greater the number of positive responses, the more frequently the respondent reported voting for the incumbent; the greater the number of negative responses, the more inclined respondents were to vote for the challenger.

The payoffs reaped by members of both houses from attention to constituents and emphasis on their personal character and performance are also evident in voters' responses to open-ended survey questions about what they like and dislike about candidates. These responses also reveal an important shift over time in the way voters typically respond to these questions. As many as five responses are coded for each question. Their distribution by type for House incumbents, challengers, and candidates for open seats in six selected elections from 1978 to 2000 are shown in Table 5–12.

Issues pertaining to job performance, experience, and district and individual services are mentioned most frequently as qualities voters liked about incumbents. Such issues are mentioned much more rarely for nonincumbents, which is not much of a surprise. A plurality of positive comments about candidates of all kinds have to do with personal characteristics, which frequently seem, at least on the surface, empty of political content. This is probably an illusion; experimental research has shown that voters form affective evaluations of candidates based on

TABLE 5–12 Voters' Mentions of Things they Liked and Disliked about House Candidates, Selected Years, 1978–2000 (in percentages)

	YEAR							CHANGE
	1978	1984	1988	1994	1996	1998	2000	1978–2000
Things Liked about Incumbents								
Personal	39	40	31	28	31	37	32	−7
Performance/experience	19	16	12	17	18	14	17	−2
District service/attention	25	22	26	22	17	15	19	−6
Party	1	3	3	4	7	5	6	5
Ideology/policy	12	12	19	23	22	24	21	9
Group associations	5	7	9	5	5	4	5	0
Number of respondents	749	969	846	694	905	394	809	
Number of mentions	859	1,106	925	875	1,160	537	1,021	
Mentions per respondent	1.15	1.14	1.09	1.26	1.28	1.36	1.26	.11
Things Disliked about Incumbents								
Personal	40	41	32	28	23	27	37	−13
Performance/experience	15	7	6	17	10	8	10	−5
District service/attention	9	7	13	5	8	1	6	−3
Party	7	10	11	12	17	14	14	7
Ideology/policy	22	29	35	35	38	43	27	5
Group associations	6	5	4	3	3	6	6	0

	YEAR							CHANGE
	1978	1984	1988	1994	1996	1998	2000	1978–2000
Number of respondents	749	969	846	694	905	394	809	
Number of mentions	190	243	171	332	412	211	289	
Mentions per respondent	.25	.25	.20	.48	.46	.53	.36	.11
Things Liked about Challengers								
Personal	58	57	45	35	36	40	43	−15
Performance/experience	6	6	4	7	10	15	5	−1
District service/ attention	3	5	7	3	5	5	4	1
Party	4	5	8	13	13	12	17	13
Ideology/policy	27	21	26	38	34	25	24	−3
Group associations	3	5	10	3	3	4	6	3
Number of respondents	749	969	846	694	905	394	809	
Number of mentions	139	298	189	254	360	179	217	
Mentions per respondent	.19	.31	.22	.39	.40	.45	.27	.08
Things Disliked about Challengers								
Personal	44	38	53	20	22	23	29	−15
Performance/experience	7	7	3	11	12	12	12	5
District service/ attention	0	11	1	1	5	3	0	0
Party	7	11	21	23	25	39	28	21
Ideology/policy	42	32	23	42	33	18	23	−19
Group associations	1	4	0	3	3	6	8	7
Number of respondents	749	969	846	694	905	394	809	
Number of mentions	122	188	88	143	307	102	133	
Mentions per respondent	.16	.19	.09	.22	.34	.26	.16	0
Things Liked about Candidates for Open Seats								
Personal	55	55	57	35	36	44	43	−12
Performance/experience	8	9	15	14	8	6	4	−4
District service/attention	6	4	1	4	6	1	1	−5
Party	4	11	12	10	13	15	24	20
Ideology/policy	18	16	14	34	31	32	26	8
Group associations	9	6	1	3	6	1	2	27
Number of espondentsa	232	228	152	308	172	128	89	
Number of mentions	143	172	86	221	112	118	95	
Mentions per respondent	.61	.75	.56	.72	.65	.92	1.07	.46
Things Disliked about Candidates for Open Seats								
Personal	42	34	41	20	17	23	26	−16
Performance/experience	12	3	5	14	4	6	2	210
District service/ attention	3	0	2	3	2	0	0	23
Party	5	9	34	29	39	28	43	38
Ideology/policy	35	45	15	32	39	40	26	29
Group associations	3	6	3	2	0	4	4	1
Number of respondentsa	232	228	152	308	172	128	89	
Number of mentions	60	67	59	113	52	53	47	
Mentions per respondent	.26	.29	.39	.37	.30	.41	.53	.27

Note: Some columns do not sum to 100 because of rounding.

[a]Number of respondents is doubled for the Open Seat Category because they comment on two candidates.

Source: National Election Studies for years listed.

campaign information and then often forget the information but remember the affective evaluation. When later asked why they like or dislike a candidate, they give some reasons that rationalize their feeling, but they are not necessarily the reasons that led to the feelings in the first place.[45]

The reasons voters give for liking or disliking candidates depend on what is on their minds at the time they are asked, and that, in turn, is determined by whatever campaign messages have caught their attention.[46] Campaigns frame the decision between candidates differently in different years. Notice that between 1978 and the mid-1990s, the proportion of both positive and negative comments about candidates' personal characteristics, performance, and district services fell, while the proportion of comments concerning party, ideology, and policy grew. These trends, summed across all three types of House candidates, are displayed in Figure 5–9. Clearly, the content of electoral politics—at least as it is refracted through the minds of voters—has become less personal, and more explicitly political, since the 1970s. Although *personal* criteria continue to predominate among positive comments, *political* criteria now tend to predominate among negative comments. In 1978, whereas 83 percent of positive comments concerned the candidate's personal characteristics, experience, service, or performance, only 12 percent concerned party, policy, or ideology. In 2000, the respective figures were 63 percent and 31 percent. Similarly, the percentage distribution of negative comments between these categories changed from 29–64 to 57–36 in 1998 before falling back to a 47–47 tie in 2000. Notice also that party, ideology, and policy are invariably more commonly mentioned as things disliked than as things liked about candidates.

These changes in the frame have worked to the detriment of incumbents. House members thrive when voters focus on their personal virtues and services to the district and its inhabitants. They become more vulnerable when the focus

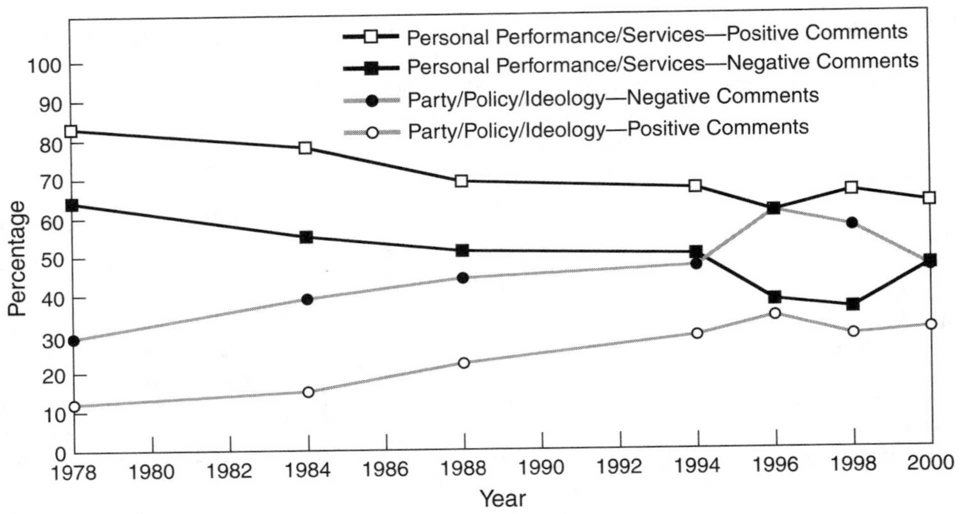

FIGURE 5–9 Criteria for Evaluating House Candidates, Selected Years, 1978–2000
Source: American National Election Studies.

is on their party, ideology, or policy stances, for these repel as well as attract voters. Notice that the incidence of negative comments about House incumbents was much higher in the 1990s (negative mentions per respondent were twice as frequent as in earlier elections). The ratio of likes to dislikes for incumbents was also much smaller in the 1990s (an average of 2.6:1, compared with more than 4.5:1 for each of the earlier election years). The changes first registered in the 1994 election were not, then, merely an artifact of the strong anti- (Democratic) incumbent sentiments prevailing that year, for they were sustained through the next two elections.

The distribution of evaluative comments about Senate candidates, displayed in Table 5–13, is not very different from the distribution of comments about House candidates during the same period. The incidence of personal comments is about the same; references to performance and experience are more common for senators, and references to services and attention are less common. References to

TABLE 5–13 Voters' Mentions of Things They Liked and Disliked about Senate Candidates, 1988–1992 (in percentages)

	INCUMBENTS	CHALLENGERS	CANDIDATES FOR OPEN SEATS
Things Liked about Candidates			
Personal	31	42	33
Performance/experience	26	13	17
District service/attention	15	4	8
Party	4	10	8
Ideology/policy	19	27	29
Group associations	5	3	3
Number of respondents	3,142	3,142	1,298
Number of mentions	3,573	1,700	1,047
Mentions per respondent	1.14	.54	.81
Things Disliked about Candidates			
Personal	34	29	28
Performance/experience	10	11	11
District service/attention	8	3	2
Party	13	27	23
Ideology/policy	29	29	34
Group associations	5	2	4
Number of respondents	3,142	3,142	1,298
Number of mentions	1,662	1,435	699
Mentions per respondent	.53	.46	.54

Note: Some columns do not sum to 100 because of rounding.

Source: Senate Election Studies, 1988, 1990, and 1992.

party, ideology, and policy are also distributed similarly. In general, it appears that the patterns for House candidates have become more like the patterns for Senate candidates in recent elections. Once again, voters do not think much differently about House and Senate candidates. They do, however, have more thoughts about Senate candidates; the number of comments per respondent is generally larger for Senate candidates, particularly nonincumbents.

Although there has been measurable decline from the remarkably high levels of regard for incumbents found in the late 1970s, survey evidence continues to confirm that all of the actions members of Congress are purported to undertake in pursuit of reelection still pay off in some way. Individual voters respond, for example, to the advertising (familiarity, contacts), credit-claiming (personal and district services), and position-taking (general and specific agreement with members' votes and issue stances) that David Mayhew identified as the characteristic means by which incumbents pursue reelection.[47] On the other hand, the home styles developed by the House members whom Fenno observed no longer seem quite so effective as they once did. Fenno found that, in the 1970s, members typically worked to project images devoid of partisan or even programmatic content, presenting themselves instead as trustworthy, hardworking people who deserve support for their experience, services, and personal qualities more than for their political beliefs or goals.[48] Partisan, policy, and ideological considerations have clearly become more prominent since Fenno did his research, and the strategy he described conspicuously failed a number of Democrats in 1994 and Republicans in 2006.

Finally, it is also apparent that the electoral strategy of discouraging the opposition before the campaign begins is effective and often effectively pursued. Even amid the upsurge in competition in the early 1990s, most incumbent House members continued to face obscure, politically inexperienced opponents whose resources fell far short of what it takes to mount a serious campaign. It is obvious from the survey data how this would ease the incumbent's task of retaining voters' support. House incumbents appear to be doubly advantaged compared with their Senate counterparts. They are more highly regarded (compare the thermometer ratings in Figures 5–7 and 5–8) and more likely to face obscure opponents (compare the figures on familiarity in Table 5–1). These are not separate phenomena. Not only do popular incumbents discourage serious opposition but, in the absence of vigorous opposition, information that might erode the incumbent's popularity seldom reaches voters.

Winning Challengers

The connection between the vigor of the challenge and the popularity of the incumbent is evident when we observe how voters respond when incumbents are seriously challenged. The most serious challenges are, by definition, the successful ones. Voters' responses to the survey questions about both challengers and incumbents in districts where the challenger won are sharply different from those in districts where the incumbent won. This is evident from the data in Table 5–14, which lists responses to selected questions about winning and losing challengers and incumbents in the 1994 House elections and 1988–1992 Senate elections.

TABLE 5–14 Voters' Responses to Winning and Losing Challengers and Incumbents (in percentages)

	1994 CHALLENGER (HOUSE)		1988–1992 CHALLENGER (SENATE)	
	Won (N = 92)	Lost (N = 609)	Won (N = 303)	Lost (N = 2,106)
Familiarity with Candidates				
Recalled challenger's name	55[a]	18	51[a]	30
Recognized challenger's name	97[a]	52	98[a]	82
Neither	3[a]	48	2[a]	18
Recalled incumbent's name	63[a]	49	59	55
Recognized incumbent's name	98	93	99	99
Neither	2	7	1	1
Contact with Challenger				
Any	90[a]	46	97[a]	84
Met personally	7	3	10	9
Received mail from challenger	54[a]	21	58	50
Read about challenger	64[a]	30	86[a]	74
Saw challenger on TV	80[a]	27	91[a]	73
Family or friends had contact with challenger	25[a]	7	—	—
Evaluations of Candidates				
Challenger's thermometer rating[b]	61[a]	52	57[a]	48
Incumbent's thermometer rating[b]	45[a]	63	51[a]	65
Likes something about challenger	49[a]	14	53[a]	29
Dislikes something about challenger	24[a]	11	38[a]	29
Likes something about incumbent	38[a]	56	45[a]	61
Dislikes something about incumbent	47[a]	26	45[a]	32

[a]Difference in responses to winning and losing challengers is significant at $p < .05$.
[b]Measured in degrees, not percentages.

Sources: National Election Study 1994 and Senate Election Studies, 1988, 1990, and 1992.

Winning challengers are much better known by voters than losing challengers are. Half the electorate can recall their names and nearly all can recognize them and rate them on the thermometer scale. Incumbents are also better known in these races—a full-scale campaign generates more information all around—but their advantage over the challenger in familiarity practically disappears. So does their advantage in voter evaluations. Not only are winning challengers better known, they are also rated significantly higher on the thermometer scale. The incumbents they have defeated are rated significantly lower, leaving the challenger with a clear advantage.

The same is true of the incidence of voters' liking or disliking something about the candidates. The data indicate that successful challengers do two things: They make voters aware of their own virtues and they make voters aware of the incumbent's shortcomings. The frequency of both positive and negative comments is significantly higher for winning than for losing challengers, but the jump in positive comments is much greater. For losing incumbents, the frequency of positive comments is significantly lower, while the incidence of negative comments is significantly higher. Again, winning challengers enjoy a clear advantage on this dimension. Finally, we observe a sharply lower job-approval rating for losing compared to winning incumbents of both houses of Congress.

When I examined the equivalent data from earlier elections for the previous editions of this book, I found that losing incumbents had *not* been rated lower than winning incumbents on most of these evaluative dimensions. Voters were just as inclined to like something about the losers as about the winners; they were also just as likely to approve of the incumbents' general job performance, to think that the incumbents would be of assistance if asked, and to remember something specific the incumbents had done for the district.[49]

In the past, incumbents did not lose by failing to elicit support on grounds of general performance and services to constituents. They lost when challengers were able to project a positive image of their own and to persuade voters that incumbents have liabilities that outweigh their usual assets. In 1994, however, voters in districts that rejected incumbents were far more critical of the incumbent's performance on all these dimensions—another indication that their circumstances had changed for the worse.

As we would expect, voters are much more likely to report contacts during a campaign with winning challengers than with losing challengers, though the differences are considerably larger for House than for Senate challengers. The most important differences for House challengers show up in contacts through the mass media: mail, newspapers, and television. In fact, winning challengers are encountered as often as incumbents via these media; compare the figures in Table 5–4. The differences that tend to remain between incumbents and winning challengers are in the modes of contact associated with holding office over a period of years: personal and staff contacts and, of course, the mail.

It is no mystery why winning challengers reached so many voters and were so much more familiar to them: They ran much better financed campaigns than did the losers. The winning House challengers in the districts covered by the survey spent more than $600,000 on average, compared to less than $140,000 for the losing challengers. The winning Senate challengers also spent significantly more money on the campaign than the losers.

In general, voters react to winning House challengers very much as they do to candidates for open seats and to most Senate challengers.[50] Competitive challengers also make it possible for more voters to make ideological and policy distinctions between House candidates, again producing contests that are more like Senate elections, in which policy issues and ideology usually play a larger role.[51] This is further evidence that differences between House and Senate elections, and among the varieties of House contests, must be attributed primarily to varying characteristics of House and Senate challengers and their campaigns. To say this is to reiterate that differences among candidacies, rather than differences in patterns of voting behavior, are what distinguish House from Senate elections.[52]

Issues in Congressional Elections

A broader implication of this argument is that congressional voters behave the way they do because politicians behave the way they do. We have seen, for example, how well voters' reactions to House incumbents fit the strategies they follow to win reelection. One explanation is that members of Congress simply understand what appeals to voters and act accordingly. However, the deviant cases (that is, challenger victories) and senatorial elections suggest that the matter is not so simple. Voters react differently, depending on the style and content (not to mention volume) of appeals that candidates make to them. Political strategies are based on assumptions about how individual voters operate; but voting behavior is constrained by the electoral context created by strategic decisions.

It is a classic case of mutual causation. As Fiorina has pointed out, converging patterns of electoral strategy and electoral behavior typical of congressional elections in the 1960s and 1970s conspired to crowd national issues out of electoral politics.[53] But this trend was not immutable. When challengers (Republicans in 1980, Democrats in 1982, Republicans in 1994, Democrats in 2006) found that they could win votes by linking the incumbent to national policy failures and unpopular leaders, national issues reentered the electoral equation.

Attitudes toward the Iraq War, for example, had a powerful influence on individual voters in 2006. To be sure, views on the war and approval of the president were strongly related to party identification ($r = 0.75$ and $r = 0.77$, respectively) and these two attitudes were tightly linked to one another ($r = 0.85$); all three of these variables had a major effect on the evaluations of incumbents' job performance. But as the equations in Table 5–15 show, with party identification,

TABLE 5–15 Opinions on the Iraq War and Voting in the 2006 Congressional Elections (Probit Equations)

House of Representatives (N=22,240)	**Coefficient**	**Standard Error**	**Effect[a]**
Intercept	.26	(.04)	
Party Identification	.60	(.02)	.45
Democrat is incumbent	.40	(.04)	.16
Republican in incumbent	−.24	(.04)	.09
Approval of incumbent's performance	.85	(.02)	.60
Approval of Bush's performance	−.64	(.04)	.25
Believe Iraq War was a mistake	.36	(.02)	.28

(continued)

TABLE 5–15 Continued

Senate (N=18,695)			
Intercept	.35	(.05)	
Party Identification	.72	(.02)	.51
Democrat is incumbent	32	(.05)	.12
Republican in incumbent	−.13	(.05)	.05
Approval of incumbent's performance	.91	(.02)	.62
Approval of Bush's performance	−.82	(.05)	.31
Believe Iraq War was a mistake	.39	(.03)	.29

Note: The dependent variable is vote for Democrat; standard errors are in parentheses. A coefficient that is at least twice its standard error is statistically significant at $p < .05$. Approval of incumbent's performance takes values if 1 (approve), 0 (unsure) and −1 (disapprove), with the signs switched for Republican incumbents; "believe Iraq War was a mistake" takes values of 1 if yes, 0 if unsure, −1 if no.

[a]Effect is the difference in the probability of voting for the Democrat between the most pro-Democratic and most pro-Republican settings on the variable, with the other variables set at their means.

Source: Cooperative Congressional Election Study.

incumbency status, and approval of the incumbent's and of the President Bush's performance all taken into account, views on the Iraq War still had a substantial effect on the probability of voting for a Democrat rather than a Republican—with estimated differences of 0.28 in House elections and 0.29 in Senate elections depending on whether the voter thought the war had been a mistake. The war's effect on the election is discussed in greater detail in the next chapter; the point here is that issues can have direct as well as indirect effects (though evaluations of the president and the incumbent) on individual voting decisions in congressional elections.

Even in the 1970s, when issues seemed to have little measurable impact on individual voting once other variables were taken into account, congressional elections had a profound impact on national policy, partly because the results were interpreted by politicians to reflect voters' preferences on policy matters. They could point to solid evidence that, in aggregate, congressional election results are highly sensitive to national issues and conditions and therefore justify such interpretations. Chapter 6 pursues a resolution to this curious paradox, along with a more complete examination of how national issues enter congressional election politics.

NOTES

1. Michael P. McDonald and Samuel Popkin, "The Myth of the Vanishing Voter," *American Political Science Review* 95 (2001): 963–974.

2. McDonald and Popkin, "The Myth of the Vanishing Voter"; Eric R.A.N. Smith and Michael Dolny, "The Mystery of Declining Turnout in American National Elections" (Paper presented at the Annual Meeting of the Western Political Science Association, Salt Lake City, March 30–April 1, 1989); Ruy Teixeira, *The Disappearing American Voter* (Washington, DC: Brookings Institution, 1992); and Warren E. Miller and J. Merrill Shanks, *The New American Voter* (Cambridge, MA: Harvard University Press, 1996), pp. 509–514.
3. Steven J. Rosenstone and John Mark Hansen, *Mobilization, Participation, and Democracy in America* (New York: Macmillan, 1993), p. 215.
4. Raymond E. Wolfinger and Steven J. Rosenstone, *Who Votes?* (New Haven, CT: Yale University Press, 1980), pp. 24–26.
5. Wolfinger and Rosenstone, *Who Votes?* p. 94.
6. Wolfinger and Rosenstone, *Who Votes?* p. 18.
7. Walter Dean Burnham, "Shifting Patterns of Congressional Voting Participation," in *The Current Crisis in American Policies*, ed. Walter Dean Burnham (New York: Oxford University Press, 1982), pp. 166–203; see also Rosenstone and Hansen, *Mobilization, Participation, and Democracy*, pp. 211–248.
8. Wolfinger and Rosenstone, *Who Votes?* pp. 104–114; see also Stephen D. Shaffer, "Policy Differences Between Voters and Non-Voters in American Elections," *Western Political Quarterly* 35 (1982): 496–510.
9. John D. Griffin and Brian Newman, "Are Voters Better Represented?" *Journal of Politics* 67 (2005): 1206–1227.
10. Teixeira, *Disappearing Voter*, pp. 86–101; and Benjamin Highton and Raymond E. Wolfinger, "The Political Implications of Higher Turnout," *British Journal of Political Science* 31 (2001): 179–223.
11. Angus Campbell, "Surge and Decline: A Study of Electoral Change," in *Elections and the Political Order*, ed. Angus Campbell et al. (New York: John Wiley, 1966), pp. 40–62.
12. Except that midterm electorates are somewhat older. See Raymond E. Wolfinger, Steven J. Rosenstone, and Richard A. McIntosh, "Presidential and Congressional Voters Compared," *American Politics Quarterly* 9 (1981): 245–255; see also Albert D. Cover, "Surge and Decline Revisited" (Paper presented at the Annual Meeting of the American Political Science Association, Chicago, September 1–4, 1983), pp. 15–17; and James E. Campbell, *The Presidential Pulse of Congressional Elections* (Lexington: University of Kentucky Press, 1993), pp. 44–62.
13. This does not mean that presidential elections do not affect congressional elections in other ways, of course; that issue is taken up in Chapter 6.
14. Gregory A. Caldeira, Samuel C. Patterson, and Gregory A. Markko, "The Mobilization of Voters in Congressional Elections," *Journal of Politics* 47 (1985): 490–509; Franklin D. Gilliam Jr., "Influences on Voter Turnout for U.S. House Elections in Non-Presidential Years," *Legislative Studies Quarterly* 10 (1985): 339–352; and Robert A. Jackson, "A Reassessment of Voter Mobilization," *Political Research Quarterly* 49 (1996): 331–349. The

anticipation of a close election itself increases turnout; see Stephen P. Nicholson and Ross A. Miller, "Prior Beliefs and Voter Turnout in the 1986 and 1988 Congressional Elections," *Political Research Quarterly* 50 (1997): 199–213.

15. See Angus Campbell, Philip E. Converse, Warren E. Miller, and Donald E. Stokes, *The American Voter* (New York: John Wiley, 1960), Chapter 6.
16. Warren E. Miller and Santa A. Traugott, *American National Election Studies Data Sourcebook 1952–1986* (Cambridge, MA: Harvard University Press, 1989), p. 81; see also Figure 5–2.
17. Morris P. Fiorina, *Retrospective Voting in American National Elections* (New Haven, CT: Yale University Press, 1981).
18. Samuel L. Popkin, John W. Gorman, Charles Philips, and Jeffrey A. Smith, "Comment: What Have You Done for Me Lately? Toward an Investment Theory of Voting," *American Political Science Review* 70 (1976): 779–805.
19. This figure includes independents who lean toward one party or the other as partisans; excluding leaners, the Democratic advantage falls from 41–23 to 35–31 from 1980 to 1994.
20. This change was the extension of a long-term trend that has seen the Republicans grow from less than 20 percent of the southern electorate in the 1950s to a majority after 1998; see Gary C. Jacobson, "Party Polarization in National Politics: The Electoral Connection," in *Polarized Politics: Congress and the President in a Partisan Era*, ed. Jon R. Bond and Richard Fleisher (Washington, DC: Congressional Quarterly Press, 2000), p. 16.
21. Alan I. Abramowitz, "The End of the Democratic Era? 1994 and the Future of Congressional Election Research," *Political Research Quarterly* 48 (1995): 873–889; and Gary C. Jacobson, "Terror, Terrain, and Turnout: Explaining the 2002 Midterm Elections," *Political Science Quarterly* 118 (Spring 2003): 12–16.
22. The sensitivity of aggregate distribution of party identification to political conditions is shown clearly in Michael B. MacKuen, Robert S. Erikson, and James A. Stimson, "Macropartisanship," *American Political Science Review* 83 (1989): 1125–1142.
23. Stephen Ansolabehere, *Cooperative Congressional Election Study—Common Content*. Palo Alto, CA: Polimetrix, Inc, 2006.
24. Robert B. Eubank, "Incumbent Effects on Individual Level Voting Behavior in Congressional Elections: A Decade of Exaggeration," *Journal of Politics* 47 (1985): 964–966; Gary C. Jacobson and Douglas Rivers, "Explaining the Overreport of Votes for Incumbents in National Election Studies" (Paper presented at the Annual Meeting of the Western Political Science Association, Pasadena, California, March 18–20, 1993); and Janet Box-Steffensmeier, Gary C. Jacobson, and J. Tobin Grant, "Question Wording and the House Vote Choice: Some Experimental Evidence," *Public Opinion Quarterly* 64 (Fall 2000): 257–270.
25. Albert D. Cover, "One Good Term Deserves Another: The Advantage of Incumbency in Congressional Elections," *American Journal of Political Science* 21 (1977): 532.

26. Gary C. Jacobson, *Money in Congressional Elections* (New Haven, CT: Yale University Press, 1980), p. 16.
27. The reasons for this decline remain obscure; see Gary C. Jacobson, "The Declining Salience of U.S. House Candidates, 1958–1994" (Paper presented at the Annual Meeting of the American Political Science Association, Boston, September 3–6, 1998).
28. John A. Ferejohn, "On the Decline of the Competition in Congressional Elections," *American Political Science Review* 71 (1977): 171; and Candice J. Nelson, "The Effects of Incumbency on Voting in Congressional Elections, 1964–1974," *Political Science Quarterly* 93 (1978/1979): 665–678.
29. Jacobson, *Money*, pp. 19–20; also Alan I. Abramowitz, "Name Familiarity, Reputation, and the Incumbency Effect in a Congressional Election," *Western Political Quarterly* 28 (1975): 668–684.
30. Thomas E. Mann, *Unsafe at Any Margin: Interpreting Congressional Elections* (Washington, DC. American Enterprise Institute for Public Policy Research, 1978), pp. 30–34.
31. For consideration of the difficulties of making comparisons over time using available data, see Morris P. Fiorina, "Congressmen and Their Constituents: 1958 and 1978," in *The United States Congress*, ed. Dennis Hale (New York: Transaction Books, 1983).
32. John R. Alford and John R. Hibbing, "The Disparate Electoral Security of House and Senate Incumbents" (Paper presented at the Annual Meeting of the American Political Science Association, Atlanta, August 31–September 3, 1989), p. 14.
33. The results are typical of every election for which we have data; see the earlier editions of this book.
34. Donald E. Stokes and Warren E. Miller, "Party Government and the Saliency of Congress," *Elections and the Political Order*, ed. Angus Campbell, et al. (New York: John Wiley, 1966), p. 205. Contrary findings are reported by Abramowitz, "Name Familiarity," pp. 673–683, and Jacobson, *Money*, p. 16.
35. Richard F. Fenno Jr., *The United States Senate: A Bicameral Perspective* (Washington, DC: American Enterprise Institute for Public Policy Research, 1983), p. 11.
36. Jonathan S. Krasno, *Challengers, Competition, and Reelection: Comparing Senate and House Elections* (New Haven, CT: Yale University Press, 1994), p. 47.
37. Fenno, *Senate*, pp. 18–19; the Senate Election Study confirms this candidate's view that voters have very similar expectations of senators and representatives; see Krasno, *Comparing Senate and House Elections*, pp. 17–35.
38. Alan I. Abramowitz, "A Comparison of Voting for U.S. Senator and Representative in 1978," *American Political Science Review* 74 (1980): 639.
39. For a comparison of probit and ordinary least-squares regression, see John Aldrich and Charles Cnudde, "Probing the Bounds of Conventional Wisdom: A Comparison of Regression, Probit, and Discriminant Analysis," *American Journal of Political Science* 19 (1975): 571–608.

40. *Personal contact* is defined as having met the candidate, attended a meeting at which he spoke, or having had contact with the candidate's staff; *mail contact* is having received something in the mail from the candidate; *mass media contact* is having learned about the candidate by reading newspapers and magazines, listening to the radio, or watching television; *indirect contact* is reporting that a family member or acquaintance has had some kind of contact with the candidate.
41. Data are from the 1994 National Election Study because it is the most recent survey that contains the contact questions; comparable analysis of earlier surveys containing these questions produces very similar results; see the second and third editions of this book.
42. For additional evidence on this point, see Gary C. Jacobson, "Enough Is Too Much: Money and Competition in House Elections, 1972–1984," in *Elections in America*, ed. Kay L. Schlozman (Boston: Allyn & Unwin, 1987), pp. 192–195; and Gary C. Jacobson, "The Effects of Campaign Spending in Congressional Elections," *American Political Science Review* 72 (1978): 480–485.
43. Campaign spending rises with a state's population but at a diminishing rate, so that the more populous the state, the lower the per-voter expenditures.
44. Abramowitz, "Voting for U.S. Senator and Representative," p. 636; Thomas E. Mann and Raymond E. Wolfinger, "Candidates and Parties in Congressional Elections," *American Political Science Review* 74 (1980): 622–629; Barbara Hinckley, "House Re-elections and Senate Defeats: The Role of the Challenger," *British Journal of Political Science* 10 (1980): 441–460.
45. Milton Lodge and Marco R. Steenbergen, with Shawn Brau, "The Responsive Voter: Campaign Information and the Dynamics of Candidate Evaluation," *American Political Science Review* 89 (1995): 309–326.
46. John Zaller and Stanley Feldman, "A Theory of Survey Response," *American Journal of Political Science* 36 (1992): 586–589.
47. David R. Mayhew, *Congress: The Electoral Connection* (New Haven, CT: Yale University Press, 1974), pp. 49–68.
48. Richard F. Fenno Jr., *Home Style: House Members in Their Districts* (Boston: Little, Brown, 1978), Chapters 3 and 4.
49. See the first edition of this book, pp. 117–118.
50. See Tables 5–1, 5–2, and 5–3.
51. Alan I. Abramowitz, "Choices and Echoes in the 1978 U.S. Senate Elections: A Research Note," *American Journal of Political Science* 25 (February 1981): 112–118; Gerald C. Wright Jr., and Michael Berkman, "Candidates and Policy in U.S. Senate Elections," *American Political Science Review* 80 (1986): 567–588; and Gary C. Jacobson, "Reagan, Reaganomics, and Strategic Politics in 1982: A Test of Alternative Theories of Midterm Congressional Elections" (Paper presented at the Annual Meeting of the American Political Science Association, Chicago, September 1–4, 1983), pp. 19–22.
52. Barbara Hinckley, "House Re-elections and Senate Defeats: The Role of the Challenger," *American Political Science Review* 74 (1980): 458–469; Alford and Hibbing, "Electoral Security," pp. 18–23; Peverill Squire, "Challengers in

Senate Elections," *Legislative Studies Quarterly* 14 (1989): 544; Krasno, *Challengers, Competition and Reelection*, pp. 154–170; and Paul Gronke, *Settings, Institutions, Campaigns, and the Vote* (Ann Arbor: University of Michigan Press, 2000).

53. Morris P. Fiorina, *Congress: Keystone of the Washington Establishment*, 2nd ed. (New Haven, CT: Yale University Press, 1989), Part I.

Chapter 6

NATIONAL POLITICS AND CONGRESSIONAL ELECTIONS

In 1995, the first Republican-controlled Congress elected in more than forty years began a sustained effort to dismantle programs and overturn policies that had accumulated under decades of Democratic rule. Their targets included welfare programs for poor families, regulations protecting the environment and consumers, and Medicare spending. Spending cuts were justified by the goal of balancing a federal budget that had been running large deficits since the early 1980s. At the same time, Republican leaders pushed for large tax cuts skewed toward upper-income families. This combination of policies would redistribute income from poorer to wealthier citizens, extending a trend initiated in 1981 under the Reagan administration. Many of the programs scheduled for elimination had first seen the light of day in the explosion of social welfare legislation that followed the 1964 elections. Others had been enacted in the 1930s as part of the New Deal, which was the last time such a radical shift in national policy had been attempted.

Each of these major changes in the direction of national policy was the product of the preceding congressional election. The New Deal, the Great Society, and the Republicans' conservative counterattack on the welfare state were all made possible by a major shift of congressional seats from one party to the other. The New Deal happened because the 1932 election gave Franklin D. Roosevelt large and cooperative majorities in Congress, with reinforcements in 1934 and 1936. Lyndon Johnson's War on Poverty went into high gear when Democrats increased their share of House seats from 59 to 68 percent in 1964; it was stopped cold when Democratic representation dropped back to 57 percent following the 1966 elections. The Reagan administration's early victories on tax and welfare spending reduction were possible because the 1980 election had given Republicans control of the Senate for the first time since 1952 and thirty-three additional House seats, raising their share in that body from 36 to 44 percent; their much broader assault on welfare and regulatory programs had to wait, however, until 1994, when they won majorities in both houses.

These pivotal election years stand out in Figures 6–1 and 6–2, which display the net Republican or Democratic seat advantage in the House and Senate following each post–Civil War election. The charts underline the crucial importance of congressional elections as collective as well as individual events. When the wins and losses in all the separate contests are added up, the sums determine

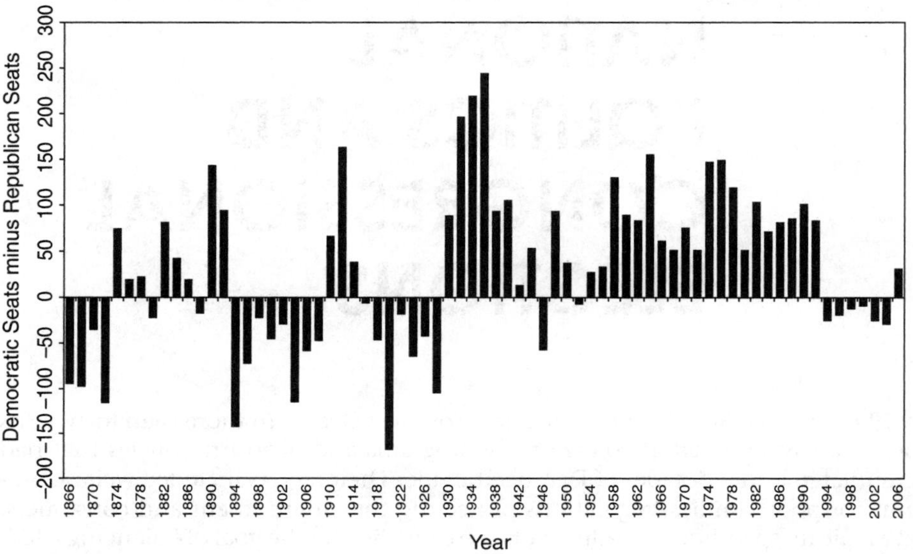

FIGURE 6–1 House Margins, 1866–2006

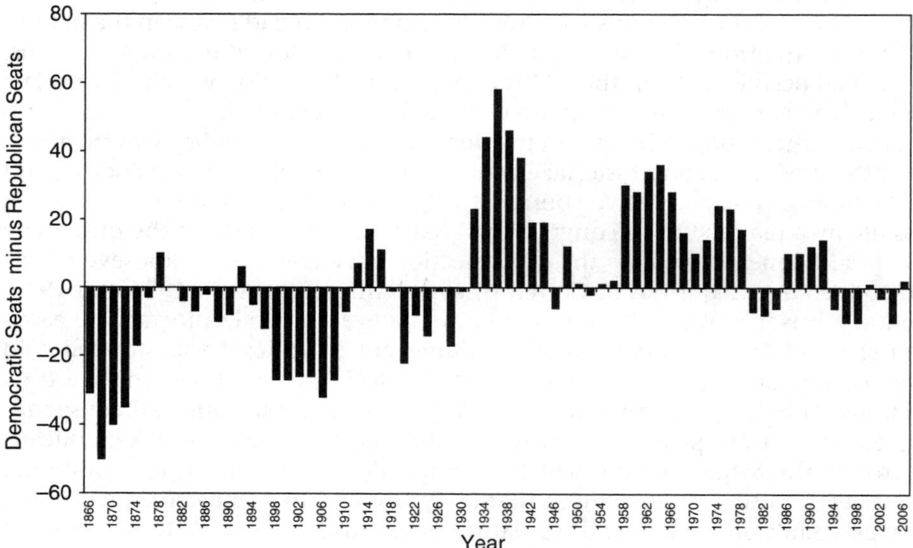

FIGURE 6–2 Senate Margins, 1866–2006

which party controls the House and Senate and with what size majority. The aggregate outcome also gives everyone in national politics at least a speculative sense of what is on the public's mind. The raw numbers and their interpretation establish the opportunities and constraints that guide the direction of national policy for at least the next two years and often a good deal longer.[1] The electoral politics of Congress may center largely on individual candidates and campaigns, but it is the collective results of congressional elections that shape the course of national politics.

This is true not only in a specific and practical sense—take, for example, the Republican gains in 1994 leading directly to reduced federal spending on social welfare programs—but also more fundamentally. The possibility of responsible representative government in the United States depends on the capacity of congressional elections to influence the course of public policy. This, in turn, is contingent on aggregate election results reflecting, in a meaningful way, the basic concerns of the public. How the millions of individual voting decisions in hundreds of distinctly individual contests combine to produce intelligible election results is the subject of this chapter.

Political Interpretations of Congressional Elections

Before the tools of survey research came into common use, politicians and political analysts had little problem interpreting aggregate congressional election results. It was widely believed that economic conditions (prosperity or recession, unemployment, or price levels) and presidential politics (the popular standing of presidents or presidential candidates—influenced by economic conditions and policy triumphs or blunders) shaped the electoral prospects of congressional candidates. Thus, it was possible to look at sets of data such as those in Figures 6–1 and 6–2 or Table 6–1 and, with a little knowledge of contemporary events, make sense of them.

Republicans triumphed in 1946 because of economic dislocation and inflation brought on by postwar demobilization; Democrats made a comeback in 1948 behind Truman's spirited campaign in defense of the New Deal and because of economic problems—strikes, rising prices—that could be blamed on the Republican Congress. Public dissatisfaction with the second Truman administration was clearly expressed in the 1950 and 1952 elections. A major recession took its toll on Republicans in 1958. The Goldwater debacle lengthened Johnson's coattails in 1964 and the Republicans came back in 1966, as discontent with Johnson's policies spread.

Republican congressional candidates were punished in 1974 for Nixon's Watergate sins and a recessionary economy. Inflation, Iran, and incompetence at the top of the ticket spelled disaster for Democrats in 1980, but they rebounded in 1982 on the strength of a recession that produced the highest unemployment levels since the Great Depression. In elections from 1984 through 1988, voters registered relative satisfaction with the status quo in both congressional and presidential elections; when they became disgusted with both parties in 1990, the administration's party naturally suffered more. With the end of divided government in 1992, popular discontent was focused fully on the Democrats as the

TABLE 6–1 Net Party Shift in House and Senate Seats, 1946–2006

Year	House	Senate	President's Party[b]
1946	56 R[a]	13 R	D[a]
1948	75 D	9 D	D
1950	28 R	5 R	D
1952	22 R	1 R	R
1954	19 D	2 D	R
1956	2 D	1 D	R
1958	49 D	15 D	R
1960	22 R	2 R	D
1962	1 R	3 D	D
1964	37 D	1 D	D
1966	47 R	4 R	D
1968	5 R	6 R	R
1970	12 D	2 R	R
1972	12 R	2 D	R
1974	49 D	4 D	R
1976	1 D	0	D
1978	15 R	3 R	D
1980	33 R	12 R	R
1982	26 D	1 R	R
1984	14 R	2 D	R
1986	5 D	8 D	R
1988	2 D	0	R
1990	8 D	1 D	R
1992	10 R	0	D
1994	54 R	8 R	D
1996	3 D	2 R	D
1998	4 D	0	D
2000	1 D	5 D	R
2002	8 R	1 R	R
2004	3 R	4 R	R
2006	31 D	6D	R

Note: Listed is the change in the number of seats won compared to the previous general election, not the number gained on election day; the two numbers sometimes differ because of changes created by special elections and party switches between elections.

[a]D indicates Democrats, R indicates Republicans.

[b]Denotes party of winning candidate in presidential election years.

Sources: Norman J. Ornstein, Thomas E. Mann, Michael J. Malbin, *Vital Statistics on Congress 1997–1998* (Washington, D.C.: Congressional Quarterly, 1998), Table 2.3; data for 1998–2006 compiled by author.

party in power, so the Republicans swept to a historic victory in 1994. Republican overreaching on the budget and on Bill Clinton's impeachment reduced their House majorities in 1996 and 1998. In 2002, George W. Bush's popularity as national leader in the war on terrorism helped Republicans pick up House seats and take control of the Senate—but in 2006, his low approval ratings, largely generated by the increasingly unpopular Iraq War, cost Republicans their majorities in both chambers. Plainly, it is no great challenge to interpret congressional elections as national events controlled by national political conditions. Most political professionals do so routinely.

Models of Aggregate Congressional Election Results

Social scientists have examined the impact of national forces on congressional elections rather more systematically without upsetting the conventional wisdom. Numerous studies have investigated the effects of national economic conditions, variously measured, on the national division of the two-party vote for representative.[2] Although the variety of approaches taken to the question (different economic indices, time periods, and control variables) has engendered important disagreements, most specifications produce the expected systematic relationship between the state of the economy and aggregate congressional election outcomes: The better the economy is performing, the better the congressional candidates of the president's party do on election day.

Edward Tufte took this work a step further by adding a measure of the popular standing of the president to the analysis. Tufte began with the familiar fact of political life that the president's party nearly always loses seats in midterm elections; the figures in Table 6–1 attest to it. The president's party lost House seats in every postwar midterm election until 1998 and 2002, dropping an average of twenty-four. And more often than not, the party of the winning presidential candidate picks up House seats in a presidential election year (the postwar average is twelve). The theory of surge and decline, outlined in Chapter 5, was an attempt to explain these phenomena as part of a single system. Investigations of individual voting behavior produced little support for the theory. The theory also failed to explain the size of the midterm swing affecting the president's party, which has varied from a gain of seven to a loss of fifty-six House seats in postwar elections.

Tufte showed that the division of the congressional vote in midterm elections was strongly and systematically related to simple measures of the economy (change in real income per capita over the election year) and presidential approval (percentage approving the president's performance in office in the Gallup Poll closest to election day). He also applied his model to presidential election years, using relative candidate evaluations in place of presidential approval ratings.[3]

The regression equation reported in Table 6–2 is an updated variant of Tufte's model. The dependent variable is the change in the percentage of House seats held by the president's party before and after the election. I include a control for the party's "exposure"—the share of seats it holds above or below its average over the previous eight elections—because the more seats a party holds, the more of its seats are vulnerable to the opposition.[4] The exposure figure has been adjusted to

TABLE 6–2 The Effects of National Conditions on U.S. House Elections, 1946–2006

Variable	Coefficient	Standard Error
Intercept	−17.34	3.14
Exposure	−.75	.11
Change in real income per capita (%)	1.29	.31
Presidential approval (%)	.25	.06
Adjusted R^2	.70	
Durbin-Watson Statistic	2.26	
Number of Cases	31	

Note: The dependent variable is the percentage of seats gained or lost by the president's party; see the text for a description of the independent variables; standard errors are in parentheses; all coefficients are statistically significant at $p < .01$, two-tailed test.

incorporate the sharp and sustained swing favoring the Republicans that followed the redistricting for the 1990s.[5] National conditions are represented by the change in real income per capita in the year preceding the election and the president's level of popular approval in the last Gallup Poll taken prior to the election.

The equation explains 70 percent of the variance in the share of House seats a party wins or loses, and all of the other variables work as expected. According to the coefficients, the difference between the highest and lowest values of presidential approval (74 percent and 32 percent) translates into a difference of forty-six House seats, and the difference between the highest and lowest values of income change (6.0 percent and –2.6 percent) translates into a difference of forty-eight House seats. Of course, the equation also leaves 30 percent of the variance unexplained, a fact of considerable importance when we turn our attention to specific election years later in this chapter.

The results of this and other analyses leave little doubt that economic conditions and presidential performance ratings affect aggregate House election results. Both also have a significant impact on aggregate Senate election results, although there is, not surprisingly, more unexplained variance on the Senate side.[6] Furthermore, congressional electorates behave rationally; the party of the administration is held responsible for the performance of its president and of the economy. Tufte recognized that "many different models of the underlying electorate are consistent with electoral outcomes that are collectively rational,"[7] but less-cautious scholars have interpreted collective rationality to be a demonstration of equivalent individual rationality. The problem with this interpretation is that it finds only modest support in survey studies of individual voters.

The strong connection between aggregate economic variables and aggregate election results naturally inspired scholars to investigate the effects of economic conditions on individual voting behavior. At least four different kinds of economic variables might influence the vote choice: personal financial experiences and expectations, perceptions of general economic conditions, evaluations of the government's economic performance, and party images on economic policies.[8]

Most aggregate-level studies are based on the assumption that personal financial well-being is the primary criterion used by voters: "Rational voters are concerned with their real income and wealth."[9] The aggregate economic variables (change in real per capita income, percentage unemployed) were chosen because they represent direct economic effects on individual citizens. Survey studies have turned up very little evidence that personal finances directly influence individual congressional voters, however. The occasional effects that do appear in some election years are generally indirect and much too weak to account for the robust relationships that Tufte and others have found between national measures of economic conditions and election outcomes.

Survey research does produce some evidence suggesting that economic conditions may influence the vote in one or more of the other ways. But the reported effects are almost always modest and explain little additional variance in the vote once other variables (of the kind examined in the previous chapter) are taken into account. Part of the reason is that views of the economy are shaped by partisanship: Voters identifying with the president's party tend to be more positive about it than those of the opposing party.[10] But whatever the reason, the behavior of individual voters does not conform to any straightforward model of economic rationality.[11]

Survey findings about the electoral effects of voter evaluations of presidents are somewhat more consistent with the aggregate evidence. Samuel Kernell found that in midterm elections from 1946 through 1966, approval or disapproval of the president's performance was correlated with congressional preferences (with party identification controlled) and that disapproval had a greater effect than approval.[12] Other evidence from elections in the 1960s also showed voter evaluation of presidents to influence congressional voting.[13] Studies from the 1970s reported contrary findings; evaluations of Ford (in 1974) and Carter (in 1978) made little difference. Since then, however, midterm assessments of presidents from Reagan to George W. Bush have had a substantial influence on the individual House vote, one that was especially large in 2006 (see Figure 6–10 later in this chapter).[14]

Various attempts have been made to account for the often feeble connection between the economic variables and individual congressional voting without abandoning the original premise of individual economic rationality; none has been fully convincing.[15] Fiorina has made the strongest empirical case, arguing that personal economic experiences "affect more general economic performance judgments, both types of judgments feed into evaluations of presidential performance, and more general judgments, at least, contribute to modifications of party identification,"[16] which is known to be strongly related to the vote. Even granting this complex process, the effects are a good deal weaker than the strong aggregate relationships would predict.

Presidential Coattails

The impact of voters' feelings about the presidential candidates is puzzling in a different way. Customarily, this has been discussed in terms of *coattail effects*. The term reflects the notion that successful candidates at the top of the ticket—in national elections, the winning presidential candidate—pull some of their party's candidates into office along with them, riding, as it were, on their coattails. Just how this works is a matter of considerable debate. Perhaps the presidential choice has a direct influence on the congressional choice; people prefer to vote for candidates sharing their presidential favorite's party affiliation. Or perhaps both choices are influenced by the same set of considerations—for example, disgust with the failures of the current administration or delight with a party platform to which both candidates are committed—and so move in the same direction. It is even conceivable that, on occasion, support for the head of the ticket spills over from support for candidates for lower offices.

Regardless of the mechanisms in operation, if a large number of fellow partisans are swept into office along with the president, political interpretation usually favors the traditional view embodied in the term itself. A presidential winner whose success is not shared by other candidates of his party is presumed to have no coattails.

The question of whether the president has strong coattails is of more than academic interest. Sheer numbers matter; administrations get more of what they want from Congress the more seats their party holds in the House and Senate. Roosevelt's New Deal, Johnson's Great Society, and Reagan's budget victories all depended on large shifts in party seats. George H. W. Bush, in contrast, had no choice but to compromise with a strongly Democratic Congress from the beginning of his presidency, and Bill Clinton was left in a similar position when his party failed to regain its congressional majorities in 1996. Aside from sheer numbers, members of Congress who believe that they were elected with the help of the president are more likely to cooperate with him, if not from simple gratitude, then from a sense of shared fate: They will prosper politically as the administration prospers. Those convinced that they were elected on their own, or despite the top of the ticket, have less reason to cooperate.

Finally, a partisan sweep that extends to Congress also sends a potent message to the incumbents who survived (and to other Washington politicians). If the electorate seems to have spoken clearly and decisively, political wisdom dictates that its message be heeded, at least for a while.[17] The resistance of recalcitrant senior Democrats to the Kennedy–Johnson programs collapsed for a time after the 1964 election. Republican gains in 1980 transformed more than a few congressional Democrats into born-again tax- and budget-cutters. The 1988 congressional election returns, in contrast, left Democrats under little pressure to follow Bush's lead, and the 1992 elections, in which the Democrats lost a net ten House seats, were scarcely a ringing endorsement of Bill Clinton's plans. Similarly, George W. Bush's narrow victories in 2000 and 2004 brought little change to the House (and were accompanied by inconsistent results in the Senate—a five-seat Democratic gain in 2000, a four-seat Republican gain in 2004) and left congressional Democrats with little reason to worry about opposing the president's policies.

How such considerations affect congressional politics is discussed more thoroughly in Chapter 7. The political significance of coattail effects (or, more precisely, the perception of them) is mentioned here because most of the aggregate evidence available indicates that coattails became increasingly attenuated between the 1950s and the 1980s. Both *cross-sectional* (relating the presidential and congressional vote at the district level) and *time-series* (relating the national presidential and congressional vote over a series of election years) studies show a diminishing connection between presidential and congressional voting over that period.[18] Evidence from elections since 1992, however, indicates that the linkage has tightened once again.

One perspective on the link between presidential and congressional elections is provided by the data in Figure 6–3, which displays the percentage of House districts that delivered split verdicts—majorities for the presidential candidate of one party, and for the House candidate of the other party—in presidential election years from 1920 through 2004. The increase between 1952 and 1972 is striking. The proportion of split results is naturally larger in years with presidential landslides—it reached peaks of 44 and 45 percent, respectively, in 1972 and 1984—but from the 1960s through the 1980s, it exceeded 30 percent even in years with comparatively close presidential contests. In the 1990s, however, the proportion of split districts fell off, and in 2004 it dropped to 14 percent, the lowest in 60 years. Clinton and George W. Bush may not have had lengthier coattails than their recent predecessors (see Table 6–1), but partisan consistency at the House district level has risen sharply over the past two decades.

Further evidence is presented in Figures 6–4 and 6–5, which show changes in the simple correlation between the district-level House and presidential vote and the incidence of ticket-splitting reported in the National Election Study (NES) surveys, from 1952 through 2004. The correlation between the House and presidential vote, which stood at 0.86 in 1952, declined to as low as 0.52 in 1972 before rising again, reaching 0.84 in 2004. This is not merely a consequence of realignment in the South—where conservative voters now vote Republican at the congressional level as they have been doing at the presidential level since Barry Goldwater's candidacy in 1964—for the same trends appear if the analysis is

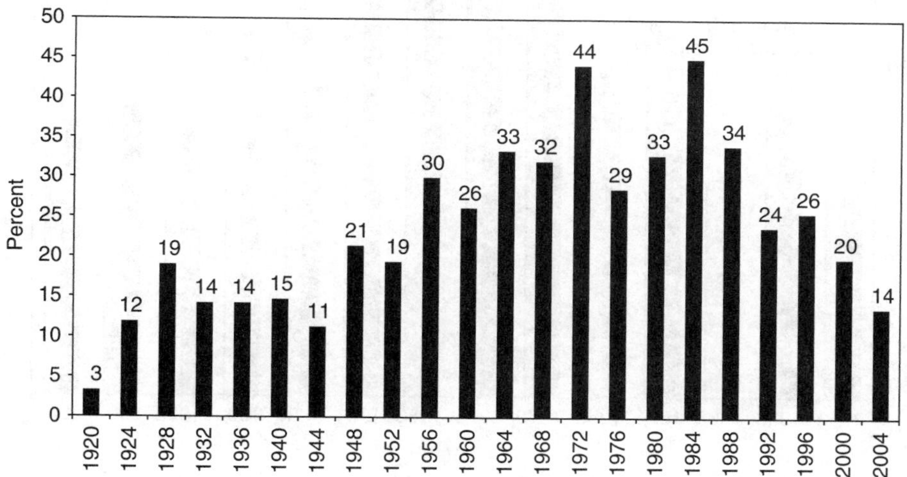

FIGURE 6–3 Proportion of Districts with Split Results in Presidential and House Elections, 1920–2004

Note: Prior to 1952, percentages are based on from 344 to 364 districts rather than the full 435 because of missing data.

Source: Norman J. Ornstein, Thomas E. Mann, Michael J. Malbin, *Vital Statistics on Congress 1997–1998* (Washington D.C.: Congressional Quarterly, 1997), Table 2–16; 2000 and 2004 data compiled by author.

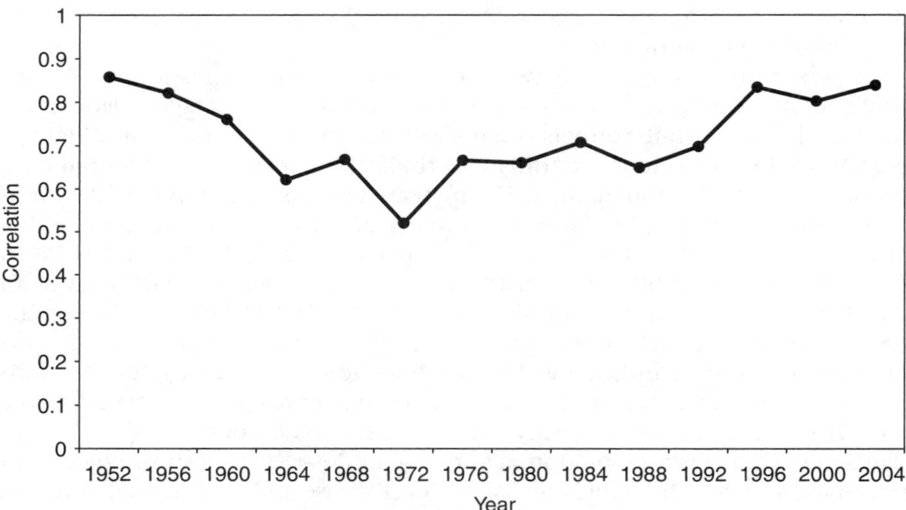

FIGURE 6–4 Correlations Between District-Level House and Presidential Voting, 1952–2004
Source: Compiled by author.

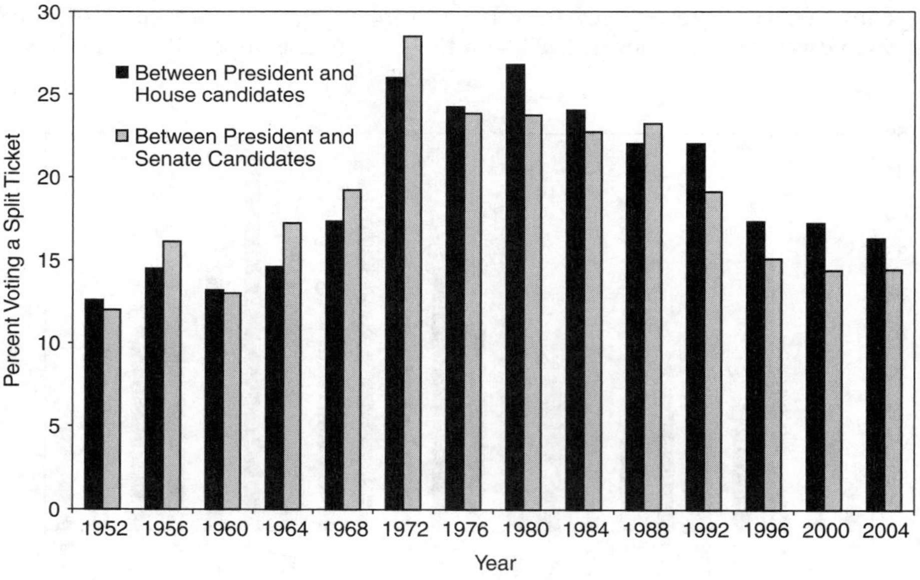

FIGURE 6–5 Ticket Splitting in National Elections, 1952–2004
Source: American National Election Studies, 1952–2004.

confined to nonsouthern districts.[19] The incidence of major party ticket-splitting—voting for a Democrat for one office, a Republican for the other—shows the same pattern inverted, with a sharp rise in ticket-splitting from the 1950s to the 1970s, followed by a decline that ended in 2004 at the lowest levels in three decades.[20]

Because the extent to which presidential and congressional election results coincide has such profound implications for national politics, it is worth considering some of the individual-level evidence in more detail. It suggests that even in elections with a high incidence of split results and split-ticket voting, presidential coattails continue to exert a pull. Still, coattail contributions to congressional victories for the president's party have been erratic and usually modest in recent elections. Understanding the reason for this will tell us something important about how national political forces influence congressional elections.

A simple test for the presence of coattail effects of some kind can be made by adding a variable representing the presidential vote to the full probit model (Equation 3) presented in Table 5–9. The results, reported and interpreted in Table 6–3, indicate that the presidential vote choice in 2000 had a large and statistically significant impact on the probability that a voter would vote for the Democratic

TABLE 6–3 Coattail Effects (Probit Estimates)

	PROBABILITY OF VOTING FOR DEMOCRATIC HOUSE CANDIDATE						
	VOTED FOR		DIFFERENCE IN PROBABILITY				
Initial Probability	Bush	Gore	2000	1996	1992	1988	1984
.10	.06	.17	.11	.17	.09	.09	.10
.25	.15	.38	.23	.32	.18	.19	.19
.40	.26	.56	.30	.39	.23	.24	.24
.50	.35	.65	.30	.40	.24	.25	.25
.60	.44	.74	.30	.39	.23	.24	.24
.75	.62	.85	.23	.32	.18	.19	.19
.90	.83	.94	.11	.17	.09	.09	.10

PROBIT EQUATION (2000)	COEFFICIENT	STANDARD ERROR
Intercept	–.53	.26
Party identification	.39	.10
Democrat is incumbent	.05	.25
Republican is incumbent	–.38	.23
Familiarity with Democrat	1.38	.26
Familiarity with Republican	–1.22	.25
Likes something about Democrat	1.05	.17
Dislikes something about Democrat	–.71	.21
Likes something about Republican	–1.17	.18
Dislikes something about Republican	.65	.21
Presidential vote	1.26	.20
Precentage correctly predicted (null=50.9)	91.3	

Source: National Election Study, 2000.

House candidate, even with party identification and the candidate-oriented variables controlled. The first column lists a range of hypothetical probabilities of voting for the Democrat (assumed to be based on the party and candidate variables) unaffected by the presidential vote. The second column shows how these probabilities change if the voter voted for Bush, the third column, for Gore. For example, a voter who otherwise (on the basis of the other variables) had a 0.5 probability of voting for the Democrat would have a 0.65 probability of doing so if he voted for Gore but only a 0.35 probability if he voted for Bush.

The difference in the probability of voting Democratic contingent on the choice between Bush and Gore is listed in the fourth column. It is characteristic of probit coefficients that their effects are largest in the middle range of probabilities. The final four columns provide the same estimates, computed from the equivalent equations for 1984, 1988, 1992, and 1996.[21] The estimated effects are virtually identical across the first three elections and they become noticeably larger in 1996 and then shrink back in 2000. The full set of variables is not available for 2004, but the closest feasible approximation of the equation for that year suggests a coattail effect even larger than in 1996.[22]

Yet another way to check for coattail effects is to observe the consequences of partisan defection in the presidential campaign on the congressional vote. The pattern for the 1952 through 2004 elections is shown in Figures 6–6 and 6–7. Clearly, party identifiers who voted for the other party's presidential candidate were a good deal more likely also to vote for the other party's House or Senate candidate as well in every election year. On average, more than 50 percent of the presidential defectors also defected in both House and Senate elections, compared with only about 13 percent of the presidential loyalists.

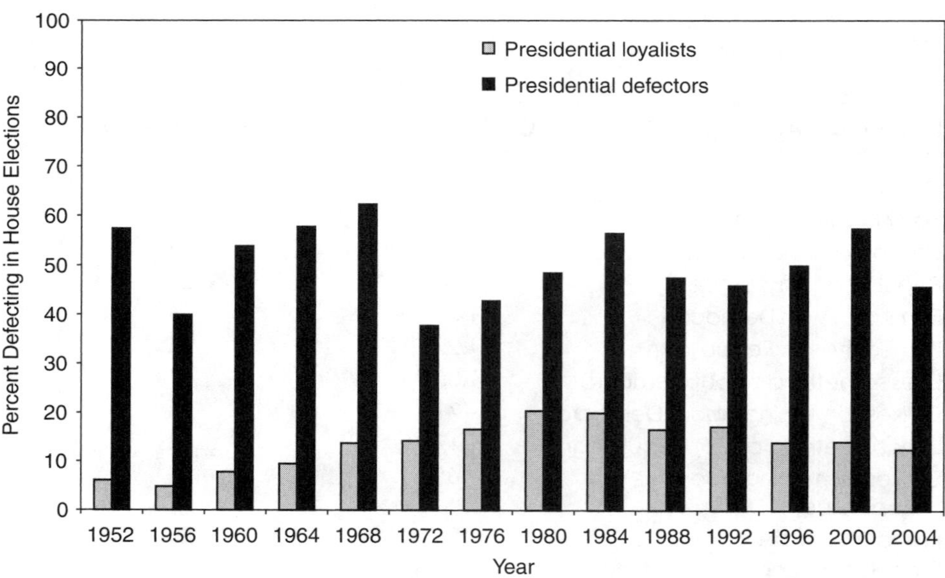

FIGURE 6–6 Partisan Defections to House Candidates, by Presidential Loyalty, 1952–2004

Source: American National Election Studies.

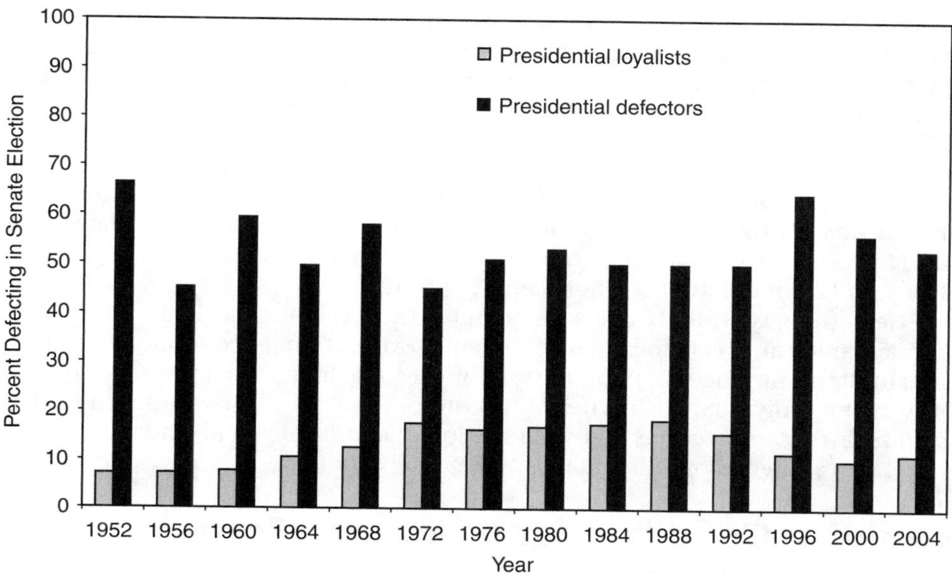

FIGURE 6–7 Partisan Defections to Senate Candidates, by Presidential Loyalty, 1952–2004

Source: American National Election Studies.

The aggregate effects of presidential coattails depend on how defection rates differ between the two parties' identifiers. For example, about 80 percent of the defectors in 1980, and 85 percent in 1984, were Democrats voting for Reagan, so this pattern must have helped Republican congressional candidates. A simple calculation shows that, had presidential defections been divided equally while other things remained the same, the reported vote for House Republicans would have been 3 percentage points lower in 1980 and 5 percentage points lower in 1984; the Republican vote for senator would have been 2 points lower in 1980 and 4 points lower in 1984. Presidential defections were more evenly balanced in 1988—about 60 percent were Democrats voting for Bush—so the net effect is smaller, adding about 1 percentage point to the Republican vote in both House and Senate contests. In 1992, 2000, and 2004, defections were so evenly balanced that neither party enjoyed any net benefit, but in 1996 the balance finally favored Democrats, adding about 2.6 percentage points to their overall House and Senate totals.

Plainly, nontrivial coattail effects have been discernible in recent elections. The effects were evidently stronger in 1984 than in the other years under examination. This is a curious result because the aggregate results imply that Reagan's coattails were considerably shorter in 1984 than they were in 1980. In 1980, Republicans picked up thirty House and twelve Senate seats; in 1984, they picked up only fourteen House seats while losing two Senate seats. Despite Reagan's huge landslide and a sharp increase in the proportion of voters calling themselves Republicans, Republicans held ten fewer House seats after 1984 than they did after 1980. Similarly, Clinton's victory in 1996 brought the Democrats only meager gains in the House, and Democrats actually lost Senate seats (see Table 6–1).

The elections of 1984 and 1996 are not the first for which aggregate and survey evidence of coattail effects conflict. In 1972, Richard Nixon won more than 60 percent of the vote, yet Republicans gained only twelve House seats and lost two Senate seats. Nonetheless, coattail effects were detectable at the level of individual voters. Just as in more recent elections, voters in 1972 who defected to the other party's presidential candidate were significantly more likely to defect to the other party's House candidates as well.[23] Almost 90 percent of the defectors were Democrats voting for Nixon; again, it is possible to calculate that, had defections been divided evenly and the other patterns remained stable, the Republican House vote would have been 5 percentage points lower.

Here, then, is evidence of a connection at the level of individual voters that is not apparent at the aggregate level, whereas for national economic conditions and midterm presidential popularity, strong aggregate relationships tend to atrophy at the individual level. The solution to both of these puzzles lies in understanding the interactions between national conditions and the career and campaign strategies of individual congressional candidates.

National Conditions and Strategic Politics

It is entirely possible for national conditions, personalities, and issues to affect congressional election results without directly impinging on individual voters at all. Samuel Kernell and I have presented the full explanation of how this can be so elsewhere—in *Strategy and Choice in Congressional Elections*[24]—so I will merely summarize it here.

A great deal of evidence, some of which was presented in Chapter 5, indicates that, in present-day congressional elections, the vote decision is strongly influenced by the voters' knowledge and evaluations of the particular set of candidates running in the district or state. National issues such as the state of the economy or the performance of the president may influence some voters some of the time—for example, voters who think that one candidate will do a better job dealing with the most important national problem almost invariably vote for that candidate—but for many voters the congressional choice is determined by evaluations of candidates as individuals, often with little reference to national policies or personalities. Even in 1994 and 2006, when national issues did shape voters' decisions to an unusual extent, the choice offered locally among a set of candidates remained crucial and, as in all recent elections, the relative political talents and campaign resources of congressional challengers were decisive in framing that choice.

Variations in the attractiveness of challengers and the vigor of their campaigns are by no means random. The decisions to run for Congress and to contribute to campaigns are subject to strategic calculation. As I pointed out in Chapter 3, the strongest potential candidates—those already holding a place on the political-career ladder—also have the greatest incentive for careful strategic behavior, for they have the most to lose if a bid for a higher office fails. Their plans are invariably conditioned by a reading of the odds on winning. People who contribute to campaigns also take full account of the candidate's electoral chances. Some clear evidence of strategic behavior on the part of candidates and contributors was presented in Table 3–4 and Figure 3–7. More experienced nonincumbent candidates run more lavishly financed campaigns when the incumbent seems vulnerable or when no incumbent is running.

Another important consideration is whether it promises to be a good or bad year for the party—and that, it is widely believed, depends on national economic and political conditions. A booming economy and a popular president (or presidential candidate) are assumed to favor the party in power; economic problems and other national failings that are blamed on the administration are costly to its congressional candidates. *Exactly those things that politicians and political scientists who look at aggregate data believe influence congressional voters also guide the strategic decisions of potential candidates and contributors.*

This means that when the partisan outlook is gloomy, shrewd and ambitious politicians figure that the normally long odds against defeating an incumbent are even worse than usual and wait for a better day. People who supply campaign resources to the party's candidates also decline to waste the resources in trying to defeat incumbents they dislike and, instead, deploy them to defend their own favorite incumbents who may be in more trouble than usual.

Politicians of the other party, sensing that electoral tides are moving in their direction, view the chances of winning as better than usual, so more and better candidates compete for the nomination to challenge incumbents.[25] One thing that encourages them to make the race is easier access to campaign funds; contributors are also more willing to invest in challenges because political conditions seem favorable. Because the marginal effects of campaign spending are so much greater for challengers than for incumbents, the contrasting offensive and defensive contribution strategies do not simply cancel one another out; rather, they add to the vote totals of the party favored by national political conditions.

Thus when conditions appear to favor one party over the other, the favored party fields an unusually large proportion of formidable challengers with well-funded campaigns, while the other party fields underfinanced amateurs willing to run without serious hope of winning. In addition, incumbents of the disadvantaged party are marginally more likely to retire when facing the prospect of a tougher-than-usual campaign; the struggle for one more term may not be worth the effort.[26] This, too, means that the disadvantaged party will have relatively fewer strong candidates.

The choice between pairs of candidates across states and districts in an election year thus varies systematically with the strategic decisions of potential candidates and associated activists. These decisions are systematically informed by perceptions of national political and economic conditions. Voters need only respond to the choice between candidates and campaigns at the local level to reflect, in their aggregate behavior, national political forces. It is not necessary for individual-level analogs of national forces—the voter's personal economic experiences and feelings about the president or presidential candidates—to influence the vote directly in order to affect the aggregate results. Some voters are no doubt moved by such considerations—the favored party's candidates certainly strive to show how national conditions affect voters' lives—but pervasive individual rationality of this sort is not essential for the process to work. The intervening strategic decisions of congressional elites provide a mechanism sufficient to explain how national forces can come to be expressed in congressional election outcomes.

The logic of this explanation is straightforward enough; there is also considerable evidence for it. Politicians routinely sniff the political winds early in the election year; speculation about what will happen in the fall is a common feature of political news in January and February, even earlier in some election years, notably 2008. Predictions are explicitly based on economic conditions and the public standing of the administration. Other information, from polls and special elections, for example, is also sifted for clues. Signs and portents are readily available, widely discussed, and taken seriously.[27]

They are also usually heeded. In 1974, for example, Watergate, recession, and Nixon's low standing in the polls made it very difficult for Republicans to recruit good candidates at all levels. Republicans expected it to be a bad year and candidates and activists refused to extend themselves in a losing cause.[28] Democrats saw it as a golden opportunity, and an unusually large proportion of experienced candidates challenged Republican incumbents.[29] Their strategic decisions contributed to the Democrats' best year in the past three decades.

Campaign contributors also respond to election year expectations. In 1974, for example, Democratic challengers typically spent more than 2.8 times as much as Republican challengers; they even outspent Democratic incumbents. Republican incumbents, on the defensive, spent 74 percent more than Democratic incumbents. In 1994, it was the Republicans' turn to go on the offensive and the Democrats' turn to try to save endangered incumbents. Republican challengers outspent Democratic challengers by 60 percent that year; Democratic incumbents spent 32 percent more than Republican incumbents. Conditions strongly favored Democrats in 2006, and their challengers raised and spent, on average, 2.3 times as much as Republican challengers, while Republican incumbents felt compelled to spend 47 percent more than their Democratic counterparts. The patterns could hardly be clearer. Campaign contributions—and hence expenditures—were sharply responsive to perceived political trends in 1974, 1994, and 2006.

Not all election years follow this pattern so decisively. For example, all the signs for 1982 pointed to a very good year for Democrats, yet Democratic challengers were not especially well funded and were actually outspent by Republican challengers. The pattern of expenditures for 1984 seems to reflect a good Republican year, and so it was; yet, as we have seen, Republican House gains were rather limited, especially compared with 1980. Overall, though, the relationship between the relative levels of spending by the two parties' challengers (measured by the ratio of Republican to Democratic challenger spending) and the size of the partisan seat swing across these elections remains quite strong ($r = 0.77$).

Campaign finance data do not exist for elections prior to 1972, so there is no way to know whether campaign contributions reflected strategic advantages and disadvantages in earlier election years. It is possible, however, to show that variations in the relative quality of each party's candidates are strongly related to national conditions and aggregate election results in the way that is necessary for the explanation to be valid. The regression equations in Table 6–4 demonstrate that the relative aggregate quality of each party's challengers reflects, among other things, national conditions.

For this analysis, the quality of a party's challengers is measured as the percentage of those who have held elective office. The independent variables are presidential approval and real income change, plus the current partisan division of House seats (to take into account the opportunities created by exposure). Because the administration's party (not just the Democratic Party) is supposed to be rewarded or punished for the administration's performance, presidential

TABLE 6–4 Determinants of the Percentage of Experienced House Challengers, 1946–2006

Variable	Democrats (Equation 1)	Republicans (Equation 2)	Democrats – Republicans (Equation 3)
Intercept	55.71[a] (11.92)	−4.65 (9.28)	60.37[a] (11.90)
Party of administration	−32.54[a] (8.48)	4.16 (6.60)	−36.71[a] (8.46)
Seats won by Democrats last election (%)	−.22 (.18)	.32[a] (.14)	−.54[a] (.18)
Change in real income per capita (2nd quarter)	.90[a] (.42)	.02 (.32)	.88[a] (.42)
Presidential approval (2nd quarter)	.29[a] (.08)	−.02 (.06)	.31[a] (.08)
1992 or later	−13.11[a] (2.73)	1.91 (2.13)	−15.02[a] (2.72)
Adjusted R^2	.50	.06	.57
Number of cases	31	31	31

Note: The dependent variable in Equations 1 and 2 is the percent of challengers of the designated party who have held elective office; for Equation 3, it is the difference between the two; the independent variables are described in the text; standard errors are in parentheses.

[a]Statistically significant at $p < .05$, one-tailed test.

approval and income change are multiplied by –1 when a Republican is in the White House, and a fourth variable, the party of the administration, is included as a control. National conditions are measured in the second quarter (April–June) of the election year because that is the period during which most *final* decisions about candidacy must be made.[30] I have also included a variable that controls the effects of the sustained shift in favor of Republicans in the 1990s, which has reduced the proportion of strong Democratic challengers.[31]

The coefficients from Equation 1 indicate that both economic conditions and the level of public approval of the president have a large and significant impact on the quality of Democratic challengers. Neither factor matters to Republicans, who are sensitive only to the opportunities offered by the current level of Democratic strength in the House (Equation 2). However, a composite variable measuring the relative quality of challengers is affected significantly by all these variables. This is the key variable because relative quality is what matters for aggregate results on election day. The evidence is in Table 6–5. The dependent variable here is the change in the percentage of House seats won by the Democrats from the prior to the current election. As before, I control for the Democrats' exposure

TABLE 6–5 National Forces, Strategic Politicians, and Inter-election Seat Swings in House Elections, 1946–2006

Variable	(Equation 1)	(Equation 2)	(Equation 3)
Intercept	66.76[a] (8.34)	50.19[a] (9.25)	21.59[a] (5.81)
Party of administration	−37.86[a] (6.67)	−27.65[a] (6.62)	
Seats won by Democrats last election (%)	−.80[a] (.11)	−.59[a] (.11)	−.41[a] (.11)
Change in real income per capita	.77[a] (.32)	.47 (.28)	
Presidential approval	.30[a] (.07)	.22[a] (.06)	
Quality of Democratic challengers		.25[a] (.10)	.52[a] (.09)
Quality of Republican challengers		−.46[a] (.14)	−.70[a] (.16)
1992 or later	−10.13[a] (1.90)	−5.90[a] (2.15)	
Adjusted R^2	.75	.83	.71
Number of cases	31	31	31

Note: The dependent variable in Equations 1 and 2 is the change in the percentage of seats won by the Democrats from the previous; standard errors are in parentheses.

[a]Statistically significant at $p < .05$, one-tailed test.

and for the party of the administration. The other variables are measured as in Table 6–4, except that real income change is the average for the election year and presidential approval is taken from the last Gallup Poll before the election.

The first equation in Table 6–5 presents another variant of the standard referendum model discussed earlier. As usual, both presidential approval and economic performance have a significant impact on party fortunes. The second equation adds the aggregate quality variable for each party's challenger; each of these variables has a strong, statistically significant impact on the House seat swing; Democrats gain more seats, the better their challengers are, and lose more seats, the better the Republican challengers are. Note in particular that the quality of Republican challengers is, if anything, more strongly related to election results than is the quality of Democratic challengers, even though high-quality Republican challengers appear to be less strategic in their behavior than high-quality Democratic challengers. Note also that the effect of real income change is reduced by nearly half (compared to Equation 1) and ceases to be statistically significant; presidential approval continues to have a significant influence, although its estimated impact is reduced somewhat.

A model that includes the quality variables but not income change or presidential approval (Equation 3) explains nearly as much (71 percent) as the model that does the opposite (Equation 1; 75 percent). That is, a full 71 percent of the variance in postwar House seat shifts can be explained by just three variables: the quality of Republican challengers, quality of Democratic challengers, and exposure. The coefficients from Equation 2 indicate that, controlling for other factors, a difference of 1 percentage point in quality of Democratic candidates is worth about one House seat; the range between its highest and lowest values (thirty-two) covers thirty-three seats. A difference of 1 percentage point in the quality of Republican challengers is worth about two House seats; the range between its highest and lowest values (sixteen) covers thirty-one seats. A graphic display of the simple relationship between relative candidate quality and party fortunes in postwar House elections appears in Figure 6–8.

In general, then, the political strategies of congressional elites are responsive to national forces and help to translate them into aggregate election results.[32] Complete evidence—on candidates, campaign finances, and voting behavior—is available only as far back as the early 1970s, and my data on experienced challengers extend back only to 1946. Recent research has found evidence of consequential strategic entry by high-quality challengers in late nineteenth and early twentieth centuries, as well, so the pattern is not unique to the post–World War II era.[33] Still, it is very likely that in some earlier electoral periods, national forces influenced voters more directly. It would be difficult to argue, for instance, that many congressional voters in 1932, 1934, or 1936 were not responding directly to their economic experiences during the Great Depression or to their feelings

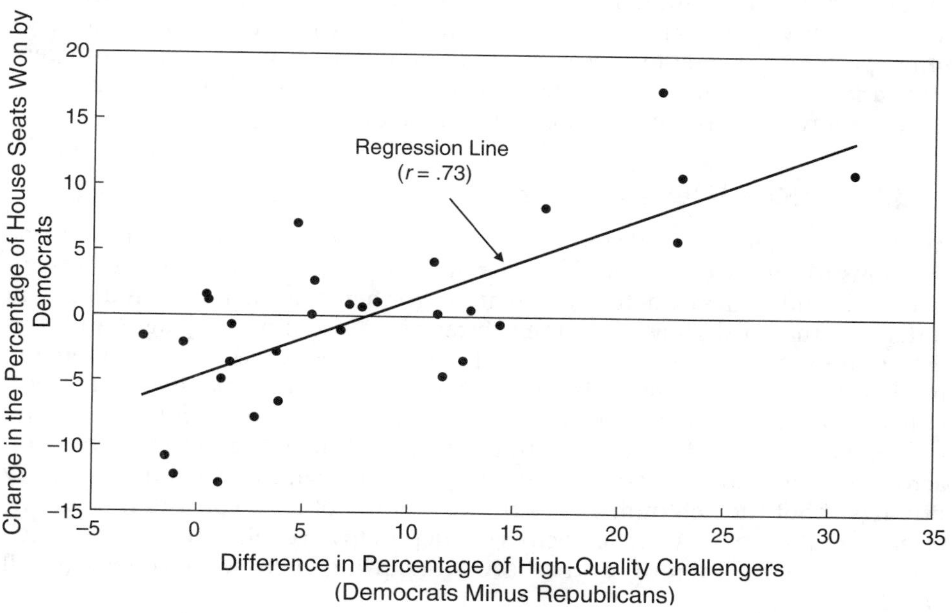

FIGURE 6–8 The Quality of Challengers and Party Fortunes in House Elections, 1946–2006

Source: Compiled by author.

about Franklin D. Roosevelt. Individual congressional candidates were important only insofar as they were committed to a position for or against the New Deal. Elections such as these were, of course, the source of the conventional wisdom about the effects of national forces on the fates of congressional candidates. Shrewd politicians would be well advised to adjust their career strategies to take advantage of favorable national tides and to avoid contrary currents.

The strong postwar trend toward a more candidate-centered style of electoral politics would reduce the electoral importance of national forces while enhancing that of individual candidates and campaigns. In a more candidate-centered electoral politics, the resources and talents of challengers would have a larger impact on district-level results. Elite strategies would thus make a greater independent contribution to a party's electoral performance.

If, over the years, individual candidates and campaigns became comparatively more important and national forces less so, politicians would not necessarily abandon their traditional strategies. They would, rather, continue to respond strategically to national trends because, increasingly as a consequence of their own strategic choices (and those of other congressional activists), their expectations about election outcomes would continue to be realized. At the extreme, their expectations could come to be based on false assumptions, their prophecies wholly self-fulfilling. National economic and political conditions might affect congressional elections only because congressional elites expect them to do so.

There is no reason to think that this point has been or will ever be reached. Electoral prophecies are self-reinforcing but not exclusively self-fulfilling. The quality of challengers has, however, become a more important part of the equation. The effects of national conditions depend to a considerable extent on what candidates do with national issues at the local level.[34] Consequently, the electorate's ability to exercise democratic control by acting as, to use V.O. Key's phrase, a "rational god of vengeance and reward"[35] has become more contingent and variable, depending on elite decisions that are only partially determined by the economy and other systematic national forces.

Campaign Themes

At the district level, in addition to shaping alternatives by influencing strategic decisions to run or contribute money, national conditions affect the success or failure of candidacies by defining the campaign themes available to candidates in different situations. They shape the substantive content of campaigns and thus determine the form in which national issues are presented to, and therefore influence, individual voters. The connections between national issues and individual voting decisions are forged by the rhetoric of campaigns and so vary as do the campaigns. Variation occurs both across districts in a single election year and across election years. Variation across election years helps to explain why survey findings about the determinants of the vote are so often inconsistent from one election to the next.[36] Variation across districts helps to explain why there is such a wide divergence among district-level vote swings between elections (recall Table 3–2).

Remember from the discussion of voting behavior in Chapter 5 that to succeed, challengers must accomplish two basic tasks: build support for themselves and undermine that of their incumbent opponents. The first task is insufficient without the second. Adverse conditions for the incumbent contribute to the first task by encouraging better-qualified challengers to run and by increasing the campaign resources available to them when they do. They contribute to the second task by giving challengers a campaign theme that has some prospect of undermining the incumbent's support.

Incumbents are, as a class, remarkably adept at taking credit for the good things that government does while avoiding responsibility for its failures. Under neutral or favorable conditions, a member of Congress who cultivates his or her district diligently and avoids personal scandal makes an extremely difficult target. But if people are sufficiently unhappy with an administration or the Congress, if the economic situation is sufficiently dire, or if a war is sufficiently unpopular, it may become a good deal more difficult to avoid guilt by association if there is an energetic challenger continually reminding voters of the connection. This is crucial. A vigorous campaign is still essential to defeat incumbents, no matter how bad the political conditions become for them personally or for their party.

Thus, national conditions continue to create problems or opportunities for congressional candidates; but how they are handled or exploited makes more difference now than in the past, and this varies among candidates, between parties, and across election years. When a party does not field enough challengers who have the resources and skills to take full advantage of the opportunities created by national conditions, partisan swings are dampened; when it does, partisan swings are enhanced. Similarly, incumbents often survive individual political or personal shortcomings if they avoid challengers capable of exploiting them. These are among the clearest lessons of recent electoral history, to which we now turn.

House Elections, 1992–2006

1992

After substantial upheavals in 1980 and 1982, House elections for the rest of the decade were uneventful, with weak challengers, low turnover, and small partisan swings (see Figure 6–1 and Table 6–1). The static results reflected national conditions that, for different reasons in different years, were not conducive to changes.[37] The cycle of uneventful House elections ended with a bang in 1992 and foreshadowed the dramatic reversal of partisan fortunes to come in 1994. The 1992 elections yielded the largest crop of new representatives in more than forty years, with 110 newcomers joining the House in January 1993. The influx of new members sharply altered the House's demographic makeup. The number of women representatives rose from twenty-eight to forty-seven; of African Americans, from twenty-five to thirty-eight; of Hispanics, from eleven to seventeen.

Despite all this turmoil, partisan change in Congress was exceedingly modest. Republicans, though losing the presidency, picked up ten seats in the House, leaving the Democrats with a reduced but still comfortable 258–176 majority. The coincidence of a large turnover in membership with a small partisan swing in the House is a historical oddity. In other postwar elections, a large turnover of House seats has been accompanied by a large partisan swing. Uniquely in 1992, a very large turnover coincided with a very small net partisan shift.[38]

The peculiarities of the 1992 congressional election reflect the converging effects of three basic environmental forces—divided government, a stagnant economy, and reapportionment—refracted through signal events (such as the Anita Hill–Clarence Thomas dispute, the House Bank scandal, and a Democratic presidential victory) and filtered through the strategic choices of political elites. The appropriate metaphor for the course of politics leading up to 1992 is not a tide but a roller coaster. The dramatic diplomatic and military successes that drove Saddam Hussein's Iraqi forces from Kuwait in early 1991 raised George H. W. Bush's performance ratings to unprecedented heights. The public standing of Congress also improved markedly, but the war issue threatened political problems for the members—almost all of them Democrats—who had voted against authorizing the president to send soldiers against Iraq. By the war's end, Bush looked unbeatable for 1992, and Republicans were relishing the prospect of recruiting Gulf War heroes to challenge Democratic doves. The war, Bush's popularity, and the prospect of reapportionment promised a banner Republican year in 1992.

The Republicans' high expectations foundered on the economy. The 1990 midterm elections had coincided with a recession; but so had midterms in five of the previous six postwar Republican administrations. (The Reagan administration in 1986 was the exception.) The Republicans' problem was that, although the economy had rebounded strongly from these earlier midterm recessions, only a feeble, fitful recovery followed the 1990 recession. The economy's annual growth rate from the bottom of the recession in the first quarter of 1991 through the third quarter of 1992 was less than 2 percent, not enough to make a dent in the high unemployment figures. The economy's annual growth rate for the entire George H. W. Bush presidency was less than 1 percent, the lowest for any administration since the Depression.

The economy's continuing weakness steadily sapped the support that the president had acquired by bringing the Gulf War to a successful conclusion. Public attention turned from foreign affairs, a venue where Republicans have enjoyed an advantage for years, to domestic economic issues, where the faltering economy played to the Democrats' strength.[39] Still, the economy fed the public's disaffection with Congress as well as with the president; polls showed that ratings of Congress and the president suffered from bad economic news at the same time and to the same degree.[40] Evidently, the public was not disposed to make distinctions when it came to allocating blame, so the weak economy was not an unalloyed Democratic advantage. Ultimately, though, it did help congressional Democrats because it contributed so much to Bill Clinton's victory.

Americans in 1992 had no shortage of reasons for disdaining Congress: bank overdrafts, pay raise subterfuges, ethical lapses, the savings-and-loan debacle, and so on. But what gave these issues their potency was something more basic: the government's apparent inability to address a host of economic problems that had driven public confidence in the economy to a seventeen-year low.[41] The difficulty for voters was that twelve years of divided government had made the assignment of blame for economic and other troubles problematic. When one party controls both Congress and the White House, the public has an obvious target for its wrath: the party running the show. Whether the ruling party is actually to blame for bad times is beside the point; for better or worse, responsibility comes with power. Divided government invites each party to blame the other, and the public ends up agreeing with both and blaming both.

The electoral consequences of a sour economy under divided government were complicated by an accident of the calendar because House seats had to be reapportioned and district boundaries redrawn for 1992 to reflect the population shifts recorded by the 1990 census. Election years that end in 2 have typically produced higher turnover in the House than have other years; members whose districts disappear or are changed in politically damaging ways are more likely than usual to retire—and more likely than usual to be defeated if they do not. Still, in recent decades, reapportionment has added, on average, only about ten new members to the House beyond the normal turnover. Two additional circumstances exaggerated the effect of redistricting for 1992. First, the effort to carve out districts in which racial minorities formed a majority of voters wherever feasible led to more radical changes in district boundaries than usual. Second, districts in several of the largest states were redrawn for 1992 by mapmakers who, in contrast to past practices, studiously ignored the interests of incumbents. In previous reapportionment cycles, state legislatures did more of the work and routinely sought to protect the incumbents of one or both parties (depending on whether one or both controlled the state government and thus had any say in the matter). Courts, largely indifferent to the fate of incumbents and parties, did far more to shape districts for the 1990s.

Both the pressure for "minority–majority" districts and court intervention worked, in principle, to the advantage of Republicans. Most African American and Hispanic voters favor Democrats, so ethnic gerrymanders concentrate Democratic votes in districts in which they are "wasted" because the party wins by many more votes than it needs—precisely what a partisan Republican gerrymander would accomplish. Courts also drew maps more congenial to Republicans than the predominantly Democratic state legislatures would have devised on their own.

By itself, redistricting would have inspired an unusually large number of House retirements and produced a bumper crop of vulnerable incumbents in 1992. But the effects of redistricting were strongly reinforced by two other circumstances: the public's overwhelming contempt for members of Congress as a class and the House Bank scandal, which gave an individual focus to many voters' otherwise diffuse disdain.

Until its abolition in 1992, the House Bank had existed in one form or another since 1830. The paychecks of members who used its services were automatically deposited in their accounts, which they could draw on by writing personal checks. For as long as anyone could remember, the bank gave members free "overdraft protection." That is, the bank honored a check even when a member's account held insufficient funds to cover it. The bank refused to cover the checks of only the most flagrant abusers of this privilege. This indulgence was a political disaster waiting to happen, and, for members of the House, it happened at the worst possible moment. Auditors' reports of hundreds of members writing thousands of overdrafts became public knowledge in 1991. Coming at a time when the public was already primed to think the worst of Congress and Republicans were desperate for any issue that might unlock the Democrats' decades-old grip on the House, damage control proved impossible. Hounded by constituents, the media, the White House, junior House Republicans hungry for an issue, and, finally, innocent members who wanted to be absolved of suspicion, the House leadership could not sidetrack the issue. Members were left with no alternative but to vote to disclose all the names of the bad check writers and the numbers of overdrafts they had written.

The combination of redistricting, widespread disgust with Congress, and the individual vulnerability of members with significant overdrafts combined to produce a dramatic increase in the overall level of competition for House seats, for the public's anger at Congress rose in plenty of time to shape the career decisions of potential candidates in 1992. Among incumbents, individual targets could be identified according to their vulnerability on the overdraft issue by mid-April 1992 at the latest. The troubles of some were known even earlier. The upheavals expected from redistricting also dictated boldness in 1992.

There was thus a remarkable jump in the sheer number of people seeking major-party nominations for Congress. The Federal Election Commission received filings from 2,950 candidates, 1,000 more than the 1982–1990 average. This surge produced a precipitous drop in the number of seats won without major party opposition in the general election. Only thirty-four seats went uncontested by one of the major parties in 1992, compared to eighty-five such seats in 1990 and an average of seventy-one for elections in the previous decade. Indeed, fewer House seats went uncontested in 1992 than in any other postwar election to that date. Postwar highs in the number of voluntary retirements from the House (sixty-six) and of incumbents defeated in primary elections (nineteen) guaranteed that the number of open seats that were up for grabs in the general election (ninety-one) also set a postwar record; the previous high was sixty-five and the 1946–1990 average was forty-four.

The quality of challengers in 1992 was also considerably improved over recent elections. In 1992, 22 percent of both parties' challengers had previously held elective office, up from the postwar low of 10 percent for both parties in 1990. Still, this percentage was lower than in other recent election years in which the incumbents of at least one party fared poorly, such as 1974 and 1982. The politically ambitious professionals had a wider selection of opportunities in 1992 because an unusual number of seats lacked incumbents, and, as always, experienced candidates flocked to compete for open seats.

Heightened competition led to closer contests. The average share of the two-party vote won by incumbents in 1992 (63.6 percent) was the lowest since 1966, and the proportion of marginal incumbents (those who won with less than 60 percent of the two-party vote) was the highest since 1964 (33.4 percent). These figures are all the more impressive because they were recorded after many of the most vulnerable incumbents had already retired from the House or been defeated in primary elections.

Reapportionment and the general disdain for Congress, which was given individual focus by the House Bank scandal, shared principal responsibility for high turnover. Reapportionment threw a record number of House incumbents into districts with other incumbents; some retired, some moved, and some (a total of nine in the primary and general elections) lost contests to other incumbents in redrawn districts. But the consequences of redistricting were greatly amplified by the publication of each member's record with the House Bank.

Table 6–6 displays the consequences of these disclosures. The likelihood of exit from Congress by every route—retirement, defeat in the primary, and defeat in the general election—increased significantly with the number of bank overdrafts. When the 103rd Congress convened in 1993, more than half the members of the 102nd whose overdrafts had reached triple digits were gone, while 83 percent of those with completely clean records reassumed their seats. Had

TABLE 6–6 House Bank Overdrafts and Membership Attrition (in percentages)

Fate of Representative	NUMBER OF OVERDRAFTS			
	None	**1–99**	**100–199**	**200 or more**
Retired from politics[a]	8.9	11.9	15.0	33.3
$X^2 = 13.09, p < .005$	(168)[b]	(219)	(20)	(27)
Defeated in primary[c]	2.0	2.2	18.8	27.8
$X^2 = 37.91, p < .001$	(146)	(181)	(15)	(18)
Defeated in general election[d]	2.8	5.6	23.1	15.4
$X^2 = 11.83, p < .01$	(140)	(172)	(13)	(13)
Not in 103rd Congress[e]	17.3	24.7	50.0	59.3
$X^2 = 28.86, p < .001$	(168)	(219)	(20)	(27)

[a]Left the House but did not run for another office.
[b]Number of cases from which percentages were calculated.
[c]Based on members seeking reelection; excludes four pairs of incumbents competing with one another because of redistricting.
[d]Based on members winning renomination; excludes five pairs of incumbents competing with one another because of redistricting.
[e]For any reason.
Note: Ted Weiss (D-NY), who died September 14, 1992, is not included; Walter B. Jones (D-NC), who died September 15, 1992, but had already announced his retirement, is included.

Source: Gary C. Jacobson and Michael Dimock, "Checking Out: The Effects of Bank Overdrafts on the 1992 House Elections," *American Journal of Political Science* 38 (1994): 606.

members with overdrafts been returned to Congress at the same rate as those without any, the 103rd would have had seventy-eight newcomers instead of 110, and turnover would have been about average for a year ending in 2.

The House Bank scandal and its consequences were profoundly ironic. Contrary to the view initially spread by the media and accepted by the public, the overdrafts violated no laws and cost the taxpayers no money.[42] Yet the scandal ended many more congressional careers than policy disasters such as the savings-and-loan debacle, which left taxpayers holding the bag for hundreds of billions of dollars, or the quadrupling of the national debt from $1 billion to $4 billion in little more than a decade. Members of Congress routinely escape individual blame for major policy failures because the legislative process diffuses responsibility; the action is so complex, the details of policy so arcane, and each individual's responsibility so obscure, that it is impossible to figure out who is culpable and who is not. Everyone with a checking account understands what it means to balance a checkbook, however, and each House member's culpability was precisely measured in the count of unfunded checks.[43]

High turnover always changes the face of Congress in some way; usually the change is partisan and generational. In 1992, the major changes were instead demographic; forty of the 110 newly elected members were ethnic minorities, women, or both. The increase of more than 50 percent in the number of African Americans and Latinos serving in the House is a direct result of the ethnic gerrymanders carried out at the behest of the courts. The "Year of the Woman," on the other hand, although helped along by redistricting, was primarily an artifact of the Thomas Hearings.

The proximate reason for the abrupt increase in the number of women elected to the House and Senate in 1992 was the abrupt increase in the number of politically talented and experienced women who sought and won nominations for congressional seats in competitive states and districts. The surge of experienced, well-financed women candidates was in turn a direct consequence of the widespread outrage that was generated by the October 1991 Senate Judiciary Committee hearings in which Anita Hill accused Supreme Court nominee Clarence Thomas of sexual harassment. The all-male committee's treatment of Hill and her accusations infuriated many women, provoking the startling surge in political activity among women that was a unique feature of the 1992 elections.

The Year of the Woman—more precisely, the year of the Democratic woman (twenty of the twenty-three newly elected women were Democrats)—was forged in the primaries. The success rate of women candidates in general elections for the House (44 percent of those running) was not dramatically higher than it had been over the previous two decades (39 percent), but the number of women running, 106, was far above the previous high of sixty-nine in 1990. More important, half of the nonincumbent women were running for open seats. In the end, nearly all the gains made by women in the 1992 House elections were the consequence of Democratic women taking open seats. Democratic women did unusually well in 1992, then, because they won an uncommonly large share of the nominations for seats that their party's candidates would have had a serious chance of winning regardless of gender—seats not defended by an incumbent.

They also did well because they were, by the standard of experience, high-quality candidates. This is evident from Table 6–7, which lists the proportion of nonincumbent candidates (by gender, party, and type of race) who had previously held some elective public office, along with their electoral fates. The Democratic women running for open seats were the most experienced of any subgroup, and their success rate was the highest of any. Observe, however, that prior elective office is strongly related to electoral success in all categories; winning is far more closely linked to experience than to gender. Women won a lot more House seats in 1992 not because being female was such a great advantage in the general election but because so many of the high-quality candidates in competitive districts were women.

Although the 1992 elections brought high turnover and sharp changes in the House's demography, they registered little partisan change. The forces that generated turnover did not have a consistent partisan thrust. Conditions that favored Republicans—reapportionment, the House Bank scandal (more Democrats than Republicans had written overdrafts), the low repute of a Congress run by Democrats, perhaps the Gulf War—were offset by conditions that favored Democrats—the stagnant economy, George H. W. Bush's unpopularity, and Bill Clinton's vigorous and successful presidential campaign.

Ross Perot's remarkable showing in the 1992 presidential election—he won 19 percent of the popular vote nationally and as much as 33 percent in his best House district—naturally raises the question of whether his candidacy had any

TABLE 6–7 Experience, Sex, and Success of Nonincumbent House Candidates, 1992 (in percentages)

	Prior Elective Office	WINNERS Prior Office	WINNERS No Prior Office
Challengers			
Democrats			
Men	24.7 (93)[a]	8.7 (23)	2.9 (70)
Women	18.5 (27)	40.0 (5)	0.0 (22)
Republicans			
Men	24.3 (181)	13.6 (44)	5.1 (137)
Women	21.4 (14)	0.0 (3)	0.0 (11)
Open Seats			
Democrats			
Men	66.7 (66)	71.4 (42)	38.2 (21)
Women	69.2 (26)	83.2 (18)	50.0 (8)
Republicans			
Men	53.3 (75)	52.5 (40)	28.6 (35)
Women	30.8 (13)	50.0 (4)	11.1 (9)

[a]Number of cases from which percentages were calculated.

Source: Gary C. Jacobson, "Unusual Year, Unusual Election," in *The Elections of 1992*, ed. Michael Nelson (Washington, D.C.: Congressional Quarterly Press, 1993), p. 171.

effect on the congressional contests. It did, but not in any way that affected who won or lost. As disdainers of politics as usual, Perot's supporters might be expected to dislike incumbents, so we would expect that the higher Perot's vote in the district, the better a challenger would do. This is what we observe to be the case, but only in districts that are not competitive in the first place. In districts where the incumbent received less than 60 percent of the vote, Perot's level of support was not related to the vote; only in districts won by more than 60 percent is the relationship substantively large and statistically significant. In the low-information context of a noncompetitive campaign, anti-establishment sentiments spilled over into House voting. But competitive House campaigns evidently framed the choices in their own terms.

1994

The 1992 elections, extraordinary as they were, turned out to be only a prelude to an even greater upheaval in 1994. For the first time in forty-two years, Republicans captured the House of Representatives. The fifty-two seat gain that gave them a 230–204 majority was the largest net partisan swing since 1948. Why did Republicans, after four decades of futility, suddenly win a clear majority of House seats? The short answer is that they won by inverting political patterns that had given Democrats comfortable House majorities despite a generation of Republican superiority in presidential elections. In an earlier edition of this book, I offered this summary explanation for the Republicans' inability to win control of the House:

> Republicans have failed to advance in the House because they have fielded inferior candidates on the wrong side of issues that are important to voters in House elections and because voters find it difficult to assign blame or credit when control of government is divided between the parties.[44]

In 1994, the Republicans won the House by fielding (modestly) superior candidates who were on the right side of the issues that were important to voters in House elections and persuading voters to blame a unified Democratic regime for government's failures. They exploited favorable national issues more successfully than any party in decades. But marketable national campaign themes did not by themselves give the Republicans their House majority. To win House seats, Republicans still needed plausible candidates with enough money to get their messages out to district voters. Even in 1994, the effects of national issues, important as they were, depended on how they were injected into local campaigns.

House Democrats had long thrived by adhering to former House Speaker Tip O'Neill's dictum that "all politics are local." All politics were *not* local in 1994. Republicans succeeded in framing the local choice in national terms, making taxes, social discipline, big government, and the Clinton presidency the dominant issues. They did so by exploiting three related waves of public sentiment that crested simultaneously in 1994. The first was public disgust with the politics, politicians, and government in Washington. The second was the widespread feeling that American economic and social life was out of control and heading in the wrong direction. The third was the visceral rejection of Bill Clinton by a crucial set of swing voters, the "Reagan Democrats" and supporters of Ross Perot.

Public contempt for members of Congress as a class had been growing for more than two decades. All the regular polling questions measuring attitudes toward government found an increasingly angry and distrustful public. Disapproval of Congress's performance reached an all-time high of 79 percent in one 1994 poll, but that was only the latest incremental extension of a long-term trend. Rising distrust and anger had been fed by several streams. One major stream flowed directly from the politics of divided government during the Reagan–George H. W. Bush years. Divided government encouraged the kind of partisan posturing, haggling, delay, and confusion that voters hate whenever Republican presidents and Democratic Congresses have faced major policy decisions. It also guaranteed that voters would wind up feeling betrayed by the inevitable compromises that made agreement possible.

The formal end of divided government in 1992 was supposed to end gridlock. It did not. Many of the Clinton administration's most ambitious plans—notoriously, health care reform—died in an agony of conflict and partisan recrimination. The truth, revealed early in the 103rd Congress when Minority Leader Bob Dole led a successful Republican filibuster against Clinton's economic stimulus package, was that divided government had not ended at all. Divided partisan control of *policy making* persists as long as the minority party holds at least 40 seats in the Senate and can therefore kill any bill it wants to kill.[45]

The illusion of unified government put the onus of failure on the Democrats; the reality of divided government let Senate Republicans make sure that the administration would fail. Clinton was elected on a promise of change. Senate

Republicans could prevent change—and they did. It was not difficult, for while everyone may agree that change is desirable, rarely do we find ready consensus on what to change *to.* If voters did not get change with Clinton—or if they did not like the changes he proposed—the alternative was to elect Republicans.

Public anger at a government paralyzed by gridlock was intensified by the widespread sense that the problems the political establishment had failed to address were indeed serious. The benefits of economic growth during the Reagan–Bush years went largely to families in the top income decile. The broad middle class had, by many measures, made little economic progress; incomes (including fringe benefits) of the families in the middle portion of the distribution were nearly flat over the two decades between 1973 and 1992.[46] Although the economy grew during the first two years of the Clinton administration, the fruits of growth again went largely to families at the upper end of the economic scale. Hence in the October *Los Angeles Times* poll, 53 percent of the respondents thought the economy remained in recession. The economic discontent that elected Clinton in 1992 had barely faded by 1994, and this time it helped to elect a Republican Congress.[47]

Economic prosperity, moreover, is not the only measure of the quality of life. The public institutions that serve ordinary people—public schools, police, courts—seemed in the early 1990s to be in trouble. The issues of crime, illegal immigration, and unmarried teenage mothers on welfare that dominated the 1994 campaigns in many places were not new, but they gained new urgency as signs that American society was out of control. For millions of Americans, government had delivered neither physical nor economic security, failing conspicuously to reverse what they saw as moral and cultural decline. The large majority that believed the nation was on the wrong rather than the right track (57 percent compared to 37 percent in the exit polls) indicated that the longing for change that put Clinton in the White House had not been satisfied. Two-thirds of those who thought the nation was on the wrong track voted for the Republican House candidate, compared to only 29 percent of those who thought the nation was on the right track.

Stagnant incomes, declining public services, and the rising fear of crime left large segments of the population with poorer lives and diminished prospects. It was in this context that the perks and peccadilloes of politicians—scandals involving senior leaders in the House and the Keating Five in the Senate, bank overdrafts, unpaid restaurant bills, post office shenanigans, and pay-raise subterfuges—were so damaging to members of Congress. The image of representatives as self-serving, easily corrupted, and indifferent to the needs of the average citizen or the good of the nation had pervaded the 1992 elections and helped produce the largest turnover in the House since World War II. Members were unable to shake that image in the 103rd Congress, and now that Democrats were ostensibly in full control of the government, they became the principal targets of popular wrath and disappointment.[48]

The Clinton Problem

Bill Clinton's reputation as a leader was, of course, the chief target and victim of the Republicans' gridlock strategy. But this was not the only problem Clinton posed for congressional Democrats. Although his overall performance ratings were not, comparatively speaking, all that bad, he had thoroughly alienated important groups of swing voters: the so-called Reagan Democrats and much of the largely male Perot constituency. The cultural symbolism portrayed by many of the administration's actions was anathema to socially conservative white men, especially in the South. The conspicuous attention to race and gender "diversity" in making appointments called to mind the affirmative-action programs they detested. Support for gays in the military, gun control, and the role and style of Hillary Rodham Clinton reminded these swing voters of the cultural liberalism that was at the core of what they did *not* like about the Democratic party. Clinton's reputation with this segment of the electorate was probably worsened by one of his most notable successes: the passage of the North American Free Trade Agreement, which put him at odds with traditional blue-collar Democratic constituents.

The 1994 National Election Study revealed that only 37 percent of southerners approved of Clinton's performance, his lowest rating in any region. Among white southern men, Clinton's approval stood at a dismal 28 percent. Moreover, the relationship between presidential approval and the House vote was notably stronger in 1994 than it had been in 1986 or 1990. Clinton's low level of approval was thus more damaging to his copartisans than usual and was concentrated among swing voters. White respondents in the NES survey reported voting 10 percentage points more Republican in 1994 than they had in 1992; support for Republicans among white southerners went up 14 points. In the exit polls, fully 44 percent of the white southern males said that their House vote was a vote against Clinton (20 percent said it was a vote for Clinton; for nonsouthern males, the comparable figures were 33 percent and 24 percent). Perot supporters, who had split their House votes evenly between the two parties in 1992, voted two-to-one Republican in 1994.[49]

Voters in 1994 were angry with government; the Democratic party was the party of government, not only because it were in charge but also because that party believes in government. Republican candidates, who like to claim that they do not believe in it, offered themselves as vehicles for expressing antigovernment rage by taking up the banner of structural panaceas—term limits, a balanced-budget amendment, cuts in congressional staff and perks—that were broadly popular and had special appeal to the alienated voters who had supported Perot. The policy issues that resonated best with voters in 1994—crime, immigration, welfare dependency, taxes, big government—were also Republican issues. Recognizing Clinton's unpopularity, especially in the South and especially among white males, Republican candidates sought to portray their opponents as Clinton clones; many of them used TV ads that showed pictures of their opponents' faces digitally morphing into Clinton's face.

Republicans were thus able to frame the choice in many swing districts as one—not between an accomplished provider of pork and diligent servant of district interests and a challenger whose ability to deliver the goods was at best doubtful—but between a supporter of liberal elitist Bill Clinton, big government, high taxes, and politics as usual and a challenger opposed to these horribles. The House Democrats' customary strategy of emphasizing the projects, grants, and programs they have brought to the district and the value of their experience and seniority not only failed but was turned against them. The more they reminded people of pork and clout, the more they revealed themselves as insiders, that loathed class of career politicians. With the choice framed this way, the old ploy of running for Congress by running against Congress—joining the chorus of criticism to put oneself apart from, and above, the institution—was rendered threadbare as well. The Democrats were unable to duck individual responsibility for the House's collective shortcomings.

Ironically, the Republicans' "Contract with America," which became so prominent in setting the Republican agenda after the election, had, in itself, little impact on the voters. On September 27, more than 300 Republican House candidates signed a pledge on the steps of the capitol to act swiftly on a grab-bag of proposals for structural and legislative change, including constitutional amendments requiring a balanced budget and imposing term limits on members of Congress, major cuts in income taxes, and reductions in spending on welfare programs for poor families. Although the contract got some attention in the media and was a target of Democratic counterattacks, most voters went to the polls blissfully unaware of its existence. The *New York Times*/CBS News poll of October 29–November 1 found that 71 percent of respondents had never heard of the contract and another 15 percent said it would make no difference in how they voted. Only 7 percent said it would make them more likely to vote for the Republican House candidate, while 5 percent said it would make them less likely to do so. The most prominent Republican effort to nationalize the campaign thus remained almost invisible to voters. This does not mean that individual parts of the contract were not used effectively by Republican campaigners; on the contrary. But the contract itself had far more impact on Republican candidates (before and after the election) than on voters.

Nationalizing the Vote

Although the contract had little to do with it, in 1994 Republicans did succeed in nationalizing the elections to a much greater degree than usual in recent elections. In effect, they ran a set of midterm congressional campaigns that mirrored their successful presidential campaigns. As a result, their House victories echoed their presidential successes far more clearly than at any time during the preceding forty years.

Most of the seats Republicans took from Democrats were in districts that leaned Republican in presidential elections. A serviceable measure of a district's presidential leanings during this period can be computed by taking the average division of its two-party vote between the presidential candidates in 1988 and 1992.[50] The national mean for this measure of district presidential voting habits is 49.9 percent Democratic; its median is 48.3 percent Democratic. As Table 6–8 shows, Republican gains in 1994 were heavily concentrated in districts where the Democrats' vote, averaged over the two elections, fell below 50 percent. For example, thirty-one open seats formerly held by Democrats were at stake. Republicans won all sixteen open Democratic seats in districts where George H. W. Bush's share of the two-party vote, averaged together for 1988 and 1992, exceeded 50 percent; they won only six of the fifteen where the Democrats' presidential average exceeded 50 percent. Republican challengers defeated 29 percent (twenty-one of seventy-three) incumbent Democrats in districts where Bush's average exceeded 50 percent, but only 9 percent (thirteen of 152) in districts where Bush's average fell short of this mark.

The handful of switches to the Democrats followed the same pattern: Democrats took four of five open Republican seats where the Democrats' average share exceeded 50 percent; they won none of other sixteen open Republican seats and defeated no Republican incumbents. The net effect of seats changing party hands in 1994 was a closer alignment of district-level presidential and House results than in any election since 1952—all the more remarkable because no presidential candidates were on the 1994 ballot.

Republicans won the House in 1994 because an unusually large number of districts voted locally as they had been voting nationally. The same is true, necessarily, of individual voters. The most notable change was a sharp increase in party loyalty among self-identified Republicans, particularly in districts with Democratic incumbents. The Republican defectors who had, in the past, helped Democrats win Republican-leaning districts deserted in large numbers. Congressional Republicans were thus finally able to cash in on their party's gains in party identifiers registered in polls a full ten years earlier.[51]

The Republican Party's successful organizational effort to nationalize the campaign was helped enormously by the new national networks of conservative talk-show hosts and conservative Christian activists. Conservatives in general and evangelical Christians in particular turned out at notably higher rates than other voters and comprised a significantly larger proportion of the electorate than in 1992.[52] Republican leaders did an outstanding job of organizing and mobilizing the groups in their coalition and of coaching their candidates in the art of using the party's themes effectively against Democrats.

Although the key to the Republican victory in 1994 lay in nationalizing the House elections, this does not mean that the candidate-centered, locally focused electoral politics was superseded. The 1994 elections were not "nationalized" in the sense that electoral forces operated consistently across districts. Although the mean district vote swing to Republicans was by recent historical standards quite large (5.9 percentage points, the largest since 1974), it was only slightly more uniform than the recent norm,[53] and the electoral value of incumbency was only slightly less impressive than usual (recall Figure 3–3). Lucky for the Democrats that it was not; the pattern of results displayed in Table 6–8 suggests that, without the incumbency advantage, the Democratic minority in the 104th Congress would have been considerably smaller.

Moreover, strategic behavior both reflected and magnified election year trends. Democrats behaved as if they expected it to be a bad year for their party and helped to make it so. Strategic Democratic retirements clearly hurt the party's overall performance. Although about the same proportion of House Democrats and Republicans retired (11 percent), most of the Republicans left to run for higher office (thirteen of twenty, 65 percent), whereas most of the departing Democrats (twenty of twenty-seven, 71 percent) did not. Among retirees who did not leave to pursue another office, age is the only variable with any predictive power for Republicans, whereas age, previous vote margin, and district presidential partisanship all contributed significantly to Democratic retirements; the closer the margin in 1992 and the more Republican the district in presidential voting, the more likely a Democrat was to retire. In simple percentages, 18 percent of the Democrats in districts that leaned Republican in presidential elections retired, compared with only 7 percent of the Democrats in districts that leaned Democratic in presidential elections. The retirements of the former group proved disastrous for the party; as Table 6–8 indicates, Republicans took every one of the sixteen seats thereby exposed. Another sign of the Democrats' strategic

TABLE 6–8 District Partisanship and Electoral Outcomes in 1994 House Elections (Percentage of Republican Victories)

	DISTRICT LEANS		
	Republican	**Democratic**	**sig.**
Seats held by Democrats			
Incumbents	28.8 (73)[a]	8.6 (152)	$p < .001$
Open Seats	100.0 (16)	40.0 (15)	$p < .001$
Seats held by Republicans			
Incumbents	100.0 (141)	100.0 (16)	n.s.
Open Seats	100.0 (16)	20.0 (5)	$p < .001$
Total	78.9 (246)	19.1 (188)	$p < .001$

[a]Number of districts from which percentages were calculated.

Note: Republican-leaning districts are defined as those in which the two-party vote for George Bush, averaged across 1988 and 1992, was greater than 50 percent; Democratic-leaning districts are those in which this average fell below 50 percent.

Source: Gary C. Jacobson, "The 1994 House Elections in Perspective," *in Midterm: Elections of 1994 in Perspective*, ed. Philip Klinkner (Boulder, Colorado: Westview Press, 1996).

response to expectations was the unusual distribution of uncontested seats. For the first time in the entire postwar era, Democrats conceded more seats to Republicans (thirty-five) than Republicans conceded to Democrats (seventeen) in the general election.

The quality of challengers also reflected rational career strategies, though as usual, potential Democratic challengers were much more sensitive to election year expectations than were Republicans. Democrats have long enjoyed a stronger "farm system" supplying experienced House candidates because they hold more of the lower-level offices that form the typical stepping stones to Congress (particularly in state legislatures). Normally, therefore, Democrats have a substantial advantage in fielding experienced challengers. On average over the previous twenty-four postwar congressional elections, 26 percent of the Republican incumbents, but only 16 percent of Democratic incumbents, faced challengers who had previously held elective public office. Prior to 1994, Republicans fielded the more experienced crop of challengers only twice: in 1966, when they picked up forty-seven seats, and in 1992, when they picked up ten seats while losing the White House. They did so again in 1994, but mainly because so few experienced Democrats were willing to take the field; only 14 percent of Republican incumbents faced experienced Democratic challengers, at the time the second-lowest proportion in any postwar election.

The Republicans' proportion of experienced challengers (16 percent) was merely average for them, but then many of their most highly touted challengers were unapologetic amateurs running as antigovernment outsiders. Despite all the rhetoric condemning "career politicians," however, experienced Republican challengers greatly outperformed the novices, picking up significantly more votes and victories. Experienced Republican challengers won 43 percent (fifteen of thirty-five) of the races they entered, compared with 11 percent (nineteen of 173) of inexperienced Republican challengers. Naturally, experienced challengers were more common in districts with Republican presidential leanings. But even controlling for local partisanship and other relevant variables, experienced challengers did significantly better than amateurs on election day.[54]

One reason experienced Republican challengers did better than the amateurs is that, as always, they raised and spent much more money. The distribution of campaign funds in 1994 followed the expected pattern for a year when campaign activists expect a strong partisan tide, so Republican challengers were significantly better funded than Democratic challengers. Not only was their average spending higher, but more of them were financed beyond the threshold usually required for a competitive campaign. Experienced Republican challengers were especially well funded, spending an average of $454,966 compared to $201,307 for the other Republican challengers. Democrats, on the defensive, channeled relatively more money to incumbents; Republican incumbents had far less to worry about and could get away with lower spending. As usual, both parties generously funded their candidates for open seats who were remotely competitive, regardless of national trends.

The strategic allocation of Republican campaign funds was also strongly influenced by local conditions. Republican challengers raised and spent more money in districts that leaned Republican in presidential elections, particularly in districts where Democratic incumbents had made themselves vulnerable by supporting their party and president on key roll-call votes. Thus Democratic loyalists in Republican-leaning districts were the principal targets of the most lavishly funded Republican challenges. Not surprisingly, the data show that they were most likely to lose the election as well.[55]

Multivariate analysis indicates that not only did support for the party's (and administration's) positions hurt Democrats indirectly by stimulating better-funded opposition, but it also hurt them directly as well. That is, House Democrats did not suffer across the board in 1994 for the alleged sins of their party and president; their difficulties were proportional to their support for the administration on the most visible issues before the 103rd Congress. Put another way, the Republicans' national campaign themes were evidently effective to the degree that individual Democrats were vulnerable to the charge of supporting the administration on controversial issues. National campaign themes were more effective in districts with a stronger inclination toward Republicans in presidential elections and where Bill Clinton was especially unpopular—the South.[56]

In sum, although all electoral politics were not local in 1994, the electoral effect of national issues varied across districts and regions, depending on incumbency, the quality of candidates, the level of campaign spending, the partisan makeup of the district, and the behavior of the incumbent. Wielding potent campaign themes drawn from national issues, Republicans needed only reasonably attractive and well-financed candidates to take seats from Democrats in districts that leaned Republican in presidential elections. Democratic retirements from such districts created a host of open-seat opportunities that well-funded Republican candidates exploited to the hilt. Against incumbent Democrats, Republicans did best where they fielded experienced, well-financed challengers against Democrats whose votes tied them to the Clinton administration in districts where the president (and his party more generally) were relatively unpopular—where, in other words, the local campaign could give their national themes the most extensive publicity and the local context gave these themes their greatest resonance.

Poorly funded Republican challengers were largely unsuccessful even in districts where the Democrat should have been vulnerable.[57] The central issues in the 1994 House elections may have been national but how they played out depended strongly on local circumstances.

After the upheavals of 1992 and 1994, the next two congressional elections appear positively mundane. Voters in both elections endorsed the status quo, retaining Republican majorities in both houses of Congress. Yet in both cases, although for different reasons, the status quo they endorsed was anything but ordinary.

1996

Despite Bill Clinton's easy reelection, Republican candidates did remarkably well in the 1996 House races. They lost only eight House seats on election day; moreover, because five Democratic opportunists had switched to the Republican side of the aisle after the 1994 election and Republicans enjoyed a net gain in special elections that were held during the 104th Congress, the party ended up with only three fewer House seats in 1996 than it had won in 1994. That a Democrat could win the White House by eight million votes without winning control of Congress would have been unthinkable only a few years earlier; every one of the twenty-six successful Democratic presidential candidates from Thomas Jefferson in 1800 through Bill Clinton in 1992 had brought Democratic majorities into the House with them. Yet by the time it happened, few informed political observers were surprised, a sign of how profoundly the balance of partisan competition had shifted in the 1990s.

Why were Democratic candidates for Congress unable to cash in on Clinton's victory? After all, Clinton's own reelection prospects had been dramatically enhanced by his victory in a showdown with the Republican Congress over the budget in 1995. When Republicans had tried to force Clinton to accept their package of tax and spending cuts by threatening to shut down the government, he had held firm. The Republicans' rhetoric (Speaker Newt Gingrich had told the Public Securities Association, "I don't care what the price is. I don't care if we have no executive offices, no bonds for 60 days."[58]) helped Clinton to paint them as extremists, and the Republican Congress absorbed most of the blame for the two government shutdowns that occurred when Clinton vetoed the Republicans' budget and the government's spending authority lapsed in late 1995. The public took Clinton's side in the dispute by decisive margins, and public ratings of Congress and Gingrich turned sharply downward. At the same time, Clinton's approval ratings rose, and he assumed a permanent lead over Bob Dole in the presidential polls; by the time Congress relented and let the government go back to work in January 1996, the presidential election was effectively decided.[59]

But if the House Republicans' mistakes reelected Clinton, why did they not also cost the Republicans control of Congress? The answer lies in changes in the structure of electoral competition for congressional seats that were both manifested and magnified by the 1994 elections and in the electoral politics of divided government during good times.

I have already noted one important structural change: the post-1990 redistricting that produced a more favorable set of districts for Republicans. But a second, related improvement in the Republicans' competitive position emerged from the 1994 election. Most of the seats the party added in 1994 were seats

Republicans should have held in the first place. We can calculate from the data in Table 6–8 that of the fifty-six districts newly taken by Republicans in 1994, thirty-seven (66 percent) had voted Republican, on average, in the two preceding elections. Democrats took back only four of these thirty-seven seats (11 percent), compared to six of the other nineteen (32 percent). Moreover, because Democrats still outnumbered Republicans in districts favoring the other party's presidential candidates (forty-eight to thirty-eight), going into 1996, the Democrats still held the large share of vulnerable seats. In 1996, they lost seven of those seats, while Republicans were losing twelve of theirs.

The Democrats' problems were compounded by another legacy of 1994: the loss of majority control. Predictably, the unaccustomed insults of minority status prompted a voluntary exodus of Democrats from the House, giving Republicans a shot at open seats in Republican-leaning districts. A higher number and proportion of Democrats than Republicans voluntarily left the House in 1996, and, as in 1994, a disproportionate share of the departing Democrats abandoned seats that had been voting Republican at the presidential level, particularly in the South; of twelve such seats opened in 1996, the Democrats lost six. Revealingly, twenty-three of the twenty-eight retiring House Democrats announced their departures before the end of 1995, while a majority of Republican retirees (eleven of twenty-one) announced theirs in 1996. Strategic retirements inspired by the Republicans' seeming ascendancy during most of 1995 made it harder for Democrats to exploit the shift in public opinion away from the Republican Congress after the budget showdown.

In addition, as we saw in Chapter 4, the Republican takeover of Congress transformed the campaign money market. Democrats no longer had the majority status and committee control to attract campaign contributions from business-oriented political action committees (PACs), which after 1994 were freer to follow the Republican hearts as well as their pocketbooks in allocating donations. Not only did such PACs have less reason to contribute to incumbent Democrats, they also had less reason to worry about contributing *against* incumbent Democrats, whose ability to retaliate against interests that funded their opponents had diminished sharply.

Finally, the shock of 1994, the prospective imbalance of campaign funds, and the expectation that they were likely to be in the minority evidently made it more difficult for the Democrats to recruit high-quality candidates to take on incumbent Republicans. As always, experienced challengers were far more successful than the rest. Democratic challengers who had previously held elective public office won 26 percent (twelve of forty-seven) of the contests they entered, compared to only 4 percent (six of 158) of the amateurs. The Democrats' problem was that only 22 percent of their challengers were experienced, a figure below their postwar average of 26 percent and not at all typical of a good Democratic year.

The Campaigns

Strategic career decisions taken by prospective Democratic congressional candidates, along with the other structural shifts in the balance of competition for seats, clearly made it harder for the Democrats to exploit Clinton's victory. But it would have been difficult to exploit in any case. The anticongressional Republican stance so helpful to Clinton was not as helpful to Democrats for several reasons. First, many potentially vulnerable House Republicans did what Democrats had routinely done to hold on to seats against contrary national tides during their forty-two years of control: run as independent champions of local district interests. Had they stuck together throughout the 104th Congress as they had in the early months on the Contract with America, the 1996 elections might have become a referendum on their collective performance as a party. In the end, however, the Republicans' brief flirtation with responsible party government succumbed to the desire of individual members to win reelection and of the party as a whole to keep its majority. After the budget debacle, Republicans with moderate constituencies bolted the party on such issues as repeal of the assault weapons ban, weakening endangered species protection, and raising the minimum wage.[60] The Contract with America, so prominent in 1994 and 1995, was conspicuous by its absence from most of the Republican incumbents' 1996 campaigns.

Second, Clinton's reelection strategy was unhelpful to congressional Democrats. The closest historical precedent for the Republican triumph of 1994 was 1946, the last time the Republicans had won control of Congress at the midterm with a Democrat in the White House. Democrats hoped, and Republicans feared, that the precedent for 1996 would be 1948, when Harry Truman's political resurrection swept the Democrats back into control of Congress. Unfortunately for the Democrats, the historical model for 1996 was not 1948, but 1984, when Ronald Reagan rode to easy reelection on a tide of good economic news while his party was picking up only fourteen seats in the House and losing three in the Senate.

Both Reagan and Clinton ran upbeat campaigns extolling a strong economy and popular policy successes. Both drew on extraordinary political skills to extend their personal appeal beyond their party's normal electoral base. Both won easy reelection. But neither of their campaigns offered much leverage to their congressional challengers. If times are good and the president deserves another term, why replace incumbents of the majority party in Congress, who can plausibly claim a share of the credit for peace, prosperity, and progress? The other status quo elections held under divided government—Dwight D. Eisenhower's reelection in 1956 and Richard Nixon's reelection in 1972—offer confirming examples. As Table 6–9 shows, every postwar president reelected to a second full term had remarkably short coattails. All four saw their party lose seats in the Senate, and their largest pickup in the House was Reagan's paltry fourteen seats in 1984.

TABLE 6–9 Congressional Results When Presidents are Elected to a Second Full Term Under Divided Government

Year	President	Vote	House	Senate
1956	Eisenhower (R)	57.7%	2 D	1 D
1972	Nixon (R)	61.8%	12 R	2 D
1984	Reagan (R)	59.2%	14 R	2 D
1996	Clinton (D)	54.5%	8 D	2 R

Note: "D" refers to Democrats, "R" to Republicans; the vote percentage is calculated from the major party vote.

Third, the difficulty for Democratic challengers was amplified by the very strategy that revived Clinton's presidency. By accepting so many of the Republicans' goals—agreeing to balance the budget by 2002, declaring that "the era of big government is over," signing a bill to end welfare entitlements that had been part of the social safety net since the New Deal, opposing gay marriages, and supporting prayer in school—Clinton took command of the political center. But by campaigning on a record indistinguishable from that of a moderate Republican, he gave voters little reason to elect more Democrats to Congress.

Clinton helped congressional Republicans in other ways, as well. His firm opposition to unpopular budget cuts, assaults on environmental regulation and the Department of Education, and kindred Republican proposals in 1995 forced Republicans to rein in their most extreme impulses and alerted them to the political danger lurking in revolutionary rhetoric and radical policy changes. Clinton's maneuvering toward consensus on the budget decisions and on issues such as welfare reform, minimum wage, and health insurance portability gave them a chance to look responsible and effective.

Moreover, the administration's aura of scandal and widespread doubts about Clinton's personal character offered voters an additional reason to keep Republicans in a position to keep an eye on him. Indeed, there is some evidence that the revelations late in the campaign of foreign contributions to the Democratic National Committee moved many late-deciding voters into the Republican column, reducing Clinton's margin of victory and thereby impeding the Democrats' effort to retake the House.[61] In addition, despite the implied affront to Dole, Republican leaders did not hesitate to make the near certainty of Clinton's reelection an argument for voting Republican for Congress. A majority of voters did so, and Republicans kept control of Congress.

1998

From one perspective, the results of the 1998 House elections were stunning. For only the second time since the Civil War, the president's party increased its strength in the House at midterm.[62] Democrats gained five seats, leaving the Republicans with a narrow 223–211 majority.[63] Shocked and angered by their losses, House Republicans drove Speaker Newt Gingrich, architect of their historic 1994 victory, to resign.

From another perspective, however, there is little remarkable about what happened in 1998. The national conditions that normally shape midterm elections had their usual effects: The voters, for good and familiar reasons, delivered a ringing endorsement of the political status quo. What makes the election nonetheless remarkable is, of course, that despite the president's involvement in a scandal that transfixed Washington throughout 1998 and led to his impeachment in the House and trial and acquittal in the Senate, the status quo that voters endorsed clearly included Bill Clinton in the White House.

That voters did opt for the status quo in 1998 is beyond question. Only six House incumbents met defeat and only seventeen House seats switched party control; the former ties the record and the latter sets the record for the least change in any midterm election. Both Democratic and Republican incumbents enjoyed an average vote gain of 2.8 percentage points over 1996. The 395 members returned to office in 1998 are the most for any midterm House election ever. The contrast between the first and second midterm elections of the Clinton presidency could scarcely be starker.

The triumph of the status quo in 1998 is fully consistent with national conditions. House Democrats went into the 1998 elections with only two more seats than they had held after their 1994 disaster, so their exposure was minimal. The economy was booming, with both inflation and unemployment at thirty-year lows. Moreover, the federal budget was in surplus for the first time in nearly thirty years, and violent crime and welfare dependency were dramatically lower than they had been just a few years earlier. Consistent with these highly favorable trends, Bill Clinton's job approval rating stood at 66 percent in the final Gallup poll taken before the election, the highest for any president in any midterm preelection poll since Gallup had begun asking the question more than 50 years before.[64] Plugging the appropriate values for 1998 into the equation in Table 6–2 generates the prediction that the Democrats would pick up nine seats, so their actual gain of six accurately reflected the fundamentals prevailing in 1998.

These fundamentals scarcely posed a threat to incumbent Republicans, however. Clinton and his fellow Democrats could not claim exclusive credit for good times because Republicans controlled the Congress. As always, the divided government divided credit or blame for the government's performance as well. Thus, as Clinton's approval ratings reached new heights, so did ratings of the Republican Congress; in early 1998, approval of Congress reached 57 percent—to that date, the highest level recorded in the twenty-five years the question had been asked. Incumbents of both parties benefited; in October, 58 percent of Gallup's respondents thought that most members of Congress deserved reelection, compared to 29 percent in 1992, 39 percent in 1994, and 55 percent in 1996.[65] With conditions so favorable to the political status quo, neither party stood to make much in the way of gains.

The 1998 election results, then, are about what we would expect if no one had ever heard of Monica Lewinsky. But this, of course, raises the central puzzles posed by the 1998 elections: Why did transgressions that led Special Prosecutor Kenneth Starr to recommend and the House to impeach Clinton fail to bring down the president's job approval and, with it, congressional Democrats? How is it that a scandal that obsessed the Washington community throughout the election year could have so little apparent impact on the results? What, if any, impact did the scandal actually have?

The Scandal and the Campaigns

News stories reporting Clinton's sexual relationship with Lewinsky, and charges that he had committed perjury and obstruction of justice to cover it up, surfaced just before the president's annual State of the Union address in January 1998. Clinton flatly and publicly denied all charges. The scandal's buzz helped boost the audience for the speech, which was watched by an estimated fifty-three million Americans. In it, Clinton resolutely ignored his personal problems, reminding people instead of the happy trends we have already noted, along with other blessings flowing from peace and prosperity during his watch. The public clearly got the message Clinton was trying to convey, and Clinton's approval ratings jumped to the highest levels of his presidency, surpassing 70 percent in some polls.

The public's reaction to the State of the Union address ended speculation that the Lewinsky affair would lead to Clinton's quick exit, but the scandal still complicated strategic election-year calculations. The customary forecasting cues available in early 1998 offered little hope for challengers of either party. Public satisfaction with the economy, the president, the Congress, and the United States in general were extraordinarily high.[66] Unless these assessments deteriorated sharply before election day, it would be very difficult to persuade voters to opt for change of any kind. But the Lewinsky scandal obviously did contain the potential for a dramatic deterioration in the public's rating of the president, leaving the predictive value of his current standing in serious doubt.

The scandal flared up just in time to discourage potential Democratic challengers not already daunted by the dismal track record of challengers representing the president's party at midterm. Mere mention of "impeachment" evoked memories of Watergate's devastating effect on the Republicans in 1974. Moreover, Clinton was far and away the Democrats' best fundraiser; if the scandal impaired his financial touch, Democratic candidates' fundraising problems would be compounded.[67]

The same considerations that spooked Democrats should have heartened Republicans. Yet potential Republican challengers faced the same uncertainty about how Clinton's self-inflicted travails would play out. Perhaps the public would finally turn against the president, taking their disaffection out on congressional Democrats. Yet nothing in the initial public reaction to the story promised a swelling Republican tide. Indeed, rather the opposite happened; Clinton's astonishing capacity to bounce back was a matter of public record. With relatively few Democratic targets vulnerable on their own, and with the public seemingly delighted with the status quo, potential Republican challengers had ample reason to question their own prospects.

As a consequence of these considerations, neither party recruited a cohort of challengers likely to take more than a handful of seats from the other side. Nearly one-quarter of House incumbents enjoyed a completely free ride; fifty-five Republicans and thirty-nine Democrats were unopposed in the general election, numbers dramatically higher than those of the preceeding three elections. Among those spared major party opposition were ten Republicans and eight Democrats who had won less than 55 percent of the vote in 1996 or who had represented districts won by the other party's presidential candidate that year. That so many such likely targets failed to draw even token challenges is strong evidence of widespread strategic capitulation by both sides in 1998.

The challengers who did show up were not a very formidable group. Only 18 percent of Republican incumbents faced Democrats with prior elective office experience, well below the 26 percent or so expected from either the postwar average or national conditions prevalent early in the election year. Democrats were apparently more skittish about their chances than the economy or Clinton's standing early in the election year would lead us to expect, suggesting that the scandal's shadow did indeed take a toll. This is probably the only way in which the Lewinsky affair actually hurt congressional Democrats in 1998.

The proportion of Democratic incumbents facing experienced Republican challengers was similar, 18 percent, and stood slightly above the postwar average (16 percent) or the proportion projected based on national conditions (15 percent). The scandal may have made Republicans a bit more optimistic than usual, but the data may also merely reflect the larger pool of experienced politicians created by Republican gains in state and local elections in the 1990s. On the whole, though, neither party fielded a large enough class of formidable challengers either to signal or to justify optimism about changing the status quo.

The public's initial reaction to the Lewinsky scandal established a pattern that persisted through the rest of the election year. People's opinions on Clinton's performance as president diverged sharply from opinions on his culpability in the affair. From the very first, more people than not believed Clinton had had an affair with Lewinsky and had lied about it under oath. As the year wore on, the proportion of skeptics grew, and views of Clinton's personal character and honesty became increasingly negative.[68]

These beliefs did not, however, lessen approval of Clinton's policies or job performance or lead to widespread demands for his departure. Instead, the public soured on Kenneth Starr and his investigation. By March, moderate Republicans had begun to worry that Starr's unpopularity might rub off on them and that anything short of an open-and-shut case for impeachment would be politically disastrous.[69] In April, with public support for Clinton undiminished, Newt Gingrich joined other conservative Republican leaders in a full-scale offensive, attacking Clinton for "the most systematic, deliberate obstruction of justice, coverup, and effort to avoid the truth we have ever seen in American history."[70] The attacks were designed to mollify the party's socially conservative core supporters and to persuade the broader public that the scandal was about perjury and obstruction of justice, not about sex. While perhaps achieving the first goal, Gingrich failed conspicuously to achieve the second.

Republicans believed they had at last struck political gold when, on August 17, Clinton testified on videotape for a grand jury and then publicly confessed to having had a relationship with Lewinsky that was "not appropriate" and lying about it to the American people. Republican candidates immediately began calling for Clinton to resign and linking their opponents to the White House. "Our intention is to brand every single Democrat in the state with the scarlet 'C,'" said the executive director of the South Carolina Republican Party. "Bill Clinton . . . has reenergized our base. . . . We will gratuitously use Clinton's face on all our literature."[71]

Congressional Democrats, feeling betrayed, publicly vented their disappointment, disgust, and embarrassment, and several called on Clinton to resign. When Starr's report, recommending impeachment for perjury and obstruction of justice and containing excruciatingly detailed descriptions of Clinton's sexual dalliance with Lewinsky, was delivered with great fanfare to the House of Representatives, 138 Democrats joined the Republicans in voting to release its full text to the public. The report was posted on the Internet on September 11; ten days later, Clinton's videotaped grand jury testimony was also made public.

To the frustration of Republicans and wary relief of Democrats, the Starr report and video testimony left public opinion about Clinton and impeachment almost unchanged. His job approval ratings remained high and in some polls even improved. The proportion of Americans wanting him out, either by impeachment or resignation, rose briefly before the contents of the report and videotape were fully exposed and then began to recede, falling back below 30 percent as election day approached. At no point did less than a solid majority want Clinton to remain in office.

Why did the Lewinsky scandal fail to undermine Clinton's support? Survey data support several complementary explanations. First, the scandal could not disillusion people who had no illusions to begin with. His August confession and the subsequent impeachment hearings merely confirmed what most people already believed and thus had already factored into their assessments of Clinton. He retained popular support not because people thought him an innocent victim of his enemies' machinations or that his behavior was excusable, but despite the common belief that he was guilty as charged and was mostly to blame for his troubles.[72]

Second, while most Americans condemned Clinton's behavior and character, most also liked what had been happening with the things that directly affected their own lives—jobs, inflation, incomes, crime rates—during his presidency. As we have seen, the public had good reason to be satisfied with national economic and social trends during the Clinton administration and to want them to continue. The positive trends continued through the election year and beyond, clearly to Clinton's benefit. At the time Clinton's trial was about to begin in the Senate, more than 60 percent of the public approved of his performance on the budget, crime, and foreign policy, and more than 80 percent approved of his performance on the economy.[73]

Third, people who liked Clinton's policies but disapproved of his behavior had a convenient way to avoid cognitive dissonance: They could adopt the view that the scandal was about sex and that the president's sex life was a private, not public, matter. In polls taken during 1998, nearly two-thirds of the public consistently took this position. And finally, Clinton was fortunate in his enemies. Over the course of the scandal, the public came to disdain Clinton's antagonists—Starr, Republican congressional leaders, the news media—even more than they did him.[74]

But most important, and basic to all these other explanations, is that the public's response to the scandal was starkly partisan. This was particularly true of people identifying themselves as Democrats; Clinton retained his support largely because ordinary people in his own party refused to turn against him. In polls taken during September and October, self-identified Democrats divided on at about 85–15 against impeachment or resignation, while Republican identifiers favored both by about 60–40.[75] The partisans who turned out to vote in 1998 were even more polarized. Among Democratic voters surveyed by the NES, 92 percent approved of Clinton's performance, 90 percent opposed his resignation, and 93 percent opposed his impeachment. Among Republican voters, only 40 percent approved of Clinton's performance, 70 percent wanted him to resign, and 63 percent wanted him impeached if he didn't resign.

With Clinton's public support holding steady, the House Republicans' decision on October 8 to hold impeachment hearings was not popular, and Congress's approval ratings, while remaining high by historical comparison, began to slide. Instead of enjoying a winning issue, congressional Republicans found themselves in a serious political bind. Their core constituency of social conservatives demanded impeachment and would be unforgiving of anything less, while the broader public was overwhelmingly opposed to removing the president.

The public's reaction to the events of August and September made it increasingly unlikely that the Clinton–Lewinsky scandal would, by itself, swing elections to Republican congressional candidates. With so much of the electorate sick of hearing about it, just bringing up the matter risked a backlash, and so candidates on both sides tended to ignore it. Mindful of the polls, most Republican candidates carefully avoided suggesting that the election should be a referendum on impeachment. Yet this left them with little else to say, for having staked victory on Clinton's troubles, they were unprepared to wage campaigns on issues that voters were saying they did care about. And those issues—notably education, HMO reform, and protecting Social Security—were the kind on which voters think Democrats do a better job than Republicans anyway. The public's distinction between Clinton the president and Clinton the person freed Democrats to campaign on Clinton's policy agenda without defending his character or behavior. A few Democratic challengers even turned the impeachment issue to their advantage. In one notable instance in New Jersey, Democratic challenger Rush Holt upset incumbent Michael Pappas in a campaign that featured TV ads showing Pappas literally singing the praises of Kenneth Starr (to the tune of "Twinkle Twinkle Little Star") on the floor of the House.[76]

Although most of the public seemed unmoved by the scandal, Republicans still hoped that it would help them by mobilizing their Clinton-hating core supporters while discouraging disaffected Democrats from voting. The party's $10 million media blitz during the last week of the campaign sought to exploit the scandal to these ends. But in the end, it was Republicans—disaffected because they opposed impeachment—who were more likely to stay home.[77]

Ultimately, then, the election was not a referendum on impeachment—to the great good fortune of the Republican Party. For a large majority of voters, strongly positive national trends trumped all other considerations, leaving them disposed to continue the political status quo by reelecting incumbents of both parties. Prospective challengers who thought it would be a tough year to pry support away from incumbents turned out to be right, although their prophecy was, as usual, in large part self-fulfilling. Republicans, trusting that Clinton's disgrace would be their ticket to victory, were left without a viable message to use against Democratic incumbents when the issue fizzled. Democrats were able to squeeze some small advantage from voters' opposition to impeachment and a favorable issue climate and so enjoyed modest but symbolically important gains.[78] Yet the Clinton–Lewinsky scandal probably scared off high-quality challengers in potentially winnable districts, leaving Democrats poorly prepared to take full advantage of their unexpected good fortune. It is worth noting in this regard that four of the five winning Democratic challengers were from that small fraction who had prior experience in elective office (as was the lone successful Republican challenger); all were generously funded.[79]

2000

The 2000 elections were as close to a dead heat across the board as we are ever likely to see. As such, they accurately represented the close partisan balance now prevailing in the United States. As we saw in Chapter 5, the substantial popular majority among party identifiers that Democrats had enjoyed since the New Deal was largely gone by the mid-1980s, a change traceable largely to realignment of southerners and social conservatives into the Republican camp.[80] Democrats have since retained a small advantage among party identifiers in most polls,[81] but because self-identified Republicans are more likely to vote than Democrats and are slightly more loyal to their party when they do, the normal electoral balance is now nearly even.

The congressional election results in 2000 mirrored this close partisan balance because national forces were essentially neutral. The narrow margin separating Bush and Gore (Bush won 49.7 percent of the major-party popular votes, 50.4 percent of the electoral votes) meant that neither party benefited nationally from presidential coattails. Nor did any other national conditions clearly favor one party over the other. Unlike 1994, but like 1996 and 1998, the electoral environment in 2000 broadly favored the congressional status quo. The economy continued to look strong through election day. Modest inflation, low unemployment, rising family incomes, a growing federal budget surplus, and declining rates of crime and welfare dependency had left the public largely content with the direction of the country and approving of its elected leaders.

In an October 2000 Gallup Poll, more than 70 percent of the public rated the economy as excellent or good, and more than 70 percent approved of Clinton's economic performance. Twice as many Americans were satisfied as were dissatisfied with the direction of the country. This was good news for the Democrats, presumably, but Clinton had to share credit with the Republican-controlled Congress, where incumbents of both parties stood to benefit from the generally high levels of public satisfaction.[82] At the time of the 2000 elections, both Clinton and the Republican Congress were enjoying unusually high levels of approval by historical standards.[83] The most plausible reason that public approval of the president and a Congress dominated by his enemies moved in rough parallel is that many Americans evaluate both branches by the same criteria—namely, the economy and the general state of the nation.[84]

The high level of public satisfaction with Congress and the absence of a discernable partisan tide had a predictably dampening effect on House competition in 2000. Only the most vulnerable incumbents attracted formidable, well-funded opponents, and in the end only six incumbents—four Republicans and two Democrats—were defeated in the general election.[85] Even many of the thirty-five open seats were not hotly contested because the districts' partisan makeup so clearly favored one of the parties. Most of these noncompetitive open seats were held by Republicans, so that although the Republicans had to defend twenty-five open seats to the Democrats' ten, they actually enjoyed a net gain of one open seat on election day.

The battle for control of the House was thus highly concentrated in a small number of seats, where unprecedented sums were spent by both the candidates and diverse independent and "voter education" campaigns operating outside the regular campaigns' purview (see Chapter 4). Most prominent among the handful of incumbents who did attract vigorous opposition were Republicans from Democratic-leaning districts who had defied the manifest wishes of a majority of their constituents by voting to impeach Clinton. Three of the four Republican incumbents who lost fell into this category: Californians Brian Bilbray and James Rogan, both representing districts where Clinton had won 55 percent of the major-party vote in 1996, and Jay Dickey of Arkansas, representing a district where Clinton had won 66 percent. But Republicans as a group escaped punishment for their widely unpopular move to oust the president by the simple fact that it failed. Most voters got what they wanted, continuation of the Clinton presidency, and saw no reason to punish Republicans wholesale for the attempt. Just as good times helped Clinton to survive the impeachment process, the strong economy probably helped protect the Republicans in Congress from any impeachment backlash by encouraging public contentment with the status quo.

Also contributing to an uneventful election was the House Republicans' shrewd defensive campaign strategy that was, ironically, almost the exact inverse of the one that had given them their majorities in 1994. Rather than campaign as a team pledged to a common program as they had with the Contract with America in 1994, Republican campaigns in 2000 centered on individual candidates and locally important issues.[86] Instead of boldly challenging Clinton, congressional Republicans sought, after impeachment, to avoid confrontations with the president at all costs. Democrats had hoped to make the Republican Congress an issue, but congressional Republicans carefully avoided battles that would remind voters either of the 1995 government shutdown or impeachment, instead curbing their ideological rhetoric and rolling out the pork barrel.[87]

In the end, relatively few seats changed party control (seventeen, tied for third lowest among the twenty-seven post–World War II congressional elections), but on balance the changes that occurred increased the partisan match between districts and members, extending one of the most important developments of the Clinton era (see Figure 6–3).

2002

In 2002, for the second midterm election in a row, the president's party gained seats in the House. Prior to 1998, this had happened only once since the Civil War,[88] and some postelection analysts read the Republicans' upset of naïve expectations based on the historical pattern as both surprising and indicative of a pro-Republican national tide.[89] But just as in 1998, nothing in the 2002 results challenged our current understanding of the processes that shape midterm congressional elections. Rather, the Republican gain of six House seats (seven more than its 2000 total) was entirely consistent with models treating midterm elections as a referendum on the administration and economy.[90] It was also more a consequence of redistricting than of any national shift in public sentiment toward the Republican Party. And it was the undeniable if unintended gift of Osama bin Laden.

In the final Gallup Poll taken before the 2002 election, 63 percent of the public approved of George W. Bush's performance as president.[91] While Bush's approval rating in 2002 was not as high as Bill Clinton's was in November 1998 (66 percent), it tied Ronald Reagan's 1986 rating for second highest in any postwar midterm election. Bush's high public approval, like that of Clinton and Reagan before him, clearly helped his party's congressional candidates, but this was in no way unusual.[92] The unusual thing was the origin of his high ratings: the terrorist attacks of September 11, 2001, on New York and Washington and Bush's response to them.

The events of September 11 and their aftermath profoundly transformed the electoral context for 2002, most importantly by redefining the Bush presidency and transforming public perceptions of the president. Bush had entered the White House only after the Republican appointees on the Supreme Court had settled the fierce partisan battle over the Florida vote count in his favor. In polls taken shortly after the election, a large majority of Americans who had voted for his Democratic opponent, Al Gore, regarded Bush's victory as illegitimate.[93] As a result, Bush never enjoyed the customary winner's honeymoon. His initial reception by the public showed the widest partisan differences for any newly elected president in polling history.[94] In the twenty-eight Gallup and CBS News/*New York Times* polls taken prior to September 11, Bush's approval ratings averaged 88 percent among self-identified Republicans but only 31 percent among Democrats.[95] This 57-point gap marked Bush as an even more polarizing figure than the former record holder, Bill Clinton (with a 52-point average partisan approval gap for the equivalent period). Among Democrats at least, Bush's competence and legitimacy remained in doubt until September 11.[96]

The shock of September 11 and the president's forceful response to the crisis rallied nearly the entire nation to his side. The terrorist attacks radically altered the context in which people responded to the approval question; the president was now to be evaluated the defender of American democracy against shadowy foreign enemies rather than a partisan figure of questionable competence and legitimacy. As Figure 6–9 shows, Bush's approval ratings jumped to record levels, as high as 90 percent in some polls. The already large supportive Republican majority grew to near unanimity, but Democrats accounted for most of the change, as their approval ratings shot up by 50 percentage points.[97] Although Bush's level of approval declined steadily after the beginning of the election year, especially among Democrats, it remained high by historical comparison.

The president's rise in public esteem improved the Republicans' prospects for 2002 in a variety of ways. It helped the administration escape the consequences of the financial scandals, epitomized by the collapse of Enron, involving Bush's political cronies and campaign contributors. It is easy to imagine how the Democrats would have exploited the president's vulnerability on this dimension had his

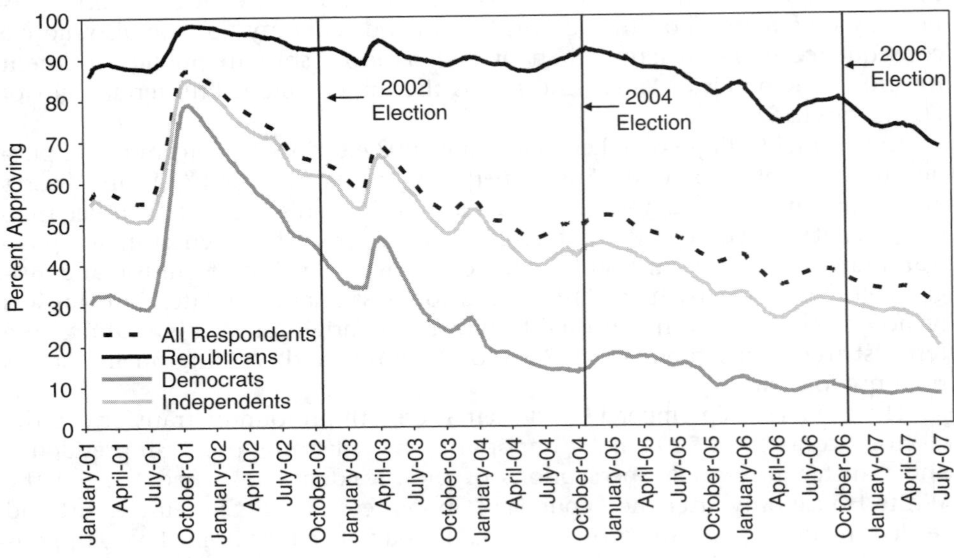

FIGURE 6–9 Approval of George W. Bush's Performance, 2001–2007
Source: Lowess-smoothed trends from 351 CBS News/*New York Times* and Gallup Polls.

status as commander-in-chief in the war on terrorism not put partisan criticism beyond the pale at the very time the scandals emerged. In the end, Democrats derived no apparent electoral benefit from scandals otherwise ideally suited to their strategy of depicting the Bush administration and congressional Republicans as agents of greedy corporations, indifferent to the jobs, investments, and pensions of ordinary Americans.

Bush's popularity also scared off high-quality Democrat challengers. Bush's sky-high ratings during the period when potential candidates had to make decisions about running evidently discouraged politically experienced and ambitious Democrats. As a result, the cohort of Democratic House challengers fielded in 2002 was the lowest quality (in terms of prior success in winning elective public office) of any postwar election, except the 1990 midterm.[98]

Other changes in the electoral environment wrought by the events of September 11 went beyond the president's rise in public esteem and were equally beneficial to Republicans. The shift in political focus from domestic issues to national defense and foreign policy moved the debates from Democratic turf to Republican turf. Asked in preelection polls which party in Congress would do a better job dealing with health care, education, Social Security, prescription drug benefits, taxes, abortion, unemployment, the environment, and corporate corruption, most respondents chose Democrats. Asked which party would do a better job dealing with terrorism, the possibility of war with Iraq, the situation in the Middle East, and foreign affairs, most preferred Republicans.[99] Voters put terrorism and the prospect of war at the top of their list of concerns, providing a major assist to the Republican cause. Without September 11, the election would have hinged on domestic issues, and the talk of invading Iraq would have seemed like "wagging the dog," a transparent attempt to deflect attention from the economy.

The war on terrorism also helped deflect blame from the administration and its congressional allies for the return of budget deficits. The extraordinary expense of dealing with the physical and economic damage inflicted by the attacks and of tightening homeland security against future threats was unavoidable. Wars, after all, are always fought on borrowed money.

The Economy

The slow economy was potentially a much greater electoral threat to Republicans than the return of red ink (to which it also of course contributed). Had Democrats succeeded in making the economy the dominant issue, they might well have run the 108th Congress. Yet once again, September 11 and its aftermath shielded the administration and Republican congressional candidates from the full force of economic discontent. Although the president sought to blame the terrorist attacks for aborting the recovery from the mild recession of 2001, he could not escape generally negative public reviews of his economic performance. Despite less than stellar grades on the economy, however, his leadership in the war on terrorism kept his overall ratings high.[100] Had the terrorist attacks not occurred, Bush's overall approval rating would have remained much closer to his approval rating on handling the economy—averaging just below 50 percent for September and October 2002, and this alone might have cost Republicans control of the House.[101]

Ironically, the economy itself—at least by the usual measures, including the growth in real disposable income, the variable used in the equation in Table 6–2—was not particularly bad by historical standards; but the bursting of the stock market bubble and the sharp rise in unemployment that followed had left the public with a decidedly negative view of the economy. In a preelection poll, only about one-quarter of Gallup's respondents rated the economy "excellent" or "good," whereas nearly three-quarters found it only "fair" or "poor," the worst net rating of the economy since 1994. Consumer confidence was at its lowest level since 1993.[102] It was all the more important, then, that Bush's approval ratings were detached from the economy and that Republicans were able to deflect attention from the domestic economy to foreign policy and defense issues.

Exposure and Redistricting

In 2002, just as in 1998, low exposure helps explain why the president's party gained rather than lost seats. George W. Bush lost the popular vote by 540,000 votes, and Republicans lost a net two House seats in 2000; because Bush had no discernable coattails and left House Republicans with no additional marginal House seats, Democrats had relatively few easy targets in 2002. Redistricting diminished the number of potential targets for Democrats even further. Indeed, as we saw in Chapter 2, redistricting, especially when combined with the high level of partisan consistency in district voting patterns, is sufficient to explain the Republican House gains in 2002.

We also saw in Chapter 2 that redistricting tended to strengthen incumbents of both parties in 2002. Consequently, the number of competitive House races was abnormally low. Usually, the shakeup set in motion by redistricting produces a bumper crop of competitive races in years ending in 2. Not in 2002; the number of districts classified by *Congressional Quarterly* as "tossup" or "leaning" prior to the election totaled only 48, compared to 103 in 1992 and 84 in 1982.[103] Redistricting patterns were a major reason for the dearth of competitive races in 2002; the shortage of plausible opportunities helps to explain why Republicans as well as Democrats fielded relatively few strong challengers and why the small number of races that were competitive attracted such a disproportionate share of campaign resources.

In the end, 2002 produced the smallest number of successful House challenges (four) of any general election in U.S. history. To be sure, incumbents did not survive redistricting entirely unscathed; four also lost general elections to other incumbents, four were defeated in primaries by other incumbents, and four were defeated in primaries by challengers. But the total number of defeated incumbents, sixteen, was less than half the average (thirty-five) for postwar election years ending in 2. The number of voluntary retirements was also lower than normal for a reapportionment year. As a consequence, only fifty-four new members entered the House when the 108th Congress met in 2003, fewer than half of the 110 newcomers seated in 1992 and well below the average for postwar reapportionment years (eighty-two).

2004

The 2004 elections left the Republican Party in its strongest position since Herbert Hoover was elected president back in 1928. George W. Bush won reelection by a modest but unambiguous margin (50.7 percent to John Kerry's 48.3 percent of the popular vote), while the Republicans solidified their congressional majorities by adding three House seats and four Senate seats. The election was not, however, a ringing electoral endorsement of the administration's or Republican Congress's performance, nor did it represent any global shift in public sentiment to the Republican side. Rather, it was the product of two salient features of American politics during the first decade of the twenty-first century: the substantial structural advantage Republicans enjoy in the struggle for control of Congress, and the extraordinarily polarized public reactions to the Bush administration, sentiments that found their fullest expression in the presidential contest but also spilled over into congressional races.

The election brought little change to the House of Representatives. Only seven of the 402 incumbents who sought reelection were defeated, and four of the seven were victims of the Republican gerrymander in Texas discussed in Chapter 2, not swings in voter sentiment. The party already in control held onto twenty-seven of the thirty-four open seats, and two of the three that were lost by Democrats were also a legacy of the Texas redistricting, as was the Republican pickup of the state's new open seat. Without the Texas remap, only eight House seats would have changed party hands, an all-time low.

The fierce battle for the White House remained in doubt until election day, but there was no similar contest for control of the House. Despite data showing Democrats with a lead among voters in both party identification and the generic House vote in polls taken during the months leading up to the election,[104] continued Republican control of the House was never in doubt. The reason is simple: the structural advantage Republicans enjoy from the more efficient distribution of their regular voters across House districts (see Figure 2–3 and the related discussion in Chapter 2). Without a strong national tide in their favor, Democrats had no serious prospect of winning control of the House.

No partisan tide was on the horizon in 2004. The economy's performance during the entire George W. Bush administration was mediocre by historical standards, but growth was solid in the year leading up to the election and the economy's earlier weakness could be blamed, in part, on the damage done to markets by the attacks of 9/11. Real per capita income grew by 2.4 percent during 2004, close to the average of 2.7 for postwar presidential election years. The net loss of jobs since Bush took office in 2001 gave Democrats something to talk about, but the modest improvements during 2004 took the edge off the issue.

President Bush's job approval ratings also fell into a politically neutral range. Although declining from the record-high rating Bush enjoyed during the immediate post-9/11 rally and the robust 63 percent registered at the time of the 2002 election, they generally remained above 50 percent until February 2004 and stayed close to this mark through the election (Figure 6–9). The relatively low performance ratings Americans gave the president on the economy (an average of 43 percent approving, August through October) continued to be offset by notably higher performance ratings on his handling of terrorism (56 percent approving), keeping the president's overall job approval at a level that offered neither party's congressional candidates a discernable advantage, even after Bush's handling of the Iraq War had become a net liability (44 percent approving during this period).[105]

More important, the *composition* of Bush's overall approval ratings promised neither party's congressional candidates any help. Bush enjoyed overwhelming support from Republicans, achieving the highest job-approval ratings within his own party of any president in the more than fifty years pollsters have been asking the question. But his approval rating among Democratic identifiers fell steeply after the post-9/11 rally and by the beginning of 2004 had dipped below 20 percent (Figure 6–9). It fell further during the campaign, reaching the lowest point the Gallup Poll ever recorded to that date among the rival party's identifiers—8 percent in one October 2004 poll. Ironically, the candidate who had pledged in his 2000 acceptance speech campaign to be "a uniter, not a divider" had become the most polarizing president on record.[106]

In such a highly polarized atmosphere, neither party could anticipate attracting many partisan defectors on election day, so the vast majority of House districts were ceded to the dominant party. The consequence was the lowest level of competition for House seats ever observed. *Congressional Quarterly* classified only thirty-seven contests as "no clear favorite" or merely "leaning" to one party, the smallest number of competitive races in the three decades the publication has been handicapping House contests.[107] Only the most vulnerable House incumbents—very few in number—attracted formidable challenges. And in a departure from past elections, even open House seat contests were relatively quiet in 2004. Only eleven of the thirty-five were classified as competitive by *Congressional Quarterly*. (In 2000 and 2002, by comparison, more than half of open seats were rated competitive.) One reason is that only nine of these seats were in the "wrong" party's hands according to the district's 2000 presidential vote; in twenty-one open districts, the 2000 presidential vote for the candidate of the party currently holding the seat exceeded 55 percent.

In sum, few districts were in play in 2004 because the ingredients of a competitive race were missing in so many places; not only was no partisan tide running, but there were few seats where local partisanship or missteps by the incumbent gave the out-party hope. In the end, five of the seven open seats that switched party control in 2004 went to the party with the 2000 presidential majority, as did the new open seat in Texas, the two Texas seats where incumbents faced off, and four of the five other seats where challengers were successful. Thus, although the House elections produced very little change, they extended the long-term trend toward increasing district-level consistency in House and presidential voting, documented in Figure 6–3, and in partisan loyalty among voters, documented in Figure 5–1.

Finally, it is worth noting that the net results of the House elections were again almost exactly what the statistical models of the effects of national forces on aggregate election outcomes. For example, the second equations in Table 6–5 predicts a three-seat gain for Democrats in 2004, just what they would have achieved were it not for the Texas redistricting (which was, of course, not factored into the model).

2006

Democrats picked up thirty House seats in 2006 to win a 233–202 majority, one seat larger that held by the Republicans in the previous Congress. They also gained six Senate seats to win a one-seat majority in the upper house. Remarkably, Democrats lost not a single seat in either chamber, the first election in U.S. history in which a party retained all of its congressional seats.

Although other factors clearly contributed to the pro-Democratic national tide—notably, scandals that weakened some Republican members and cast a negative light on the whole congressional party—its primary source was the electorate's unhappiness with the Iraq War and the president responsible for it. Midterm elections are usually at least to some extent popular referendums on the current administration, although as noted earlier in this chapter, the electoral effects of attitudes toward the president vary from year to year. But by any measure, the degree to which opinions on Bush's job performance shaped individual voting in 2006 was extraordinarily large.

Well before the election, surveys provided ample reason for believing that opinions of Bush would have an unusually large effect on voters in 2006, especially among those holding negative views of his performance. Figure 6–10 shows that, compared to electorates in previous midterms going back to 1982, voters in 2006 were more likely to say that their congressional vote would be about the president (54 percent, compared to between 34 and 46 percent in the earlier midterms); more important, voters totaling more than one-third said that their vote for Congress would be a vote against Bush, a noticeably larger proportion than for any of his three predecessors at midterm, including Bill Clinton in 1994. The reversal from 2002, when an unusually high proportion of voters said their vote would be an expression of *support* for President Bush, is especially notable.

Post-election surveys found that voters did what they said they would do. The proportion of the electorate whose vote for U.S. representative was consistent with their evaluations of President Bush—voting Republican if they approved of his performance, voting Democratic if they disapproved—reached about 85 percent,

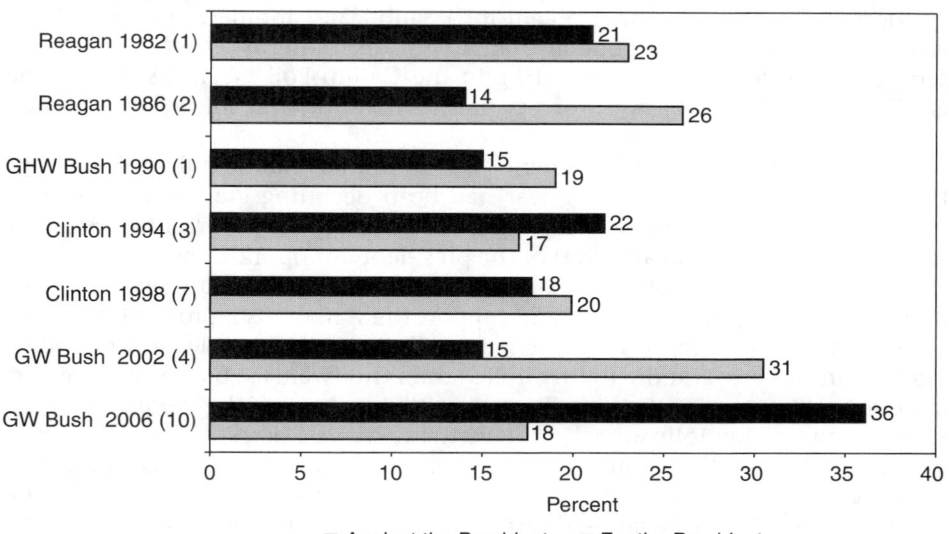

FIGURE 6–10 Is Your Vote For Congress a Vote For or Against the President?
Note: The number of surveys averaged is in parentheses.

Source: Pew Research Center for the People & the Press, "October 2006 Survey on Electoral Competition: Final Topline," October 17–22, 2006, at http://people-press.org/reports/questionnaires/293.pdf, accessed November 15, 2006.

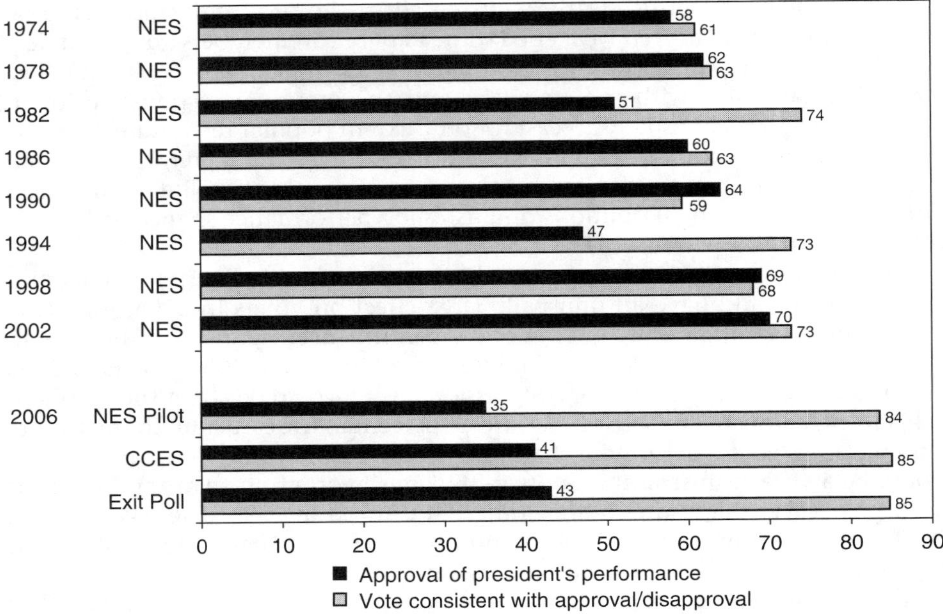

FIGURE 6–11 Consistency of Presidential Approval with the House Vote in Midterm Elections, 1974–2006

more than 10 percentage points higher than in any of the previous eight midterm elections (Figure 6–11). The problem for Republican candidates was that Bush was also considerably less popular than any of his midterm predecessors in this set; Bush's 38 percent approval rating in the Gallup Poll taken just before the election was in fact the lowest for any president at midterm since Harry Truman in 1950.

The main reason for the president's low rating was public unhappiness with the war in Iraq. Support for the war had been declining gradually for several years and by the 2006 election averaged a little less than 40 percent. As support for the war ebbed, so did approval of the president, for opinions on the president and the war remained tightly linked. The proportion of Americans giving consistent responses—approve of Bush and support the war, or disapprove of Bush and oppose the war—averaged 84 percent in polls spanning the election period.[108] These opinions are far more tightly linked than they were for Bush's predecessors in comparable situations—Harry Truman with the Korean War (60 percent consistent) and Lyndon Johnson with the Vietnam War (64 percent consistent).[109]

Opinions on both war and the president (see Figure 6–9) also continued to split decisively along party lines, and these divisions were fully expressed in the voting booth in 2006. Table 6–10 displays some pertinent comparative data; the comparisons between 2006 and elections during the recent period of Republican dominance (1994 onward) are the most informative, because prior to then, majority status and the incumbency advantage gave Democratic candidates a boost among Republicans and independents.[110] Republican Party identifiers remained as loyal to their House candidates in 2006 as they have been in midterm

TABLE 6–10 Partisanship and Voting in Midterm House Elections, 1994–2006 (Percent Voting for the Republican)

	Republicans	Democrats	Independents
1974 NES	77	14	37
1978 NES	72	17	48
1982 NES	84	17	46
1986 NES	72	16	45
1990 NES	71	12	41
1994 NES	88	18	54
1998 NES	86	24	53
2002 NES	84	16	52
2006 NES Pilot	88	4	41
2006 CCES	86	11	41
2006 Exit Poll	92	8	41

elections since 1994. Democrats were even more inclined to vote with their party, defecting at substantially lower rates than in past midterms. This obviously benefited Democratic candidates, but their support among independent voters was probably more important. Notice that in Figure 6–9, Bush's standing among independents was much closer to that among Democrats (about 20 points higher) than among Republicans (about 50 points lower). This segment of the electorate, which had given Republican House candidates 52–54 percent of their votes in midterms since 1994, shifted decisively to the Democratic side in 2006.

These voting patterns did not appear spontaneously, but reflected national and local campaigns mounted by candidates, their parties, and allied interest groups. As always, each side sought to frame the decision in terms that favored its candidates. Democrats urged voters to use their franchise to express their unhappiness with the war, the president, and the Republican members of Congress who supported them; their goal was to nationalize the election. Most Republican incumbents sought keep the election a local affair, emphasizing their independence, devotion to local interests, and record of delivering valued projects and services to constituents. Democrats won this framing contest, producing the most nationalized election since 1994. In national campaigning, Republican leaders sought to replace the war in Iraq with terrorism and homeland security as the dominant electoral focus, recapitulating themes that had helped their party in 2002 and 2004, but in 2006, the Democrats' criticism of the Iraq War and the Republican Congress found the larger audience.

Strategic Politicians in 2006

The unpopularity of Bush and the war were necessary to the Democrats' victory but not by themselves sufficient; as always, taking seats from the opposition required qualified, well-financed challengers capable of exploiting a national tide locally and thus depended on the party's effective recruitment of candidates and strategic distribution of campaign resources. But the influx of candidates and resources on the Democratic side was also itself a reflection of the intensity of their opposition to the president and the war.

The Democrats had reason to believe early on that 2006 would be a good year for them, allowing plenty of time to mobilize candidates and resources. Responses to the generic House vote question—asking respondents which party's candidate they would vote for if the election were held today without specifying any candidate's name—typically gave them a wide lead well before the election year, a good five points ahead of where they had been at comparable periods heading into other recent elections (Figure 6–12). Even discounting for the fact that generic polls always tend to exaggerate the Democrats' support, the lead was large enough by the end of 2005 to conclude that majority status was within reach.

This atmosphere helped with recruitment of candidates and fundraising, and Rahm Emanuel, the chair of the Democratic Congressional Campaign Committee, did an effective job on both fronts. The proportion of Democratic House challengers with experience in elective office was only average for recent decades (17 percent), but as always, experienced candidates were much more likely to be found in open seats and potentially competitive districts. Emanuel's main innovation was to encourage and support candidacies of moderate-to-conservative Democrats in districts where mainstream national Democrats would have faced poor prospects.

More important, though, was that the campaigns of a large proportion of Democratic candidates showing any promise at all were amply financed through some combination of contributions and independent spending by party or outside organizations. The campaigns of fifty-four of the sixty-two Democrats pursing

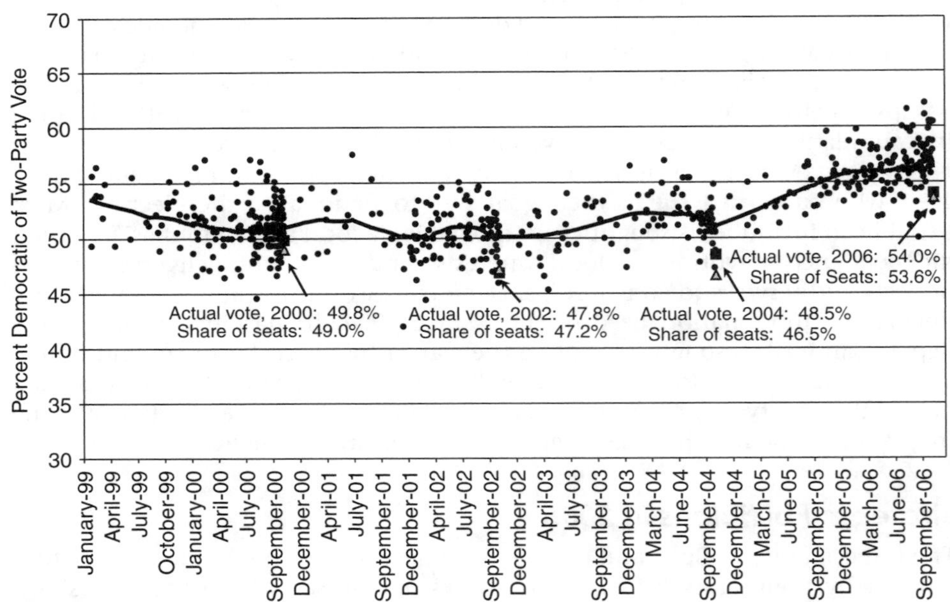

FIGURE 6–12 Generic House Vote Intention, 1999–2006 (Registered/Likely Voters)

Source: Complied by author, largely from data reported at http://www.pollingreport.com, various dates.

Republican-held House seats who ended up with at least 45 percent of the major-party vote were backed by more than $1 million in contributions and party and independent spending. Of the remaining eight, three won anyway. For only four or five House races do the financial data suggest that party officials overlooked a promising candidate who might have won with a more generous infusion of cash, an impressive record considering that the number of seats estimated to be in play by election handicappers kept growing as the election drew nearer.[111]

Republicans also invested massively to defend their vulnerable House seats—the losing Republican incumbents on average outspent their Democratic challengers by more than 30 percent[112]—and it is conceivable that their efforts saved some incumbents, for nine Democratic challengers won more than 49 percent of the major-party vote but fell short of a majority. In general, however, the outcomes of campaigns abundantly funded by both sides—as were all ten of these contests—are not determined by who spends more, but by voters' responses to the candidates and the messages the money is spent to promote (see Chapter 3).

The strong pro-Democratic national tide was running in 2006 was not by itself sufficient to deliver control of Congress to the Democrats. The Democrats' share of the total House vote nationally increased by nearly 5 percentage points over 2004, and the vote swing to Democrats in districts contested in both 2004 and 2006 averaged a little less than 5 points. But only five of the thirty Democratic pickups would have been achieved with a five-point increase in the Democratic vote over 2004; nineteen required swings of 10 or more points to put the Democrat above 50 percent. The actual swing in the districts Democrats took from Republicans averaged 14 points, exceeding 10 points in twenty-four of them. These results underline the crucial contribution of the Democrats' strategic deployment of campaign resources—candidates, money, personnel—to their success in turning a favorable partisan tide into the victories that produced their House majority. The tide by itself was not enough; in most districts, it had to be effectively exploited by Democratic candidates at the district level to effect the outcome. Nonetheless, a couple of low-spending, relatively obscure Democrats did win unexpected victories, not so much because local voters had changed their opinions of the Republican incumbent but because so many former supporters thought it more important this time to vote their opposition to the Republican regime and its leader.[113]

The 2006 election did disprove one familiar canard: that partisan gerrymandering has virtually eliminated competitive House districts. The number of House seats won with less than 55 percent of the major-party vote in 2006 (sixty) was the highest since 1948. The election also confirmed that incumbents' electoral safety is contingent rather than automatic; fourteen of the twenty-two losing Republican incumbents had coasted in with more than 60 percent of the vote in 2004. But it is also true that it required a powerful partisan tide to offset the Republicans' structural advantage in enough districts to produce such results. That advantage remains firmly in place and will make it difficult for Democrats to keep their majority under less-favorable conditions.

Conclusion: House Election Patterns, 1980–2006

Stepping back from the dramatic details of the most recent elections and viewing the wider set going back to 1980, we can see the broader patterns that have shaped aggregate House election outcomes during the past two decades. Table 6–11 leaves no doubt about what it takes for elections to change the makeup of the House: potent issues combined with vigorous challenges. Both are necessary. Issues won't do it by themselves (1984, 1990, 1996); neither will strong challenges (1982 Republicans). But when they are combined, turnover is sharply higher, incumbents become much more vulnerable, and, if the issues favor one party over the other, we observe a large net swing to the favored party.

No matter how favorable the issues are to the challenger's party, a vigorous challenge is almost always necessary to knock off an incumbent. This is evident from Table 6–12, which lists the percentage of winning challengers in years favorable to the challenger's party,[114] depending on whether the incumbent was marginal (won more or less than 60 percent of the vote in the last election) and whether the challenge was strong (the challenger had held elective office or spent at least $400,000 in 2006). Plainly, the strength of the challenger's candidacy is far more important than the marginality of the incumbent. Even in good years, few challengers merely float in on the rising partisan tide, while strong challengers have an impressive record of success even against nonmarginal incumbents. Marginal incumbents do attract serious challengers more frequently (70 percent compared to 26 percent for nonmarginal incumbents), which is just what our understanding of career strategies would lead us to expect. But in the absence of a serious challenger, even a marginal incumbent has an excellent prospect of surviving a strong contrary partisan tide.

TABLE 6–11 Issues, Challenges, and Turnover in House Elections, 1980–2006

Year	Issues Useful to Challengers?	Strong Challenges?	Turnover	Incumbents Defeated	Net Swing
1980	Yes – R	Yes – R	74	30	34 R
1982	Yes – D	Yes – D, R	81	23	26 D
1984	Yes – R	No	43	16	14 R
1986	No	No	50	6	5 D
1988	No	No	28	6	2 D
1990	Yes – D, R	No	35	15	9 D
1992	Yes – D, R	Yes – D, R	110	24	10 R
1994	Yes – R	Yes – R	86	34	52 R
1996	Yes – D	No	74	21	9 D
1998	No	No	40	6	6 D
2000	No	No	34	6	2 D
2002	No	No	53	8	6 R
2004	No	No	14	7	3 R
2006	Yes – D	Yes – D	31	22	31 D

TABLE 6–12 Successful Challenges in Election Years Favorable to the Challenger's Party, 1972-2006 (In Percentages)

Challenge	Marginal Incumbent	Nonmarginal Incumbent	Total
Strong	32.6 (270)[a]	20.4 (211)	27.2 (482)
Weak	8.0 (113)	1.3 (590)	2.4 (704)
Total	25.1 (383)	6.4 (801)	12.5 (1186)

[a]Number of cases from which percentages were calculated.
Note: Marginal seats are those in which the incumbent won less than 60 percent of the two-party vote in the previous election. Strong challenges are show in which the challenger spent at least $400,000 (in 2006 dollars) or had previously held elective public office.

Senate Elections, 1980–2006

Senate elections since 1980 illustrate yet another quirk in the translation of national forces into congressional election outcomes. They show that presidential coattails and other national forces can have different aggregate effects in different election years because the distribution as well as the size of the vote for a party's congressional candidates determines its aggregate total of wins and losses. The distribution of votes (and vote shifts) is, of course, strongly affected by local circumstances—candidates, campaigns, and other idiosyncratic factors. Although true of House elections, this is most clearly the case among Senate elections because of both the great differences in state populations and the underlying competitiveness of so many states. The ebb and flow of Senate representation in elections since 1980 (see Figure 6–2) offers a particularly striking illustration of how sensitive aggregate election results can be to small changes in voting behavior—and therefore to national or local conditions that influence voters.

In 1980, Republicans took over the Senate in dramatic fashion by winning twenty-two of the thirty-four seats at stake, taking twelve seats from the Democrats and losing none of their own. Yet they did not win a majority of votes cast nationally for U.S. senators. Republican victories were concentrated in smaller states and were won by narrower margins. Republican candidates won eleven of the fourteen contests in which the winner received 52.1 percent or less of the vote. A shift of only 50,000 votes, properly redistributed, would have given the Democrats seven additional seats and a 54–46 majority.[115] Although strong candidates and campaigns were essential to the Republican victories,[116] with so many cliffhangers, even the relatively small coattail effects estimated for Senate contests in 1980 (Reagan supplying about 2 additional percentage points across the electorate) were large enough to have been decisive in producing the Republican majority.[117]

The parties broke even in 1982 Senate contests, each party picking up two seats from the opposition. The Republicans held on to the Senate by once again winning the close ones. They took eight of the ten tightest races; redistribution of fewer than 35,000 votes would have given Democrats control of the Senate. In 1984, Republicans finally won a majority of the votes cast nationwide for senators. The survey evidence examined in this chapter indicates that Reagan's victory added about 4 percentage points to their total. Yet they suffered a net loss of two Senate seats and were defeated in four of the six contests won with less than 55 percent of the two-party vote. The reason is not that Reagan's triumph was unhelpful but that Republican opportunities were much more limited in 1984 than they had been in 1980. Democrats defended only fourteen seats and most of the vulnerable incumbents were Republicans.

Considering the number of seats they had at risk, Republicans emerged from the 1984 Senate elections with their prospects for long-term control of the Senate seemingly enhanced. Five of the seven Republican senators whom Democrats had serious hopes of defeating were reelected, all but one (Jesse Helms) by a wide margin. Reagan may have helped Republican Senate candidates as much, if not more, in 1984 as in 1980, but local circumstances were so different that his coattails had a smaller effect on the number of seats changing hands.

In 1986, Democrats recaptured six of the Senate seats they had lost in 1980 and took three others from Republicans, losing only one of their own, for a net pickup of eight seats and a 55–45 majority. Once again, however, a switch of only 55,000 votes, properly redistributed, would have left the Senate in Republican hands. This time the Democrats won the close ones, taking nine of eleven races won with less than 52 percent of the vote. Although this might appear to be an instance of surge and decline—Republicans riding in on the Reagan surge in 1980, riding out in the midterm election six years later—these elections hinged largely on the local candidates and campaigns. Some of the surprise Republican victors from 1980 won easy reelection; others were defeated soundly. The difference reflected the variations in the quality of the incumbents (several of the losing Republican incumbents proved themselves to be inept politicians), as well as of the challengers.[118] The Democratic challengers won mainly by raising local issues and persuading voters that the Republican incumbents cared more about ideological goals than local interests.[119]

Unlike 1986, the 1988 Senate elections left the partisan balance in the Senate unchanged. Democrats took four seats from Republicans, defeating three incumbents and taking one open seat. Republicans took three seats from Democrats, defeating one incumbent and taking two open seats. The net result was a standoff, leaving a 55–45 Democratic majority, as had the 1986 election before Senator Zorinsky died and a Republican, David Karnes, was appointed in his place. But once again, with changes in only a handful of votes, the net outcome could have been quite different. Four seats were won with less than a 51 percent of the major party vote, three by Republicans. A shift of fewer than 3 percentage points in selected states could have elected three more Republicans or four more Democrats. It would have taken a switch of about 180,000 votes to give Republicans effective control in 1988 (fifty seats plus the vice presidency)—about 0.3 percent of the more than sixty-five million votes cast for Senate candidates.

The 1990 Senate elections further underlined the idiosyncrasy of Senate contests. Voters endorsed the status quo to a greater extent than they had in any election since senators had been chosen by popular vote. Despite a public mood hostile to officeholders and the historically greater vulnerability of Senate incumbents, only a single incumbent—Rudy Boschwitz, a Minnesota Republican—was defeated. No other seats changed party control; thirty-one incumbents were reelected, and Republicans retained control of their three open seats. In contrast to other recent senate elections, 1990 produced relatively few close contests; only four seats were won with less than 52 percent of the two-party vote, and twenty-two of the thirty-five winners received more than 60 percent. It would have taken a shift of more than 350,000 votes to give Republicans effective control of the Senate.

The 1992 Senate elections, like the House elections, brought striking demographic changes without altering the partisan balance. Of the twelve newly elected senators, four were women, one of them (Carol Mosely-Braun of Illinois) an African American; the election tripled the number of women senators from two to six. Another of the entering senators, Ben Nighthorse Campbell of Colorado, was the first Native American ever elected to the Senate. Yet the elections again produced no net partisan change at all, leaving the Democrats with the same 57–43 majority they had enjoyed before election day.

As in the House, the advances made by women in the Senate were rooted in the primaries. Three of the four newly elected women—all Democrats—won open Senate seats; the fourth, Dianne Feinstein of California, defeated an appointed senator, John Seymour, who was an incumbent in name only. In contrast, the six women (five Democrats, one Republican) who faced elected incumbent senators in the general election lost. (The lone incumbent woman, Barbara Mikulski of Maryland, won reelection.) All the victors had previously held elective office, whereas four of the six losers were pursuing their first.[120]

Only one of the new women senators—Feinstein, who had narrowly lost a race to be California's governor in 1990—would have been a sure bet to win nomination without the special stimulus of the Anita Hill–Clarence Thomas confrontation. Carol Mosely-Braun defeated incumbent Democrat Alan Dixon, who had voted to confirm Thomas, in the Illinois primary and then held on to win the general election against a relatively obscure first-time candidate. Patty Murray's self-described status as "a mom in tennis shoes" helped her to emerge on top in Washington's "jungle" primary (in which candidates from all parties run on a single ballot, with the top Democratic and Republican vote-getters winning each party's nomination). Barbara Boxer took the California nomination despite having 143 overdrafts at the House Bank, in large part because of the attention and support her gender attracted in the primary.

Apart from putting a record number of women into the upper house, the 1992 Senate elections were not unusual. The average level of competition is always higher in Senate than in House elections—stronger challengers, closer elections, incumbents defeated more frequently—and 1992 was no exception. But neither was it special: The numbers of newcomers (twelve) and successful challengers (four) were about average. The incidence of marginal incumbents—56 percent received less than 60 percent of the vote—was about 10 points higher than it was in the 1980–1990 period, but that is the only sign of unusually intense competition.

A surprising aspect of the 1992 Senate elections was the absence of net partisan change, for the seats at stake in 1992 were the same that had given control of the Senate to the Republicans with a twelve-seat swing in 1980 and to the Democrats with an eight-seat swing in 1986. This time, they produced no net partisan change at all. The balance of national partisan forces had something to do with this stasis, but the customary idiosyncrasy of Senate elections had more to do with it.

Republicans had initially expected to cash in on both the Gulf War and the fact that the Democrats had more seats to defend (twenty-one of thirty-six), nine of which had been won only narrowly in 1986. Later in the campaign, Democrats anticipated picking up some seats with the help of anger over the Thomas hearings, the faltering economy, and Clinton's coattails. In the end, both parties were probably helped a little by their particular issues, and the net result was a wash. The two Democratic senators who lost (Terry Sanford of North Carolina and Wyche Fowler of Georgia) were among the three southern Democrats who had opposed authorizing the president to use military force against Iraq (Ernest Hollings of South Carolina, the third, won with just 52 percent of the vote). How much this vote contributed to their defeats is uncertain because both Sanford and Fowler had been narrow victors in 1986 and had had other serious electoral problems. Still, if not decisive, their vote against going to war was certainly a political liability.

On the Democratic side, the economy and Clinton's strength probably helped Russ Feingold to defeat Bob Kasten, the Republican incumbent, in Wisconsin. Some of Dianne Feinstein's landslide margin over John Seymour in California is attributable to her gender and to Clinton's appeal in California, but she was the stronger candidate by almost any standard and would have won in 1992 without any help from national forces. If there was any helpful Democratic trend in 1992, it showed up mainly in the narrowness of some Republican incumbents' escapes and the relative ease with which most of the Democrats who had once seemed vulnerable won reelection. Six of the Republican winners got no more than 52 percent of the two-party vote; all but one of the Democratic winners (Ernest Hollings of South Carolina) enjoyed wider margins of victory. Democrats were aided by the departure of two scandal-ridden incumbents (Alan Cranston of California and Brock Evans of Washington) and their replacement by stronger Democratic nominees. Both parties held on to all of their open Senate seats.

The 1994 Republican tide flowed just as strongly in Senate as in House elections. Republicans took control of the Senate by taking eight seats from the Democrats, immediately adding a party-switching opportunist (Richard Shelby of Alabama) to end up with a 53–47 majority, which grew to 54–46 a few months later, when Democrat Ben Nighthorse Campbell of Colorado also switched sides. The Republican Senate victory was less surprising than the House victory, to be sure, because the party had controlled the Senate from 1981 to 1987 and because most Senate seats can be won by either party under the right conditions. But it was just as decisive.

As in the House elections, open seats made the difference. Republicans won all six open seats vacated by Democrats, defeated two of sixteen Democratic incumbents, and kept all the seats they already held (ten incumbents, three open seats). Also as in the House, Senate Democrats tended to retire where constituency voting patterns promised to make life difficult. Democrats vacated six of twelve seats in states where, on average, the two-party vote for Democratic presidential candidates fell below 50.5 percent; they vacated none of the ten seats where the presidential vote exceeded this amount. Strategic retirements thus hurt Democrats in Senate as well as House elections.

It could have been even worse for the Democrats. Three of their winners received less than 52 percent of the vote; only one winning Republican cut it that close. Still, it would not have taken a shift in very many votes to alter the results. A careful redistribution of about 174,000 votes (0.3 percent of the votes cast) would have let the Democrats retain four seats and thus their majority; but then a shift of only 112,000 votes (0.2 percent of those cast) could have given the Republicans three additional seats.

As usual, experienced candidates both reflected and enhanced the competitiveness of these elections. Although much was made of the victories of two political novices in Tennessee (Fred Thompson, a lawyer and actor, and Bill Frist, a surgeon), seven of the eleven new Republican senators had served in the House and another had been his state's governor.

In 1996, despite Clinton's victory, the Republicans added two new seats to the majority they had won in 1994, increasing their margin to 55–45. Democrats were hurt by the luck of the draw as well as by retirements. Thirteen senators retired in 1996, the largest number of voluntary departures since 1914, when senators were first directly elected by voters. Eight of the thirteen were Democrats, four of them from the South. The timing of their retirement announcements again suggests strategic withdrawal; all eight of the Democrats, but only one of the Republicans, announced their retirements before Clinton's successful showdown with the Republican Congress in late 1995. Republicans won three of the seats vacated by Democrats, two in the South (Alabama and Arkansas) and one in Nebraska, a state won handily by Bob Dole. Republican Senator Larry Pressler of South Dakota was the only incumbent defeated in the general election, and his was the only Republican Senate seat lost in 1996.

Democrats were also unlucky in the class of Senate seats up in 1996, for Senate and presidential outcomes tended to coincide. Republicans won fourteen of the seventeen seats at stake in states won by Dole, while Democrats won ten of the seventeen states won by Clinton. The Republicans' good fortune was that states won by Dole were more likely than other states to have Senate contests. Only three of Dole's nineteen states lacked a Senate race, compared to fourteen of Clinton's thirty-one states. By the luck of the draw, the Democrats were poorly positioned to take advantage of whatever help Clinton's victory might have provided their Senate candidates.

In 1998, the parties broke even in the Senate, preserving the status quo and the Republicans' 55–45 majority. Democrats defeated two Republican incumbents but lost two open seats. Republicans defeated one Democratic incumbent while losing one open seat. Although six Senate seats thus changed hands, the switches were much more a consequence of local issues and personalities than of any general thirst for change. Still, the outcome was disappointing to Republicans, for Democrats were defending most of the vulnerable seats, and Republicans had entertained dreams of winning a filibuster-proof sixty-seat majority.[121] There is some evidence that popular opposition to Clinton's impeachment hurt Republican Senate candidates even more than it did Republican House candidates, even though the Senate had not yet addressed the issue.[122] The potential effect of the issue was limited, however, because the number of close elections was comparatively small—only nine were won with less than 55 percent of the two-party vote, compared to fifteen in 1996—and only two contests were won by margins of less than 38,000 votes. In contrast to the 1994 and 1996 elections, the 1998 elections disturbed neither the partisan nor the ideological balance in the Senate.

Unlike the uneventful House elections, the Senate elections shook up the status quo in 2000. Republicans lost five seats, leaving the Senate evenly divided between the parties for only the second time in U.S. history. Democrats had picked up one seat in July, when Republican Paul Coverdell of Georgia died and Georgia's Democratic governor appointed Democrat Zell Miller to take his place; Miller easily won a special election on November 7 to fill out the remaining four years of Coverdell's term. The Democrats gained four additional seats on election day, defeating five incumbent senators to the Republicans' one, with each party losing a single open seat.

The 2000 Senate elections were the first test for several of the staunchly conservative Republicans who were first elected on the strong Republican tide in 1994. Three of the five Republican losers in 2000—John Ashcroft of Missouri, Rod Grams of Minnesota, and Spencer Abraham of Michigan—were members of this class. All three were burdened with images that put them well to the right of their constituents. Part of the reason Democrats pulled even in the Senate is that the strong Republican tide that had prevailed in 1994 was no longer running.

The other Republican incumbents to lose in 2000 were William V. Roth of Delaware and Slade Gorton of Washington. Roth's bid for a sixth term at age seventy-nine was damaged when he fainted during two public appearances late in the campaign, a sign that he might no longer be up to the job physically. He lost to Thomas Carper, a popular governor and former U.S. representative. Gorton had the rare experience of losing as a Senate incumbent for the second time. Elected in 1980, defeated in 1986, then elected to Washington's other Senate seat in 1988 and 1994, Gorton was beaten in 2000 by Maria Cantwell, a former congresswoman turned Internet executive, in a contest so close that it took almost as long to resolve as the presidential race in Florida. The Democrats lost one Senate incumbent, Charles Robb of Virginia. Robb's defeat, combined with the standoff in open-seat contests (each party picked up one from the other, Republican John Ensign winning a Nevada seat, Democrat Bill Nelson a Florida seat) killed Democrats' hopes of winning a Senate majority in 2000.

The 50–50 tie raised some interesting possibilities as the presidential contest went unresolved for five weeks after the election. The vice president casts the tie-breaking vote on organizational matters such as which party's members will chair Senate committees. With a Bush victory, that vote would be cast by Republican Dick Cheney. If Gore had won, his running mate, Joe Lieberman, would have had to resign his Connecticut Senate seat in order to become vice president. Lieberman's successor would then have been appointed by Connecticut Governor John Rowland, a Republican who would have chosen someone from his own party, thus giving the Republicans a 51–49 majority.

The 2000 Senate elections produced several historic firsts: Hillary Clinton, by winning the New York Senate seat left open by the retirement of Democrat Daniel Patrick Moynihan, became the first First Lady to be elected to any public office, let alone the Senate. In Missouri, Ashcroft lost to a dead man. Ashcroft's opponent, Democratic Governor Mel Carnahan, had been killed in a plane crash on October 16. The Democratic lieutenant governor thereby became governor and quickly promised voters he would appoint Carnahan's widow, Jean Carnahan, to the seat if the late governor, whose name remained on the ballot, were to win, which he did. Finally, victories by Clinton, Cantwell, Carnahan, and Debbie Stabenow (who defeated Abraham in Michigan) raised the number of women senators from nine to thirteen, then an all-time high. Considering that until 1993 no more than two women had ever sat in the Senate at the same time, these gains extended a notable trend.

There was a modest but observable relationship between statewide presidential and Senate results. The incumbent party lost six of fourteen Senate seats in states won by the other party's presidential candidate but only two of nineteen seats in states won by its own party's presidential candidate. One of the two was Florida, where Gore may actually have been the voters' first choice (we'll never know). The other was Missouri, which Bush won by a narrow margin. With the exception of Missouri's Ashcroft, every losing incumbent was from a state won by the other party's presidential candidate. Overall, twenty-four of thirty-four states cast a plurality of their votes for Senate and presidential candidates of the same party, precisely the same as in 1992 and 1996.

It is also possible to detect traces of the impeachment struggle in the Senate results. Twelve Republican incumbents represented states won by Clinton in 1996. The two who voted against conviction were reelected easily. Five of the ten voting for conviction lost, as did Bill McCollum, the House impeachment manager who tried to move up to the Senate in Florida. Five Republican incumbents represented states that Dole had won in 1996; all of them voted for conviction, and all were reelected. This is not to say that impeachment was a decisive issue in any of these races, but votes for conviction may have contributed to the impression that Republican conservatives such as Grams, Abraham, Ashcroft, and McCollum were ideologically out of step with their pro-Clinton constituencies.

Democrats won the close elections in 2000, taking five of six seats won with less than 52 percent of the major party vote. With the exceptions of Clinton, Carnahan, and Jon Corzine, who spent more than $60 million on his election, both parties' newcomers were experienced politicians; three were former governors, five were former U.S. representatives.

2002–2006

The Senate tie was broken in May 2001 when James Jeffords of Vermont abandoned the Republican Party to become an Independent who would vote with the Democrats on organizational matters. Jeffords's defection set the stage for a titanic battle for control of the Senate, provoking the huge investment of campaign resources by candidates, parties, and outside groups that was examined in Chapter 4. The Republicans came out on top, adding a net two seats by defeating two incumbent Democrats (Jean Carnahan of Missouri, running for the remainder of the term to which she had been appointed in 2000, and Max Cleland of Georgia) and adding an open seat while losing one incumbent of their own (Tim Hutchinson, defeated by Mark Pryor in Arkansas). Their open-seat pickup was in Minnesota, where Democratic incumbent Paul Wellstone, ahead in most polls, had died in a plane crash eleven days before the election; Republican Norm Coleman defeated former Senator and Vice President Walter Mondale, hastily chosen to replace Wellstone. The results left the Republicans with fifty-one seats and thus control of the Senate.

The key to Republican victories in Minnesota, Missouri, and Georgia, as well as in several states where Republican Senate seats had been at risk was superior mobilization of Republican voters. Bush's near-universal approval among Republicans, his energetic fundraising, and frenzied last-minute campaigning in competitive states, combined with effective Republican grassroots drives to get out the vote, put Republicans over the top.[123] The Republicans also made effective use of the homeland security issue in races against Cleland and Carnahan (see Chapter 4); as in the House elections, the legacy of September 11 clearly worked to the Republicans' benefit.

It was a narrow victory. Republicans took a larger share of the close ones, winning four of the six contests won by less than 53 percent of the vote. Redistribution of about 40,000 votes (less than 0.1 percent of the total votes cast), properly allocated, could have given Democrats control of the Senate or given Republicans two additional seats. Still, Senate outcomes, like those of House contests in 2002, usually reflected the constituency's underlying partisan balance; of the thirteen Senate races considered to be in doubt in October, ten went to the party that had won the state's presidential vote in 2000.[124] Minnesota was the only state won by Gore (barely, with 51 percent of the vote) where Republicans took a Senate seat from the Democrats.

The same trend toward greater consistency in voting for president and U.S. representative in 2004 (Figure 6–3) appeared in Senate elections as well, resulting in a four-seat addition to the Republicans' Senate majority. Although Democrats had entertained some hope of adding the two seats they needed to become the majority party, they would have had to win all of the close ones. Instead, Republicans won five of the six races classified by *Congressional Quarterly* as toss-ups and another classified as leaning Democratic (majority leader Tom Daschle's seat). The Democrats' main problem was again structural They had to compete with the more-efficient distribution of Republican voters. Although Gore had won the national vote in 2000, Bush carried thirty of the fifty states, including twenty-two of the thirty-four states with Senate contests in 2004. Democrats had to defend ten seats in states Bush had won, including five left open by retirements, all in the South, where support for Democrats has been eroding for several decades. Meanwhile, Republicans were defending only three seats in states won by Gore. In the end, Republicans won all five of the open southern Democratic seats, plus Daschle's. Democrats picked up two open Republican seats with Barak Obama's victory over Alan Keyes in Illinois and Ken Salazar's over Peter Coors in Colorado. Seven of the eight Senate seats that changed party hands in 2004 went to the party that won the state in the 2000 and 2004 presidential elections; Salazar's victory was the lone exception.

Most devastating to Democrats' hopes was the loss of the open seats they were defending in the South. Figure 6–13 shows why they were shut out. For many years, a substantial proportion of Southerners who preferred Republican presidential candidates had nonetheless been willing to vote for Democrats for Senate; between 1960 and 1992, an average of 40 percent did so. After the Republican takeover of the Senate in 1994, that average fell to 15 percent; in 2004, it was down to 8 percent and, if the analysis is confined to open seats, it becomes a mere 4 percent.[125] Consequently, the five Democrats defending open Senate seats in the South ran only slightly ahead of Kerry (3 percentage points on average), dooming their candidacies in states where Bush was very popular and won handily.[126] Tom Daschle's narrow defeat by John Thune in South Dakota (49.4 percent to 50.6 percent) was also probably a consequence of tightening party lines. Daschle had run 92,000 votes ahead of Bill Clinton in 1992 but outpolled Kerry by only 44,000 in 2004, not enough in a state that Bush won with 61 percent of the major party vote.

More generally, twenty-seven of the thirty-four Senate contests were won by the party whose presidential candidate won the state's electoral votes, tying 1964

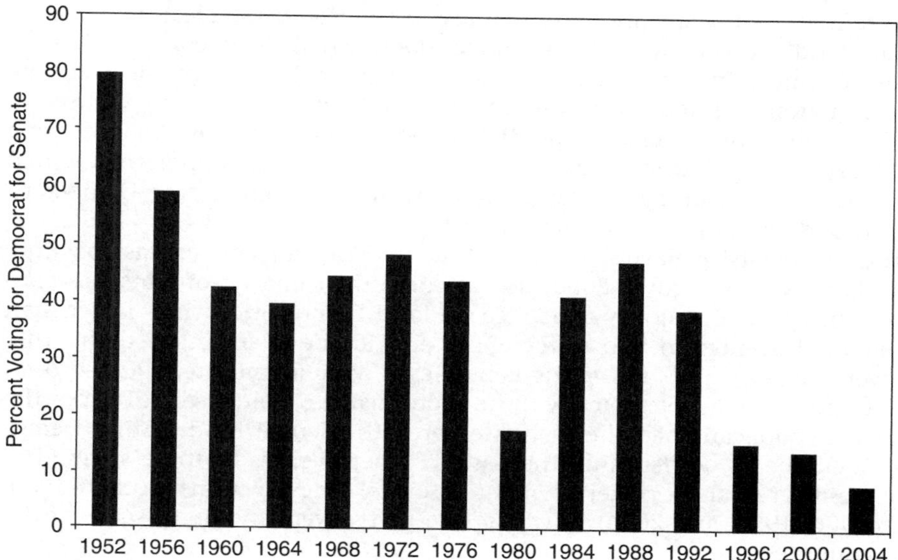

FIGURE 6–13 Ticket Splitting by Republican Presidential Voters in the Southern Senate Elections, 1952–2004
Source: National Election Studies.

for the highest level of congruence in president–Senate election results in the past half century. When the 2004 winners were added to the continuing Senate membership, fully 75 percent of Senators represented states where their party's candidate won the most recent presidential election, the highest proportion in at least fifty years.

In 2006, it was the Democrat's turn to sweep the competitive races. They took six seats from Republican incumbents and lost only one of the hotly contested races (Harold Ford of Tennessee came up short with 48.6 percent of the vote in his attempt to become the first African American elected to the Senate from the South). As in the 2006 House races, national conditions—the Iraq War, Bush's unpopularity, congressional scandals—gave Democrats a strong edge. And as in House races, Democrats fielded formidable challenges to Republican Senators wherever prospects looked at all promising,[127] and the campaign of every Democrat (and Republican) in any of the Senate races where the outcome was at all in doubt was lavishly funded through a combination of contributions, party spending, and independent spending campaigns. The amounts put into the campaigns of competitive Democrats ranged from more than $9 million in the low-population states of Montana and Rhode Island to more than $23 million (Missouri); their Republican opponents were at least as well funded. No Senate candidate in even the most marginally competitive race could reasonably complain about a shortage of campaign resources in 2004.

Statewide exit polls indicate that independent voters were the key to Democratic victories over Republican Senate incumbents in several Republican-leaning states (Montana, Missouri, Virginia), although in Ohio the Democrat's margin of victory was large enough that a disproportionate share of independent votes was not essential. Democrats also won handily in the Democratic-leaning states of Rhode Island and Pennsylvania. In Rhode Island, where Democrats have a two-to-one advantage in party identifiers, unhappiness with the Republican regime in Washington was too strong for incumbent Lincoln Chafee to withstand. Despite having the lowest presidential support score and most liberal voting record of any Republican senator, his former Democratic supporters deserted him in droves. According to exit polls, he won 46 percent of the Democrats' votes in 2000 but only 15 percent in 2006.[128]

The Democrats' average share of the total vote cast for senator was up a little more than five points over 2000, the last time the same set of seats was contested. Their Senate majority depended on local Democratic swings larger than the national average in two states (Ohio and Rhode Island), but their other takeovers came in states where the Republicans' vote margin in 2000 had been narrow enough to be overcome with no more than a 5-point swing. Four of the defeated Republicans had themselves entered the Senate by defeating Democratic incumbents, underlining the basic competitiveness of these states. The Senate results repeat the pattern evident in several other elections (notably 1980, 1982, 1986, 1994, and 2004) in which one party swept the lion's share of the hotly-contested races.

Maintaining the Balance

The Senate has changed party hands six times since 1980. In three instances, 1980, 1994, and 2006, the switch was part of a broader partisan tide that was visible in other elections as well. In contrast, when the Democrats won control in 1986, the shift was entirely idiosyncratic to the Senate elections. The switch in 2001 was set up (though not accomplished until Jeffords's defection) by Democratic gains in 2000, an election with no perceptible partisan tide at all. Republicans benefited by a modest national swing in 2002, a consequence of differential turnout and issues put on the agenda by the attacks of September 11, but they probably would have controlled the Senate only by the grace of Vice President Cheney had Paul Wellstone not died in a plane crash. There have also been a couple elections since 1980—namely 1982 and 1984—when the Senate swings, though small, actually went *against* the national partisan trend. Clearly, the close competitive balance in so many states creates a potential for dramatic swings in party fortunes. Yet at the same time, along with the idiosyncratic variety offered by local candidates, campaigns, and issues, it can also allow large swings to occur without strong partisan tides and partisan tides to surge without producing large partisan swings.

NOTES

1. Midterms can be as important as presidential election years in this regard; see Andrew E. Bush, Horses in *Midstream: U.S. Midterm Elections and Their Consequences, 1894–1998* (Pittsburgh: University of Pittsburgh Press, 1999).
2. Gerald H. Kramer, "Short-Term Fluctuations in U.S. Voting Behavior," American Political Science Review 65 (1971): 131–143; G. J. Stigler, "General Economic Conditions and National Elections," *American Economic Review* 63 (1973): 160–167; Francisco Arcelus and Allan H. Meltzer, "The Effects of Aggregate Economic Variables on Congressional Elections," *American*

Political Science Review 69 (1975): 1232–1239; Howard S. Bloom and H. Douglas Price, "Voter Response to Short-Run Economic Conditions: The Asymmetric Effect of Prosperity and Recession," *American Political Science Review* 69 (1975): 1240–1254; Douglas A. Hibbs Jr., "President Reagan's Mandate from the 1980 Elections: A Shift to the Right?" *American Politics Quarterly* 10 (1982): 387–420; and Brian Newman and Charles Ostrom Jr., "Explaining Seat Changes in the U.S. House of Representatives, 1950–98," *Legislative Studies Quarterly* 27 (August 2002): 383–405.

For arguments that the economy makes no difference in midterm elections, see Alberto Alesina and Howard Rosenthal, "Partisan Cycles in Congressional Elections and the Macroeconomy," *American Political Science Review* 83 (1989): 373–398; Robert S. Erikson, "Economic Conditions and the Congressional Vote: A Review of the Macrolevel Evidence," *American Journal of Political Science* 34 (1990): 373–399; Kenneth Scheve and Michael Tomz, "Electoral Surprise and the Midterm Loss in U.S. Congressional Elections," *British Journal of Political Science* 29 (1999): 507–521; and G. Patrick Lynch, "Midterm Elections and Economic Fluctuations: The Response of Voters over Time," *Legislative Studies Quarterly* 27 (May 2002): 265–294.

For critiques of these arguments, see Gary C. Jacobson, "Does the Economy Matter in Midterm Elections?" *American Journal of Political Science* 34 (1990): 400–407; and Gary C. Jacobson, *The Electoral Origins of Divided Government: Competition in House Elections, 1946–1988* (Boulder, CO: Westview Press, 1990), pp. 77–80. For a study examining state-level data, see Andrew Rudalevige, "Revisiting Midterm Loss: Referendum Theory and State Data," *American Political Research* 29 (January 2001): 25–46.

3. Edward R. Tufte, *Political Control of the Economy* (Princeton, NJ: Princeton University Press, 1978), Tables 5–2 and 5–4; see also Edward R. Tufte, "Determinants of the Outcomes of Midterm Congressional Elections," *American Political Science Review* 69 (1975): 812–826.
4. Bruce I. Oppenheimer, James A. Stimson, and Richard W. Waterman, "Interpreting U.S. Congressional Elections: The Exposure Thesis," *Legislative Studies Quarterly* 11 (1986): 227–247.
5. Gary C. Jacobson, "Reversal of Fortune: The Transformation of U.S. House Elections in the 1990s," in *Continuity and Change in Congressional Elections*, ed. David Brady, John Cogan, and Morris P. Fiorina (Stanford, CA: Stanford University Press, 2000), Table 1. Based on this analysis and updating it through 1998, I estimate that the "expected" number of seats held by House Democrats fell by 42 after 1990. All the coefficients in the equation remain statistically significant without this adjustment, but with it, the adjusted R^2 rises from 0.50 to 0.71.
6. Alan I. Abramowitz and Jeffrey A. Segal, "Determinants of the Outcomes of U.S. Senate Elections," *Journal of Politics* 48 (1986): 433–439.
7. Tufte, "Midterm Congressional Elections," p. 826.
8. M. Stephen Weatherford, "Social Class, Economic Conditions, and Political Translation: The 1974 Recession and the Vote for Congress" (Paper presented at the Annual Meeting of the Western Political Science Association, Portland, Oregon, March 22–24, 1979), pp. 3–7.

9. Arcelus and Meltzer, "Congressional Elections," p. 1234.
10. Partisan differences on the economy were especially large during the G. W. Bush administration; see Gary C. Jacobson, *A Divider Not a Uniter: George W. Bush and the American People* (New York: Pearson, 2007), p. 249.
11. See Morris P. Fiorina, "Economic Retrospective Voting in American National Elections," American Journal of *Political Science* 22 (1978): 426–443; Donald R. Kinder and D. Roderick Kiewiet, "Economic Discontent and Political Behavior: The Role of Personal Grievances and Collective Economic Judgments in Congressional Voting," *American Journal of Political Science* 23 (1979): 495–527; M. Stephen Weatherford, "Economic Conditions and Electoral Outcomes: Class Differences in the Political Response to Recession," *American Journal of Political Science* 22 (1978): 917–938; Weatherford, "The 1974 Recession and the Vote for Congress"; Gary C. Jacobson, "Reagan, Reaganomics, and Strategic Politics in 1982: A Test of Alternative Theories of Midterm Congressional Elections" (Paper presented at the Annual Meeting of the American Political Science Association, Chicago, September 1–4, 1984); Alan I. Abramowitz, "Economic Conditions, Presidential Popularity, and Voting Behavior in Midterm Congressional Elections," *Journal of Politics* 47 (1985): 31–43; D. Roderick Kiewiet, *Macroeconomics and Micropolitics* (Chicago: University of Chicago Press, 1983), Chapter 6; and David W. Romero and Stephen J. Stambaugh, "Personal Economic Well-Being and the Individual Vote for Congress: A Pooled Analysis, 1980–1990," *Political Research Quarterly* 49 (1996): 607–616.
12. Samuel Kernell, "Presidential Popularity and Negative Voting: An Alternative Explanation of the Midterm Congressional Decline of the President's Party," *American Political Science Review* 71 (1977): 44–66.
13. Robert B. Arseneau and Raymond E. Wolfinger, "Voting Behavior in Congressional Elections" (Paper presented at the Annual Meeting of the American Political Science Association, New Orleans, September 4–8, 1973); and Candice J. Nelson, "The Effects of Incumbency on Voting in Congressional Elections, 1964–1974" (Paper presented at the Annual Meeting of the American Political Science Association, San Francisco, September 2–5, 1975).
14. Morris P. Fiorina, *Retrospective Voting in American National Elections* (New Haven, CT: Yale University Press, 1981), p. 165; Gary C. Jacobson, "Congressional Elections 1978: The Case of the Vanishing Challengers," in *Congressional Elections*, ed. Louis Sandy Maisel and Joseph Cooper (Beverly Hills, CA: Sage Publications, 1981), p. 238; Jacobson, "Reagan, Reaganomics, and Strategic Politics in 1982," p. 16; Abramowitz, "Voting Behavior in Midterm Congressional Elections," p. 36; Gary C. Jacobson and Samuel Kernell, "National Forces in the 1986 U.S. House Elections," *Legislative Studies Quarterly* 15 (1990): 74–82; Alan I. Abramowitz, "It's Monica, Stupid: The Impeachment Controversy and the 1998 Midterm Election," *Legislative Studies Quarterly* 26 (May 2001): 211–226; and Gary C. Jacobson and Sean Cain, "September 11 and the U.S. House Elections of 2002" (Paper presented at the Annual Meeting of the American Political Science Association, Philadelphia, August 28–31, 2003); Gary C. Jacobson, "Referendum: The 2006 Midterm Congressional Elections," *Political Science Quarterly* 122 (2007): 1–24.

15. See Gary C. Jacobson and Samuel Kernell, *Strategy and Choice in Congressional Elections*, 2nd ed. (New Haven, CT: Yale University Press, 1983), pp. 12–13.
16. Morris P. Fiorina, "Short- and Long-Term Effects of Economic Conditions on Individual Voting Decisions," in *Contemporary Political Economy*, ed. D.A. Hibbs and H. Fassbender (Amsterdam: North Holland, 1981), pp. 73–100.
17. James A. Stimson, Michael B. MacKuen, and Robert S. Erikson, "Dynamic Representation," *American Political Science Review* 89 (1995): 543–565; Lawrence J. Grossback, David M. Peterson, and James A Stimson, *Mandate Politics* (New York: Cambridge University Press, 2006).
18. Walter Dean Burnham, "Insulation and Responsiveness in Congressional Elections," *Political Science Quarterly* 90 (1975): 411–435; Randall L. Calvert and John A. Ferejohn, "Coattail Voting in Recent Presidential Elections," *American Political Science Review* 77 (1983): 407–419; John A. Ferejohn and Randall L. Calvert, "President Coattails in Historical Perspective," *American Journal of Political Science* 28 (1984): 127–146; George C. Edwards III, *Presidential Influence in Congress* (San Francisco: W. H. Freeman, 1980), pp. 74–75; Richard Born, "Reassessing the Decline of Presidential Coattails: U.S. House Elections, 1952–1980," *Journal of Politics* 46 (1984): 60–79; James E. Campbell, "Predicting Seat Gains from Presidential Coattails," *American Journal of Political Science* 30 (1986): 397–418; Jacobson, *Electoral Origins of Divided Government*, pp. 80–81; and Gregory N. Flemming, "Presidential Coattails in Open-Seat Elections," *Legislative Studies Quarterly* 20 (1995): 197–212.
19. Gary C. Jacobson, "Party Polarization in National Politics: The Electoral Connection," in *Congress and the President in a Partisan Era*, ed. Jon R. Bond and Richard Fleisher (Washington, DC: Congressional Quarterly Press, 2000), p. 21.
20. Ticket-splitting rates are of course higher in years with substantial independent or third-party presidential candidacies (1968, 1980, 1992, and 1996) if we include these candidates' supporters in the analysis. Such voters are forced to split their tickets if they vote in the House election because there is no House candidate of their presidential favorite's party to vote for. Even if we include the Perot voters in the 1996 analysis, however, the incidence of ticket-splitting is only 22 percent, tying 1988 for the lowest of any year since 1964.
21. For the actual equations, see the second, third, fourth, and fifth editions of this book, respectively.
22. Controlling for partisanship, incumbency, and feeling thermometer ratings of the candidates (set at 50 degrees for respondents who could not recognize and rate the candidate), a probit equation using NES data estimates that, with the other variables set at their means, the probability of voting for the Democratic House candidate would be 0.30 if the respondent voted for John Kerry, 0.84 if the respondent voted for Bush, a difference of 0.54.
23. Gary C. Jacobson, "Presidential Coattails in 1972," *Public Opinion Quarterly* 40 (1976): 194–200; Calvert and Ferejohn, "Coattail Voting," p. 415.
24. Jacobson and Kernell, *Strategy and Choice*, p. 33.
25. Jacobson and Kernell, *Strategy and Choice*, p. 33.

26. Jacobson and Kernell, *Strategy and Choice*, pp. 49–59.
27. Jacobson and Kernell, *Strategy and Choice*, pp. 27–29.
28. "Running Hard in Watergate's Shadow," *Congressional Quarterly Weekly Report* 32 (February 16, 1974): 353; and "Southern Republicans: Little Hope This Year," *Congressional Quarterly Weekly Report* 32 (October 26, 1974): 2959–2961.
29. Linda L. Fowler, "Candidate Perceptions of Electoral Coalitions: Limits and Possibilities" (Paper presented at the Conference on Congressional Elections, Rice University and the University of Houston, January 10–12, 1980), p. 11; and Jacobson and Kernell, *Strategy and Choice*, p. 32.
30. Jacobson, *Electoral Origins of Divided Government*, p. 73.
31. Jacobson, "Reversal of Fortune," p. 12.
32. For further evidence to these points, see Gary C. Jacobson, "Strategic Politicians and the Dynamics of U.S. House Elections, 1946–1986," *American Political Science Review* 83 (1989): 775–793; and Michael Berkman and James Eisenstein, "State Legislators as Congressional Candidates: The Effects of Prior Experience on Legislative Recruitment and Fundraising," *Political Research Quarterly* 52 (1999): 481–498.
33. Jamie L. Carson and Jason M. Roberts, "Strategic Politicians and U.S. House Elections, 1874–1914," *Journal of Politics* 67 (2005): 474–496; Jamie L. Carson, Eric J. Engstron, and Jason M. Roberts, "Redistricting, Candidate Entry, and the Politics of Nineteenth-Century U.S. House Elections," *American Journal of Political Science* 50 (2006): 283–293.
34. Jacobson, "Strategic Politicians," pp. 787–790; Jacobson, *Electoral Origins of Divided Government*, pp. 55–57; Gary Cox and Jonathan Katz, "Why Did the Incumbency Advantage in U.S. House Elections Grow?" *Journal of Politics* 40 (May 1996): 478–497.
35. V.O. Key, Jr., with Milton Cummings, *The Responsible Electorate* (Cambridge, MAs: Harvard University Press, 1966), p. 7.
36. Morris P. Fiorina, "Who Is Held Responsible? Further Evidence on the Hibbing–Alford Thesis," *American Journal of Political Science* 27 (1983): 158–164; and Kiewiet, *Macroeconomics and Micropolitics*, pp. 102–108.
37. For a more detailed discussion of these elections, see the fifth edition of this book.
38. Gary C. Jacobson, "Congress: Unusual Year, Unusual Election," in *The Elections of 1992*, ed. Michael Nelson (Washington, DC: Congressional Quarterly Press, 1983), pp. 153–182.
39. John Petrocik, "Divided Government: Is It All in the Campaigns?" in *The Politics of Divided Government*, ed. Gary W. Cox and Samuel Kernell (Boulder, CO: Westview Press, 1991), pp. 20–30.
40. Jacobson, "Congress," pp. 162–164.
41. James Risen, "Numbers Don't Add Up for Bush," *Los Angeles Times*, September 25, 1992, p. A22.
42. Adam Clymer, "Public Believes Worst on Bank Scandal," *New York Times*, April 2, 1992, p. A1.

43. Gary C. Jacobson and Michael A. Dimock, "Checking Out: The Impact of Bank Overdrafts on the 1992 House Elections," *American Journal of Political Science* 38 (1994): 601–624.
44. Gary C. Jacobson, *The Politics of Congressional Elections*, 3rd ed. (New York: HarperCollins, 1992), p. 239.
45. Keith Krehbiel, "Institutional and Partisan Sources of Gridlock: A Theory of Divided and Unified Government," *Journal of Theoretical Politics* 8 (1996): 7–40.
46. Paul Richter, "It Just *Seems* Like We're Worse Off," *Los Angeles Times*, January 26, 1995, p. A25.
47. In 1992, 79 percent of the voters (in the national exit polls) thought the economy was in bad shape, and 62 percent of them voted for a Democrat for the House. In 1994, 75 percent said they were no better off financially than they had been two years before; 57 percent thought the economy was still in bad shape, and 62 percent of this group voted for the Republican. See Gary Langer, "'94 Vote: Republicans Seize the Reins of Discontent," ABC News Analysis, reported in *Hotline*, November 11, 1994.
48. In 1992, angry and dissatisfied voters had voted Democratic in House elections 56 percent to 44 percent; in 1994, they voted Republican, 64 percent to 36 percent. See Ibid.
49. Langer, "'94 Vote"; and *New York Times*, November 13, 1994, p. A15.
50. The 1988 district presidential vote was recomputed for each district to adjust for redistricting after 1990; the data are from Michael Barone and Grant Ujifusa, *The Almanac of American Politics 1994* (Washington, DC: National Journal Press, 1993).
51. Gary C. Jacobson, "1994 House Elections in Perspective," *Political Science Quarterly* 111 (1996), p. 8; Jacobson, "Reversal of Fortune"; and James E. Campbell, "The Presidential Pulse and the 1994 Congressional Election," *Journal of Politics* 59 (1997): 830–857.
52. According to a survey sponsored by the Christian Coalition, 33 percent of the 1994 voters were "religious conservatives," up from 24 percent in 1992 and 18 percent in 1988; see *Congressional Quarterly Weekly Report* 52 (November 19, 1994): 3364. In the 1994 exit poll, 38 percent identified themselves as "conservatives," compared with 30 percent in 1992; see Langer, "'94 Vote."
53. The standard deviation of the inter-election vote swing across districts between 1992 and 1994 was 7.8 percentage points, compared to an average of 8.8 percentage points for the previous ten elections.
54. Jacobson, "1994 House Elections," p. 15.
55. Jacobson, "1994 House Elections," p. 14
56. Jacobson, "1994 House Elections"; see also Paul Gronke, Jeffrey Koch, and J. Matthew Wilson, "Follow the Leader? Presidential Approval, Presidential Support, and Representatives' Electoral Fortunes," *Journal of Politics* 65 (2003): 785–808.
57. Against incumbent Democrats in Republican-leaning districts, 49 percent (nineteen of thirty-nine) Republican challengers who spent in excess of

$300,000 won, whereas only 6 percent (two of thirty-two) of the challengers who spent less than this sum managed to defeat the incumbent. If analysis is further confined to Democratic incumbents who supported the Clinton administration on at least two of three key votes, the respective percentages are 52 percent (fourteen of twenty-seven) and 13 percent (two of fifteen).

58. George Hager, "GOP Ready to Take Debt Limit to the Brink and Beyond," *Congressional Quarterly Weekly Report* 53 (September 23, 1995): 2865.
59. Gary C. Jacobson, "The 105th Congress: Unprecedented and Unsurprising," in *The Elections of 1996*, ed. Michael Nelson (Washington, DC: Congressional Quarterly Press, 1997), pp. 144–147.
60. Jonathan D. Salant, "House Republicans Stray from the 'Contract' Terms," *Congressional Quarterly Weekly Report* 54 (July 6, 1996): 1929–1933.
61. According to the national exit polls, voters who made their decisions in the last few days before the election voted for Dole over Clinton, 40 percent to 35 percent. See *Los Angeles Times*, November 7, 1996, p. 22. An additional 1 percent of the vote would have put the Democratic candidate over 50 percent in eleven House districts; an additional 2 percent would have put the Democrat over the top in twenty-two districts. For additional evidence of party balancing in 1996, see Charles E. Smith Jr., Robert D. Brown, John M. Bruce, and L. Marvin Overby, "Party Balancing and Voting for Congress in the 1996 National Election," *American Journal of Political Science* 43 (1999): 737–764.
62. The Democrats picked up seats in 1934 during the New Deal realignment; both parties had added seats in 1902 when the House grew by 29 seats, but the president's Republicans had picked up fewer than the opposition Democrats and so were relatively weaker after the election.
63. Bernard Sanders, the lone independent who normally votes with the Democrats, was also reelected.
64. Gary C. Jacobson, "Impeachment Politics in the 1998 Congressional Elections," *Political Science Quarterly* 114 (1999): 33–40.
65. The Gallup Poll, October 9–12, 1998, at *http://www.gallup.com/POLL_ARCHIVES/9810912.htm*.
66. Gary C. Jacobson, "Public Opinion and the Impeachment of Bill Clinton," *British Elections and Parties Review* 10, ed. Philip Cowley et al. (London: Frank Cass, 2000), pp. 7–11.
67. Jeffrey Katz and Dan Carney, "Clinton's Latest, Worst Troubles Put His Whole Agenda on Hold," *Congressional Quarterly Weekly Report* 56 (January 24, 1998): 165.
68. Jacobson, "Impeachment Politics," p. 43.
69. Dan Carney with Carroll J. Doherty, "GOP Struggles to Find Strategy to Deal with Starr Fallout," *Congressional Quarterly Weekly Report* 56 (March 14, 1998): 643–644.
70. "Thrust and Parry: Gingrich v. Clinton," *Congressional Quarterly Weekly Report* 56 (May 2, 1998): 1128.
71. Karen Foerstel, "Clinton's Address Fails to Defuse Ticking Time Bomb of Starr Report," *Congressional Quarterly Weekly Report* 56 (August 22, 1998): 2281.

72. Jacobson, "Public Opinion and Impeachment," pp. 4–6.
73. Jacobson, "Public Opinion and Impeachment," pp. 9–11.
74. Jacobson, "Public Opinion and Impeachment," pp. 11–15.
75. Jacobson, "Public Opinion and Impeachment," p. 18.
76. Sung to the tune of "Twinkle, Twinkle Little Star," the lyrics were

    Twinkle, twinkle, Kenneth Starr,
    Now we see how brave you are.
    We could not see which way to go,
    If you did not lead us so,
    Twinkle, twinkle Kenneth Starr,
    Now we see how brave you are.

    Iver Peterson, "An Upset is Traced, in Part, to a Partisan Song," *New York Times*, November 5, 1998, p. B16.
77. Alan I. Abramowitz, "It's Monica, Stupid: Voting Behavior in the 1998 Midterm Election" (Paper presented at the Annual Meeting of the American Political Science Association, Atlanta, September 2–5, 1999), p. 5.
78. Abramowitz, "It's Monica, Stupid," pp. 6–8.
79. According to Federal Election Commission data, the six successful challengers had already spent between $954,693 and $1.59 million each.
80. Alan I. Abramowitz, "The End of the Democratic Era? 1994 and the Future of Congressional Election Research," *Political Research Quarterly* 48 (December 1995): 873–889; and Warren E. Miller and J. Merrill Shanks, *The New American Voter* (Cambridge, MA: Harvard University Press, 1996), Chapter 7.
81. In twenty Gallup polls taken between January and September 2000, the Democrats averaged 51.5 percent of the major-party identifiers (with leaners included among the partisans); the two-party split among voters in the 2000 National Election Study sample was 53–47, but the survey probably overstates Democratic strength, as the presidential vote was reported as 50.6 percent for Gore, 45.5 percent for Bush.
82. Monika L. McDermott and David R. Jones, "Do Public Evaluations of Congress Matter? Retrospective Voting in Congressional Elections," *American Politics Research* 31 (March 2003): 155–177.
83. Gary C. Jacobson, "A House and Senate Divided: The Clinton Legacy and the Congressional Elections of 2000," *Political Science Quarterly* 116 (Spring 2001): 8.
84. Analysis of the 2000 NES data reveals a positive and significant association between approval of Clinton and Congress once party identification is controlled.
85. Three other incumbents, two Democrats and a Republican, lost primary elections.
86. Bob Benenson, "Proudly Worn Party Label Missing in Key Contests," *CQ Weekly* 22 (September 2000): 2182–2185.
87. Andrew Taylor, "Sound Like a Moderate, Vote Like a Conservative," *CQ Weekly* (August 5, 2000): 1930–1934; and Mike Christensen, "Congress's Cornucopia: A Sampler of Spending Add-ons," *CQ Weekly* (October 7, 2000): 2322–2323.

88. See note 62 above.
89. See, for example, James Carney and John Dickerson, "W. and the 'Boy Genius,'" *Time* (November 11, 2002): 41–45; and Howard Fineman, "How Bush Did It," *Newsweek* (November 11, 2002): 29–31.
90. A version of the equation in Table 6–2 using data from 1946–2000 predicts a nine-seat Republican House gain in 2002.
91. His average rating in the fourteen polls taken during the month preceding the election by Gallup (four), CBS News/*New York Times* (two), Pew Research Center (two), *Newsweek* (two), ABC News/*Washington Post* (two), NBC/*Wall Street Journal* (one), and CNN/*Time* (one) was also 63 percent approving; see *http://www.pollingreport.com/BushJob.htm*, August 7, 2003.
92. Democrats picked up five House seats in 1998; Reagan's Republicans lost only five seats, the best performance at the midterm for any Republican administration before 2002.
93. Jacobson, "A House and Senate Divided," p. 19.
94. Gary C. Jacobson, "Partisan Polarization in Presidential Support: The Electoral Connection," *Congress and the Presidency* 30 (Spring 2003): 1–36.
95. The average among independents was 50 percent approving.
96. As late as June 2001, among Democrats, 68 percent thought Bush could not be trusted to keep his word, 59 percent thought he did not have strong leadership qualities, 78 percent doubted his ability to deal wisely with an international crisis, 70 percent thought he did not have the skills needed to negotiate with world leaders, and 54 percent doubted his judgment under pressure. See "Bush and the Democratic Agenda," CBS News/*New York Times* Poll, June 14–18, 2001, at *http://www.cbsnews.com/htdocs/pdf/bushbac.pdf*.
97. The ratings of independents are usually within a percentage point or two of the president's overall ratings; thus approval by independents rose from about 50 percent before to about 85 percent after September 11 and then declined gradually to about 64 percent by November 2002.
98. Only 10.8 percent of Republican incumbents were opposed in 2002 by Democrats who had ever held elective public office—a figure 1.9 standard deviations below the postwar mean of 24.9 percent. The postwar low was 10.1 percent in 1990.
99. Jeffrey M. Jones, "Republicans Trail in Congressional Race Despite Advantage on Issues," Gallup News Service, September 26, 2002, at *http://www.gallup.com/poll/releases/pr020926.asp?Version=p*; Lydia Said, "National Issues May Play Bigger-Than-Usual Role in Congressional Elections," Gallup News Service, October 31, 2002, at *http://www.gallup.com/poll/releases/pr021031.asp?Version=p*.
100. Jacobson, *Divider*, pp. 84–86.
101. The model in Table 6–2 would predict Republicans to lose the House if Bush's overall approval rating were less than 50 percent.
102. Consumer Research Center News Release, October 29, 2002, at *http://www.crc-conquest.org/consumer_confidence*.
103. "CQ Ratings: The House," *CQ Weekly* (October 26, 2002): 2795.

104. Generic polls ask whether, if the election were held today, the respondent would vote for the Republican or Democratic candidate without mentioning the candidate's names. In the sixteen CBS News/*New York Times* polls taken between January 2004 and the election, the Democrats' share of party identifiers averaged 53 percent; in thirty generic House polls taken between August 1 and the election, an average of 51.4 percent said they would vote for the Democrat. See *http://www.pollingreport.com.*
105. Based on 20 surveys taken between August 1 and October 30, 2004, by the CBS News/*New York Times* Gallup, ABC News/*Washington Post, Los Angeles Times,* and Pew Research Center for the People & the Press polls. Figure 3 includes data from these organizations plus the NBC News/ *Wall Street Journal, Newsweek,* Marist, and Bloomberg polls; all sample all adults 18 years and older.
106. Jacobson, *Divider,* pp. 5–7.
107. *Congressional Quarterly* classifies seats as safe Republican, Republican favored, leaning Republican, no clear favorite, leaning Democratic, Democrat favored, or safe Democratic. These classifications are usually quite accurate; in 2004, all of the seats classified as safe or favored went to the party so designated; only three of the thirty classified as leaning to a party were won by the other party. The 1980–2002 average for the middle three categories was sixty-nine. For 2004, the data are from *http://www.nytimes.com/packages/html/politics/2004_ELECTIONGUIDE_GRAPHIC/index_HOUSECQ.html;* for earlier years, they are from the October election previews in the *CQ Weekly Report.*
108. In secondary analysis of 107 of these polls, mean consistency was 83.8 percent with a standard deviation of 2.9 percent.
109. See Gary C. Jacobson, "Public Opinion and the War in Iraq," presented at the Annual Meeting of the American Political Science Association, Philadelphia, August 30th–September 3, 2006, p. 25.
110. The independent category includes partisan leaners in these data to allow comparisons to the Exit Poll results.
111. The five were Larry Kissel (NC 8, 49.9%), Victoria Wulsin (OH 2, 49.4%), Sharon Reiner (MI 07, 48.4%) Nancy Ann Skinner (MI 9, 47.3%), and Larry Grant (ID 1, 47.2%). By Charlie Cook's calculations, the number of Republican seats in play (defined as tossup or leaning Democratic) grew from 11 in May to 42 in October; see *The Cook Political Report,* at *http://www.cookpolitical.com/races/house/default.php,* (accessed November 6, 2006).
112. "House Winners Raised a Record Average of $1.1 Million," press release, Campaign Finance Institute, November 8, 2006, at *http://www.cfinst.org/pr/110806b.html* (accessed November 27, 2006).
113. This category would include Carol Shea-Porter who defeated Joseph Bradley III in New Hampshire and David Loebsack who defeated James Leach in Iowa.
114. A favorable year is defined as one in which the challenger's party increased its share of the national two-party vote for House candidates by at least 3 percentage points; by this criterion, 1974, 1982, 1996, and 2006 were

favorable to Democrats and 1980, 1984, and 1994 were favorable to Republicans.

115. Thomas E. Mann and Norman J. Ornstein, "Sending a Message: Voters and Congress in 1982," in *The American Elections of 1982*, ed. Thomas E. Mann and Norman J. Ornstein (Washington, DC: American Enterprise Institute for Public Policy Research, 1983), p. 136.
116. Jacobson and Kernell, *Strategy and Choice*, p. 82.
117. See also James E. Campbell and Joe A. Sumners, "Presidential Coattails in Senate Elections," *American Political Science Review* 84 (1990): 513–524; Campbell and Sumners argue that presidential coattails can be credited with twelve Republican Senate victories between 1972 and 1988, including four in 1980.
118. The quality of challengers makes an important difference in Senate as well as House elections; see Peverill Squire, "Challengers in Senate Elections," *Legislative Studies Quarterly* 14 (1989): 531–547; Gary C. Jacobson and Raymond E. Wolfinger, "Information and Voting in California Senate Elections," *Legislative Studies Quarterly* 14 (1989): 509–529.
119. Rob Gurwitt, "Voters Restore Democrats to Senate Control," *Congressional Quarterly Weekly Report* 44 (November 8, 1986): 2811–2814; see also Patricia A. Hurley, "Partisan Representation, Realignment, and the Senate in the 1980s" (Paper presented at the Annual Meeting of the Midwest Political Science Association, Chicago, April 14–16, 1988).
120. Jacobson, "Congress," p. 173.
121. Karen Foerstel, "Senate: GOP on the March," *Congressional Quarterly Weekly Report* 56 (October 24, 1998): 2868–2872.
122. Abramowitz, "Monica," p. 8.
123. Mary Clare Jalonick, "Senate Changes Hands Again," *CQ Weekly* (November 9, 2002): 2907–2909; and Rebecca Adams, "Georgia Republicans Energized by 'Friend to Friend' Campaign," *CQ Weekly* (November 9, 2002): 2892–2893.
124. "Six Tossups Muddy Forecast for the Senate," *CQ Weekly* (October 26, 2002): 2792–2793; the exceptions were Minnesota, Arkansas, and South Dakota (lost by Republican challenger John Thune by 534 votes).
125. The same trend shown in Figure 6–13 is evident in southern voting for U.S. representative, although it is not so pronounced and was lowest in 1996, not 2004.
126. According to the 2004 NES survey, Bush's approval rating was 63.9 percent in these five states, compared to 49.4 percent elsewhere.
127. The list of Democratic challengers in the seven tightest races includes three candidates who had held statewide offices (governor, attorney general, auditor), two U.S representatives, a president of the state senate, and a former secretary of the Navy. The Democrats who retained open seats for the party were also experienced candidates: the attorney general for Minnesota's largest county and two U.S. Representatives (counting Bernie Sanders, an Independent who caucuses with the Democrats).
128. Jacobson, "Referendum," pp. 20–22.

Chapter 7

ELECTIONS, REPRESENTATION, AND THE POLITICS OF CONGRESS

Congressional elections matter because the U.S. Congress matters. Though often overshadowed in the popular imagination by forceful presidents, Congress retains so much of its institutional autonomy that it remains, in Morris P. Fiorina's apt phrase, the "keystone of the Washington establishment." Any lingering doubts about that have been laid to rest by what happened during the Clinton administration. Republicans advanced their agenda far more effectively controlling Congress but not the White House than they ever did by controlling the White House but not Congress. Even during the George W. Bush administration, when defense against terrorism and the prosecution of wars in Afghanistan and Iraq vastly increased the power and status of the executive branch, Congress's influence over domestic policy remained decisive; the president was by no means uniformly successful in achieving his legislative goals even with both houses in Republican hands. Congress's performance as an institution therefore has a profound effect on how—and how well—the United States is governed.

The workings of Congress, and its strengths and weaknesses as a governing institution, are in turn intimately connected to how its members win and hold office. This chapter examines how the electoral politics depicted in the first six chapters affects the workings of the House and Senate as institutions and the policy choices they make. Its central point is simple: How members win and hold office powerfully affects the internal organization of the houses of Congress, the kind of legislation they produce, and the kind of representation Americans therefore receive.

Representation

Congress is a representative assembly. Put most simply,[1] it is a representative assembly because its members are chosen in competitive popular elections, and if voters do not like what the members are doing, they can vote them out of office. Voters can hold representatives accountable for their actions as long as members care about their own reelection or their party's future, and nearly every member does. Representation is an effect of electoral politics; the electoral system determines the kind of representation Congress provides.

Reflecting the multidimensional electoral system described in earlier chapters, representation in Congress is also multidimensional and its main elements, while always present, have varied in importance over time. The electoral politics of the late 1960s and 1970s invited a focus on representation of the interests, values, and needs of local constituencies. Since that time, the growing electoral involvement of organized interest groups has increasingly directed members' attention to issues and concerns extending beyond the boundaries of their districts and states. Even more importantly, the expanding electoral role of national parties, both organizationally and as the locus of intensified ideological conflict, has made the partisan component of representation much more salient than it was a generation ago.

Policy Congruence

During the era when candidate-centered electoral politics was at its peak, political scientists paid the most attention to one aspect of representation: policy congruence. The central question they addressed involved the extent to which the policy views of people in a state or district are reflected in the policy stances (usually measured by roll-call votes) of the people they elect to Congress. This has never been an easy question to answer. Information on constituency opinion is scarce and often unreliable, and it is doubtful that there is any "constituency opinion" on many of the issues Congress faces. Measuring constituents' attitudes has challenged the ingenuity of a generation of scholars because the one obvious solution—regular, adequately sized sample surveys of a large number of states and districts—has, at least until recently, simply been too expensive.[2]

Demographic indicators, simulations, referendum voting, and aggregated national survey data have all been used to estimate state and district attitudes. So have small-sample district- and state-level surveys.[3] Each of these approaches has drawbacks, and there is the additional problem of establishing some kind of comparability between any of these measures and measures of congressional behavior.[4] Still, a number of general conclusions can be drawn from this work. Most research suggests that congressional roll-call votes are indeed related to estimated district opinion, although the strength of the connection varies across issue dimensions and is never overwhelmingly large. The relationships are strongest when votes and attitudes are combined and reduced to a few general dimensions—for example, domestic welfare policy or civil rights for minorities—and weaker for specific votes on single pieces of legislation.[5] The connection is also stronger if the constituency is defined as the member's supporters (defined by voting or partisanship).[6]

All of these findings make intuitive sense. Members of Congress develop differentiated images of their constituencies and have a fair notion of who keeps them in office. It is no surprise that they are more responsive to some groups than to others. There is no great pressure to vote district (or supporting constituency) preferences on every vote, especially because on many specific votes constituency preferences are unknown or unformed. Members need only take care to cast "explainable" votes. On the other hand, anyone who consistently votes contrary to the wishes of his or her constituents is likely to run into trouble. Voters, in aggregate, do form passably accurate notions of their representatives' voting patterns, and members who stray too far from home suffer at the polls.[7]

Few members do so unawares, for most become adept at anticipating how their voters will respond to their actions. As Fenno pointed out, the pursuit of reelection is what makes representation of this sort possible:

> There is no way that the act of representing can be separated from the act of getting elected. If the congressman cannot win and hold the votes of some people, he cannot represent any people. Further, he cannot represent any people unless he knows, or makes an effort to know, who they are, what they think, and what they want; and it is by campaigning for electoral support among them that he finds out such things. During the expansionist stage of his constituency career, particularly, he probably knows his various constituencies as well as it is possible to know them. It is, indeed, by such campaigning, by going home a great deal, that a congressman develops a complex and discriminating set of perceptions about his constituents.[8]

This knowledge is the basis for making judgments about what constituents want or need from politics. Two-way communication is essential to representation. The stress that members of Congress put on their accessibility invites communication from constituents, at the same time as it attracts their support. The knowledge and work it takes to win and hold a district not only establish the basis for policy congruence but also let the member know when it is irrelevant or unnecessary.

Research by Fenno and other scholars also makes it clear that there is much more to representation than policy congruence. Members certainly "represent" their constituents in important ways by helping them cope with the federal bureaucracy, by bringing in public works projects, by helping local governments and other groups to take advantage of federal programs, or by helping an overseas relative get permanent resident status. Particularized benefits, as these are called, are still benefits and an important part of representation is making sure one's constituents get their share.

Interests and Causes

Representation of still another kind is provided by members who become spokespeople for interests and causes not confined to their constituencies. Some African American members of Congress, for example, try to speak for all African Americans. Senator Sam Brownback takes it upon himself to champion the values of the religious right. Representative Henry Hyde–spent much of his career leading the legislative fight against abortion for the right-to-life movement. Senator Barbara Boxer tirelessly promotes the feminist position on women's issues. Most members are not so careless that their commitment to a group or cause upsets their supporting constituency; more often it becomes a way of pleasing constituents (especially their core supporters) and so coincides nicely with electoral necessities. But not always. A few members invite consistently strong opposition and regularly court defeat in representing their vision of the national interest. The electoral process, however, tends to weed them out.

On a somewhat more mundane level, the current electoral structure gives representation of a sort to any group that can mobilize people or money to help in campaigns. The views of conservative Christian leaders enjoy much more respectful attention now that they have demonstrated their ability to deliver millions of votes. Various groups—corporate political action committees (PACs), trade associations, labor unions, and ideological groups that supply campaign resources—help to elect congenial candidates and acquire access to them, helping to ensure that these groups' interests are represented in Congress. It is a matter of debate whether this is a benign or pernicious phenomenon, and the controversy is not likely to die down as long as interest groups continue their heavy and growing involvement in pivotal congressional races. But it would be hard to argue that some mechanism for representing the enormous variety of economic and political interests that cannot be encompassed within the framework of single-member districts is not essential.

Representation by Referendum

Congress is broadly representative on another dimension. As we saw in Chapter 6, aggregate election results are responsive to national economic and political conditions. When citizens are unhappy with the government's performance, the administration's party suffers the consequences. The opposing party picks up more seats, and even those who remain in Congress get the message that they had better recognize new realities. Reagan was able to win budget victories not only because more Republicans sat in the 97th Congress but also because the remaining Democrats read the election results as a demand that something drastic be done about taxes and inflation. The issue in 1981 was not whether the budget and taxes would be cut, but which package of cuts—those of the administration or those of the House Democrats—would be adopted.[9] Similarly, the influx of new House Republicans in 1994 made cuts in domestic spending and action on other items in the Contract with America the top priorities for many of the holdovers as well. And after 2006, some congressional Republicans began to go their own way on the Iraq War, abandoning the unwavering support for the Bush administration's policies that had been common only a couple of years earlier.

Aggregate representation of this kind is necessarily crude and rests on somewhat shaky foundations, depending, as it does, partly on the self-reinforcing expectations of congressional elites. And it can operate only when there is some visible public consensus on the general direction of policy, which is by no means always the case. The energy crisis, designated by Carter as the "moral equivalent of war," was certainly the dominant national issue when gas lines developed and energy prices skyrocketed. But Congress could not produce any systematic plan to cope with it because all of the proposed solutions would impose major costs on politically powerful groups. Budget politics during the Reagan–George H. W. Bush years assumed a similar character, with the public fed up with the problem—continuing deficits—but badly divided on the solution. Moreover, aggregate shifts are subject to misinterpretation; Clinton's victory in 1992 was, it turned out, no mandate for liberal domestic policies, nor was the Republican victory in 1994 a mandate for dismantling the welfare state. The message of 2006 was to change direction on Iraq, but there was no clear signal regarding what the new direction should entail.

Descriptive Representation

In one particular way, Congress does not represent the American public well at all: demographically. Congress contains a much greater proportion of white, male, college-educated, professional, higher-income people than the population as a whole; the Senate is especially unrepresentative by these criteria. Even the creation of minority–majority districts after 1990 did not eliminate racial under-representation in the House, although the gap did narrow. African Americans comprise 12 percent of the voting-age citizens, 9 percent of the House; Latinos make up 7 percent of the voting-age citizens, 6 percent of the House. Only one African American, Barack Obama of Illinois, sat in the Senate in the 110th Congress (2007–2008). And despite the dramatic success of women candidates in 1992 and further gains thereafter, women, who make up a majority of the voting-age population (52 percent), held only 17 percent of House seats and 16 percent of Senate seats in the 110th. Occupationally, 37 percent of House members and 59 percent of Senators are lawyers; a blue-collar background or an advanced science degree is rare. Congress also boasts a much higher proportion of millionaires than the population at large.

Yet Congress is probably quite representative of the kinds of people who achieve positions of leadership in the great majority of American institutions. It would be unlikely in the extreme for an electoral system such as the one described in this book to produce a Congress that looks anything like a random sample of the voting-age population. What it does produce is a sample of local elites from a remarkably diverse nation. And from this perspective, at times the electoral politics of Congress generates legislative bodies that are *too* representative of the myriad divisions in American society.

Like the members of Congress whom we elect, we Americans have wanted to have it both ways. We enjoy the programs and benefits that the federal government provides, but we dislike paying the price in the form of increased taxes, higher inflation, and greater government regulation. Public opinion polls routinely find solid majorities in favor of national health insurance, government guarantees of jobs, and current or greater levels of spending on the environment, education, the homeless, and health care. The same polls find equally solid majorities believing that the federal government is too large, spends too much money, and is too intrusive in people's lives. We like a balanced budget, but we want it to be achieved without increased taxes or reduced services.[10] When Congress is stalemated, produces self-contradictory policies, or tolerates large budget deficits, it accurately reflects our own disagreement, confusion, and self-contradictory preferences. As Mayhew pointed out, "half the adverse criticism of Congress . . . is an indirect criticism of the public itself."[11]

Policy Consequences

Particularism

Among the most familiar targets for congressional critics' scorn is members' notorious affection for policies that produce particularized benefits.[12] Electoral logic inspires members to promote narrowly targeted programs, projects, and tax breaks for constituents and supporting groups without worrying about their impact on spending or revenues. Recipients notice and appreciate such specific and identifiable benefits and show their gratitude to the legislator responsible at election time. Because the benefits come at the expense of general revenues, no one's share of the cost of any specific project or tax break is large enough to notice. It thus makes political sense for members to pursue local or group benefits that are paid for nationally even if the costs clearly outweigh the benefits. Conversely, there is no obvious payoff for opposing any particular local or group benefit because the savings are spread so thinly among taxpayers that no one notices.

The influence of Congress's fondness for particularized benefits goes beyond public works and tax breaks. Virtually any proposal will attract more support if the benefits it confers can be sliced up and allocated in identifiable packages to individual states and districts. Because everyone in Washington knows this, policies are deliberately designed to distribute particularized benefits broadly even when that makes no objective sense. As a consequence, resources are not concentrated where they are needed most (or where they can be used most efficiently by any objective criterion). They are wasted and their impact is diluted. Grandly conceived programs emerge in a form that often ensures that they will fail to achieve their objectives, feeding doubts that the federal government can do anything well.[13]

A more fundamental problem with particularized benefits is that Congress is forever tempted to overproduce them. Individual members gain politically by logrolling, supporting each other's projects or tax breaks in return for support for their own. But when everyone follows such an individually productive strategy, all may end up in worse shape politically when shackled with collective blame for the aggregate consequences. Spending rises, revenues fall, the deficit grows, inefficient government programs proliferate, and the opposition attacks the logrolling coalition—in practice, the majority party—for wastefulness and incompetence.

Attacks on the traffic in particularized benefits, under the more familiar pejorative label *pork*, are routinely included in indictments of Congress. In reality, spending for traditional pork-barrel projects has been a small part of the federal budget for years, and such projects contributed relatively little to the large deficits of the 1980s and early 1990s or of the George W. Bush administration. The $29 billion spent on 9,963 earmarked projects in the 2006 budget set a new record but still amounted on only about 1 percent of federal outlays.[14] As symbols of "waste," however, pork-barrel projects are irresistible; for example, the $223 million earmarked in an appropriations bill for a "bridge to nowhere" in Alaska became the target of universal ridicule that contributed to the congressional Republicans' woes in 2006.[15]

Many of the Republicans first elected in the 1990s portrayed themselves as scourges of pork, but few of them declined to support local projects that would benefit their constituents. For example, Enid Green Waldholtz of Utah, while celebrating her part in a vote to balance the budget, circumvented a Transportation Appropriations Subcommittee rule against earmarked highway projects to secure a $5 million grant for work on Interstate 15 in Salt Lake City.[16] George Nethercutt, who had upset Speaker Tom Foley in 1994, fought hard to spare a $436,000 wheat research facility in his Washington district that had been targeted by Republican budget cutters. And Greg Ganske of Iowa fought to continue funding for local mass transit and recreational projects initiated by an incumbent he had tagged a wasteful spender and defeated in 1994. As Ganske put it,

"I see my primary role as trying to [help] government be more fiscally responsible than it has been in the past," but "it's also part of a congressman's job to represent his district."[17] Exactly.

Even when stringent budget constraints limit potential for pork, members care very much about snaring a share of whatever is available. During the 104th Congress, for example, the best opportunity came in military spending, the one area where Republicans wanted to spend more than the Clinton administration. Members made the most of it by adding, for example, projects not requested by the military to the military construction bill for fiscal 1996. When Ed Royce of California, a self-described "porkbuster," sought to cut $10.4 million earmarked for construction of a new physical fitness center at the Bremerton Puget Sound Naval Shipyard, he was pointedly reminded of his own plea to the chair of the House National Security Military Research and Development Subcommittee for a local project not requested by the Pentagon: "Could you see your way fit to put $34 million in this year's bill, because it will really help me out back in my district?"[18]

With the budget finally back in balance in 1998, members of both houses and both parties reveled in the opportunity provided by authorization of a six-year, $217.9 billion surface transportation bill to deliver particularized benefits to their districts and states. The House version of the bill contained more than 1,500 highway and bridge projects, the Senate's version, about 300.[19] Under much tighter budgetary conditions in 2003, senators added $675 million in pork barrel spending (later reduced to $355 million in conference) to the $78.5 billion supplemental spending bill meant to cover the cost of the war in Iraq.[20] Even in wartime, the search for particularized benefits persists.

Serving the Organized

Another important consequence of electoral politics—and routine target of criticism—is that Congress serves the vocal, organized, and active.[21] The system naturally favors any politically attentive group that is present in significant numbers in a large number of states or districts. The best examples are veterans (widely distributed, well organized) and Social Security recipients (widely distributed, large numbers, consistent voters). Large numbers are not, however, essential for groups to be influential. Organization and money also matter. It is easy to exaggerate the threat that PACs pose to democracy,[22] but their electoral importance is undeniable, and it would be surprising if their political clout was not proportionate. They need not "buy" members with their contributions to be effective. Some of the most successful groups—the National Rifle Association (zealous opponents of gun-control legislation) and anti-abortionists are examples—win by the implicit threat to finance and work for the opponents of members who do not support their positions. A few instances where such groups have helped to defeat seemingly entrenched incumbents are sufficient to keep most members representing districts where such groups are a force from taking them on.

The prospect of being targeted by any group with formidable campaign resources is unsettling; most members prefer to keep a low profile, avoiding votes that consistently offend active, well-organized interests. During the 1970s, for example, Environmental Action, a conservation lobbying group, compiled and publicized a list of the "Dirty Dozen," twelve congressmen who had (by

Environmental Action's standards) bad records on environmental issues and who seemed vulnerable. Over the course of five elections, twenty-four of the fifty-two who made the Dirty Dozen list were defeated. A consultant who worked on the campaigns claimed that the tactic "was very effective at making congressmen think twice about certain votes. There were numerous examples of members or their staff calling and saying 'Is the congressman close to being on the list?' or 'Is this vote going to be used to determine the list?'"[23] The League of Conservation Voters (LCV) revived the tactic in 1996, again with considerable success. In elections from 1996 through 2006, thirty-nine of the eighty-one candidates targeted were eventually defeated, including twenty-nine incumbents and seven House members trying to move up to the Senate. The tactic's potential was underlined by the reaction of Bob Dornan, a flamboyant conservative with a career LCV score of about 10 on a 100-point scale, to being put on the list in 1998. "In my heart," he said, "I'm a Greenpeace kind of guy."[24]

Keeping a low profile to avoid becoming a target became more difficult after the congressional reforms of the 1970s. Rule changes intended to open congressional activities to greater public scrutiny worked; the action became more visible, with more public meetings and more recorded votes. Members were thereby exposed to more pressure from interest and constituency groups. Lobbyists were quick to take advantage; there was a notable increase in the sophistication and effectiveness of Washington lobbyists. Shrewd interest groups learned to combine their work in Washington with work at the grassroots level, organizing a stream of messages from the district that, at the very least, encourages members to listen attentively to the pitch made by the group's Washington agent. Conducting such campaigns has become easier with the spread of modern communications technology and the emergence of professionals who organize grassroots campaigns for a living—if a group has the money to pay for them.

The growth of interest group activity, combined with the expanding financial role of PACs, transformed Congressional lobbying. Raymond Bauer, Ithiel de Sola Pool, and Lewis A. Dexter's classic study of lobbying in the 1950s described a process dominated by insiders. It was mainly a matter of friends talking to friends. Lobbyists worked through allies in Congress, encouraging them to pursue legislative projects that they were already inclined to favor by helping them do the necessary work. Opponents were ignored; pressure tactics in the insulated social world of Congress were felt to be counterproductive. Not surprisingly, members regarded lobbying as basically benign, and lobbyists as a resource to be exploited.[25]

Few members would take such a sanguine view today. Insiders still lobby in the old way, although most of them now supplement their work with outside activities. Some PACs have been created at the behest of Washington lobbyists, who view them as a means to making inside work more effective.[26] But they have been joined by the host of activists and organizations working to influence Congress from the outside. An effective outside strategy does not rely on maintaining friendly relations with incumbents, so outsiders are free to use pressure tactics, including explicit threats of electoral revenge, against members who oppose their views.

All of these developments reduce members' political maneuverability. The visibility of action and the growing capacity of organized groups to raise electoral trouble make it harder to engage in a politics of accommodation and compromise. It is not surprising that congressional enthusiasm for sunshine waned in the 1980s and that much of the important legislative action moved back behind closed doors, nor that House Democrats became increasingly inclined to adopt more restrictive rules on bills sent to the floor. Nor is it surprising that Republican leaders, having seen how health lobbyists mobilized public opposition to help them kill the Clinton health care reforms in 1994, provided only the sketchiest information about Medicare reforms before bringing them to a vote in 1995. In more recent years, the party leaders have sought to exercise tight control over the entire legislative process in order, among other goals, to minimize opportunities for interest groups to persuade back-benchers to bolt the party on bills important to the leadership.

Responsiveness without Responsibility

The scramble for local benefits, the sensitivity to organized interests, and the dilemmas created by a public demanding mutually contradictory policies point to the fundamental danger in the kind of representation encouraged by candidate-centered electoral politics: individual responsiveness without collective responsibility. The safest way to cope with contradictory policy demands is to be acutely sensitive to what constituents and other politically important groups want in taking positions or providing benefits but to avoid responsibility for the costs they would impose. It does not help matters when members are rewarded individually for taking pleasing positions but are not punished for failing to turn them into national policy or, when they do become policy, for seeing that they work.[27] Nor does it help when members thrive by delivering concentrated benefits to localities or special interests without being held accountable for the diffuse costs they impose on everyone else. As long as members are not held individually responsible for their collective performance in governing, a crucial form of representation is missing. Responsiveness is insufficient without responsibility.

The only instruments we have managed to develop for imposing collective responsibility on legislators are political parties. There is nothing original about this observation; it is a home truth to which students of congressional politics inevitably return.[28] Morris Fiorina put the case cogently:

> A strong political party can generate collective responsibility by creating incentives for leaders, followers, and popular supporters to think and act in collective terms. First, by providing party leaders with the capability (e.g., control of institutional patronage, nominations, etc.) to discipline party members, genuine leadership becomes possible. Legislative output is less likely to be a least common denominator—a residue of myriad conflicting proposals—and more likely to consist of a program actually intended to solve a problem or move the nation in a particular direction. Second, the subordination of individual office holders to the party lessens their ability to separate themselves from party actions. Like it or not their performance becomes identified with the performance of the collectivity to which they belong. Third, with individual candidate variation greatly reduced, voters have less incentive to support individuals and more to support or oppose the party as a whole. And fourth, the circle closes as party line voting in the electorate provides party leaders with the incentive to propose policies which will earn the support of a national majority, and party backbenchers with the personal incentive to cooperate with leaders in the attempt to compile a good record for the party as a whole.[29]

Pristine party government has never been characteristic of American politics, to be sure, but all of its necessary elements eroded with the electoral changes of the

1960s and 1970s. The emerging issues raised by the civil rights movement, the Vietnam War, the energy crisis, the environmental movement, *Roe v. Wade*, and the women's movement initially split both parties, but they cut across people, states, districts, and thus members of Congress in different ways. Coherent and consistent battle lines were absent, so policy coalitions tended to be ad hoc and fluid.[30] Conditions encouraged members to operate as individual political entrepreneurs and rewarded them when they did.

These developments exacerbated the unresolved tension between individual and collective goals inherent in congressional life. Although members win and hold seats in good part through their own personal efforts, it is what they achieve collectively, not individually, that shapes their parties' reputations and determines Congress's institutional significance. The problem is that party reputations or Congress's institutional strength are, for members, collective goods. Everyone in the majority benefits if their party builds a reputation for governing well, and all members benefit from belonging to a powerful and respected legislative body. Members enjoy these benefits, however, regardless of whether they contribute to achieving them.

The electoral needs of individual members and the practices required to make the House and Senate effective governing institutions often generate conflicting demands. The potential cost of ignoring the former is specific and personal: loss of office. The potential cost of ignoring the latter is diffuse and collective: an imperceptible marginal weakening of authority or decline in party stature. It is obvious where the balance of incentives lies. David Mayhew spelled out the danger in his classic book, *Congress: The Electoral Connection*, more than thirty years ago: "Efficient pursuit of electoral goals by members gives no guarantee of institutional survival. Quite the contrary. It is not too much to say that if all members did nothing but pursue their electoral goals, Congress would decay or collapse."[31] The same holds true for the congressional parties.

The Congressional Parties: Decline and Revival

Congress has not collapsed. Because its members do care about more than reelection, they adopt institutional structures and processes designed to harness individual energies to collectively important ends. The most important of these institutional structures by far are the congressional parties. Even in periods when party government as outlined by Fiorina has not been remotely descriptive of American realities, the congressional parties have been at the center of collective action. Party leaders are responsible for producing results that bolster the party's collective reputation in the face of persistent incentives for individual members to ride free on the efforts of others.[32] Moreover, Congress's decentralized, specialized legislative committee systems—another set of institutions offering incentives for individual members to provide collectively beneficial goods[33]—could not work effectively without some means for coordinating the activities of its diverse parts. The fragmented activity must be reduced to some order, the membership welded together from time to time into majority coalitions, if Congress is to share in governing.

Members of Congress recognize that the parties make a vital contribution to partisan and institutional achievement, and not a little of the deference accorded party leaders derives from that knowledge.[34] Still, party leaders face the basic reality that members keep their jobs by pleasing *voters*, not the congressional party. Leaders can count on loyalty only to the degree that members believe that the ultimate career payoff is higher for loyalty than for defection.

To be effective, party leaders need the authority to reward cooperation with, or punish defection from, the party's collective enterprise. Just how much authority members are willing to delegate to leaders depends on how worried they are that leaders might use it in ways harmful to their careers or commitments. In general, the more unified that party members are in terms of ideology and policy preferences, the more authority they are willing to delegate to leaders. The more internally divided a party, the more reluctant its members are to give leaders the resources necessary to enforce party discipline, for who knows what a leader representing the "wrong" faction might do with them?

During the 1950s and 1960s, Democratic leaders had to contend with a fractious membership whose differences were rooted in the diverse constituencies they were elected to represent. Hence they considered it their job not so much to compel members to toe a party line as to discover it, to find and promote policies that party members could willingly support because doing so enhanced their own local reputations as well as their party's image. They were quick to recognize electoral necessity; members were expected to "vote the district first" when conflicts with the party's position arose, and they were encouraged to serve their constituents diligently in order to keep the seat for the party. There was nothing odd about this, for Democratic leaders were chosen to serve their party's members as they wish to be served. Such permissiveness simply reflected a widely acknowledged necessity arising from the diversity of the party's national coalition and its members' notions about how to win reelection.

The Democrats were well aware of the costs as well as the benefits of tolerant party leadership and in the 1970s introduced changes designed to strengthen the party's hand. The Speaker, who leads the majority party in the House, was given effective control of the Rules Committee, which directs the flow of legislation coming to the floor of the House, and dominant influence on the caucus's Steering and Policy Committee, which, among other things, makes committee assignments. The Speaker was also authorized to appoint ad hoc committees to manage specific pieces of legislation, allowing sensitive and controversial bills to be handled by a committee whose members were chosen for their willingness to cooperate. The party's whip organization was enlarged substantially, and the custom of organizing separate task forces to help push through legislation of special importance to the party took root. These changes gave the party leaders more tools to coordinate the work of a fragmented legislative body and to exercise party control over lawmaking.

Democrats were willing to strengthen their party's capacity to act collectively because the division that had threatened to split the New Deal Coalition from the beginning—between northern liberals and southern conservatives—had begun to fade. The southern Democrats' ideological distinctiveness was gradually undermined by the influx of northerners, industrial development, the movement of conservative southern white voters from the Democratic into the Republican camp, and the Voting Rights Act, which brought African American voters into southern Democratic electorates. As the electoral constituencies of Democrats became more similar across regions, their electoral interests became more consonant. The result was greater party cohesion permitting stronger leadership.[35] House Democrats also accepted stronger leadership in the 1980s because they recognized the need to act collectively to make a public record as they contended with hostile Republican presidents and, from 1981 to 1987, a Republican Senate. Still, Democratic leaders rarely found it easy to assemble legislative coalitions on major issues, for the party was and remains a diverse coalition of groups and interests.[36]

Republicans delegated much more authority to their leaders when they took over the House in 1995. Unified by the party's Contract with America, as well as by their shared conservative ideology, House Republicans made Newt Gingrich the most powerful Speaker since the revolt against Joseph Cannon in 1910. Meeting in caucus, the Republicans ignored seniority in appointing committee chairs, ratifying without dissent the slate proposed by Gingrich. Gingrich was also given a strong say in committee assignments, which he used to stack committees with junior allies firmly committed to the Contract with America.

House Republicans gave their leader an unusually strong hand because they believed that his strategy—embodied not only in the Contract with America but also in the guidance he had given so many of them through GOPAC—had given them their majority; they also believed that their performance on the promises in the contract would determine whether they would keep it. Although the contract's influence on voters was small (see Chapter 6), its impact on the Republican House was enormous, for its promise of quick, focused action made strong leadership indispensable. It did not, however, guarantee that the Speaker would always get his way; for the most zealous of the new Republican representatives, commitment to the spirit of the contract was even more powerful than commitment to Gingrich, and they resisted every compromise on the ground that voters would punish them for selling out if they did not. Gingrich had to squash back a bench coup in 1997 and eventually resigned from the speakership and Congress after the Republicans' loss of House seats in 1998 was blamed on his mishandling of the impeachment issue. Gingrich's successor, Dennis Hastert, relying on the political skills and strong-arm tactics of Tom DeLay (chief whip in the 104th–107th Congresses, majority leader in the 108th and part of the 109th), maintained high levels of party discipline through the last Congress of the Clinton administration and the first three Congresses of George W. Bush's administration.

Even the Senate's tradition of unbridled individualism was disturbed by the winds of change flowing from 1994. In July 1995, the Republican majority imposed six-year term limits on committee chairs and voted to adopt a formal legislative agenda at the start of each Congress. Committee chairs would also henceforth be subject to ratification by a secret vote of the Republican Conference (all Republican members meeting in caucus). These changes (and several more rejected unsuccessful proposals) were intended to make senior members more responsive to party majorities, making it easier for the party to act collectively. In the 104th Congress, even Senate Republicans were acting as if they had an expanded personal stake in their party's collective performance.[37]

The Revival of Party Cohesion, 1980–2006

Clearly, the organizational basis for much stronger party government, particularly in the House, developed during the last quarter of the twentieth century. The strengthening of congressional party organizations coincided with, and contributed to, the clarification of partisan divisions and the increase in party conflict that followed the election of Ronald Reagan in 1980. The budget crunch brought on by the energy crisis of the 1970s deserves a good deal of the credit for the initial change. Congress's electoral and institutional needs mesh most harmoniously when politics can focus on distributing benefits. In periods of prosperity and growth, public and private resources expand together, and members can busy themselves with the happy chore of figuring out how to divide up a growing pie. Universalistic distributive criteria—something for everyone, regardless of party—are applicable, and logrolling coalitions are relatively easy to assemble. The 1960s were just such a period. The 1970s, however, brought slower growth, higher inflation, and the need for higher taxes to pay for the benefits so generously provided when the economy was booming. Instead of the pleasant prospect of distributing benefits, Congress increasingly faced the bleak task of distributing costs.

Constraints on distributive politics drew even tighter in the 1980s and, although many sources of political cleavage remained, party coherence made a notable comeback. It did so in part because of a development that erected yet another barrier to responsible party government in the full sense, however: the division of government between a Republican White House and a Democratic Congress. After the brief period in 1981 when the Reagan administration won its major budget initiatives by splitting the House Democrats, divided government helped to unify both parties in both houses. On roll-call votes, Republicans continued to line up loyally behind their president. Democrats became increasingly loyal to their party throughout the 1980s and by the 1990s were achieving the highest party unity scores since *Congressional Quarterly* began keeping track in 1954.

The rise of party cohesion in Congress is documented in Figures 7–1 and 7–2, which display the percentage of party unity votes (votes in which majorities of Democrats and Republicans took opposite sides) and the percentage of votes in which party members voted with their party's majority on these votes in the House and Senate since 1954. After falling to a low point during the Nixon and Ford administrations, party unity in both parties and houses has grown steadily, rising by about 14 percentage points in both chambers. The proportion of party unity votes also grew through the Clinton administration before falling off during the George W. Bush administration, in part because of consensual votes on homeland security issues put on the agenda by the terrorist attacks of September 11, 2001.

In addition to incentives for the majority party to resist administrations controlled by their rivals and to project an image of party competence, party unity was enhanced by the structure of decision-making under divided government. When the White House and Congress (or one of its houses) are controlled by opposing parties, major policy conflicts have to be worked out through high-level negotiation between the president and congressional leaders. The need for high-level negotiation centralizes decision processes, strengthening the hand of the top leadership. Restrictive rules and other procedural devices designed to prevent elaborately negotiated deals from unraveling are easier to justify and enforce. Omnibus legislation leaves only all-or-nothing choices to back benchers.[38]

Members may have also found it more expedient to be loyal to their parties in recent Congresses because of the expanded role of national party committees, leadership PACs, and other allied PACs in recruiting, training, and financing

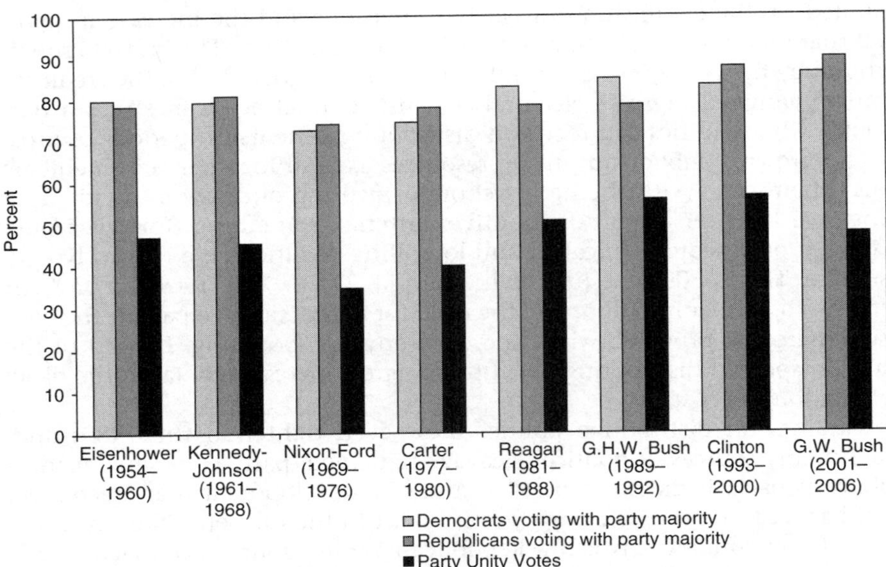

FIGURE 7–1 House Party Unity, Eisenhower through George W. Bush Administrations

Sources: Compiled by author from data in Norman J. Ornstein, Thomas E. Mann, and Michael J. Malbin, *Vital Statistics on Congress 2001–2002* (Washington, D.C.: American Enterprise Institute. 2002). Table 8–4 and "Party Unity Background." *CQ Weekly* (January 1, 2007): 38–39.

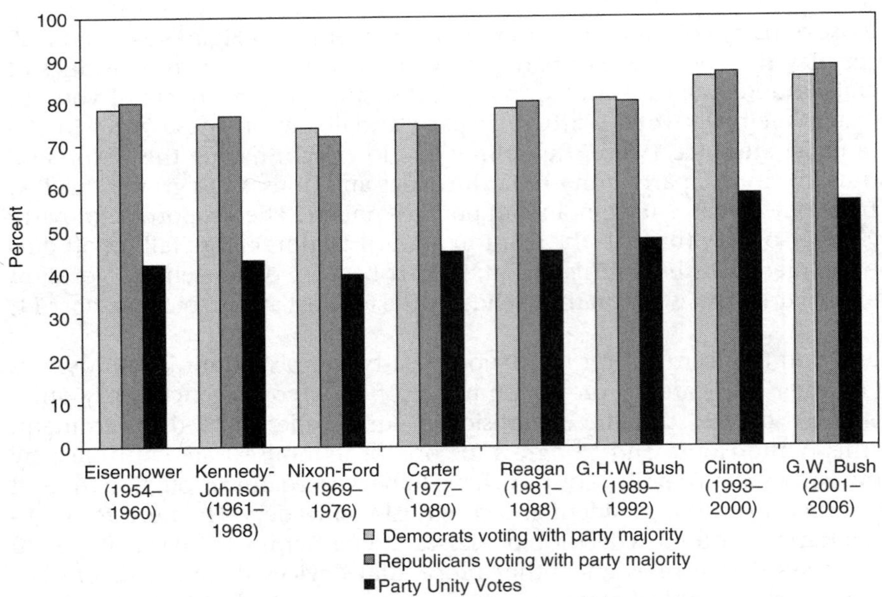

FIGURE 7–2 Senate Party Unity, Eisenhower through George W. Bush Administrations

Sources: Compiled by author from data in Norman J. Ornstein, Thomas E. Mann, and Michael J. Malbin, *Vital Statistics on Congress 2001–2002* (Washington, D.C.: American Enterprise Institute, 2002), Table 8–4 and "Party Unity Background," *CQ Weekly* (January 1, 2007): 38–39.

congressional candidates. Members elected as part of a team, using common campaign themes and issues, and with considerable help from party committees, should be more disposed to cooperate on legislative matters. Members hoping for generous party assistance in future campaigns should be more susceptible to persuasion by leaders who influence the distribution of the party's funds.[39]

Ideological Polarization in Congress and the Electorate

As the parties became more unified, they also became more polarized along ideological lines. The ideological gap between the parties in both houses has widened appreciably since the 1970s, as Figures 7–3 and 7–4 demonstrate. The figures display party averages on Poole and Rosenthal's first-dimension DW-Nominate score in the House and Senate, respectively, in the 80th–109th Congresses. The scores are calculated from all non-unanimous roll-call votes cast during the period and locate each member for each Congress on a liberal–conservative scale that ranges from –1.0 to 1.0; the higher the score, the more conservative the member.[40]

Republicans grew, on average, steadily more conservative. Democrats became more liberal as their party's conservative southern members were gradually replaced in Congress by Republicans, leaving the remaining southern Democrats ideologically more similar to other congressional Democrats. Figure 7–5 shows how the gap between the two parties' average ideological locations has grown in both houses of Congress over the past three decades. The congressional parties are now more distinct, ideologically, than at any time since the early years of the twentieth century.

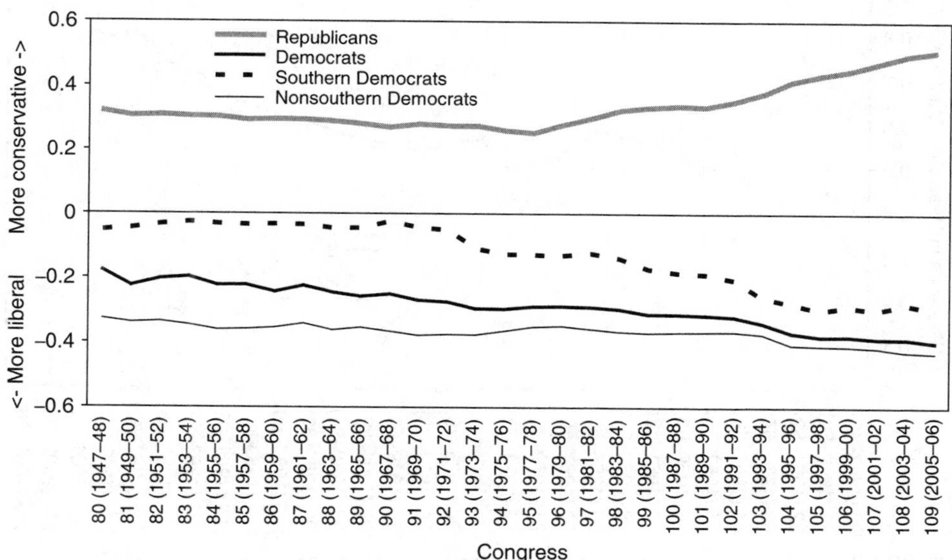

FIGURE 7–3 Ideological Positions of House Party Coalitions, 80th–109th Congresses
Source: Keith T. Poole, at *http://voteview.uh.edu/dwnomin.htm.*

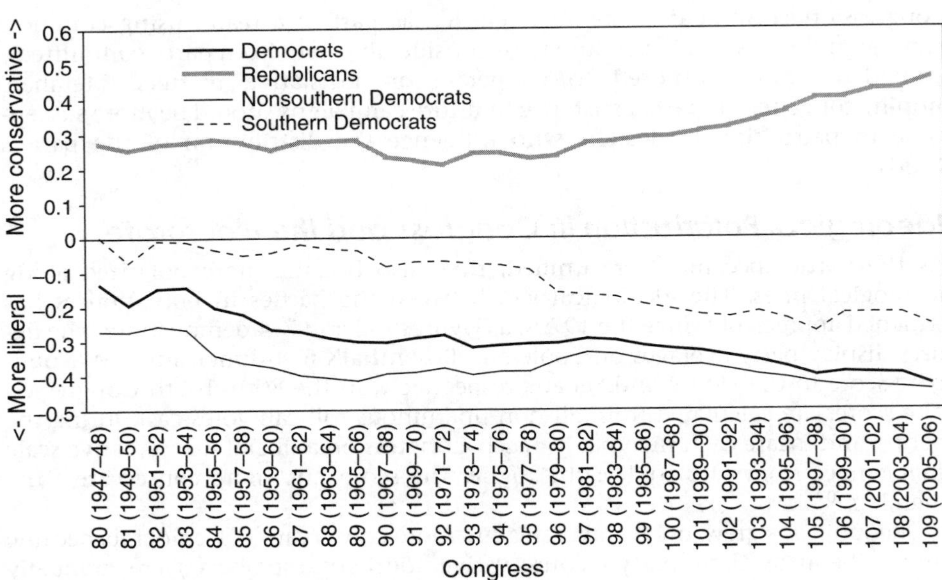

FIGURE 7–4 Ideological Positions of Senate Party Coalitions, 80th–109th Congresses
Source: Keith T. Poole, at *http://voteview.uh.edu.dwnomin.htm.*

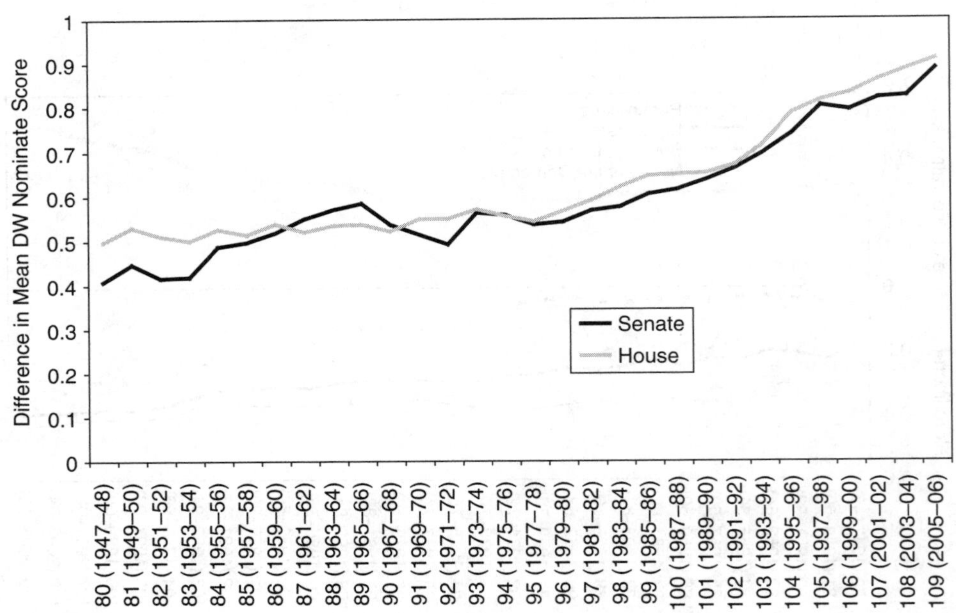

FIGURE 7–5 Ideological Differences between the Congressional Parties, 80th–109th Congresses
Source: Keith T. Poole, at *http://voteview.uh.edu.dwnomin.htm.*

Polarization in Presidential Support

A parallel and related trend has been the growing partisan disparity in congressional support for presidential initiatives and preferences, as displayed in Figures 7–6 through 7–8. For this analysis, presidential support is measured as the percentage of votes for the president's position on conflictual roll calls, defined as those on which fewer than 80 percent of members in a chamber voted with the president.[41] Despite some noticeable differences, the figures reveal the same pattern of increasing partisan polarization in presidential support scores that we observe in DW-Nominate scores. The trends are clearest in Figure 7–8, which traces the partisan gap in average presidential support scores from the Eisenhower through the first session of the 109th Congress during the George W. Bush administrations. The House parties were somewhat more polarized on presidential initiatives than on ideology during the Kennedy and Johnson administrations, and the Senate parties were somewhat less polarized on presidential initiatives than on ideology during Bill Clinton's first Congress. Still, the widening partisan disparity in presidential support from the Nixon administration onward is unmistakable, and party differences were greater during the Bush administration than in any other in the series. Both the president's partisans and opposition partisans contributed to the trend.

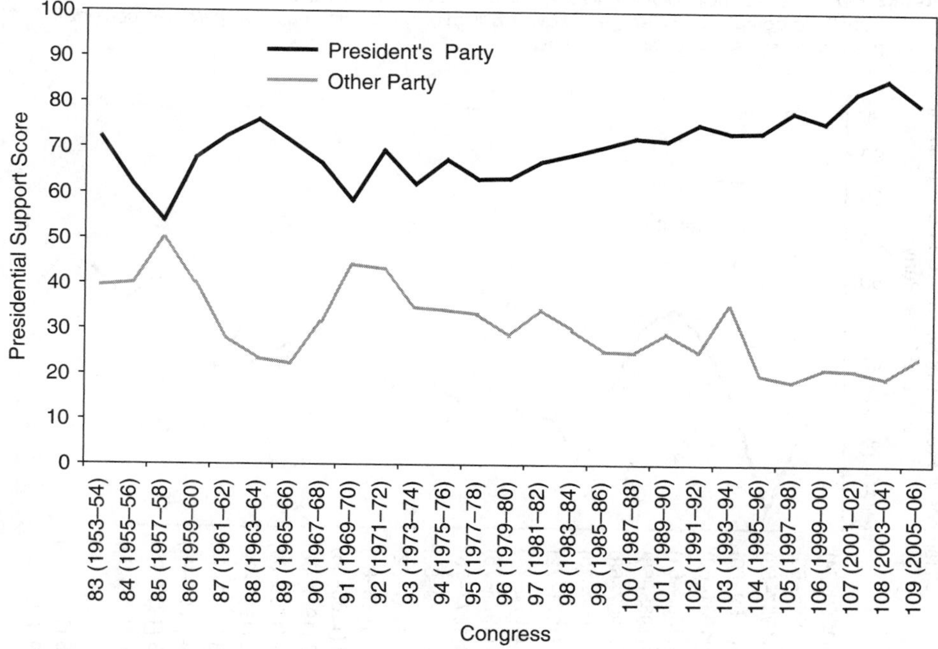

FIGURE 7–6 Presidential Support in the House of Representatives, 83rd–109th Congresses

Source: Data compiled by George C. Edwards III, at *http://bush.tamu.edu/cps/cps/archivedata/index.html;* annual scores are averaged for each Congress.

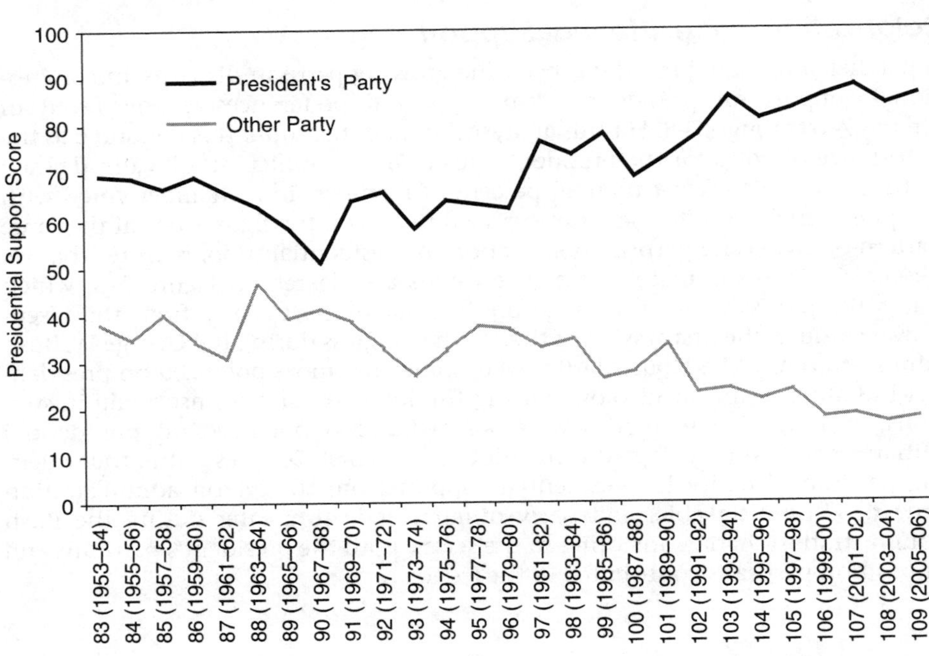

FIGURE 7–7 Presidential Support in the Senate, 83rd–109th Congresses

Source: Data compiled by George C. Edwards III, at *http://bush.tamu.edu/cps/cps/archivedata/index.html;* annual scores are averaged for each Congress.

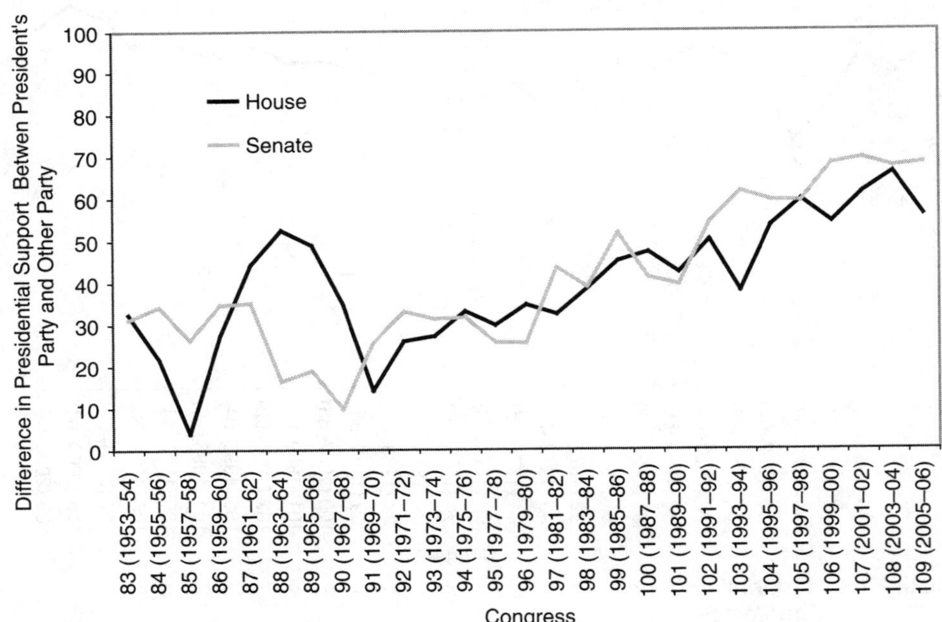

FIGURE 7–8 Partisan Differences in Presidential Support, 83rd–109th Congresses

Source: Data compiled by George C. Edwards III, at *http://bush.tamu.edu/cps/cps/archivedata/index.html;* annual scores are averaged for each Congress.

Party Polarization: The Electoral Connection

Plainly, policy representation in Congress has taken on an increasingly partisan cast over the past several decades. If elections shape congressional behavior as strongly as I have argued in this book, then growing party divisions in Congress must reflect concurrent changes in electoral politics, as indeed they do. But the sharpening of partisan conflict in Congress also affects electoral politics by shaping and clarifying the choices faced by voters.

The standard explanation for the rise in party cohesion in Congress since the 1970s is party realignment in the South, which left both congressional parties with more politically homogeneous electoral coalitions, reducing internal disagreements and making stronger party leadership tolerable. This explanation is certainly correct as far as it goes. The realignment of southern political loyalties and electoral habits has been thoroughly documented.[42] Starting from almost nothing in the 1950s, Republicans now enjoy solid majorities of southern partisans, as well as of House and Senate seats.[43] Realignment in the South certainly contributed to the increasing ideological homogeneity of the parties, but it is by no means the whole story. Other forces have also necessarily been at work, for the parties have become more homogeneous outside the South as well.

Both aggregate and survey data reveal a clear constituency basis for the widening of party and ideological divisions in the House and Senate. For example, the district-level presidential vote, taken as a proxy for district partisanship, shows a growing partisan disparity in the electoral constituencies of House Republicans and Democrats (Figure 7–9).[44] In 1972, for instance, the vote for Richard Nixon was only 7.6 percentage points higher in districts won by Republicans than in districts

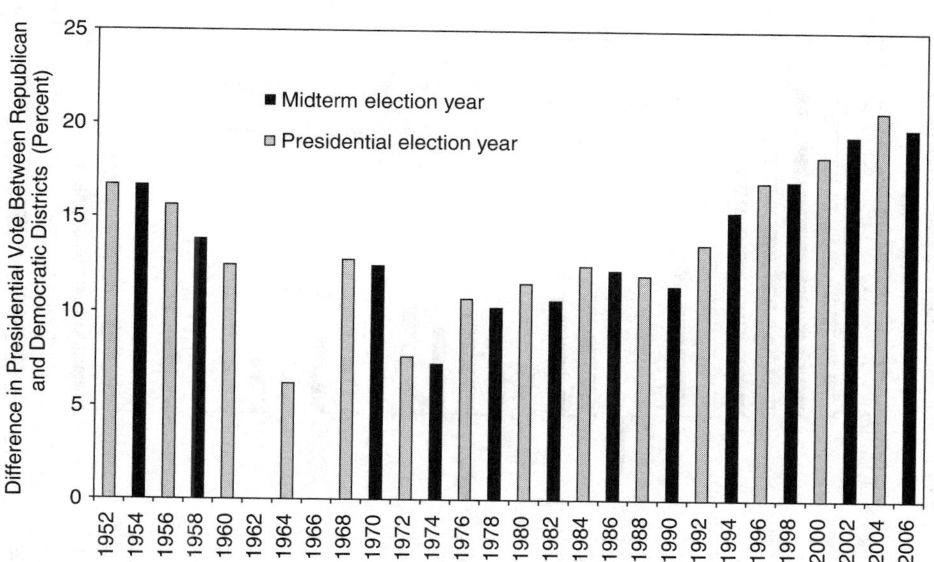

FIGURE 7–9 The Polarization of U.S. House Districts, 1952–2006
Note: Data for 1962 and 1966 are unavailable because of redistricting.
Source: Compiled by author.

won by Democrats. After a steep increase since then, the difference is now about 20 percentage points. Similarly measured, the electoral bases of the Senate parties have also become more polarized, although in absolute terms the differences are considerably smaller than those in the House (Figure 7–10).[45] Differences of this sort in the respective congressional parties' electoral bases are strongly related to party differences in presidential support as well as in roll-call ideology, so these trends have clearly contributed to partisan polarization in Congress.[46]

Survey data also provide evidence that the congressional parties represent increasingly distinctive electoral constituencies. Between 1972 and 2004, the National Election Studies have asked respondents to place themselves on a 7-point ideological scale ranging from extremely liberal to extremely conservative.[47] On average, nearly 80 percent of respondents who say they voted in the House elections are able to locate their position on the scale (and the proportion of voters able to place themselves on the scale has grown over time). Analysis of these data shows that the relationships among voters' ideological self-placement, party identification, views on political issues, and voting decisions have all become stronger over the past thirty years. Citizens sort themselves into the appropriate party (given their ideological leanings and positions on issues) a good deal more consistently now than they did in the 1970s, with the largest increases in consistency occurring in the 1990s.[48] In particular, voters locating themselves to the right on the liberal–conservative scale have become much more Republican in their voting habits, as Figure 7–11 demonstrates. Comparable data from the exit polls conducted between 1980 and 2006 show the same pattern of change.

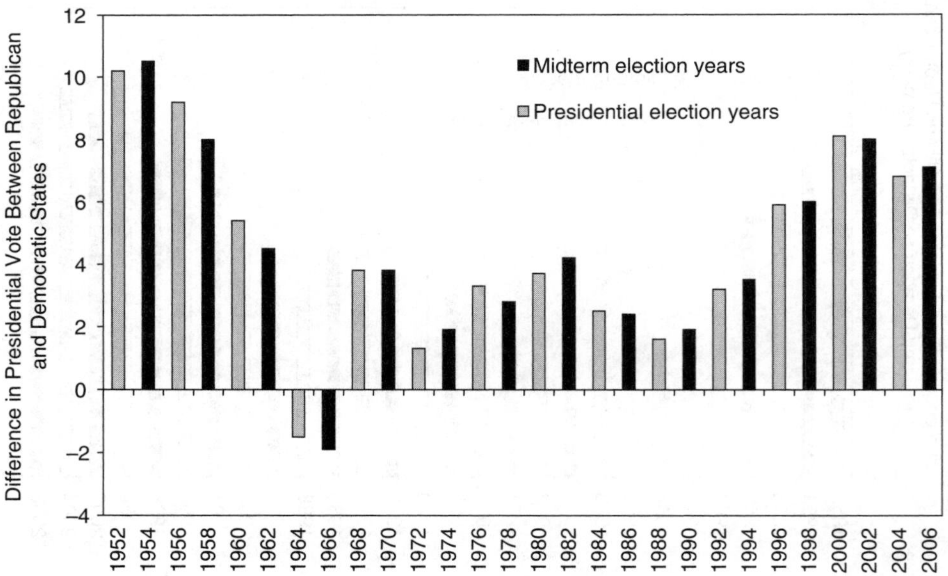

FIGURE 7–10 The Polarization of State Constituencies, 1952–2006
Source: Compiled by author.

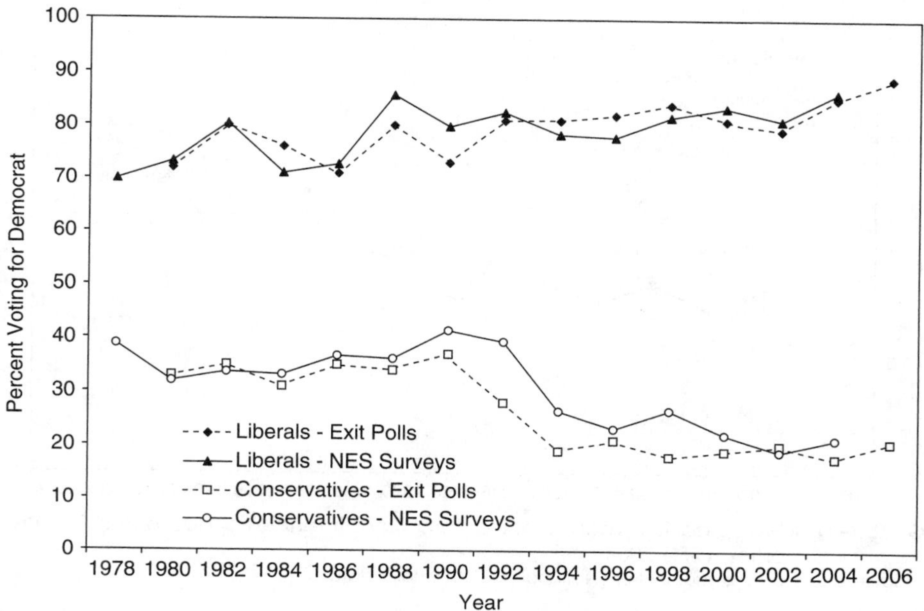

FIGURE 7–11 Ideology and the House Vote, 1978–2006
Sources: National Election Studies, 1978–2002; "Portrait of the Electorate," *New York Times* (November 13, 1994): A15; and Voter News Service Exit Polls, 1996–2002; National Election Pool Poll, 2004–2006.

Diverging Electoral Constituencies

The growth in partisan coherence, consistency, and loyalty (see Chapter 5) among voters has made the two parties' respective electoral constituencies—that is, the voters who supported the party's winning candidates—politically more homogeneous and more dissimilar. Differences in the ideological makeup of electoral constituencies can be measured by subtracting the mean ideological self-placement of NES respondents who voted for one set of winning candidates from the mean for respondents who voted for another set of winning candidates. Figure 7–12 displays the changes in the ideological distinctiveness of the electoral constituencies of House and Senate Republicans and Democrats since 1972. In the 1970s, the ideological differences between the two parties' electoral constituencies were modest, in the neighborhood of 0.5 points on this 7-point scale. By 2004, the gaps had nearly tripled, to 1.5 points. Realignment in the South explains only part of this change, since the gap between Republican and Democratic constituencies outside the South also grew (from 0.7 to 1.5 points in the House, from 0.6 to 1.4 in the Senate).[49]

Greater partisan consistency in voting has also reduced the proportion of electoral constituents shared by the president and members of Congress representing the opposition party. Figures 7–13 and 7–14 display this trend. For example, when Ronald Reagan took office in 1981, he faced a Congress in which 34 percent of House Democrats' voters and 37 percent of Senate Democrats' voters had also voted for him. When George W. Bush took office in 2001, he shared only 19 percent of the House Democrats' voters and only 14 percent of the

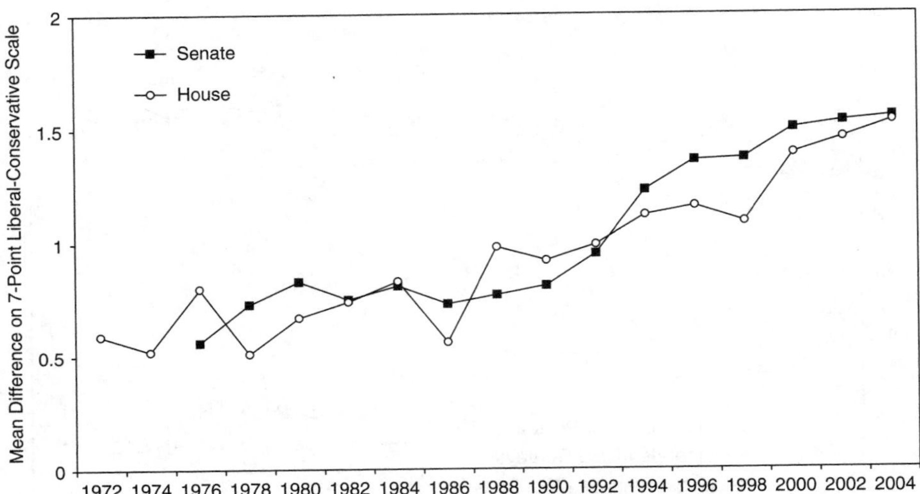

FIGURE 7–12 Ideological Divergence of Electoral Constituencies of House and Senate Parties, 1972–2004

Source: Compiled by author from National Election Studies data.

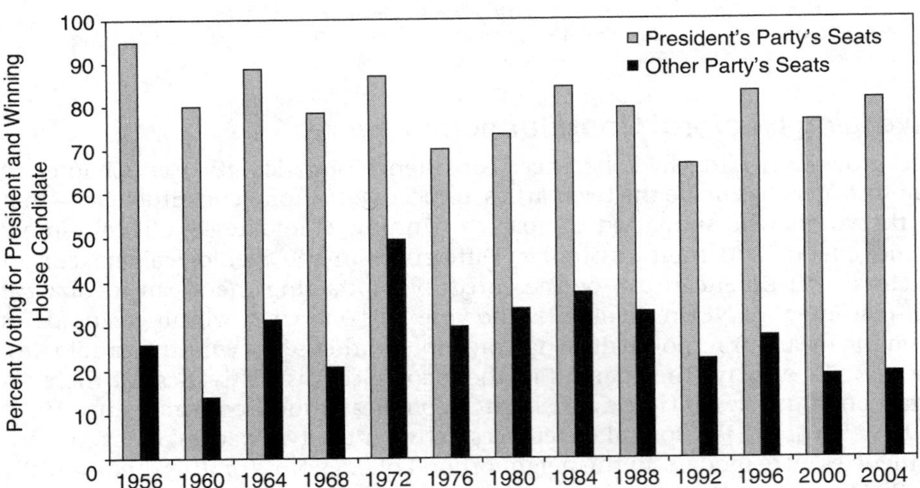

FIGURE 7–13 Shared Electoral Constituencies, U.S. Representative and President, 1956–2004

Source: Compiled by author from National Election Studies data.

Senate Democrats' voters. This represents the lowest proportion of overlapping electoral constituencies since 1960 and the second lowest in the entire time series; the overlap was only slightly larger after 2004. The decline in presidential support among opposition-party senators and representatives displayed in Figures 7–6 and 7–7 thus accurately reflects changes in their electoral constituencies; with fewer of their own voters favoring the president, they have less reason to support his initiatives.

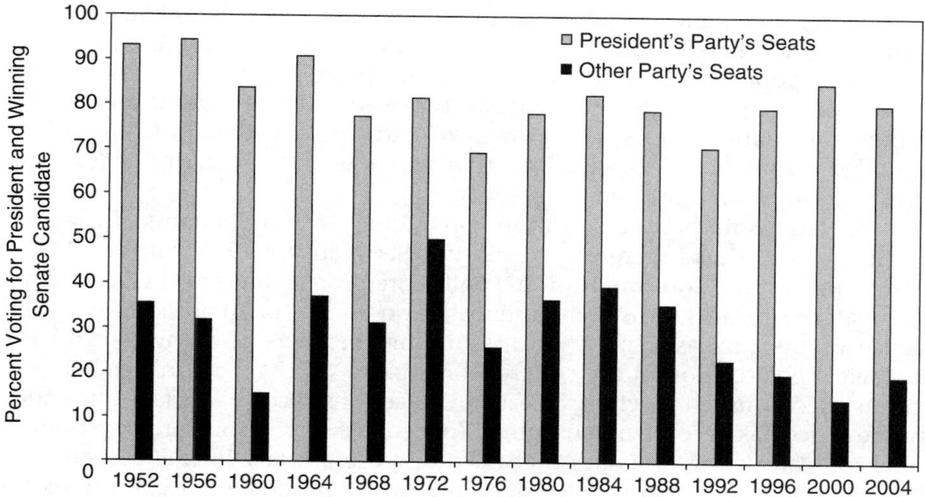

FIGURE 7–14 Shared Electoral Constituencies, U.S. Senator and President, 1952–2004
Source: Compiled by author from National Election Studies data.

Chicken or Egg?

The survey evidence, then, is consistent with the idea that partisan polarization in Congress reflects electoral changes that have left the parties with more homogeneous and more dissimilar electoral coalitions. When the focus of analysis is Congress, electoral change seems to be the independent variable: Changes in roll-call voting reflect changes in electoral coalitions. When the focus is on elections, however, it becomes apparent that causality works at least as strongly in the opposite direction: Voters sort themselves out politically by responding to the alternatives represented by the two parties.

Realignment in the South *followed* the national Democratic Party's decision to champion civil rights for African Americans and the Republican Party's choice of Senator Barry Goldwater, who voted against the Civil Rights Act of 1964, as its standard-bearer that year. Partisan divisions on the abortion issue emerged first in Congress and then in the electorate.[50] Electorates diverged ideologically after the parties had diverged ideologically; the divisions in Congress during and after the Reagan years left the two parties with more distinctive images, making it easier for voters to recognize their appropriate ideological homes. Conservatives moved into the Republican ranks, while liberals remained Democrats.[51]

This is not to say, however, that members of Congress simply followed their own ideological fancies, leaving voters no choice but to line up accordingly. As vote-seeking politicians, they naturally anticipated voters' potential responses and so were constrained by them. The Republican "southern strategy" emerged because Republican candidates sensed an opportunity to win converts among conservative white southerners. Ambitious Republicans adopted conservative positions on social issues to attract voters alienated by the Democrats' tolerance of nontraditional lifestyles but indifferent at best to Republican economic policies. Democrats emphasized "choice" on abortion because they recognized its appeal to well-educated, affluent voters who might otherwise think of themselves as Republicans. In the budgetary wars of the past three decades, Democrats have vigorously defended middle-class entitlements such as Social Security and Medicare, while Republicans have championed tax cuts because each position has a large popular constituency. In adopting positions, then, politicians are guided by the opportunities and constraints presented by configurations of voter opinion on political issues. The growth of party polarization in Congress has depended on members' expectations that voters would reward, or at least not punish, voting with one's party's majority.[52]

The relationship between partisan consistency within Congress and within the electorate is thus inherently interactive. Between the 1970s and the 1990s, changes in electoral and congressional politics reinforced one another, encouraging greater partisan consistency and cohesion in both. An important consequence of the increased party loyalty among members of Congress and the ideological polarization of the congressional parties is that the linkage between citizens' decisions on election day and the actions of the winners once they assume office has become much tighter. Indeed, election results predict congressional roll-call voting on issues that fall along the primary liberal–conservative dimension accurately enough to meet one of the fundamental conditions for responsible party government. This is evident when we regress DW-Nominate scores on two variables, party and the district-level presidential vote, and observe how much of the variance they explain. The presidential vote stands here as a serviceable if somewhat imprecise measure of district ideology; the higher the Republican share of the vote in any given election, the more conservative the district. The results are summarized in Figure 7–15, which tracks the proportion of variance in first-dimension DW-Nominate scores explained by party and presidential vote, individually and in combination, in the Congresses immediately following each presidential election since 1952.

As we would expect from the information in Figures 7–3 and 7–5, the capacity of a party to account for roll-call voting on the liberal–conservative

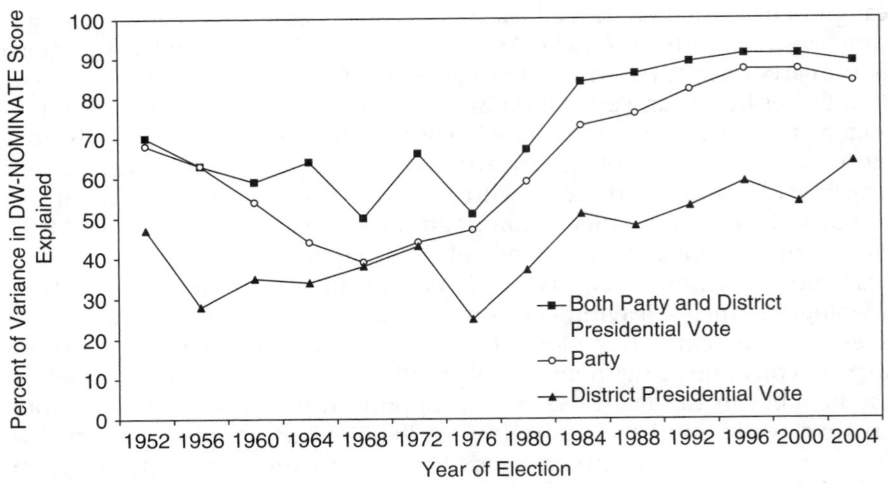

FIGURE 7–15 Variance in Roll Call Ideology, Explained by District Presidential Vote and Party, 1952–2004

Source: Compiled by author.

dimension declined from the 1950s to the 1970s but has since risen to a high level. The predictive accuracy of the district-level presidential vote remained lower than that of party through most of the period, reaching a low point in 1976 (a consequence of Jimmy Carter's initial appeal to conservative southerners) but then rising to its highest levels in the time series in 2004. The *relative* contribution of district ideology to explaining House members' positions on the liberal–conservative dimension tended to be greatest in the 1960s and 1970s, when party's contribution was lowest. After 1976, both variables became increasingly accurate predictors of congressional voting, to the point where, in recent Congresses, party and presidential vote can account for about 90 percent of the variance in representatives' positions on the scale.

The voting patterns of House members, then, are increasingly predictable from elementary electoral variables—the party of the winner and the district's ideology as reflected in its presidential leanings (with these two variables themselves correlated in 2000 at the highest level since the 1950s). With this development, voters have a much clearer idea of how their collective choices in national elections will translate into congressional action on national issues. Because party labels are so much more predictive of congressional behavior than they were in the 1970s, voters have good reason to use them more consistently to guide voting decisions.

Party Polarization and the Politics of Impeachment

The attempt of the Republican Congress to impeach and remove Bill Clinton from the presidency epitomized the sharp partisan divisions that now split the Congress and thus provides an ideal case study of congressional responses to increasingly partisan constituencies. In December 1998, when the House of Representatives voted to impeach President Bill Clinton, all but four Republicans voted for at least one of the four articles of impeachment; only five Democrats voted for any of them. On what everyone claimed was a conscience vote, 98 percent of Republican consciences dictated a vote to impeach the president, while 98 percent of Democratic consciences dictated the opposite. The Senate's verdict after the impeachment trial was only slightly less partisan. Every Democrat voted for acquittal, while 91 percent of the Republicans voted for conviction on at least one article.

Although the public as a whole steadfastly opposed the impeachment and conviction of Clinton in every national poll taken on the question, typically by margins of nearly two-to-one, it was, we saw in Chapter 6, sharply divided along partisan lines as well. In a dozen CBS News/*New York Times* polls between September 1998 and February 1999 asking respondents, "Are Bill Clinton's actions enough to warrant impeachment and removal?" an average of 86 percent of the self-identified Democrats said "no," and an average of 61 percent of self-identified Republicans said "yes."[53] Virtually identical partisan splits appeared in responses to questions about special prosecutor Kenneth Starr's impartiality and whether Clinton's transgressions were a public or private matter.[54]

The stark partisan division among voters on the impeachment issue goes a long way toward explaining partisan polarization on the issue in Congress. The strong pro-Clinton consensus among Democratic identifiers was instrumental in keeping Democrats in Congress from deserting him. Clinton's relationship with his party's congressional delegation was never particularly close. Many of them blamed him for their loss of majority status in 1994 and felt abandoned by his strategy of "triangulation"—moving to positions between the Republicans and traditional Democrats on issues such as welfare reform and balancing the budget—for winning reelection in 1996. No Democrat could (or wished to) defend his behavior in the Lewinsky scandal and many reasonably feared that his downfall would take them down with him. Thus, in August, when Clinton was finally forced to admit to having the affair and lying about it, more than a few congressional Democrats prepared to abandon ship. According to journalist Bob Woodward, Senate Minority Leader Tom Daschle "counted as many as seven Democrats who were running around with speeches or statements in various states of completion calling for Clinton to resign for the good of the party."[55] Woodward estimates that as many as half of the Senate's Democrats privately hoped that Clinton would resign.

Had Clinton's public support evaporated and, especially, had Democratic voters turned against him, Democrats in Congress, facing reelection in November, would almost certainly have deserted him en masse. But as polls continued to show widespread public approval of Clinton's presidency and opposition to his impeachment, so Democrats warily returned to the fold. In September, 138 of the 206 House Democrats had joined the unanimous Republicans in voting to release the full text of Kenneth Starr's salaciously detailed report recommending impeachment to the public. In October, thirty-one House Democrats voted to authorize impeachment hearings. In December, only five Democrats voted for any one of the four articles of impeachment. In February, not a single Democratic senator voted for conviction on any article of impeachment. Plainly, constituency opinion powerfully influenced Democratic politicians' actions on impeachment. All but a handful of congressional Democrats ended up expressing the same position taken by most citizens and an overwhelming majority of Democratic identifiers—the position that Clinton's behavior deserved condemnation but not impeachment and removal from office.[56]

Congressional Republicans, on the other hand, doggedly pursued impeachment despite its continuing unpopularity with the general public. Even the November election, in which the strategy designed to exploit Clinton's disgrace fell flat (see Chapter 6), did not stop them; neither did the near certainty that the effort to remove Clinton would fail. Although their determination might be explained by the visceral loathing many of them felt toward the president, their actions were also in line with the preferences of a strong majority of their core supporters and, particularly, their activists. We can see from Table 7–1 how partisan differences on the impeachment issue translated into differences in the views of each congressional party's electoral coalition. Although a majority of voters in districts won by Republicans in 1998 opposed impeachment, more than two-thirds of those who said they had voted for the Republican candidate favored impeachment. More than two-thirds of the voters in districts represented by Democrats opposed impeachment, with 87 percent of those who said they voted for the Democrat taking that position.

Republicans, then, in pursuing Clinton's impeachment and conviction, may have ignored the wishes of most Americans and even most of their constituents,

TABLE 7–1 Opinions on Impeachment of House Republican and Democratic Electoral Coalitions

"Just from the way you feel right now, do you think President Clinton's actions are serious enough to warrant his being impeached and removed from the Presidency, or not?" (voters only)

	Republican Districts		Democratic Districts	
	All constituents	*Republican voters*	*All constituents*	*Democratic voters*
Yes	45.3%	**67.2%**	32.8%	12.8%
No	54.7%	32.8%	67.2%	**87.2%**
N	1792	1051	1473	939

Sources: CBS News and CBS News/*New York Times* surveys completed November 17, 1998, December 15, 1998, December 17, 1998, January 4, 1999, and February 7, 1999.

but they were certainly acting as large majorities of their own partisans and their own voters desired. Forced into the unhappy choice between offending their core supporters and offending the broader public, they chose the second option. Strong pressure from party leaders encouraged them to take this course, for the Republican leadership in the House treated the impeachment vote as a party-defining event—anyone who opposed impeachment was not a real Republican—and refused to permit a vote on a resolution of censure that would have given back benchers an alternative to voting for impeachment or no sanction at all.

The public's strongly partisan reaction to the Lewinsky scandal and Clinton's impeachment echoed the intense partisan conflict that dominated national politics during the Clinton years. Responding to this echo and thus the preferences of their core supporters, members of Congress split nearly perfectly along party lines, reinforcing the impression that the move to impeach Clinton was merely a particularly nasty case of ordinary party politics. This reaction made it impossible for Republicans to turn the impeachment and expulsion of Bill Clinton into a bipartisan enterprise, dooming the effort to failure.

Representing Polarized Opinions on the Iraq War after 2006

Congress's approach to the Iraq War in early 2007 offers a second example of how party polarization in Congress reflects divisions in Republican and Democratic electoral constituencies. Leaders of the new Democratic majority made the unprecedented and potentially risky decision to try to compel President Bush to wind down U.S. involvement in the Iraq War. Members of Congress are rarely so assertive, and for good reason: Challenging a president's use of force once a war has started opens them to the charge of undercutting American troops while they are in harm's way, and it makes them targets for blame if they succeed in altering policy and things turn out badly. Iraq is not short on grim scenarios for what might happen were the United States to withdraw and leave the competing religious and ideological factions to fight it out; if Democrats succeeded in

TABLE 7–2 Opinions on the Iraq War of House Republican and Democratic Electoral Coalitions in 2007

	Republican Districts		Democratic Districts	
Was the Iraq War a Mistake?				
	All constituents	*Republican voters*	*All constituents*	*Democratic voters*
Yes	48.0%	19.2%	61.2%	**82.5%**
No	44.0%	**69.8%**	31.5%	11.6%
Should the U.S. Withdraw from Iraq Within a Year?				
Yes	51.4%	27.9%	62.2%	**81.1%**
No	48.5%	**72.1%**	37.8%	18.9%
N	12,391	7,236	11,791	8,070

Source: Cooperative Congressional Election Study 2006.

shaping policy, they could not avoid sharing responsibility for the consequences. That most congressional Democrats were willing to take this risk reflected a strong consensus among the voters who elected them rejecting the war and the president who started it. Congressional Republicans, in siding with the president and opposing the Democrats' efforts reduce U.S involvement in an increasingly unpopular war, represented an opposite yet almost equally strong consensus among the people who had elected them.

Table 7–2 displays data from a post-election survey comparing the responses of voters in districts won by Republicans and Democrats—and the subsets who said they voted for the winner—to two issues about the Iraq War: whether it a mistake and whether the United States should withdraw within a year. Huge majorities of the House Democrats' electoral constituents offered negative opinions of the war and favored disengagement. Only a small minority of the Republicans' electoral constituents shared these views, although majorities of their full constituencies leaned slightly against the war. The positions on the war taken by both parties thus represented the overwhelming consensus of their supporters; most members would have been out of step with their voters if they did *not* side with their party's leaders in the showdown over the war's direction. As with impeachment, however, House Republicans were in the riskier political position because their position was not supported by majorities of their full constituencies.

Reforming Congress

The Republicans took over Congress in 1994 by persuading voters to hold Democrats collectively responsible for the sorry state of Congress as well as of the nation. By the early 1990s, Congress had become more widely distrusted and disdained than at any time since the advent of scientific polling. Politicians by trade, members of Congress have never inspired much respect as a class, but the degree of suspicion and contempt expressed in polls and other venues (call-in talk shows, focus groups, letters to editors) was extraordinary by any standard. Solid majorities of citizens believed that most members were financially corrupt, misused office to enrich themselves, and lied when the truth would hurt them politically. Even larger majorities believed that the people they elected to Congress quickly lost touch and cared more about keeping power and serving themselves than about the welfare of the nation or their constituents.[57]

The public's image of members of Congress as indifferent and out of touch was deeply ironic to anyone aware of the enormous investment of effort most members put into keeping in touch with constituents, their devotion to casework, and their sensitivity to district opinion on policy issues. Yet individual responsiveness of this sort evidently failed to penetrate deeply enough to counteract the general image of members as a bunch of self-serving, pampered, overpaid, arrogant hacks. Republicans took advantage of this image in their 1994 campaigns, making internal reforms of Congress "aimed at restoring the faith and trust of the American people in their government" the first element in the Contract with America.[58] The proposed reforms included ending Congress's exemption from workplace laws, reducing the number of committees and committee staff, limiting terms of committee chairs, and banning the casting of proxy votes in committee, all of which were quickly adopted.

Term Limits

The most radical reform, limiting House and Senate terms, failed to win enough votes to move forward, however. Although the Contract with America promised only a vote on a constitutional amendment limiting terms, the idea had been an official part of the 1988 and 1992 Republican platforms, and many Republican candidates had campaigned in 1994 as avid supporters of congressional term limits, so the distinction between "voting on" and "voting for" was probably lost on most of the public. However, many senior House Republicans as well as a majority of Democrats opposed term limits, and the only option of the four voted upon to get even a simple majority of votes (twelve-year limits for both the House and Senate) still fell sixty-one votes short of the required two-thirds.

There is no mystery as to why so many Republican candidates championed term limits in 1994. The public loves the idea. Opinion surveys typically find overwhelming majorities in favor of limiting legislative terms, and term limit measures have passed in every state where they have been put up to a popular vote. By 1995, when the Supreme Court struck down state-imposed term limits on federal officials as unconstitutional, twenty-two states had adopted them.[59]

The logic behind the idea is curious. Its supporters claim that the high success rates of incumbent House candidates has given us an ossified ruling clique, out of touch with voters and responsive only to the special interests whose money keeps them in office. The only way to ensure change is to limit tenure. But Congress was scarcely starved for new blood at the time; more than half of the representatives in the 104th Congress (1995–1996) had served fewer than three terms, and more than half of the senators were in their first or second term. Moreover, in 1992, 1994, and 2006, voters demonstrated that they could limit terms the old-fashioned way, by voting out incumbents or compelling them to retire in the face of almost certain defeat.

Beyond that, it seems strange to expect better representation from members who must give up their seats regardless of how well they perform; what quality of work should be expected from an employee who is sure to be fired on a certain date no matter how well he or she does the job? Moreover, it strains credulity to imagine that someone who will soon be looking for a new job, probably in the private sector, will be less solicitous of "special interests" than someone whose future is controlled by voters. It seems equally doubtful that we would receive better representation from elected officials inferior in knowledge and experience to unelected bureaucrats, congressional staff, and professional lobbyists. Boosting the number of open seats, which begets the most expensive campaigns, seems an odd way to reduce the electoral importance of money (and hence the political clout of donors). Finally, it seems unlikely that representatives would be more responsive to district sentiments when casting votes or taking position in Washington if the political cost of ignoring constituents were reduced. Indeed, for some proponents, the chief virtue of term limits lies in freeing members to do the right thing regardless of what constituents want.[60] Members would, of course, become equally free to do the wrong thing.

Term limits would have their most profound effect on representation, however, by diminishing members' opportunities and incentives for developing strong ties with constituents. As Fenno has so vividly shown, it takes years of time and effort simply to learn who one's constituents are, what they want, and what they need. Even after this has been accomplished, keeping in touch is an endless, labor-intensive chore. Only the prospect of a lengthy series of future elections makes the effort worthwhile. Given the size (averaging more than 690,000 residents) and diversity of most present-day House districts, authentic "citizen legislators" would begin with little knowledge of the opinions, lives, and values of most of their constituents. With a limited electoral future in the district, they would have little reason to invest in learning more. The only "people" they would perhaps be closer to are those in their own limited social or occupational circles. This hardly seems a recipe for better representation for everyone else.

Constituents, from their side, would know even less about their representatives than they do now, in part because the faces would change more often, and in part because incumbents would put less effort into making themselves known. Voting decisions would thus be, on average, less informed than they are today. Jeffrey Mondak and Carl McCurley have shown that elections now tend to filter out the more incompetent and corrupt incumbents over time; the average quality of members remaining in each electoral class increases with each election they survive. Truncating House careers would interrupt this filtering process, reducing the aggregate quality of House members significantly.[61] This hardly seems a recipe for better representation, either.

These are mostly obvious points, but they do little to undermine support for term limits because it rests on emotion, not analysis. The idea provided a focus for public anger at members of Congress as a class and at the more general failure of the political establishment in Washington to solve major national problems. It is no accident that the movement arose at a time when responsibility was blurred by divided government. In an ironic inversion of the usual pattern, even people who continued to like and support their own representatives could still support a move to punish politicians wholesale by automatically firing them after a fixed period.

After 1995, the drive toward congressional term limits stalled. The Supreme Court declared state-level action imposing term limits on federal officials to be unconstitutional. Improving economic and other social conditions reduced voters' anger at politicians; by 1998, political experience was an electoral plus once more. Republicans' enthusiasm for term limits faded with their enjoyment of majority status, and several from the class of 1994 who had promised to serve only three terms renounced their pledges and sought reelection in 2000. Term-limit advocacy groups vowed to campaign heavily against them,[62] but none was defeated; three members who had promised to leave in 2000 were still in office in 2004, and one lasted until 2007. Even if public support for term limits returns to the level of intensity of the early 1990s, however, amending the Constitution is never easy, particularly when the prime victims of the amendment would have to provide two-thirds majorities.

If the term limits were ever imposed, it is doubtful that either their proponents or the public would like the consequences. Term limits would probably make the parties much more important in congressional elections and politics than they are today. The irony is, of course, that most term-limit advocates despise political parties as much as they despise career politicians. With less information about incumbents and with a larger number of open seats to contend with, voters would rely more heavily on cheap information shortcuts, the readiest of which is the party label, to sort out the candidates. With higher turnover, interest groups would see less advantage in cultivating individual members and more in cultivating parties and factions, redeploying their resources accordingly. With weaker ties to constituents, representatives would be freer to follow the party line; and with less time to develop their own sophisticated understanding of policy issues, they would be more open to party or ideological guidance. It would be a fine irony indeed if a populist movement inspired by fantasies of government by citizen legislators finally ushered in something like the British-inspired "responsible two-party system" advocated by an earlier generation of political scientists.[63]

The Public's Evaluations of Congress

While failing on term limits, the zealous Republicans of the class of 1994 did succeed in forcing votes on a rule banning all manner of gifts from lobbyists and legislation, tightening up their registration and reporting requirements, which then passed overwhelmingly. Like Republicans in 2004, Democrats in 2006 exploited public unhappiness with Congress by promising to reform the institution, tighten the regulation of lobbying activities and ending secret legislative earmarking. However, there is no reason to think that gestures of this sort do much to restore public faith in Congress. In the most thorough study of congressional unpopularity to date, John Hibbing and Elizabeth Theiss-Morse argued that the public objects chiefly to the way Congress does its normal business.

Hibbing and Theiss-Morse found that people want legislators to be fair and efficient. Fairness means looking out for the interests of "the people," not "special interests." Efficiency means making policy without the posturing, haggling, threatening, and compromise it normally entails—that is, without the politics.[64] Insofar as internal reforms, staff reductions, gift bans, campaign finance reform, or term limits are thought to make members of Congress less insulated, and more responsive to ordinary people, they should improve Congress's public image. But if Hibbing and Theiss-Morse are right, as long as Congress remains the venue in which intense political disagreements are thrashed out in public view, Congress will continue to be unpopular. "Just as people want governmental services without the pain of taxes, they also want democratic procedures without the pain of witnessing what comes along with those procedures."[65] Thus:

> a major part of [the public's] distaste for Congress is endemic to an open legislative body in a large and complicated modern democratic polity. When the issues are complex and far-reaching, and when interests are diverse and specialized, the democratic process will be characterized by disagreements and a pace that can be charitably described as deliberate. And these disagreements will likely be played out by surrogates rather than by ordinary people.
>
> The public performs no useful purpose by adopting the attitude that these surrogates, whether they be members of Congress, leaders of the parties, or officials of interest groups, have messed everything up and all would be right if they would only listen to ordinary people again. The truth is that ordinary people disagree fundamentally on vital issues. The noise and acrimony we despise so much in politics is a reflection of our own diversity and occasional convictions.[66]

From this perspective, Congress's standing is bound to suffer from the inevitable conflicts that arise when it tries to make national policy.[67] Moreover, the very things people don't like about Congress are exacerbated by divided government, which popular majorities consistently say they do like. The Democratic takeover of Congress in 2006 from an unpopular Republican majority boosted the institution's job-approval ratings modestly for a couple of months, but they soon fell back into the 20s as the Democratic majorities battled the Republican president and his allies in the House and Senate over the direction of the Iraq War and issues of governance and domestic policy. Ordinary Republicans disdained the Democratic Congress for what it was trying to do, ordinary Democrats soured on it for not succeeding in doing it, and nearly everyone could scorn the confrontational politics that were, in reality, the inevitable result of deeply rooted partisan differences on issues of fundamental national importance.

2008 and Beyond: A Matter of Geography

Elections since 2000 have revealed an electorate nearly evenly divided between the parties nationally but with strong regional biases that reflect clearly defined differences in cultural and political values. Polling data from these elections show Republican voters to be disproportionately white, male, fond of guns, religiously conservative, rural, married, and affluent. People with such characteristics are concentrated in states of the South, Plains, and Mountain West. Democratic voters are disproportionately female, African American, Latino, secular, unmarried, unarmed, and of modest means. They are concentrated in the states of the Northeast, Mid-Atlantic, and West Coast.[68]

The strongly regional character of current alignments is the culmination of a decades-long shift in regional voting patterns in which the two parties have gradually exchanged areas of dominance. These changes are displayed in Figures 7–16 and 7–17, which show the regional distribution of House and Senate seats since 1946. Republican gains in the South, Plains, and Mountain West put the party in control of Congress in 1994—and even after 2006 it dominated these regions. The Democrats have become dominant in the Northeast, Mid-Atlantic,

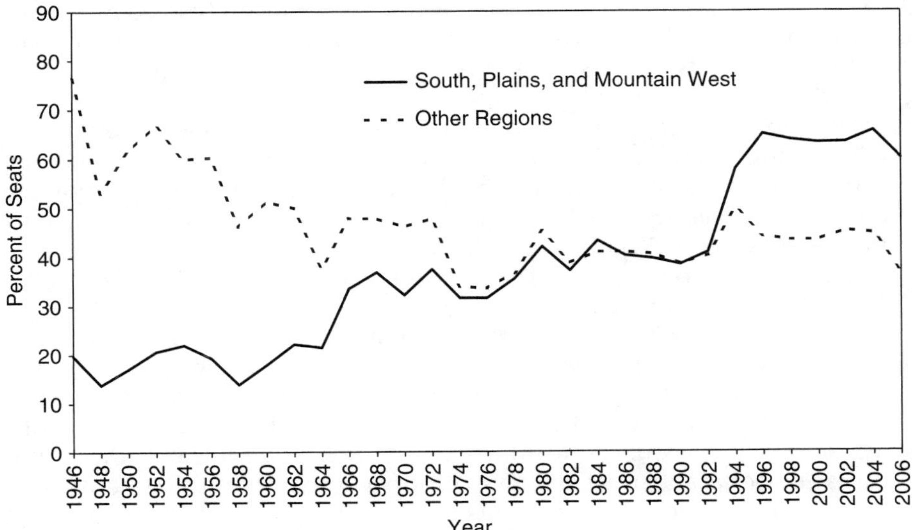

FIGURE 7–16 Republicans' Share of House Seats, by Region, 1946–2006
Source: Compiled by author.

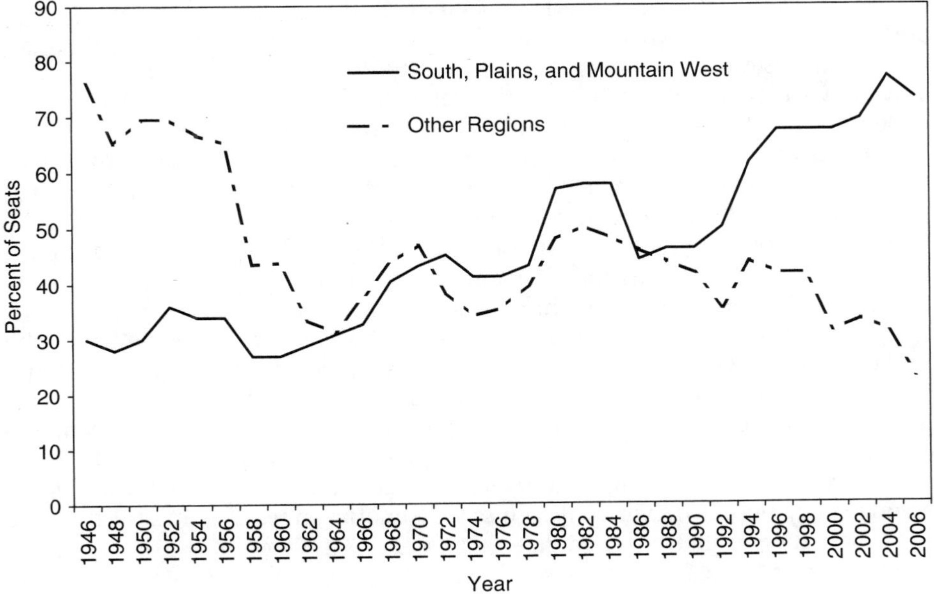

FIGURE 7–17 Republicans' Share of Senate Seats, by Region, 1946–2006
Source: Compiled by author.

Midwest, and West Coast. After the 2006 election, Republicans held 60 percent of House Seats and 73 percent of Senate seats in the South, Plains, and Mountain West, while Democrats held 63 percent of House seats and 73 percent of Senate seats outside of these regions.[69]

A closely divided electorate leaves control of Congress up for grabs every two years. The strong cultural and ideological divisions between the party coalitions make for high electoral stakes, which should stimulate vigorous competition for House and Senate seats. In reality, however, structural features of the current electoral system give the Republicans a distinct advantage in the contest for control of both houses and confine real competition, at least in the House, to a relatively small proportion of seats.

In Chapter 2, we saw that Republicans currently enjoy a structural advantage because their voters are distributed more efficiently, for the party's purposes, than are Democratic voters (recall Figure 2–3). Democrats thus have to win a significant number of seats against the partisan grain in order to control the Congress, a task that has become more difficult with the increase in party-line voting and consistency of presidential and congressional outcomes at the state and district level. It is not an impossible task, of course; with a powerful pro-Democratic tide running in 2006, they won a larger share of Republican-leaning seats than in any election since 1992 (Table 7–3). More than half of their thirty-seat pickup came in Republican-leaning districts (seven were in Democratic-leaning districts, and seven were in balanced districts). But this left their majority at serious risk in future elections when conditions might not be so favorable to their party. After 2006, forty-seven Democrats represented Republican leaning districts, whereas only five Republicans represented Democratic-leaning districts; if we include seats in balanced districts, Republicans would theoretically have sixty-eight potential targets in 2008, while Democrats would have only nineteen. Unless voters are as unhappy with Republicans in 2008 as they were in 2006, the next election promises to be major test of how far the advantages of incumbency now enjoyed by the newly elected Democrats can protect the party's majority.

Democrats also suffer a structural disadvantage in the Senate. As Alan Abramowitz has noted, the equal representation of states in the Senate now favors Republicans because Democrats do relatively better in states with large populations, while Republicans do relatively better in states with small populations. In the 50–50 election of 2000, Gore won six of the nine states with the most people; Bush won fifteen of the twenty with the fewest.[70] As noted in Chapter 2, Bush, with less than half the national vote, took thirty states in 2000; Gore took only twenty.

In Senate as in House elections, the Democrats' problem is compounded by the trend toward greater consistency in voting across federal offices. Again as in House elections, that trend was reversed at least temporarily in 2006, when Democrats picked up three seats in Republican-leaning states. The greater competitiveness—and idiosyncrasy—of Senate elections leaves plenty of room for surprise. In 2008, Democrats will be defending only twelve Senate seats, while Republicans must defend twenty-two. However, only four of the Republican seats are in states won by the Democratic presidential candidate in 2000 or 2004, whereas five of the Democratic seats were in states that went for Bush both times. As of this writing, the battle for control of the Senate promises to be intense, with the Democrats maintaining the advantage if the divisive and unpopular Iraq War continues to be regarded by most Americans as the most important national problem.

TABLE 7–3 At-Risk and Safe House Seats, 1992-2006, by Party

Electoral risk as determined by presidential vote	1992	1994	1996	1998	2000	2002	2004	2006	Change, 1992–2006
At Risk									
Democrats	67	36	40	36	36	28	31	47	−20
Republicans	14	20	22	18	24	12	13	5	−9
Total	81	56	62	54	60	40	44	52	−29
Competitive									
Democrats	49	32	27	31	26	19	14	21	−28
Republicans	23	40	29	27	27	19	20	16	−7
Total	72	72	56	58	53	38	34	37	−35
Safe									
Democrats	143	137	141	145	151	151	158	165	22
Republicans	139	170	176	178	171	198	199	181	42
Total	282	307	317	323	322	357	357	346	64

Note: "At Risk" seats are those in which the winning party's presidential candidate received at least 2 percent less than his average across all districts; "Safe" seats are those in which the winning party's presidential candidate got at least 2 percent more than his average across all districts; "Competitive" seats fall in between these ranges. The 1992 major-party presidential vote is used for 1992 and 1994, the 1996 major-party presidential vote is used for 1996, 1998; the 2000 vote is used for 2000 and (recalculated for the new districts) 2002; the 2004 vote is used for 2004 and 2006. The district presidential vote has been adjusted where necessary for changes in district boundaries required by court decisions after the initial post-1990 and post-2002 redistrictings.

Although a large majority of senators and representatives remain electorally secure, party majorities in Congress have proven to be anything but secure. In 2008, as was the case in 2000, any conceivable combination of party control of the House, Senate, and White House seems possible. The stakes will be reflected in the intensity of the pivotal campaigns at all of these levels.

NOTES

1. It is a complicated concept. See Hanna Pitkin, *The Concept of Representation* (Berkeley: University of California Press, 1967).
2. A combination of the huge National Annenberg Election Study (N = 70,945) and Knowledge Networks (N=29,869) shows some promise of helping here, but the Annenberg study's identification of House districts is error-prone; see Joshua D. Clinton, "Representation in Congress: Constituents and Roll Calls in the 106th House," *Journal of Politics* 68 (2006): 397–409.
3. For an account of this literature, see Walter J. Stone, "Measuring Constituency– Representative Linkages: Problems and Prospects," *Legislative Studies Quarterly* 4 (1979): 624.
4. Walter J. Stone, "Measuring Constituency–Representative Linkages," pp. 624–626; Catherine Shapiro, David W. Brady, Richard Brody, and John A. Ferejohn, "Linking Constituency Opinion and Senate Voting Scores: A Hybrid Explanation," *Legislative Studies Quarterly* 15 (1990): 599–622; and Larry M. Bartels, "Constituency Opinion and Congressional Policy Making: The Reagan Defense Buildup," *American Political Science Review* 84 (1991): 457–474.
5. Compare Stone, "Linkages," with Gillian Dean, John Siegfried, and Leslie Ward, "Constituency Preference and Potential Economic Gain: Cues for Senate Voting on the Family Assistance Plan," *American Politics Quarterly* 9 (1981): 341–356.
6. Stone, "Linkages," pp. 632–634. One recent study finds Republicans much more responsive to their own partisans' ideologies, while Democrats are more responsive to their opposition ideologies; see Clinton, "Representation," 404.
7. Robert S. Erikson, "Roll Calls, Reputations, and Representation in the U.S. Senate," *Legislative Studies Quarterly* 15 (1990): 623–642; Patricia Hurley, "Partisans Representation, Realignment, and the Senate in the 1980s," *Journal of Politics* 53 (1991): 3–33; Robert A. Bernstein, "Limited Ideological Accountability in House Races: The Conditioning Effect of Party," *American Political Quarterly* 20 (1992): 192–204; Amy B. Schmidt, Lawrence W. Kenny, and Rebecca B. Morton, "Evidence on Electoral Accountability in the U.S. Senate: Are Unfaithful Agents Really Punished?" *Economic Inquiry* 34 (July 1996): 545–567; and Brandice Canes-Wrone, David Brady, and John F. Cogan, "Out of Step, Out of Office: Electoral Accountability and House Members' Voting," *American Political Science Review* 96 (March 2002): 127–140.
8. Richard F. Fenno Jr., *Home Style: House Members in Their Districts* (Boston: Little, Brown, 1978), p. 233.
9. Barbara Sinclair, "Agenda Control and Policy Success: Ronald Reagan and the 97th House," *Legislative Studies Quarterly* 10 (August 1985): 291–314.

10. Gary C. Jacobson, *The Electoral Origins of Divided Government* (Boulder, CO: Westview Press, 1990), pp. 106–112.
11. David R. Mayhew, *Congress: The Electoral Connection* (New Haven, CT: Yale University Press, 1974), p. 140.
12. Mayhew, *Congress*, pp. 53–54.
13. See, for examples, R. Douglas Arnold, "The Local Roots of Domestic Policy," in *The New Congress*, ed. Thomas E. Mann and Norman J. Ornstein (Washington, DC: American Enterprise Institute, 1981), p. 272.
14. "Of Pork, Pride, and Kindred Spirits," *CQ Weekly* 59 (March 17, 2001): 577.
15. The bridge would connect the small Alaskan city of Ketchikan (population 14,770) to an island with about 50 residents, which also has the city's airport, replacing a seven-minute ferry ride.
16. "Enid Green Waldholtz," *Congressional Quarterly Weekly Report* 53 (October 28, 1995): 3273.
17. Juliana Gruenwald, "Freshmen Walk Tightrope to Satisfy Voters," *Congressional Quarterly Weekly Report* 53 (May 27, 1995): 1524–1526.
18. Donna Cassata, "Military Construction Bill Keeps Most Pet Projects," *Congressional Quarterly Weekly Report* 53 (June 24, 1995): 1857.
19. Alan K. Ota, "Senators Pile On the Take-Home Projects after Coaxing House to Reduce Its List," *Congressional Quarterly Weekly Report* (May 30, 1998): 1465.
20. Niels C. Sorrells, "Lawmakers Not Eager to Revisit Iraq Supplemental Soon," *CQ Weekly* (April 19, 2003): 940.
21. Mayhew, *Congress*, pp. 130–131.
22. Michael J. Malbin, "Of Mountains and Molehills: PACs, Campaigns, and Public Policy," in *Parties, Interest Groups, and Campaign Finance Laws*, ed. Michael J. Malbin (Washington, DC: American Enterprise Institute for Public Policy Research, 1980), pp. 152–210; and Frank J. Sorauf, *Money in American Elections* (Glenview, IL: Scott, Foresman, 1988), pp. 307–317.
23. Bill Keller, "The Trail of the 'Dirty Dozen,'" *Congressional Quarterly Weekly Report* 39 (March 21, 1981): 510.
24. League of Conservation Voters, *www.lev.org/dirtydozen/callahan_postmt.htm*, June 3, 1999; more recent data are at http://www.lcv.org/campaigns/endorsements (accessed October 23, 2006).
25. Raymond A. Bauer, Ithiel de Sola Pool, and Lewis Anthony Dexter, *American Business and Public Policy* (New York: Atherton, 1968).
26. Theodore J. Eismeier and Philip H. Pollock III, "Political Action Committees: Varieties of Organization and Strategy," in *Money and Politics in the United States*, ed. Michael J. Malbin (Washington, DC: American Enterprise Institute for Public Policy Research, 1984), pp. 124–126.
27. Mayhew, *Electoral Connection*, p. 115.
28. Mayhew, *Electoral Connection*, pp. 174–177; and Morris P. Fiorina, "The Decline of Collective Responsibility in American Politics," *Daedalus* 109 (Summer 1980): 25–45.
29. Fiorina, "Decline of Collective Responsibility," pp. 26–27.

30. Barbara Sinclair, "Coping with Uncertainty: Building Coalitions in the House and Senate," in *The New Congress*, ed. Thomas E. Mann and Norman J. Ornstein (Washington, DC: American Enterprise Institute for Public Policy Research, 1981), p. 215.
31. David R. Mayhew, *Congress: The Electoral Connection* (New Haven, CT: Yale University Press, 1974), p. 141.
32. Gary W. Cox and Mathew D. McCubbins, *Legislative Leviathan: Party Government in the House* (Berkeley: University of California Press, 1993), Chapter 5.
33. Mayhew, *Congress*, pp. 85–96.
34. Mayhew, *Congress*, pp. 145–149.
35. Cox and McCubbins, *Legislative Leviathan*, pp. 153–157.
36. David W. Rohde, *Parties and Leaders in the Postreform House* (Chicago: University of Chicago Press, 1991), pp. 162–177.
37. David S. Cloud, "GOP Senators Limit Chairmen to Six Years Heading Panel," *Congressional Quarterly Weekly Report* 52 (July 22, 1995): 2147. There is some evidence that majority party supporters, at least, do have an electoral stake in the Senate's collective reputation; see Monika L. McDermott and David R. Jones, "Congressional Performance, Incumbent Behavior, and Voting in Senate Elections, *Legislative Studies Quarterly* 30 (2005): 235–257.
38. Barbara Sinclair, *Unorthodox Lawmaking: New Legislative Processes in the U.S. Congress* (Washington, DC: Congressional Quarterly Press, 1997), Chapter 5.
39. Paul S. Herrnson, *Party Campaigning in the 1980s* (Cambridge, MA: Harvard University Press, 1988); and Kevin Leyden and Stephen A. Borelli, "An Investment in Good Will: Party Contributions and Party Unity among U.S. House Members in the 1980s," *American Politics Quarterly* 22 (1994): 421–452.
40. For an explanation of the methodology for computing these scores and justification for their interpretation as measures of liberal–conservative ideology, see Nolan M. McCarty, Keith T. Poole, and Howard Rosenthal, *Income Redistribution and the Realignment of American Politics* (Washington, DC: American Enterprise Institute Press, 1997); and Keith T. Poole and Howard Rosenthal, *Congress: A Political History of Roll Call Voting* (New York: Oxford University Press, 1997), Chapters 3 and 11.
41. The data were compiled by George C. Edward III and are available at *http://presdata.tamu.edu/*. For these charts, the annual scores are averaged for each Congress.
42. Earle Black and Merle Black, *Politics and Society in the South* (Cambridge, MA: Harvard University Press, 1987); Paul Frymer, "The 1994 Aftershock: Dealignment or Realignment in the South," in *Midterm: The Elections of 1994 in Context*, ed. Philip A. Klinkner (Boulder, CO: Westview Press, 1995); Richard Nadeau and Harold W. Stanley, "Class Polarization among Native Southern Whites, 1952–1990," *American Journal of Political Science* 37 (August 1993): 900–919; Harold W. Stanley, "Southern Partisan Changes: Dealignment, Realignment, or Both?" *Journal of Politics* 50 (February 1988): 64–88; Martin P. Wattenberg, "The Building of a Republican Regional Base in the South: The Elephant Crosses the Mason-Dixon Line," *Public Opinion Quarterly* 55 (1991): 424–431; and M.V. Hood III, Quentin Kidd, and Irwin

L. Morris, "Of Byrd[s] and Bumpers: Using Democratic Senators to Analyze Political Change in the South, 1960–1995," *American Journal of Political Science* 43 (1999): 456–487.

43. Gary C. Jacobson, "Party Polarization in National Politics: The Electoral Connection," in *Congress and the President in a Partisan Era*, ed. Jon R. Bond and Richard Fleisher (Washington, DC: Congressional Quarterly Press, 2000); in the 2004 National Election Study, 69 percent of white southern voters identified themselves as Republicans, 36 percent as Democrats.

44. Entries for midterm elections are calculated from the presidential vote in the previous election, adjusted for changes in district boundaries, if any; the statistic could not be calculated for 1962 and 1966 because information for reconfigured districts is not available.

45. The presidential vote gap between the parties' Senate constituencies is smaller than for House districts in part because, with two senators each, some states have split delegations, netting out to zero. But the growth in electoral consistency has also produced a decrease in the proportion of split Senate delegations; at the high point in the 96th Congress (1979–1980), 54 percent of the states' Senate delegations were split between the parties; by the 108th Congress (2003–2004), only 24 percent remained split, the lowest proportion since the mid-1950s.

46. Jacobson, "Partisan Polarization in Presidential Support," pp. 8–11.

47. The categories are extremely liberal, liberal, slightly liberal, moderate or middle of the road, slightly conservative, conservative, and extremely conservative.

48. Jacobson, "Party Polarization."

49. Entries for Senate electoral constituencies are calculated from the three biennial surveys up to and including the year indicated on the chart, so that data from voters electing the entire Senate membership are used to calculate each observation.

50. Greg D. Adams, "Abortion: Evidence of an Issue Evol[illegible] [illegible]can *Journal of Political Science* 41 (1997): 718–773.

51. Alan I. Abramowitz and Kyle L. Saunders, "Ide[illegible]
U.S. Electorate," *Journal of Politics* 60 (1998)[illegible]
Carmines and Geoffrey C. Layman, "Iss[illegible]
Politics: Old Certainties and Fresh Te[illegible]
Politics in the Very Late Twentieth C[illegible]
Chatham House, 1997). Geoffr[illegible]
that the ideological realignm[illegible]
partisans; see their "Party P[illegible]
American Electorate," *Am*[illegible]
786–802.

52. For an interesting discu[illegible]
district preferences ov[illegible]
and Charles Stewart [illegible]
American Journal of [illegible]

53. The partisan gap [illegible]
cent of Democra[illegible]
supported it. S[illegible]

of Bill Clinton," *British Elections & Parties Review* 10, ed. Philip Cowley, et al. (London: Frank Cass, 2000), Figure 10d.

54. Jacobson, "Public Opinion," Figures 10b and 10c.
55. Bob Woodward, *Shadow: Five Presidents and the Legacy of Watergate, 1974–1999* (New York: Simon & Schuster, 1999), p. 469.
56. Jacobson, "Impeachment Politics," p. 46.
57. "A Public Hearing on Congress," *The Public Perspective* 3 (November/December 1992), p. 82.
58. Clide Wilcox, *The Latest American Revolution? The 1994 Elections and Their Implications for Governance* (New York: St. Martin's Press, 1995), p. 69.
59. *U.S. Term Limits v. Thornton* (514 US 779, 1995).
60. George F. Will, *Restoration: Congress, Term Limits, and the Recovery of Deliberative Democracy* (New York: The Free Press, 1992).
61. Jeffrey Mondak, "Competence, Integrity, and the Electoral Success of Congressional Incumbents," *Journal of Politics* 57 (1995): 1043–1069; Jeffrey Mondak and Carl McCurley, "Inspected by #118406313: The Influence of Incumbents' Competence and Integrity in U.S. House Elections," *American Journal of Political Science* 39 (1995): 864–885.
62. Kristian Brainerd, "Several Term Limit Supporters Recant Vows to Leave the House, Saying Their Work Is Not Yet Done," *Congressional Quarterly Weekly Report* (June 19, 1999): 1444.
63. Committee on Political Parties of the American Political Science Association, "Towards a More Responsible Two-Party System," *American Political Science Review* 44 (1950): Part 2.
64. John R. Hibbing and Elizabeth Theiss-Morse, *Congress as Public Enemy: Political Attitudes Toward American Political Institutions* (New York: Cambridge University Press, 1995), pp. 14–20.
65. Hibbing and Theiss-Morse, *Congress as Public Enemy*, p. 19.
66. Hibbing and Theiss-Morse, *Congress as Public Enemy*, p. 82.
67. See Robert H. Durr, John B. Gilmour, and Christina Wolbrecht, "Explaining Congressional Approval," *American Journal of Political Science* 41 (1997): 175–207.
68. Jacobson, "Partisan Polarization in Presidential Support," pp. 8–11.
69. The South includes Alabama, Arkansas, Florida, Georgia, Kentucky, Louisiana, Mississippi, North Carolina, Oklahoma, South Carolina, Tennessee, Texas, and Virginia; the Plains include Kansas, Nebraska, North Dakota, and South Dakota; the Mountain West includes Alaska, Arizona,
orado, Idaho, Montana, Nevada, New Mexico, Utah, and Wyoming.
theast includes Connecticut, Delaware, Maine, Maryland,
tts, New Hampshire, New Jersey, New York, Pennsylvania,
d Vermont; the Midwest includes Illinois, Indiana, Iowa,
Missouri, Ohio, Wisconsin, and West Virginia; the
ifornia, Hawaii, Oregon, and Washington.

Mountain West because it has far more in
lly, and politically—with the Mountain

November 7, 2002.

BIBLIOGRAPHY

Abramowitz, Alan I. "A Comparison of Voting for U.S. Senator and Representative," *American Political Science Review* 74 (1980): 633–640.

______. "Choices and Echoes in the 1978 U.S. Senate Elections: A Research Note," *American Journal of Political Science* 25 (1981): 112–118.

______. "Economic Conditions, Presidential Popularity, and Voting Behavior in Midterm Congressional Elections," *Journal of Politics* 47 (1985): 31–43.

______. "The End of the Democratic Era? 1994 and the Future of Congressional Elections," *Political Research Quarterly* 48 (1995): 873–889.

______. "Explaining Senate Election Outcomes," *American Political Science Review* 82 (1988): 385–403.

______. "It's Monica, Stupid: Voting Behavior in the 1998 Midterm Election," *Legislative Studies Quarterly* 26 (May 2001): 211–226.

______. "Name Familiarity, Reputation, and the Incumbency Effect in a Congressional Election," *Western Political Quarterly* 28 (1975): 668–684.

______. "National Issues, Strategic Politicians, and Voting Behavior in the 1980 and 1982 Elections," *American Journal of Political Science* 28 (1984): 710–721.

______. "Partisan Redistricting and the 1982 Congressional Elections," *Journal of Politics* 45 (1983): 767–770.

Abramowitz, Alan I., Alexander, Brad, and Gunning, Mathew Gunning, "Incumbency, Redistricting, and the Decline of Competition in U.S. House Elections," *Journal of Politics* 68 (2006): 75–88.

Abramowitz, Alan I., and Cribbs, Kenneth J. "Don't Worry, Be Happy: Evaluations of Senate and House Incumbents in 1988" (Paper presented at the Annual Meeting of the American Political Science Association, Atlanta, August 31–September 3, 1989).

Abramowitz, Alan I., and Segal, Jeffrey A. "Determinants of the Outcomes of U.S. Senate Elections," *Journal of Politics* 48 (1986): 433–439.

Achen, Christopher H. "Measuring Representation," *American Journal of Political Science* 22 (1978): 475–510.

Ahuja, Sunil, Beavers, Staci L., Berreau, Cynthia, Dodson, Anthony, Hourigan, Patrick, Showalter, Steven, Waltz, Jeff, and Hibbing, John R. "Modern Congressional Election Theory Meets the 1992 House Elections," *Political Research Quarterly* 47 (1994): 909–921.

Alesina, Alberto, and Rosenthal, Howard. "Partisan Cycles in Congressional Elections and the Macroeconomy," *American Political Science Review* 83 (1989): 373–398.

Alford, John R., and Hibbing, John R. "The Disparate Electoral Security of House and Senate Incumbents" (Paper presented at the Annual Meeting of the American Political Science Association, Atlanta, August 31–September 3, 1989).

Anagnoson, J. Theodore. "Federal Grant Agencies and Congressional Election Campaigns," *American Journal of Political Science* 26 (1982): 547–561.

Ansolabehere, Stephen, and Gerber, Alan. "The Effects of Filing Fees and Petition Requirements on U.S. House Elections," *Legislative Studies Quarterly* 21 (1996): 249–264.

______. "The Mismeasure of Campaign Spending: Evidence from the 1990 U.S. House Elections," *Journal of Politics* 56 (1994): 1106–1118.

Ansolabehere, Stephen, Snowberg, Eric C., and Snyder, James M. Jr. "Television and the Incumbency Advantage in the U.S. House," *Legislative Studies Quarterly* 31 (2005): 469–490.

Ansolabehere, Stephen, Snyder, James M., Jr., and Steward, Charles III. "Candidate Positioning in U.S. House Elections," *American Journal of Political Science* 45 (January 2001): 136–159.

______. "Old Voters, New Voters, and the Personal Vote: Using Redistricting to Measure the Incumbency Advantage," *American Journal of Political Science* 44 (January 2000): 17–34.

Arcelus, Francisco, and Meltzer, Allan H. "The Effects of Aggregate Economic Variables on Congressional Elections," *American Political Science Review* 69 (1975): 232–239.

Arnold, R. Douglas. *The Logic of Congressional Action* (New Haven, CT: Yale University Press, 1990).

Banks, Jeffrey S., and Kiewiet, D. Roderick. "Explaining Patterns of Candidate Competition in Congressional Elections," *American Journal of Political Science* 33 (1989): 997–1015.

Bauer, Monica, and Hibbing, John R. "Which Incumbents Lose in House Elections: A Reply to Jacobson's 'The Marginals Never Vanished,'" *American Journal of Political Science* 33 (1989): 262–271.

Berch, Neil. "The 'Year of the Woman' in Context," *American Politics Quarterly* 24 (1996): 169–193.

Berkman, Michael, and Eisenstein, James. "State Legislators as Congressional Candidates: The Effects of Prior Experience on Legislative Recruitment and Fundraising," *Political Research Quarterly* 52 (1999): 481–498.

Bianco, William T. "Party Campaign Committees and the Distribution of Tally Program Funds," *Legislative Studies Quarterly* 24 (1999): 451–469.

______. "Strategic Decisions on Candidacy in U.S. Congressional Districts," *Legislative Studies Quarterly* 9 (1984): 351–364.

Biersack, Robert, Herrnson, Paul S., and Wilcox, Clyde. "Seeds for Success: Early Money in Congressional Elections," *Legislative Studies Quarterly* 18 (1993): 535–551.

Bloom, Howard S., and Price, H. Douglas. "Voter Response to Short-Run Economic Conditions: The Asymmetric Effect of Prosperity and Recession," *American Political Science Review* 69 (1975): 1240–1254.

Bond, Jon R. "The Influence of Constituency Diversity on Electoral Competition in Voting for Congress, 1974–1978," *Legislative Studies Quarterly* 8 (1983): 201–218.

Bond, Jon R., Covington, Cary, and Fleisher, Richard. "Explaining Challenger Quality in Congressional Elections," *Journal of Politics* 47 (1985): 510–529.

Bond, Jon R., and Fleisher, Richard H. *The President in the Legislative Arena* (Chicago: University of Chicago Press, 1990).

Bond, Jon R., Fleisher, Richard H., and Talbert, Jeffrey C. "Partisan Differences in Candidate Quality in Open Seat House Races, 1976–1994," *Political Research Quarterly* 50 (1997): 281–299.

Born, Richard. "Assessing the Impact of Institutional and Election Forces on the Evaluations of Congressional Incumbents," *Journal of Politics* 53 (1991): 764–799.

______. "Congressional Incumbency and the Rise of Split Ticket Voting." *Legislative Studies Quarterly* 25 (2000): 365–387.

______. "House Incumbents and Inter-Election Vote Change," *Journal of Politics* 39 (1977): 1008–1034.

______. "Partisan Intentions and Election Day Realities in the Congressional Redistricting Process," *American Political Science Review* 79 (1985): 305–319.

______. "Reassessing the Decline of Presidential Coattails: U.S. House Elections, 1952–1980," *Journal of Politics* 46 (1984): 60–79.

______. "Strategic Politicians and Unresponsive Voters," *American Political Science Review* 80 (1986): 599–612.

______. "Surge and Decline, Negative Voting, and the Midterm Loss Phenomenon: A Simultaneous Choice Model," *American Journal of Political Science* 34 (1990): 615–645.

Bovitz, Gregory. "Electoral Consequences of Porkbusting in the U.S. House of Representatives," *Political Science Quarterly* 117 (Fall 2002): 455–477.

Box-Steffensmeier, Janet, Jacobson, Gary C., and Grant, J. Tobin. "Question Wording and the House Vote Choice: Some Experimental Evidence," *Public Opinion Quarterly* 64 (Fall 2000): 257–270.

Box-Steffensmeier, Janet M., Radcliffe, Peter M., and Bartels, Brandon L. "The Incidence and Timing of PAC Contributions to Incumbent U.S. House Members," *Legislative Studies Quarterly* 30 (2005): 549–580.

Brady, David W. "A Reevaluation of Realignments in American Politics: Evidence from the House of Representatives," *American Political Science Review* 79 (1985): 28–49.

Brunell, Thomas L. "Partisan Bias in U.S. Congressional Elections: Why the Senate Is Usually More Republican Than the House of Representatives," *American Politics Quarterly* 27 (1999): 316–337.

Bullock, Charles S., III. "The Impact of Changing the Racial Composition of Congressional Districts on Legislators' Roll Call Behavior," *American Politics Quarterly* 23 (1995): 141–158.

______. "Redistricting and Congressional Stability," *Journal of Politics* 37 (1975): 569–575.

Burden, Barry C., and Kimball, David C. *Why Americans Split Their Tickets: Campaigns, Competition, and Divided Government* (Ann Arbor: University of Michigan Press, 2002).

Burnham, Walter Dean. "Insulation and Responsiveness in Congressional Elections," *Political Science Quarterly* 90 (1975): 411–435.

Busch, Andrew E. *Horses in Midstream: U.S. Midterm Elections and Their Consequences, 1894–1998* (Pittsburgh: University of Pittsburgh Press, 1999).

Cain, Bruce E. "Assessing the Partisan Effects of Redistricting," *American Political Science Review* 79 (1985): 320–333.

______. *The Reapportionment Puzzle*. (Berkeley: University of California Press, 1984).

Caldeira, Gregory A., Patterson, Samuel C., and Markko, Gregory A. "The Mobilization of Voters in Congressional Elections," *Journal of Politics* 47 (1985): 490–509.

Calvert, Randall L., and Ferejohn, John A. "Coattail Voting in Recent Presidential Elections," *American Political Science Review* 77 (1983): 407–419.

Campbell, Angus, Converse, Philip E., Miller, Warren E., and Stokes, Donald E. *Elections and the Political Order.* New York: John Wiley, 1966.

Campbell, James E. "Predicting Seat Gains from Presidential Coattails," *American Journal of Political Science* 30 (1986): 397–418.

______. *The Presidential Pulse of Congressional Elections* (Lexington: University of Kentucky Press, 1993).

______. "The Presidential Pulse and the 1994 Midterm Congressional Election," *Journal of Politics* 59 (1997): 830–857.

______. "The Presidential Surge and its Midterm Decline in Congressional Elections," *Journal of Politics* 53 (1991): 477–487.

______. "The Return of the Incumbents: The Nature of the Incumbency Advantage," *Western Political Quarterly* 36 (1983): 434–444.

Campbell, James E., Alford, John R., and Henry, Keith. "Television Markets and Congressional Elections," *Legislative Studies Quarterly* 9 (1984): 665–678.

Campbell, James E., and Sumners, Joe A. "Presidential Coattails in Senate Elections," *American Political Science Review* 84 (1990): 513–524.

Canon, David T. *Actors, Athletes, and Astronauts: Political Amateurs in the United States Congress* (Chicago: University of Chicago Press, 1990).

______. *Race, Redistricting, and Representation* (Chicago: University of Chicago Press, 1999).

______. "Sacrificial Lambs or Strategic Politicians? Political Amateurs in U.S. House Elections," *American Journal of Political Science* 37 (1993): 1119–1141.

Carson, Jamie L. "Strategy, Selection, and Candidate Competition in U.S. House Elections," *Journal of Politics* 67 (2005): 1–28.

Carson, Jamie L, Engstrom, Erik J., and Roberts, Jason M. "Redistricting, Candidate Entry, and the Politics of Nineteenth-Century U.S. House Elections," *American Journal of Political Science* 50 (2006): 283–293.

Carson, Jamie L., and Roberts, Jason M. "Strategic Politicians and U.S. House Elections, 1874–1914," *Journal of Politics* 67 (2005): 474–496.

Clarke, Harold D., Feigert, Frank B., Seldon, Barry J., and Stewart, Marianne C. "More Time with My Money: Leaving the House and Going Home in 1992 and 1994," *Political Research Quarterly* 52 (1999): 67–85.

Clarke, Peter, and Evans, Susan. *Covering Campaigns: Journalism in Congressional Elections* (Stanford, CA: Stanford University Press, 1983).

Clem, Alan L., ed. *The Making of Congressmen: Seven Campaigns of 1974* (North Scituate, MA: Duxbury Press, 1976).

Clinton, Joshua D. "Representation in Congress: Constituents and Roll Calls in the 106th House," *Journal of Politics* 68 (2006): 397–409.

Cnudde, Charles F., and McCrone, Donald J. "The Linkage between Constituency Attitudes and Congressional Voting Behavior: A Causal Model," *American Political Science Review* 60 (1966): 66–72.

Coleman, John J. "The Importance of Being Republican: Forecasting Party Fortunes in House Midterm Elections," *Journal of Politics* 59 (1997): 497–519.

Collie, Melissa P. "Incumbency, Electoral Safety, and Turnover in the House of Representatives, 1952–1976," *American Political Science Review* 75 (1981): 119–131.

Conway, M. Margaret, and Wyckoff, Mikel L. "Voter Choice in the 1974 Congressional Elections," *American Politics Quarterly* 8 (1980): 3–14.

Copeland, Gary. "Activating Voters in Congressional Elections," *Political Behavior* 5 (1983): 391–402.

Cover, Albert D. "Contacting Congressional Constituents: Some Patterns of Perquisite Use," *American Journal of Political Science* 24 (1980): 125–135.

______. "One Good Term Deserves Another: The Advantage of Incumbency in Congressional Elections," *American Journal of Political Science* 21 (1977): 523–542.

Cover, Albert D., and Brumberg, Bruce S. "Baby Books and Ballots: The Impact of Congressional Mail on Constituency Opinion," *American Political Science Review* 76 (1982): 347–359.

Cover, Albert D., and Mayhew, David R. "Congressional Dynamics and the Decline of Competitive Congressional Elections," in *Congress Reconsidered,* 2nd ed., ed. Lawrence C. Dodd and Bruce I. Oppenheimer (Washington, DC: Congressional Quarterly Press, 1981).

Cox, Gary W., and Katz, Jonathan. *Elbridge Gerry's Salamander: The Electoral Consequences of the Reapportionment Revolution* (Cambridge, UK: Cambridge University Press, 2002).

______. "The Reapportionment Revolution and Bias in U.S. Congressional Elections," *American Journal of Political Science* 43 (1999): 812–840.

______. "Why Did the Incumbency Advantage in U.S. House Elections Grow?" *American Journal of Political Science* 40 (1996): 478–497.

Cox, Gary, and Kernell, Samuel, ed. *Divided Government* (Boulder, CO: Westview Press, 1991).

Cox, Gary W., and Magar, Eric. "How Much Is Majority Status in the U.S. Congress Worth?" *American Political Science Review* 93 (1999): 299–309.

Cox, Gary, and McCubbins, Mathew. *Legislative Leviathan: Party Government in the House*. 2nd ed. (Cambridge: Cambridge University Press, 2007).

Cummings, Milton C., Jr. *Congressmen and the Electorate*. New York: The Free Press, 1966.

Dabelko, Kristen la Cour, and Herrnson, Paul S. "Women's and Men's Campaigns for the U.S. House of Representatives," *Political Research Quarterly* 50 (1997): 121–135.

Damore, David F., and Hansford, Thomas G. "The Allocation of Party Controlled Campaign Resources in the House of Representatives, 1989–1996," *Political Research Quarterly* 52 (1999): 371–385.

De Boef, Suzanna, and Stimson, James A. "The Dynamic Structure of Congressional Elections," *Journal of Politics* 57 (1995): 630–648.

Desposato, Scott W., and John R. Petrocik. "The Variable Incumbency Advantage: New Voters, Redistricting, and the Personal Vote," *American Journal of Political Science* 47 (January 2003): 18–32.

Dimock, Michael A., and Jacobson, Gary C. "Checks and Choices: The House Bank Scandal's Impact on Voters in 1992," *Journal of Politics* 57 (1995): 1143–1159.

Dwyre, Diana. "Spinning Straw into Gold: Soft Money and U.S. House Elections," *Legislative Studies Quarterly* 21 (1996): 409–424.

Edwards, George C., III. *Presidential Influence in Congress* (San Francisco: W. H. Freeman, 1980).

Eismeier, Theodore J., and Pollack, Philip H., III. *Business, Money, and the Rise of Corporate PACs in American Elections* (New York: Quantum Books, 1988).

Elling, Richard C. "Ideological Change in the U.S. Senate: Time and Electoral Responsiveness," *Legislative Studies Quarterly* 7 (1982): 75–92.

Engstrom, Richard N., and Christopher Kenny. "The Effects of Independent Expenditures in Senate Elections," *Political Research Quarterly* 55 (December 2002): 885–905.

Epstein, David, and O'Halloran, Sharon. "Measuring the Electoral Impact of Majority–Minority Voting Districts," *American Journal of Political Science* 43 (1999): 367–395.

Erikson, Robert S. "The Advantage of Incumbency in Congressional Elections," *Polity* 3 (1971): 395–405.

______. "Constituency Opinion and Congressional Behavior: A Reexamination of the Miller-Stokes Representation Data," *American Journal of Political Science* 22 (1978): 511–535.

______. "Economic Conditions and the Congressional Vote: A Review of the Macrolevel Evidence," *American Journal of Political Science* 34 (1990): 373–399.

______. "The Electoral Impact of Congressional Roll Call Voting," *American Political Science Review* 65 (1971): 1018–1032.

______. "Is There Such a Thing as a Safe Seat?" *Polity* 9 (1976): 623–632.

______. "Malapportionment, Gerrymandering, and Party Fortunes in Congressional Elections," *American Political Science Review* 66 (1972): 1234–1245.

______. "Measuring Constituency Opinion: The 1978 U.S. Congressional Election Survey," *Legislative Studies Quarterly* 6 (1981): 235–246.

Erikson, Robert S., and Palfrey, Thomas R. "Campaign Spending and Incumbency: An Alternative Simultaneous Equations Approach," *Journal of Politics* 60 (1998): 355–373.

Erikson, Robert S., and Sigelman, Lee. "Poll-Based Forecasts of the House Vote in Presidential Election Years, 1952–1992 and 1996," *American Politics Quarterly* 24 (1996): 520–531.

Erikson, Robert S., and Wright, Gerald F., Jr. "Policy Representation of Constituency Interests," *Political Behavior* 1 (1980): 91–106.

Eubank, Robert E. "Incumbent Effects on Individual Level Voting Behavior in Congressional Elections: A Decade of Exaggeration," *Journal of Politics* 47 (1985): 958–967.

Eulau, Heinz, and Karps, Paul D. "The Puzzle of Representation: Specifying Components of Responsiveness," *Legislative Studies Quarterly* 2 (1977): 233–254.

Feldman, Paul, and Jondrow, James. "Congressional Elections and Local Federal Spending," *American Journal of Political Science* 28 (1984): 147–163.

Fenno, Richard F., Jr. *Congress at the Grassroots: Representational Change in the South, 1970–1998* (Chapel Hill: University of North Carolina Press, 2000).

______. *Home Style: House Members in Their Districts* (Boston: Little, Brown, 1978).

______. *The United States Senate: A Bicameral Perspective* (Washington, DC: American Enterprise Institute, 1982).

Ferejohn, John A. "On the Decline of Competition in Congressional Elections," *American Political Science Review* 71 (1977): 166–176.

Ferejohn, John A., and Calvert, Randall L. "Presidential Coattails in Historical Perspective," *American Journal of Political Science* 28 (1984): 127–146.

Ferejohn, John A., and Fiorina, Morris P. "Incumbency and Realignment in Congressional Elections," in *The New Direction in American Politics*, ed. John E. Chubb and Paul E. Peterson (Washington, DC: The Brookings Institution, 1985).

Fiorina, Morris P. "The Case of the Vanishing Marginals: The Bureaucracy Did It," *American Political Science Review* 71 (1977): 177–181.

______. *Congress: Keystone of the Washington Establishment*, 2nd ed. (New Haven, CT: Yale University Press, 1989).

______. *Divided Government*, 2nd ed. (Boston: Allyn and Bacon, 1996).

______. "Economic Restrospective Voting in American National Elections: A Micro Analysis," *American Journal of Political Science* 22 (1978): 426–443.

______. *Representatives, Roll Calls, and Constituencies* (Lexington, MA: D. C. Heath, 1974).

______. *Retrospective Voting in American National Elections* (New Haven, CT: Yale University Press, 1981).

______. "Short- and Long-Term Effects of Economic Conditions on Individual Voting Decisions," in *Contemporary Political Economy*, ed. D. A. Hibbs and H. Fassbender (Amsterdam: North Holland, 1981).

______. "Some Problems in Studying the Effects of Resource Allocation in Congressional Elections," *American Journal of Political Science* 25 (1981): 543–567.

______. "Who Is Held Responsible? Further Evidence on the Hibbing–Alford Thesis," *American Journal of Political Science* 27 (1983): 158–164.

Fiorina, Morris P., and Rohde, David, ed. *Home Style and Congressional Work* (Ann Arbor: University of Michigan Press, 1989).

Fishel, Jeff. *Party and Opposition: Congressional Challengers in American Politics* (New York: David McKay, 1973).

Flemming, Gregory H. "Presidential Coattails in Open Seat Elections," *Legislative Studies Quarterly* 20 (1995): 197–211.

Fowler, Linda L. "Candidates' Perceptions of Electoral Coalitions," *American Politics Quarterly* 8 (1980): 483–494.

Fowler, Linda L., and McClure, Robert D. *Political Ambition: Who Decides to Run for Congress* (New Haven, CT: Yale University Press, 1989).

Fox, Richard Logan. *Gender Dynamics in Congressional Elections* (Thousand Oaks, CA: Sage Publications, 1997).

Franklin, Charles H. "Eschewing Obfuscation? Campaigns and the Perception of U.S. Senate Incumbents," *American Political Science Review* 85 (1991): 1193–1214.

Frantzich, Stephen. "Opting Out: Retirement from the House of Representatives, 1966–1974," *American Politics Quarterly* 6 (1978): 251–273.

Froman, Lewis A., Jr. *Congressmen and Their Constituencies* (Chicago: Rand McNally, 1963).

Frymer, Paul, Kim, Thomas P., and Bimes, Terri L. "Party Elites, Ideological Voters, and Divided Government," *Legislative Studies Quarterly* 22 (1997): 195–216.

Gaddie, Ronald Keith. "Congressional Seat Swings: Revisiting Exposure in House Elections," *Political Research Quarterly* 50 (1997): 699–710.

______. "Economic Interest Group Allocations in Open-Seat Senate Elections," *American Politics Quarterly* 25 (1997): 347–362.

______. "Investing in the Future: Economic Political Action Committee Contributions to Open-Seat House Candidates," *American Politics Quarterly* 23 (1995): 339–354.

Gaddie, Ronald Keith, Charles S. Bullock III, and Scott E. Buchanan. "What Is So Special About Special Elections?" *Legislative Studies Quarterly* 24 (February 1999): 103–112.

Gelman, Andrew, and King, Gary. "Estimating the Incumbency Advantage without Bias," *American Journal of Political Science* 34 (1990): 1142–1164.

Gerber, Alan. "Estimating the Effects of Campaign Spending on Senate Election Outcomes Using Instrumental Variables," *American Political Science Review* 92 (1998): 401–411.

Gilliam, Franklin D., Jr. "Influences on Voter Turnout for U.S. House Elections in Non-Presidential Years," *Legislative Studies Quarterly* 10 (1985): 339–352.

Gilmour, John B., and Rothstein, Paul. "A Dynamic Model of Loss, Retirement, and Tenure in the U.S. House of Representatives," *Journal of Politics* 58 (1996): 54–68.

Glazer, Amihai, and Robbins, Marc. "Congressional Responsiveness to Constituency Change," *American Journal of Political Science* 29 (1985): 259–273.

______. "Voters and Roll Call Voting: The Effect on Congressional Elections," *Political Behavior* 4 (1983): 377–390.

Goidel, Robert K., and Gross, Donald A. "A Systems Approach to Campaign Finance in U.S. House Elections," *American Politics Quarterly* 22 (1994): 125–153.

______. "Reconsidering the 'Myths and Realities' of Campaign Finance Reform," *Legislative Studies Quarterly* 21 (1996): 129–149.

Goldenberg, Edie, and Traugott, Michael. *Campaigning for Congress* (Washington, DC: Congressional Quarterly Press, 1984).

______. "Congressional Campaign Effects on Candidate Recognition and Evaluation," *Political Behavior* 1 (1980): 61–90.

______. "Normal Vote Analysis of U.S. Congressional Elections," *Legislative Studies Quarterly* 6 (1981): 247–258.

Goldstein, Ken, and Paul Freedman. "New Evidence for New Arguments: Money and Advertising in the 1996 Senate Elections," *Journal of Politics* 62 (November 2000): 1087–1108.

Goodliffe, Jay. "The Effect of War Chests on Challenger Entry in U.S. House Elections," *American Journal of Political Science* 45 (October 2001): 830–844.

Goodman, Saul, and Kramer, Gerald H. "Comment on Arcelus and Meltzer, The Effect of Aggregate Economic Conditions on Congressional Elections," *American Political Science Review* 69 (1975): 255–265.

Green, Donald P., and Jonathan S. Krasno. "Rebuttal to Jacobson's 'New Evidence for Old Arguments,'" *American Journal of Political Science* 34 (1990): 363–372.

______. "Salvation for the Spendthrift Incumbent," *American Journal of Political Science* 32 (1988): 844–907.

Griffin, John D. "Senate Apportionment as a Source of Political Inequality," *Legislative Studies Quarterly* 31 (2006): 405–432.

Griffin, John D., and Newman, Brian. "Are Voters Better Represented?" *Journal of Politics* 67 (2005): 1206–1227.

Grofman, Bernard, Brunell, Thomas L., and Koetzle, William. "Why Gain in the Senate But Midterm Loss in the House? Evidence from a Natural Experiment," *Legislative Studies Quarterly* 23 (1998): 79–89.

Gronke, Paul. *Settings, Institutions, Campaigns, and the Vote: A Unified Approach to House and Senate Elections* (Ann Arbor: University of Michigan Press, 2000).

Gronke Paul, Koch, Jeffrey and Wilson, J. Matthew. "Follow the Leader? Presidential Approval, Presidential Support, and Representatives' Electoral Fortunes," *Journal of Politics* 65 (2003): 785–808.

Groseclose, Timothy, and Krehbiel, Keith. "Golden Parachutes, Rubber Checks, and Strategic Retirements from the 102nd House," *American Journal of Political Science* 38 (1994): 75–99.

Heberlig, Eric S, and Larson, Bruce A. "Redistributing Campaign Funds by U.S. House Members: The Spiraling Costs of the Permanent Campaign," *Legislative Studies Quarterly* 30 (2005): 597–624.

Herndon, James F. "Access, Record and Competition as Influences on Interest Group Contributions to Congressional Campaigns," *Journal of Politics* 44 (1982): 996–1019.

Herrick, Rebekah. "Is There a Gender Gap in the Value of Campaign Resources?" *American Politics Quarterly* 24 (1996): 68–80.

Herrnson, Paul S. *Congressional Elections: Campaigning at Home and in Washington,* 4th ed. (Washington, DC: Congressional Quarterly Press, 2004).

______. "Do Parties Matter? The Role of Party Organizations in Congressional Elections," *Journal of Politics* 48 (1986): 612–613.

______. *Party Campaigning in the 1980s* (Cambridge, MA: Harvard University Press, 1988).

Hershey, Marjorie Randon. "Incumbency and the Minimum Winning Coalition," *American Journal of Political Science* 17 (1973): 631–637.

______. *The Making of Campaign Strategy* (Lexington, MA: Lexington Books, 1974).

______. *Running for Office: The Political Education of Campaigners* (Chatham, NJ: Chatham House, 1984).

Hetherington, Marc J., Larson, Bruce, and Globetti, Suzanne. "The Redistricting Cycle and Strategic Candidate Decisions in U.S. House Races, "*Journal of Politics* 65 (2003): 1221–1234.

Hibbing, John R. *Congressional Careers: Contours of Life in the U.S. House of Representatives* (Chapel Hill: University of North Carolina Press, 1991).

______. "The Liberal Hour: Electoral Pressures and Transfer Payment Voting in the U.S. Congress," *Journal of Politics* 46 (1984): 846–865.

______. "Voluntary Retirements from the House in the Twentieth Century," *Journal of Politics* 44 (1982): 1020–1034.

Hibbing, John R., and Alford, John R. "Constituency Population and Representation in the United States Senate," *Legislative Studies Quarterly* 15 (1990): 581–598.

______. "The Electoral Impact of Economic Conditions: Who Is Held Responsible?" *American Journal of Political Science* 25 (1981): 423–439.

Hibbing, John R., and Brandes, Sara L. "State Population and the Electoral Success of U.S. Senators," *American Journal of Political Science* 27 (1983): 808–819.

Hibbing, John, and Theiss-Morse, Elizabeth. *Congress as Public Enemy: Public Attitudes Toward American Political Institutions* (Cambridge, UK: Cambridge University Press, 1995).

Hill, Keven A. "Does the Creation of Majority Black Districts Aid Republicans? An Analysis of the 1992 Congressional Elections in Eight Southern States," *Journal of Politics* 57 (1995): 384–401.

Hinckley, Barbara. "The American Voter in Congressional Elections," *American Political Science Review* 74 (1980): 641–650.

______. *Congressional Elections* (Washington, DC: Congressional Quarterly Press, 1981).

______. "House Re-elections and Senate Defeats: The Role of the Challenger," *British Journal of Political Science* 10 (1980): 441–460.

______. "Incumbency and the Presidential Vote in Senate Elections: Defining Parameters of Subpresidential Voting," *American Political Science Review* 64 (1970): 836–842.

______. "Issues, Information Costs, and Congressional Elections," *American Politics Quarterly* 4 (1976): 131–152.

Hinckley, Barbara, Hofstetter, Richard, and Kessel, John. "Information and the Vote: A Comparative Election Study," *American Politics Quarterly* 2 (1974): 131–158.

Huckshorn, Robert J., and Spencer, Robert C. *The Politics of Defeat* (Amherst: University of Massachusetts Press, 1971).

Hurley, Patricia A. "Electoral Change and Policy Consequences: Representation in the 97th Congress," *American Politics Quarterly* 12 (1984): 177–194.

______. "Partisan Representation, Realignment, and the Senate in the 1980s," *Journal of Politics* 53 (February 1991): 3–33.

Hurley, Patricia A., and Hill, Kim Quaile. "The Prospects for Issue Voting in Contemporary Congressional Elections: An Assessment of Citizen Awareness and Representation," *American Politics Quarterly* 8 (1980): 425–449.

Hutcheson, Richard G., III. "The Inertial Effect of Incumbency and Two-Party Politics: Elections to the House of Representatives from the South, 1952–1974," *American Political Science Review* 69 (1975): 1399–1401.

Jackson, Brooks. *Honest Graft: Big Money and the American Political Process*, updated ed. (Washington, DC: Farragut Publishing Company, 1990).

Jackson, Robert A. "The Mobilization of Congressional Electorates," *Legislative Studies Quarterly* 21 (1996): 425–445.

Jacobson, Gary C. "The 1994 House Elections in Perspective," *Political Science Quarterly* 111 (1996), 203–223.

______. "The 105th Congress: Unprecedented and Unsurprising," in *The Elections of 1996*, ed. Michael Nelson (Washington, DC: Congressional Quarterly Press, 1997), 143–167.

______. "All Quiet on the Western Front: Redistricting and Party Competition in California House Elections" in *Redistricting in the New Millennium*, ed. Peter Galderisi (Lanham, MD: Lexington Books, 2005), 217–244.

______. "Campaign Spending Effects in U.S. Senate Elections: Evidence from the National Annenberg Election Survey," *Electoral Studies* 25 (June 2006), 195–226.

______. "Competition in U.S. Congressional Elections," *The Marketplace of Democracy*, ed. Michael P. McDonald and John Samples (Washington, DC: The Brookings Institution, 2006), 26–52.

______. "Congress: A Singular Continuity," in *The Elections of 1988*, ed. Michael Nelson (Washington, DC: Congressional Quarterly Press, 1989) 127–152.

______. "Congress: Elections and Stalemate," in *The Elections of 2000*, ed. Michael Nelson (Washington, DC: Congressional Quarterly Press, 2001) 185–209.

______. "Congress: Politics after a Landslide Without Coattails," in *The Elections of 1984*, ed. Michael Nelson (Washington, DC: Congressional Quarterly Press, 1985) 215–237.

______. "The Congress: The Structural Basis of Republican Success," in *The Elections of 2004*, ed. Michael Nelson (Washington, DC: Congressional Quarterly Press, 2005), 163–186

______. "Congress: Unusual Year, Unusual Election," in *The Elections of 1992*, ed. Michael Nelson (Washington, DC: Congressional Quarterly Press, 1993) 153–182.

______. "Deficit Cutting Politics and Congressional Elections," *Political Science Quarterly* 108 (1993): 375–402.

______. "The Effect of the AFL-CIO's 'Voter Education' Campaigns on the 1996 House Elections," *Journal of Politics* 61 (1999): 185–194.

______. "The Effects of Campaign Spending in Congressional Elections," *American Political Science Review* 72 (1978): 469–491.

______. "The Effects of Campaign Spending in House Elections: New Evidence for Old Arguments," *American Journal of Political Science* 34 (1990): 334–362.

______. *The Electoral Origins of Divided Government: Competition in U.S. House Elections, 1946–1988* (Boulder, CO: Westview Press, 1990).

______. "Enough Is Too Much: Money and Competition in House Elections, 1972–1984," in *Elections in America*, ed. Kay L. Schlozman (New York: Allen & Unwin, 1987) 173–195.

______. "The First Congressional Elections after BCRA," *One Election Later: 2004 Politics after the Bipartisan Campaign Reform Act*, ed., Michael Malbin. (Lanham, MD: Rowman & Littlefield, 2006), 185–203.

______. "A House and Senate Divided: The Clinton Legacy and the Congressional Elections of 2000," *Political Science Quarterly* 116 (Spring 2001): 5–27.

______. "Impeachment Politics and the 1998 Congressional Elections," *Political Science Quarterly* 114 (1999): 31–51.

______. "The Marginals Never Vanished: Incumbency and Competition in Elections to the U.S. House of Representatives, 1952–1982," *American Journal of Political Science* 31 (1987): 126–141.

______. "Measuring Campaign Spending Effects in U.S. House Elections," in *Capturing Campaign Effects*, ed. Henry Brady and Richard Johnston (Ann Arbor: University of Michigan Press, 2006), 199–220.

______. "Money and Votes Reconsidered: Congressional Elections, 1972–1982," *Public Choice* 47 (1985): 7–62.

______. *Money in Congressional Elections* (New Haven, CT: Yale University Press, 1980).

______. "Parties and PACs in Congressional Elections," in *Congress Reconsidered*, 4th ed., ed. Lawrence C. Dodd and Bruce I. Oppenheimer (Washington, DC: Congressional Quarterly Press, 1989), 117–152.

______. "Partisan Polarization in Presidential Support: The Electoral Connection," *Congress and the Presidency* 30 (Spring 2003): 1–36.

______. "Party Organization and Distribution of Campaign Resources: Republicans and Democrats in 1982," *Political Science Quarterly* 100 (1985–1986): 603–625.

______. "Party Polarization in National Politics: The Electoral Connection," in *Polarized Politics*, ed. Jon R. Bond and Richard Fleisher (Washington, DC: Congressional Quarterly Press, 2000), 9–30.

______. "Polarized Politics and the 2004 Congressional Elections," *Political Science Quarterly* 120 (2005): 199–218.

______. "Presidential Coattails in 1972," *Public Opinion Quarterly* 40 (1976): 194–200.

______. "Referendum: The 2006 Midterm Congressional Elections," *Political Science Quarterly* 122 (2007): 1–24.

______. "Reversal of Fortune: The Transformation of U.S. House Elections in the 1990s," in *Continuity and Change in Congressional Elections*, ed. David W. Brady, John Cogan, and Morris P. Fiorina (Stanford, CA: Stanford University Press, 2000), 10–38.

______. "Running Scared: Elections and Congressional Politics in the 1980s," in *Congress: Structure and Policy*, ed. Mathew McCubbins and Terry Sullivan (New York: Cambridge University Press, 1987), 34–81.

______. "Strategic Politicians and the Dynamics of House Elections, 1946–86," *American Political Science Review* 83 (1989): 773–793.

______. "Terror, Terrain, and Turnout: Explaining the 2002 Midterm Elections," *Political Science Quarterly* 118 (Spring 2003): 1–22.

Jacobson, Gary C., and Dimock, Michael A. "Checking Out: The Effects of Overdrafts on the 1992 House Elections," *American Journal of Political Science* 38 (1994): 601–624.

Jacobson, Gary C., and Kernell, Samuel. "National Forces in the 1986 U.S. House Elections," *Legislative Studies Quarterly* 15 (1990): 72–85.

______. *Strategy and Choice in Congressional Elections*, 2nd ed. (New Haven, CT: Yale University Press, 1983).

Jacobson, Gary C., Kernell, Samuel, and Lazarus, Jeffrey. "Assessing the President's Role as Party Agent in Congressional Elections: The Case of Bill Clinton in 2000," *Legislative Studies Quarterly*, 29 (May 2004), 159–184.

Jacobson, Gary C., and Wolfinger, Raymond E. "Information and Voting in California Senate Elections," *Legislative Studies Quarterly* 14 (1989): 509–524.

Johannes, John R. *To Serve the People: Congress and Constituency Service* (Lincoln: University of Nebraska Press, 1984).

Johannes, John R., and McAdams, John C. "The Congressional Incumbency Effect: Is It Casework, Policy Compatibility, or Something Else?" *American Journal of Political Science* 25 (1981): 512–542.

Jones, Charles O. *Every Second Year* (Washington, DC: Brookings Institution, 1967).

______. "Inter-Party Competition for Congressional Seats," *Western Political Quarterly* 17 (1964): 461–476.

______. "A Suggested Scheme for Classifying Congressional Campaigns," *Public Opinion Quarterly* 26 (1962): 126–132.

Kahn, Kim Fridkin. "Does Being Male Help? An Investigation of the Effects of Candidate Gender and Campaign Coverage on Evaluations of U.S. Senate Candidates," *Journal of Politics* 54 (1992): 497–517.

______. "Senate Elections in the News: Examining Campaign Coverage," *Legislative Studies Quarterly* 16 (1991): 349–374.

Kahn, Kim Fridkin, and Kenney, Patrick J. "The Importance of Issues in Senate Campaigns: Citizens' Reception of Issue Messages," *Legislative Studies Quarterly* 26 (November 2001): 573–597.

______. "A Model of Candidate Evaluations in Senate Elections: The Impact of Campaign Intensity," *Journal of Politics* 59 (1997): 1173–1205.

______. *No Holds Barred:* Negativity *in U.S. Senate* Campaigns (Upper Saddle River, N.J Prentice Hall, 2004).

______. *The Spectacle of U. S. Senate Campaigns* (Princeton, NJ: Princeton University Press, 1999).

Kayden, Xandra. *Campaign Organization* (Lexington, MA: D.C. Heath, 1978).

Kazee, Thomas A., ed. *Who Runs for Congress? Ambition, Context, and Candidate Emergence* (Washington, DC: Congressional Quarterly Press, 1994).

Kazee, Thomas A., and Thornberry, Mary C. "Where's the Party? Congressional Candidate Recruitment and American Party Organization," *Western Political Quarterly* 43 (1990): 61–80.

Kenny, Christopher, and McBurnett, Michael. "Up Close and Personal: Campaign Contact and Candidate Spending in U.S. House Elections," *Political Research Quarterly* 50 (1997): 75–96.

Kernell, Samuel. "Presidential Popularity and Negative Voting: An Alternative Explanation of the Midterm Congressional Decline of the President's Party," *American Political Science Review* 71 (1977): 44–66.

Kiewiet, D. Roderick. *Macroeconomics and Micropolitics* (Chicago: University of Chicago Press, 1983).

______. "Policy-Oriented Voting in Response to Economic Issues," *American Political Science Review* 75 (1981): 448–459.

Kiewiet, D. Roderick, and McCubbins, Mathew D. "Congressional Appropriations and the Electoral Connection," *Journal of Politics* 47 (1985): 59–82.

Kim, Thomas P. "Clarence Thomas and the Politicization of Candidate Gender in the 1992 Senate Elections," *Legislative Studies Quarterly* 23 (1998): 399–418.

Kinder, Donald R., and Kiewiet, D. Roderick. "Economic Discontent and Political Behavior: The Role of Personal Grievances and Collective Economic Judgments in Congressional Voting," *American Journal of Political Science* 23 (1979): 495–527.

King, Gary, and Browning, Robert X. "Democratic Representation and Partisan Bias in Congressional Elections," *American Political Science Review* 81 (1987): 1251–1273.

Kingdon, John W. *Candidates for Office: Beliefs and Strategies* (New York: Random House, 1968).

Koetzle, William. "The Impact of Constituency Diversity Upon the Competitiveness of U.S. House Elections, 1962–96," *Legislative Studies Quarterly* 23 (1998): 561–573.

Kolodny, Robin. *Pursuing Majorities: Congressional Campaign Committees in American Politics* (Norman: University of Oklahoma Press, 1998).

Kostroski, Warren Lee. "Party and Incumbency in Post-war Senate Elections: Trends, Patterns, and Models," *American Political Science Review* 67 (1973): 1213–1234.

Kramer, Gerald H. "Short-Term Fluctuations in U.S. Voting Behavior, 1896–1964," *American Political Science Review* 65 (1971): 131–143.

Krasno, Jonathan S. *Challengers, Competition, and Reelection: Comparing Senate and House Elections* (New Haven, CT: Yale University Press, 1994).

Kritzer, Herbert M., and Eubank, Robert B. "Presidential Coattails Revisited: Partisanship and Incumbency Effects," *American Journal of Political Science* 23 (1979): 615–626.

Kuklinski, James H., and McCrone, Donald J. "Policy Salience and the Causal Structure of Representation," *American Politics Quarterly* 8 (1980): 139–164.

Kuklinski, James H., and West, Darrell M. "Economic Expectations and Mass Voting in United States House and Senate Elections," *American Political Science Review* 75 (1981): 436–447.

Larson, Bruce A. "Incumbent Contributions to the Congressional Campaign Committees, 1990–2000," *Political Research Quarterly* 57 (2004): 155–161.

Lau, Richard R., and Pomper, Gerald M. "Effectiveness of Negative Campaigning in U.S. Senate Elections," *American Journal of Political Science* 46 (January 2002): 47–66.

______. "Effects of Negative Campaigning on Turnout in U.S. Senate Elections, 1988–1998," *Journal of Politics* 63 (August 2001): 804–819.

______. *Negative Campaigning: An Analysis of Senate Elections* (Lanham, MD: Rowman & Littlefield, 2004).

Lazarus, Jeffrey. "Unintended Consequences: Anticipation of General Election Outcomes and Primary Election Divisiveness," *Legislative Studies Quarterly* 30 (2005): 435–461.

Lee, Frances E., and Oppenheimer, Bruce I. "Senate Apportionment: Competitiveness and Partisan Advantage," *Legislative Studies Quarterly* 22 (1997): 3–24.

Leuthold, David A. *Electioneering in a Democracy: Campaigns for Congress* (New York: John Wiley, 1968).

Leveaux-Sharpe, Christine. "Congressional Responsiveness to Redistricting Induced Constituency Change: An Extension into the 1990s," *Legislative Studies Quarterly* 26 (May 2001): 275–286.

Levy, Dena, and Squire, Peverill. "Television Markets and the Competitiveness of U.S. House Elections," *Legislative Studies Quarterly* 25 (May 2000), 313–325.

Lewis-Beck, Michael, and Rice, Tom W. "Forecasting U.S. House Elections," *Legislative Studies Quarterly* 9 (1984): 475–486.

Lockerbie, Brad. "Prospective Economic Voting in U.S. House Elections," *Legislative Studies Quarterly* 16 (1991): 239–262.

Lublin, David. "The Election of African Americans and Latinos to the U.S. House of Representatives, 1972–1994," *American Politics Quarterly* 25 (1997): 269–286.

______. "Quality, Not Quantity: Strategic Politicians in U.S. Senate Elections, 1952–1990," *Journal of Politics* 56 (1994): 228–241.

Lyons, Michael, and Galderisi, Peter F. "Incumbency, Reapportionment, and U.S. House Redistricting," *Political Research Quarterly* 48 (1995): 857–871.

Maestas, Cherie D., Fulton, Sarah, Maisel, L. Sandy, and Stone, Walter J. "When to Risk It" Institutions, Ambitions, and the Decision to Run for the U.S. House," *American Political Science Review* 100 (2006): 195–208.

Maestas, Cherie D., Maisel, L. Sandy, and Stone, Walter J. "National Party Efforts to Recruit State Legislators to Run for the U.S. House," *Legislative Studies Quarterly* 30 (0000): 277–300.

Mattei, Laura Winsky, and Mattei, Franco. "If Men Stayed Home . . . The Gender Gap in Recent Congressional Elections," *Political Research Quarterly* 51 (1998): 411–436.

McAdams, John C., and Johannes, John R. "The 1980 House Elections: Reexamining Some Theories in a Republican Year," *Journal of Politics* 45 (1983): 143–162.

______. "The Voter in the 1982 House Elections," *American Journal of Political Science* 28 (1984): 778–781.

McDermott, Monika L., and Jones, David R. "Congressional Performance, Incumbent Behavior, and Voting in Senate Elections, *Legislative Studies Quarterly* 30 (2005): 235–257.

McLeod, Jack M., Brown, Jane D., and Becker, Lee B. "Watergate and the 1974 Congressional Elections," *Public Opinion Quarterly* 41 (1977): 181–195.

McPhee, William, and Glaser, William A., ed. *Public Opinion and Congressional Elections* (New York: The Free Press, 1962).

Magleby, David B., and Monson, J. Quin, ed. *The Last Hurrah? Soft Money and Issue Advocacy in the 2002 Congressional Elections* (Washington DC: The Brookings Institution, 2004).

Magleby, David B., Monson, J. Quin, and Patterson, Kelly, ed. *Dancing Without Partners: How Candidates Parties and Interest Groups Interact in the New Campaign Finance Environment* (Provo, UT: Brigham Young University, Center for the Study of Elections and Democracy, 2005).

Magleby, David B., and Nelson, Candice J. *The Money Chase: Congressional Campaign Finance Reform* (Washington, DC: The Brookings Institution, 1990).

Magleby, David B., and Patterson, Kelly, ed. *War Games: Issues and Resources in the Battle for Control of Congress* (Provo, UT: Brigham Young University, Center for the Study of Elections and Democracy, 2007).

Maisel, Louis Sandy. "Congressional Elections in 1978: The Road to Nomination, the Road to Election," *American Politics Quarterly* 8 (1981): 23–48.

______. *From Obscurity to Oblivion: Running in the Congressional Primaries* (Knoxville: University of Tennessee Press, 1982).

Maisel, Louis Sandy, and Cooper, Joseph, ed. *Congressional Elections* (Beverly Hills, CA: Sage Publications, 1981).

Maisel, L. Sandy, and Stone, Walter P. "Determinants of Candidate Emergence in U.S. House Elections: An Exploratory Study," *Legislative Studies Quarterly* 22 (1997): 72–96.

Malbin, Michael J., ed. *Money and Politics in the United States: Financing Elections in the 1980s* (Washington, DC: American Enterprise Institute, 1984).

______. *Parties, Interest Groups, and Campaign Finance Laws* (Washington, DC: American Enterprise Institute, 1980).

Mann, Thomas E. *The American Elections of 1982* (Washington, DC: American Enterprise Institute, 1983).

______. *Unsafe at Any Margin: Interpreting Congressional Elections* (Washington, DC: American Enterprise Institute, 1977).

Mann, Thomas E., and Wolfinger, Raymond E. "Candidates and Parties in Congressional Elections," *American Political Science Review* 74 (1980): 617–632.

Mattei, Franco. "Senate Apportionment and Partisan Advantage: A Second Look," *Legislative Studies Quarterly* 26 (August 2001): 391–409.

Mayhew, David R. *Congress: The Electoral Connection* (New Haven, CT: Yale University Press, 1974).

______. "Congressional Elections: The Case of the Vanishing Marginals," *Polity* 6 (1974): 295–317.

Miller, Warren E., and Stokes, Donald E. "Constituency Influence in Congress," *American Political Science Review* 57 (1963): 45–57.

Mondak, Jeffrey. "Presidential Coattails in Open Seats: The District-Level Impact of Heuristic Processing," *American Politics Quarterly* 21 (1993): 307–319.

Mondak, Jeffrey, and McCurley, Carl. "Cognitive Efficiency and the Congressional Vote: The Psychology of Coattail Voting," *Political Research Quarterly* 47 (1994): 151–175.

Nelson, Candice. "The Effects of Incumbency on Voting in Congressional Elections," *Political Science Quarterly* 93 (1978/1979): 665–678.

Nice, David. "Competitiveness in House and Senate Elections with Identical Constituencies," *Political Behavior* 6 (1984): 95–102.

Nicholson, Stephen P., and Miller, Ross A. "Prior Beliefs and Voter Turnout in the 1986 and 1988 Congressional Elections," *Political Research Quarterly* 50 (1997): 199–213.

Niemi, Richard G., and Abramowitz, Alan I. "Partisan Redistricting and the 1992 Congressional Elections," *Journal of Politics* 56 (1994): 811–817.

Nokken, Timothy. "Ideological Congruence vs. Electoral Success: Distribution of Party Organization Contributions in Senate Elections, 1990–2000," *American Politics Research* 31 (January 2003): 3–26.

Oppenheimer, Bruce I., Stimson, James A., and Waterman, Richard W. "Interpreting U.S. Congressional Elections: The Exposure Thesis," *Legislative Studies Quarterly* 11 (1986): 227–247.

Ornstein, Norman J., Mann, Thomas E., and Malbin, Michael J. *Vital Statistics on Congress 2001–2002* (Washington, DC: American Enterprise Institute, 2002).

Owens, John R. "Economic Influences on Elections to the U.S. Congress," *Legislative Studies Quarterly* 9 (1984): 123–150.

Paletz, David. "The Neglected Context of Congressional Campaigns," *Polity* 3 (1971): 195–218.

Paolini, Philip. "Group-Salient Issues and Group Representation: Support for Women Candidates in the 1992 Senate Elections," *American Journal of Political Science* 39 (1995): 294–313.

Parker, Glenn R. "The Advantage of Incumbency in House Elections," *American Politics Quarterly* 8 (1980): 449–464.

______. *Homeward Bound: Explaining Changes in Congressional Behavior* (Pittsburgh: University of Pittsburgh Press, 1986).

______. "Interpreting Candidate Awareness in U.S. Congressional Elections," *Legislative Studies Quarterly* 6 (1981): 219–234.

Parker, Glenn R., and Davidson, Roger H. "Why Do Americans Love Their Congressmen So Much More Than Their Congress?" *Legislative Studies Quarterly* 4 (1979): 53–61.

Parker, Glenn R., and Parker, Suzanne L. "Correlates and Effects of Attention to District by U.S. House Members," *Legislative Studies Quarterly* 10 (1985): 223–242.

Payne, James L. "The Personal Electoral Advantage of House Incumbents, 1936–1976," *American Politics Quarterly* 8 (1980): 465–482.

Peters, John G., and Welch, Susan. "The Effects of Charges of Corruption on Voting Behavior in Congressional Elections," *American Political Science Review* 74 (1980): 697–708.

Petrocik, John R., and Desposato, Scott. "Incumbency and Short-Term Influences on Voters," *Political Research Quarterly* 57 (2004): 363–373.

______. "The Partisan Consequences of Majority-Minority Redistricting in the South, 1992 and 1994," *Journal of Politics* 60 (1998): 613–633.

Piereson, James E. "Presidential Popularity and Midterm Voting at Different Electoral Levels," *American Journal of Political Science* 19 (1975): 683–693.

Pothier, John T. "The Partisan Bias in Senate Elections," *American Politics Quarterly* 12 (1984): 89–100.

Powell, Lynda W. "Issue Representation in Congress," *Journal of Politics* 44 (1982): 658–678.

Prior, Marcus. "The Incumbent in the Living Room: The Rise of Television and the Incumbency Advantage in U.S. House Elections, "*Journal of Politics* 68 (2006): 657–673.

Ragsdale, Lyn. "The Fiction of Congressional Elections as Presidential Events," *American Politics Quarterly* 8 (1980): 375–398.

______. "Incumbent Popularity, Challenger Invisibility, and Congressional Voters," *Legislative Studies Quarterly* 6 (1981): 201–218.

Robeck, Bruce W. "State Legislator Candidates for the U.S. House: Prospects for Success," *Legislative Studies Quarterly* 7 (1982): 507–514.

Roberds, Stephen C. "Incumbent Scandals in U.S. House Elections" (Paper presented at the Annual Meeting of the Midwest Political Science Association, Chicago, April 15–17, 1999).

Robertson, Andrew W. "American Redistricting in the 1980s: The Effect on Midterm Elections," *Electoral Studies* 2 (1983): 113–129.

Romero, David W. "The Case of the Missing Reciprocal Influence: Incumbent Reputation and the Vote," *Journal of Politics* 58 (1996): 1198–1207.

______. "Divisive Primaries and the House District Vote: A Pooled Analysis," *American Politics Research* 31 (March 2003): 178–190.

______. "The Prospects-Based Dynamics of the House Candidacy Decision," *American Politics Research* 32 (2004): 119–141.

Romero, David W., and Sanders, Francine. "Loosened Partisan Attachments and Receptivity to Incumbent Behaviors: A Panel Analysis, 1972–1976," *Political Research Quarterly* 47 (1994): 177–192.

Romero, David W., and Stambough, Stephen J. "Personal Economic Well-Being and the Individual Vote for Congress: A Pooled Analysis, 1980–1990," *Political Research Quarterly* 49 (1996): 607–616.

Schantz, Harvey L. "Contested and Uncontested Primaries for the U.S. House," *Legislative Studies Quarterly* 5 (1980): 545–562.

Scheve, Kenneth, and Michael Tomz. "Electoral Surprise and the Midterm Loss in U.S. Congressional Elections," *British Journal of Political Science* 29 (1999): 507–521.

Schoenberger, Robert A. "Campaign Strategy and Party Loyalty: The Electoral Relevance of Candidate Decision Making in the 1964 Congressional Elections," *American Political Science Review* 63 (1969): 515–520.

Segura, Gary M., and Nicholson, Stephen P. "Sequential Choices and Partisan Transitions in U.S. Senate Delegations, 1972–1988," *Journal of Politics* 57 (1995): 86–100.

Serra, George. "What's in it for Me?" *American Politics Quarterly* 22 (1994): 403–420.

Serra, George, and Cover, Albert D. "The Electoral Consequences of Perquisite Use: The Casework Case," *Legislative Studies Quarterly* 17 (1992): 233–246.

Shields, Todd G., Goidel, Robert K., and Tadlock, Barry. "The Net Impact of Media Exposure on Individual Voting Decisions in U.S. Senate and House Elections," *Legislative Studies Quarterly* 20 (1995): 415–430.

Simon, Dennis M., Ostrom, Charles W., Jr., and Marra, Robin F. "The President, Referendum Voting, and Subnational Elections in the United States," *American Political Science Review* 85 (1991): 1177–1192.

Sinclair, Barbara. "Agenda Control and Policy Success: Ronald Reagan and the 97th House," *Legislative Studies Quarterly* 10 (1985): 291–314.

______. "Washington Behavior and Home-State Reputation: The Impact of National Prominence on Senators' Visibility and Likability," *Legislative Studies Quarterly* 15 (1990): 475–494.

Sorauf, Frank J. *Money in American Elections* (Glenview, IL: Scott, Foresman, 1988).

Squire, Peverill. "Challenger Quality and Voting Behavior in U.S. Senate Elections," *Legislative Studies Quarterly* 17 (1992): 247–264.

______. "Challengers in Senate Elections," *Legislative Studies Quarterly* 14 (1989): 531–547.

______. "Preemptive Fund-raising and Challenger Profile in Senate Elections," *Journal of Politics* 53 (1991): 1150–1164.

Squire, Peverill, and Smith, Eric R.A.N. "Repeat Challengers in Congressional Elections," *American Politics Quarterly* 12 (1984): 51–70.

Steen, Jennifer A. *Self-Financed Candidates in Congressional Elections* (Ann Arbor: University of Michigan Press, 2006.

Stein, Robert, and Bickers, Kenneth N. "Congressional Elections and the Pork Barrel," *Journal of Politics* 56 (1994): 349–376.

Stewart, Charles, III, and Reynolds, Mark. "Television Markets and U.S. Senate Elections," *Legislative Studies Quarterly* 15 (1990): 495–524.

Stimson, James A., MacKuen, Michael B., and Erikson, Robert S. "Dynamic Representation," *American Political Science Review* 89 (1995): 543–565.

Stone, Walter J. "The Dynamics of Constituency: Electoral Control in the House," *American Politics Quarterly* 8 (1980): 399–424.

______. "Measuring Constituency–Representative Linkages: Problems and Prospects," *Legislative Studies Quarterly* 4 (1979): 623–639.

Stone, Walter J., and Maisel, L.Sandy. "The Not-So-Simple Calculus of Winning: Potential U.S. House Candidates' Nomination and General Election Prospects," *Journal of Politics* 65 (2003): 951–977.

Sulkin, Tracy. "Explaining Campaign Intensity," *American Politics Research* 29 (November 2001): 608–624.

Sullivan, John L., and Uslaner, Eric M. "Congressional Behavior and Electoral Marginality," *American Journal of Political Science* 22 (1978): 536–553.

Swain, John W., Borrelli, Stephen A., and Reed, Brian C. "Partisan Consequences of the Post-1990 Redistricting for the U.S. House of Representatives," *Political Research Quarterly* 51 (1998): 945–967.

Taylor, Andrew J., and Barrington, Lowell W. "The Personal and the Political in Repeat Congressional Candidacies," *Political Research Quarterly* 58 (2005): 599–605.

Thomas, Martin. "Election Proximity and Senatorial Roll Call Voting," *American Journal of Political Science* 29 (1985): 96–111.

Tidmarch, Charles M., and Karp, Brad S. "The Missing Beat: Press Coverage of Congressional Elections in Eight Metropolitan Areas," *Congress and the Presidency* 10 (1983): 47–61.

Tufte, Edward R. "Determinants of the Outcomes of Midterm Congressional Elections," *American Political Science Review* 69 (1975): 812–826.

______. *Political Control of the Economy* (Princeton, NJ: Princeton University Press, 1978).

______. "The Relationship Between Seats and Votes in Two-Party Systems," *American Political Science Review* 67 (1973): 540–554.

Uslaner, Eric. "'Ain't Misbehavin': The Logic of Defensive Issue Strategies in Congressional Elections," *American Politics Quarterly* 9 (1981): 3–22.

Uslaner, Eric M., and Conway, M. Margaret. "The Responsible Electorate: Watergate, the Economy, and Vote Choice in 1974," *American Political Science Review* 79 (1985): 788–803.

Waterman, Richard. "Comparing Senate and House Electoral Outcomes: The Exposure Thesis," *Legislative Studies Quarterly* 15 (1990): 99–114.

Weatherford, M. Stephen. "Economic Conditions and Electoral Outcomes: Class Differences in the Political Response to Recession," *American Journal of Political Science* 22 (1978): 917–938.

Welch, Susan, and Hibbing, John R. "The Effects of Charges of Corruption on Voting Behavior in Congressional Elections, 1982–1990," *Journal of Politics* 59 (1997): 226–239.

Westlye, Mark C. "Competitiveness of Senate Seats and Voting Behavior in Senate Elections," *American Journal of Political Science* 27 (1983): 253–283.

______. *Senate Elections and Campaign Intensity* (Baltimore: Johns Hopkins University Press, 1991).

Wilcox, Clyde. "I Owe It All to Me: Candidates' Investments in Their Own Campaigns," *American Politics Quarterly* 16 (1988): 266–279.

Wolfinger, Raymond E., and Rosenstone, Steven J. *Who Votes?* (New Haven, CT: Yale University Press, 1980).

Wolfinger, Raymond E., Rosenstone, Steven J., and McIntosh, Richard A. "Presidential and Congressional Voters Compared," *American Politics Quarterly* 9 (1981): 245–255.

Wolpert, Robin M., and Gimpel, James G. "Information, Recall, and Accountability: The Electorate's Response to the Clarence Thomas Nomination," *Legislative Studies Quarterly* 22 (1997): 535–550.

Wright, Gerald C., Jr. "Candidates' Policy Positions and Voting in U.S. Congressional Elections," *Legislative Studies Quarterly* 3 (1978): 445–464.

______. "Constituency Response to Congressional Behavior: The Impact of the House Judiciary Committee Impeachment Votes," *Western Political Quarterly* 30 (1977): 401–410.

______. *Electoral Choice in America* (Chapel Hill, NC: Institute for Research in Social Science, 1974).

Wright, Gerald C., and Berkman, Michael B. "Candidates and Policy in U.S. Senate Elections," *American Political Science Review* 80 (1986): 567–588.

Yiannakis, Diana Evans. "The Grateful Electorate: Casework and Congressional Elections," *American Journal of Political Science* 25 (1981): 568–580.

INDEX

Note: Initial *n* denotes endnotes

H

I

J

K

L

Q

R

S